D0423277

The Urbana Free Library

To renew: call 217-367-4057
or go to *"urbanafreelibrary.org"*
and select "Renew/Request Items"

That's the Way It Is

That's the Way It Is

A HISTORY OF TELEVISION NEWS IN AMERICA

CHARLES L. PONCE DE LEON

The University of Chicago Press
Chicago and London

Charles L. Ponce de Leon is professor of
history and American studies at California
State University, Long Beach.

The University of Chicago Press, Chicago 60637
The University of Chicago Press, Ltd., London
© 2015 by The University of Chicago
All rights reserved. Published 2015.
Printed in the United States of America

24 23 22 21 20 19 18 17 16 15   1 2 3 4 5

ISBN-13: 978-0-226-47245-4 (cloth)
ISBN-13: 978-0-226-25609-2 (e-book)

DOI: 10.7208/chicago9780226256092.001.0001

Library of Congress Cataloging-in-Publication Data
Ponce de Leon, Charles L. (Charles Leonard), author.
That's the way it is : a history of television news in
America / Charles L. Ponce de Leon.
pages; cm
Includes bibliographical references and index.
ISBN 978-0-226-47245-4 (cloth : alk. paper) —
ISBN 0-226-47245-0 (cloth : alk. paper) —
ISBN 978-0-226-25609-2 (e-book)   1. Television
broadcasting of news—United States—History.
2. Television broadcasting of news—Social
aspects—United States. I. Title.
HE8700.8.P66 2015
070.1′950973—dc23

                    2014040798

♾ This paper meets the requirements of ANSI/NISO
Z39.48–1992 (Permanence of Paper).

CONTENTS

PROLOGUE

Like many people my age, I grew up with television news. My parents watched it every night at dinnertime, and I remember well the luminous glow of our black-and-white screen and the grim visages of the anchormen we welcomed into our home. My father liked *The Huntley-Brinkley Report* on NBC, and was especially fond of Chet Huntley. My mother cheerfully submitted to his viewing preferences—though when he began to travel more frequently for business, she switched to *The CBS Evening News with Walter Cronkite*. After Huntley's retirement in 1970, my father watched CBS, too.

It's Cronkite's program that I recall most vividly. It was in the late 1960s that I began to watch the news rather than merely notice it in the background as I played with toys or daydreamed at the dinner table. And it was *The CBS Evening News* that helped to shatter the illusion that I lived in a cloistered, idyllic world. Cronkite and his intrepid correspondents made me aware of Vietnam, of the civil rights and anti-war movements, and of new social and cultural trends that, to a child, seemed bewildering. They told me about the crime and violence that were sweeping the nation, and were often on hand to describe and explain riveting events like the assassinations of Martin Luther King Jr. and Robert F. Kennedy and the mayhem that occurred at the Democratic National Convention in August 1968. I remember the RFK shooting particularly well. My mother was very fond of him, and she allowed me to stay up late to watch the election returns and see him declare victory in our home state's primary. So I was awake and watching when, shortly after his victory speech, we were told he had been shot—and even got a quick glimpse of him lying, fatally wounded, on the Ambassador Hotel's kitchen floor.

I remember television providing us with good news, too, including the momentous Apollo 11 moon landing. Our family had closely followed the progress of the American space program, and its success in putting a man on the moon was truly awe-inspiring—despite our having to wait for what seemed like an eternity while the TV displayed the same unchanging image and Cronkite and his associates struggled to fill the hours with information and commentary. But it seemed to bring us mostly bad news, and by the early 1970s we tuned in with a sense of trepidation, as the political and cultural upheavals of the era were soon accompanied by economic problems and evidence that the era of postwar prosperity was over.

By the mid-1970s I not only watched the evening news every night but also read our local newspaper—and, on many days, the *San Francisco Chronicle*, which I delivered as a paperboy. I avidly followed the Watergate scandal and the revelations unearthed by the many congressional hearings that were held in the wake of the Vietnam War. The more I learned, the more I came to perceive a blurring between the once distant public world covered by journalists and my own adolescent private world. As we waited in line for gas, drove by the squalid urban ghettos of San Francisco or Oakland, or encountered the increasing number of disaffected young people whose contempt for the postwar "American Way of Life" was readily evident in their appearance and rebellious posturing, I began to see myself, my friends, and my family as participants in the grand drama of our national life, a drama conveyed so evocatively by journalists. Somehow or another, everything seemed connected—though, at the time, I scarcely understood how and, distracted by adolescence, made few efforts to figure it out.

Gradually, however, I stopped watching television news. In my first couple of years in college, I even stopped reading newspapers. I would watch Walter Cronkite—and then Dan Rather—when I was home and my parents did. But the rhythms of college life and postcollegiate young adulthood weren't compatible with my old news habit. When I began my graduate studies in the mid-1980s, I would sometimes tune into the *CBS Evening News*, but I found it less satisfying, and I soon embraced a jaundiced view of TV news that reflected my professional aspirations as a PhD student and budding academic—that television news was bland and insipid and a poor substitute for the more substantive intellectual nourishment provided by "prestige" newspapers and magazines. Accordingly, when I resumed following the news in the late 1980s, it was by becoming a regular reader of the *New York Times*.

I still watched TV news from time to time. My wife and I especially enjoyed *60 Minutes*, and we turned on Dan Rather or Peter Jennings when something big occurred—like the fall of the Berlin Wall—or for election coverage. If a story was particularly big, we would tune in for several days, sometimes even weeks, to follow it to its conclusion. In the early 1990s, when we finally got cable, we also started watching CNN. Yet when I watched TV news, even CNN, I couldn't help but notice that it had changed since the days when I had been an avid viewer. The changes became especially apparent in the mid-1990s, when the networks and CNN feasted on the O. J. Simpson case. It got to the point where I could hardly watch at all.

There was a ready explanation for what had happened. I first encountered it in the late 1980s in articles about the television industry that I read in the *Times*, and it gained wider currency when several retired television journalists, including Cronkite, invoked it their memoirs and in often testy interviews. It was picked up and embellished by TV critics and much of the intellectual community, of which, as a young historian, I was now a part. Louis Menand calls it the "decline-of-TV-news narrative." It argues that TV news was "dumbed-down" and transformed into "infotainment," and that the people responsible for this were the "suits," the corporate executives who gained control of the networks in the 1980s and 1990s and demanded that news programs generate higher ratings and make money.

According to "declinists," if TV news changed for the worse, it was no fault of television journalists, who were powerless to resist the heavy hand of corporate influence. And, in most accounts, it was no fault of the public, who largely rejected the new-style TV news of the 1990s in spite of network efforts to pander to them. This is why, declinists claim, the audience for network news has plummeted since the early 1980s. Like me, viewers were turned off by the very features that producers had added to make television news more "interesting" and "entertaining." Between the lines of many versions of the decline-of-TV-news narrative is an unspoken assumption that the public is hankering for "real" news, and that a courageous return to principles can reverse the industry's decline and somehow recreate the national community that we like to think huddled around their TV sets in the days of Cronkite and Huntley and Brinkley.

It's a seductive tale and comports with many of the facts. It's true that the new owners who took over the networks instituted major changes and insisted that their news divisions make a profit—and that, as a result, the content, format, and "look" of TV news programs changed in many of the ways noted by declinists. And it's true that at least some viewers were alienated by the new emphasis on "infotainment" and "news you can use."

But most accounts of TV news' decline downplay the larger context and the industry's complex history, and convey only half of the truth. The aim of this book is to tell the whole story—to situate television news in its appropriate historical context and see its evolution without the mythic blinders that have led many to regard the era of Cronkite as a kind of golden age.[1]

That means facing up to some important facts. The first is that "infotainment" has been a feature of television news from the outset. This is because television was conceived mainly as a medium of entertainment—not just by the men in charge of the industry but by the vast majority of the public, who made their preferences very clear as early as the mid-1950s. The predominance of entertainment programming on TV made news, which often deals with disturbing facts, an awkward fit, especially when journalists sought to do more than provide pictures of big events and ventured into interpretive and analytic reporting. To make their programs compatible with the sitcoms, dramas, and variety shows that dominated the medium, the producers of TV news were compelled to make at least some news programs entertaining as well as informative, usually by mixing hard news and soft features. This was a formula that had been successful in mass-circulation print journalism, and its use by television journalists made perfect sense at the time. Its effectiveness on TV exerted a powerful influence on all subsequent news programming. It was the key to the success of *Today* and *60 Minutes*, and following this path became irresistible when the industry became more competitive in later years.

This brings us to the second important fact to acknowledge about the history of TV news. During the years when infotainment was kept at least partially at bay—confined to only some news programs, and outweighed on most others by hard news—it was because of peculiar historical and institutional factors that limited competition and allowed network executives to be unusually supportive and indulgent of their news divisions. A kind of protective cocoon enabled the network news divisions to grow and inspired television journalists to become increasingly ambitious about joining the journalistic establishment and providing viewers with something more than a headline service. It was in this period, the early 1960s through the late 1970s, that the producers of TV news developed their most sophisticated programs, and sought, as much as possible, to draw a sharp line between their programs and those broadcast by the entertainment divisions.

In the 1970s, however, the broader social, economic and political context began to change, and the TV news industry began to be affected by new forces, including heightened competition from local news and cable TV. The protective cocoon in which the networks' news divisions had briefly flourished was battered and began to unravel, and television journalists felt a new pressure to shift the balance toward soft news. And in the 1980s, amid the rush to deregulate industries and increase consumer choice, the competition from cable became even more intense.

This might not have been a problem if the television news habit among Americans had been deeply engrained, and if most of them had appreciated the efforts of network journalists to provide a reasonably broad and sophisticated overview of the day's most important news stories. But that habit was *not* deeply engrained, and, from the start, many Americans were suspicious and resentful of network journalists and did not like the brand of news they produced, disconcerting facts that journalists were forced to confront when the spread of cable gave viewers more choices, and, after a peak in 1981, the percentage of "television households" watching news programs progressively declined. Not surprisingly, the only network news programs that retained their audience were prime-time newsmagazines and the morning news programs—the ones most infused with entertainment values. Meanwhile, the minority of Americans who liked following the news on TV found a more congenial source of it, CNN, one of the great success stories of cable television.

This brings us to the third and perhaps most important fact that needs to be understood about the history of TV news. If large numbers of Americans watched the networks' evening newscasts during the Cronkite era, it was because, for many years, they had virtually no other options. Before cable, few television markets had more than a handful of stations, and in most markets, the networks broadcast their flagship evening newscasts at exactly the same time. Equally important, the Federal Communications Commission actively protected the networks from would-be competitors and forced their affiliates to abide by relatively strict "public-interest" requirements that made broadcasting at least some news a necessity. There were also cultural and political forces encouraging Americans to follow the news. Politicians, educators, ministers, prominent corporate executives, and the leaders of numerous community organizations ardently believed that knowledge of local, national, and international developments was a civic obligation, and they were hopeful that television in particular would help to create more informed and responsible citizens. They promoted this belief throughout the 1950s and 1960s, and though many Americans never embraced it, others fell under its sway.

When, thanks largely to cable and the FCC's deregulation of broadcasting, viewers suddenly had options, they gradually stopped watching television news, especially the network newscasts that had commanded such a large audience in previous decades. And, in the early 2000s, when Americans turned en masse to the Internet, the exodus from television news accelerated. By 2010, a dwindling number of mostly elderly Americans watched news on television—or even on cable. People were getting their news from other sources, or not at all. Competition and consumer choice had robbed television journalists of their audience—despite their best efforts to hang on to it.

But broader changes in the culture were important, too. For a variety of reasons, the broad elite consensus that had encouraged Americans to follow the news disintegrated. Television journalists began to be accused of bias, and many people lost respect for the both the news media and the institutions they routinely covered. The allure of self-interest and private life—always powerful and a potential distraction from the responsibilities of citizenship—became overwhelming as Americans came to embrace a new expressive individualism and found more varied ways of engaging in the "pursuit of happiness." By the 1990s, many people didn't feel obliged to follow the news, and new intellectual trends seemed to justify this withdrawal from public life. For many, keeping up with the news, particularly with more than the briefest headlines, was too much work. Instead, they devoted their time and energy to more enjoyable and personally meaningful activities. And many who continued to read newspapers or watch TV news felt little guilt about only paying attention to subjects that were interesting to them—like the O. J. Simpson case, rather than, say, the complicated American health care crisis or developments in the Middle East that were contributing to the growth of radical Islamist groups like al-Qaeda.

The point of this book is that TV news didn't degenerate into infotainment. It changed—in some respects for the better, in other respects for the worse—largely in response to the preferences of viewers. These changes, in turn, recalibrated the expectations of viewers and encouraged them to accept additional ones, providing journalists with further justification for innovation. Without the protection of a regulatory cocoon and cultural forces encouraging civic engagement and knowledge of the wider world, the television news industry became subject to market forces, like so many other things in America during the latter decades of the twentieth century. It was adapted to a larger media culture—indeed, an entire economy—that places the highest priority on giving people what they want.

This isn't necessarily a bad thing. The imperative to satisfy the diverse tastes of the consuming public has made cable TV in particular astonishingly diverse—the antithesis of the "vast wasteland" that network TV was in the early 1960s. And though there is more dreck on television than ever before, and the worst programs are far more puerile and vulgar than anything broadcast in the network era, the number of interesting and distinguished programs that have appeared on cable since the 1990s boggles the mind. But it's an open question whether news, as opposed to entertainment, is something that should be determined entirely by the market, particularly since some knowledge of national and international affairs is essential to be a thoughtful and autonomous citizen in a representative democracy. Can a nation where most people don't want to know about things that don't interest them remain a functioning democracy?

This book is not a comprehensive history of television news. It neglects to mention many noteworthy programs and individuals, and its discussion of some important trends is perfunctory—academic experts in the field might even say superficial. From a scholarly perspective, a comprehensive history may be sorely needed. But it would be so massive and detailed that few nonexperts would have the stamina to read it, and my highest priority is reaching a relatively wide audience.

Nor it is a species of "media studies." It does not provide in-depth readings of particular "texts" or present an argument about the "meanings" embedded in television journalism. And it is notably lacking in its reliance on theory. I'm quite familiar with this literature, and learned from it in the course of my research. But I'm a historian, and I've come to value a feature of my discipline that differentiates it from most other academic fields—its capacity for storytelling, for marshaling evidence from disparate sources to tell us what happened and why.

Accordingly, this book is a narrative history. It tells a story. It chronicles the rise and evolution of television news from the 1940s through the first decade of the new millennium. It focuses mostly on the networks and the cable news channels, but I also discuss local news and some syndicated programming, especially when it was influential. Unlike a comprehensive history, it dwells on the highlights and most significant trends, and it pays special attention to the executives, producers, and journalists who were responsible for the field's most important innovations—figures such as Reuven Frank, Don Hewitt, Fred Friendly, Richard Salant, Roone Arledge, Ted Turner, Roger Ailes, Katie Couric, and Jon Stewart. Most important of all, it documents their work in a way that is true to their lived experience—as professionals committed to public enlightenment who worked for organizations that were also forced to compete for viewers and ratings.

To produce it, I consulted a wide range of sources: oral histories, memoirs, and autobiographies; newspaper, magazine, and trade press articles; detailed reports and data on the television industry available on various websites; books about specific programs, genres, and news organizations; and more general works about the media and American society and culture. And I watched lots of TV news, much of it online, but also at selected archives. This was an eye-opening experience. I had never seen many early news programs, and my opinions of some, like *See It Now*, had been based on inaccurate assumptions about their content. I was also startled by some of the interesting and unusual topics that journalists have covered—some them utterly ridiculous, but others remarkably timely and prescient. And I was amazed at how producers in the industry's early years, despite limited technology, were able to produce such compelling programs.

This is what the publishing industry calls a "synthetic" history, drawn in large part from the yeoman work of others. I didn't conduct any interviews, nor did I attempt to access the written archives of news organizations or the personal papers of important figures. Lacking the time and resources for such research, I decided to make do with more readily available sources. Thankfully, they were quite revealing, providing me with a well-rounded picture of the forces that have shaped television journalism over the years. But the book presents a new argument, and it connects the history of television news to the broader currents of recent US history, a subject I have been teaching and writing about for twenty years. It's my knowledge of the latter that differentiates it from virtually all other books written about the subject and makes it potentially interesting to readers who are neither scholars nor media industry insiders.

I conceived this book in the summer of 2009 after a research trip to Syracuse University, where I went to examine a collection of oral histories of television industry pioneers. At the time, I was looking for a new book project and was vaguely interested in writing about some facet of television. The oral histories were quite provocative, and I was struck in particular by the insights of people who had worked in television news. There, right in front of me, was evidence that seemed to contradict the "decline-of-TV-news" narrative. I was intrigued, and in subsequent weeks, after additional research, I resolved to figure out exactly what happened. This book is the fruit of that project, my effort to correct a widespread misperception I once shared. It would be nice if there had been a cohesive, well-informed national community back in TV's "golden age," and if television news had played an important role in forging it. But that doesn't seem to have been the case—no matter how much we might wish it to be true. And that's the way it is, to borrow from Walter Cronkite's nightly sign-off.

Learning about television news has been a sobering experience. Fully understanding the challenges they faced, I came to really admire many executives, producers, and journalists. And I gained a greater appreciation of the constraints that impinge on virtually everyone who works in the mass media and commercial popular culture industries. It's a tough business that requires them to respond to the whims of public taste and the market. Give the people what they want. It's a logical mandate, and in many fields it can inspire feats of remarkable ingenuity. But, for very good reasons, it makes many journalists anxious. Perhaps it should make us anxious, too.

ACKNOWLEDGMENTS

Compared to that of most of my colleagues, my version of the schol-   xix
arly life is rather solitary. I'm not one for the conference circuit, and I
didn't circulate early versions of my book manuscript very widely for
feedback. But I was the beneficiary of important advice and support,
and I'd like to take this opportunity to thank some of the individuals
and institutions that made this book possible.

First, I'd like to commend the archivists at the Special Collections
Research Center at Syracuse University. Their television industry oral
histories were pivotal in enabling me to conceive this project. I owe
even more to John Lynch and his staff at the Vanderbilt Television
News Archive in Nashville. They were unflaggingly helpful and made
my research there rewarding and pleasurable. I also want to thank archivists at UCLA's Film and Television Archive and at the Paley Center
for Media in Beverly Hills. Though I never visited their new brick-and-
mortar facility, I was also assisted by curators and archivists at the Museum of Broadcast Communications in Chicago; their online archive
of programs predating 1968 was invaluable to me, and I appreciated
their willingness to help me deal with various technical snafus that I
experienced while conducting online research. Jaka Bartolj was especially helpful, and I'm very grateful to him for assistance with some
of the book's illustrations. Finally, I want to thank Roman Kochan,
Tracey Mayfield, and the staff of the California State University, Long
Beach, Library, who provided me with interlibrary loans and access to
hard-to-find periodical sources.

I want to thank several friends and colleagues who discussed this
project with me and gave me sage advice, particularly in its earliest

stages, when I hardly knew what I was doing: Thomas LeBien, Louis Masur, Jackson Lears, and especially Richard Wightman Fox. I want to express particular gratitude to Dan Einstein at the UCLA Film and Television Archive, who steered me to a number of different sources and archives. After a panel discussion in October 2007, my old Purchase College colleague Michelle Stewart suggested that I write a book on television news—a suggestion I dismissed out of hand because, subscribing to the "declinist" view, I thought the subject would be too "negative." Kudos to Michelle for planting that particular seed, though it took a while for it to sprout. I wrote this book while assuming a new job at Long Beach State, and I'm grateful to the administration and my new colleagues in the Department of History for providing support and creating an atmosphere that allowed me to complete it.

Doug Mitchell was enthusiastic about this project from the moment he first heard about it, and I want to thank him and others at the University of Chicago Press for help getting it through the pipeline and finally reaching the public. Carol Fisher Saller was a discerning copyeditor, and I'm grateful for her sharp eye and admirable attention to detail. I also want to thank the anonymous readers of the proposal and two versions of the manuscript. They provided invaluable advice and helped me from making some embarrassing errors.

Finally, I want to thank my family for their love and emotional support. This is the first book of mine that my children, now in or just out of college, are actually eager to read, and I hope they realize the many ways in which their presence in my life made it possible. My wife, Lynn, read the entire manuscript, and I'm grateful for the time she set aside from her busy schedule to provide advice and editorial comments. More important, I'm grateful for her love, understanding, and willingness to put up with my persistent self-absorption and absentmindedness, maladies that become particularly acute when I'm in the throes of a book project. Lynn, this one's for you.

1

BEGINNINGS

Few technologies have stirred the utopian imagination like television. Virtually from the moment that research produced the first break-throughs that made it more than a science fiction fantasy, its pro-moters began gushing about how it would change the world. Perhaps the most effusive was David Sarnoff. Like the hero of a dime novel, Sarnoff had come to America as a nearly penniless immigrant child, and had risen from lowly office boy to the presidency of RCA, a lead-ing manufacturer of radio receivers and the parent company of the nation's biggest radio network, NBC. More than anyone else, it was Sarnoff who had recognized the potential of "wireless" as a form of broadcasting—a way of transmitting from a single source to a geo-graphically dispersed audience. Sarnoff had built NBC into a jugger-naut, the network with the largest number of affiliates and the most popular programs. He had also become the industry's loudest cheer-leader, touting its contributions to "progress" and the "American Way of Life." Having blessed the world with the miracle of radio, he prom-ised Americans an even more astounding marvel, a device that would bring them sound and pictures over the air, using the same invisible frequencies.[1]

In countless speeches heralding television's imminent arrival, Sar-noff rhapsodized about how it would transform American life and en-courage global communication and "international solidarity." "Tele-vision will be a mighty window, through which people in all walks of life, rich and poor alike, will be able to see for themselves, not only the small world around us but the larger world of which we are a part," he proclaimed in 1945, as the Second World War was nearing an end and

Sarnoff and RCA eagerly anticipated an increase in public demand for the new technology.[2]

Sarnoff predicted that television would become the American people's "principal source of entertainment, education and news," bringing them a wealth of program options. It would increase the public's appreciation for "high culture" and, when supplemented by universal schooling, enable Americans to attain "the highest general cultural level of any people in the history of the world." Among the new medium's "outstanding contributions," he argued, would be "its ability to bring news and sporting events to the listener while they are occurring," and build on the news programs that NBC and the other networks had already developed for radio. He saw no conflicts or potential problems. Action-adventure programs, mysteries, soap operas, situation comedies, and variety shows would coexist harmoniously with high-toned drama, ballet, opera, classical music performances, and news and public affairs programs. And they would all be supported by advertising, making it unnecessary for the United States to move to a system of "government control," as in Europe and the UK. Television in the US would remain "free."[3]

Yet Sarnoff's booster rhetoric overlooked some thorny issues. Radio in the US wasn't really free. It was thoroughly commercialized, and this had a powerful influence on the range of programs available to listeners. To pay for program development, the networks and individual stations "sold" airtime to advertisers. Advertisers, in turn, produced programs—or selected ones created by independent producers—that they hoped would attract listeners. The whole point of "sponsorship" was to reach the public and make them aware of your products, most often through recurrent advertisements. Though owners of radios didn't have to pay an annual fee for the privilege of listening, as did citizens in other countries, they were forced to endure the commercials that accompanied the majority of programs.

This had significant consequences. As the development of radio made clear, some kinds of programs were more popular than others, and advertisers were naturally more interested in sponsoring ones that were likely to attract large numbers of listeners. These were nearly always entertainment programs, especially shows that drew on formulas that had proven successful in other fields—music and variety shows, comedy, and serial fiction. More off-beat and esoteric programs were sometimes able to find sponsors who backed them for the sake of prestige; from 1937 to 1954, for example, General Motors sponsored live performances by NBC's acclaimed "Symphony of the Air." But most cultural, news, and public affairs programs were unsponsored, making them unprofitable for the networks and individual stations. Thus in the bountiful mix envisioned by Sarnoff, certain kinds of broadcasts were more valuable than others. If high culture and news and public affairs programs were to thrive, their presence on network schedules would have to be justified by something other than their contribution to the bottom line.[4]

The most compelling reason was provided by the Federal Communications Commission (FCC). Established after Congress passed the Federal Communications Act in 1934, the FCC was responsible for overseeing the broadcasting industry and the nation's airwaves, which, at least in theory, belonged to the public. Rather than selling frequencies, which would have violated this principle, the FCC granted individual parties station licenses. These allowed licensees sole possession of a frequency to broadcast to listeners in their community or region. This system allocated a scarce resource — the nation's limited number of frequencies — and made possession of a license a lucrative asset for businessmen eager to exploit broadcasting's commercial potential. Licenses granted by the FCC were temporary, and all licensees were required to go through a periodic renewal process. As part of this process, they had to demonstrate to the FCC that at least some of the programs they aired were in the "public interest." Inspired by a deep suspicion of commercialization, which had spread widely among the public during the early 1900s, the FCC's public-interest requirement was conceived as a countervailing force that would prevent broadcasting from falling entirely under the sway of market forces. Its champions hoped that it might protect programming that did not pay and ensure that the nation's airwaves weren't dominated by the cheap, sensational fare that, reformers feared, would proliferate if broadcasting was unregulated.[5]

In practice, however, the FCC's oversight of broadcasting proved to be relatively lax. More concerned about NBC's enormous market power — it controlled two networks of affiliates, NBC Red and NBC Blue — FCC commissioners in the 1930s were unusually sympathetic to the businessmen who owned individual stations and possessed broadcast licenses and made it quite easy for them to renew their licenses. They were allowed to air a bare minimum of public-affairs programming and fill their schedules with the entertainment programs that appealed to listeners and sponsors alike. By interpreting the public-interest requirement so broadly, the FCC encouraged the commercialization of broadcasting and unwittingly tilted the playing field against any programs—including news and public affairs—that could not compete with the entertainment shows that were coming to dominate the medium.[6]

Nevertheless, news and public-affairs programs were able to find a niche on commercial radio. But until the outbreak of the Second World War, it wasn't a very large or comfortable one, and it was more a result of economic competition than the dictates of the FCC. Occasional news bulletins and regular election returns were broadcast by individual stations and the fledgling networks in the 1920s. They became more frequent in the 1930s, when the networks, chafing at the restrictions placed on them by the newspaper industry, established their own news divisions to supplement the reports they acquired through the newspaper-dominated wire services.[7]

By the mid-1930s, the most impressive radio news division belonged not to Sarnoff's NBC but its main rival, CBS. Owned by William S. Paley, the wealthy son of a cigar magnate, CBS was struggling to keep up with NBC, and Paley came to see news as an area where his young network might be able to gain an advantage. A brilliant, visionary businessman, Paley was fascinated by broadcasting and would soon steer CBS ahead of NBC, in part by luring away its biggest stars. His bold initiative to beef up its news division was equally important, giving CBS an identity that clearly distinguished it from its rivals. Under Paley, CBS would become the "Tiffany network," the home of "quality" as well as crowd-pleasers, a brand that made it irresistible to advertisers.[8]

Paley hired two print journalists, Ed Klauber and Paul White, to run CBS's news unit. Under their watch, the network increased the frequency of its news reports and launched news-and-commentary programs hosted by Lowell Thomas, H. V. Kaltenborn, and Robert Trout. In 1938, with Europe drifting toward war, CBS expanded these programs and began broadcasting its highly praised *World News Roundup*; its signature feature was live reports from correspondents stationed in London, Paris, Berlin, and other European capitals. These programs were well received and popular with listeners, prompting NBC and the other networks to follow Paley's lead.

The outbreak of war sparked a massive increase in news programming on all the networks. It comprised an astonishing 20 percent of the networks' schedules by 1944. Heightened public interest in news, particularly news about the war, was especially beneficial to CBS, where Klauber and White had built a talented stable of reporters. Led by Edward R. Murrow, they specialized in vivid on-the-spot reporting and developed an appealing style of broadcast journalism, affirming CBS's leadership in news. By the end of the war, surveys conducted by the Office of Radio Research revealed that radio had become the main source of news for large numbers of Americans, and Murrow and other radio journalists were widely respected by the public. And though network news people knew that their audience and airtime would decrease now that the war was over, they were optimistic about the future and not very keen to jump into the new field of television.[9]

This is ironic, since it was television that was uppermost in the minds of network leaders like Sarnoff and Paley. The television industry had been poised for takeoff as early as 1939, when NBC, CBS, and DuMont, a growing network owned by an ambitious television manufacturer, established experimental stations in New York City and began limited broadcasting to the few thousand households that had purchased the first sets for consumer use. After Pearl Harbor, CBS's experimental station even developed a pathbreaking news program that used maps and charts to explain the war's progress to viewers. This experiment came to an abrupt end in 1942, when the enormous shift of public and private resources to military production forced the networks to curtail and eventually shut down their television units, delaying television's launch for several years. [10]

Meanwhile, other events were shaking up the industry. In 1943, in response to an FCC decree, RCA was forced to sell one of its radio networks—NBC Blue—to the industrialist Edward J. Noble. The sale included all the programs and personalities that were contractually bound to the network, and in 1945 it was rechristened the American Broadcasting Company (ABC). The birth of ABC created another competitor not just in radio, where the Blue network had a loyal following, but in the burgeoning television industry as well. ABC joined NBC, CBS, and DuMont in their effort to persuade local broadcasters—often owners of radio stations who were moving into the new field of television—to become affiliates.[11]

In 1944, the New York City stations owned by NBC, CBS, and DuMont resumed broadcasting, and NBC and CBS in particular launched aggressive campaigns to sign up affiliates in other cities. ABC and DuMont, hamstrung by financial and legal problems, quickly fell behind as most station owners chose NBC or CBS, largely because of their proven track record in radio. But even for the "big two," building television networks was costly and difficult. Unlike radio programming, which could be fed through ordinary phone lines to affiliates, who then broadcast them over the air in their communities, linking television stations into a network required a more advanced technology, a coaxial cable especially designed for the medium that AT&T, the private, government-regulated telephone monopoly, would have to lay throughout the country. At the end of the war, at the government's and television industry's behest, AT&T began work on this project. By the end of the 1940s, most of the East Coast had been linked, and the connection extended to Chicago and much of the Midwest. But it was slow going, and at the dawn of the 1950s, no more than 30 percent of the nation's population was within reach of network programming. Until a city was linked to the coaxial cable, there was no reason for station owners to sign up with a network; instead, they relied on local talent to produce programs. As a result, the television networks grew more slowly than executives might have wished, and the audience for network programs was restricted by geography until the mid-1950s. An important breakthrough occurred in 1951, when the coaxial cable was extended to the West Coast and made transcontinental broadcasting possible. But until microwave relay stations were built to reach large swaths of rural America, many viewers lacked access to the networks.

Access wasn't the only problem. The first television sets that rolled off the assembly lines were expensive. RCA's basic model, the one that Sarnoff envisioned as its "Model T," cost $385, while top-of-the-line models were more than $2,000. With the average annual salary in the mid-1940s just over $3,000, this was a lot of money, even if consumers were able to buy sets through department-store installment plans. And though the price of TVs would steadily decline, throughout the 1940s the audience for television was restricted by income. Most early adopters were from well-to-do families—or tavern owners who hoped that their investment in television would attract patrons.

Still, the industry expanded dramatically. In 1946, there were approximately 20,000 television sets in the US; by 1948, there were 350,000; and by 1952, there were 15.3 million. Less than 1 percent of

American homes had TVs in 1948; a whopping 32 percent did by 1952. The number of stations also multiplied, despite an FCC freeze in the issuing of station licenses from 1948 to 1952. In 1946, there were six stations in only four cities; by 1952, there were 108 stations in sixty-five cities, most of them recipients of licenses issued right before the freeze. When the freeze was lifted and new licenses began to be issued again, there was a mad rush to establish new stations and get on the air. By 1955, almost 500 television stations were operating in the US.[12]

The FCC freeze greatly benefited NBC and CBS. Eighty percent of the markets with TV at the start of the freeze in 1948 had only one or two licensees, and it made sense for them to contract with one or both of the big networks for national programming to supplement locally produced material. Shut out of these markets, ABC and DuMont were forced to secure affiliates in the small number of markets—usually large cities—where stations were more plentiful. By the time the FCC starting issuing licenses again, NBC and CBS had established reputations for popular, high-quality programs, and when new markets were opened, it became easier for them to sign up stations with the most desirable frequencies, usually the lowest "channels" on the dial. Meanwhile, ABC languished for much of the 1950s, with the fewest and poorest affiliates, and the struggling DuMont network ceased operations altogether in 1955.[13]

News programs were among the first kinds of broadcasts that aired in the waning years of the war, and virtually everyone in the industry expected them to be part of the program mix as the networks increased programming to fill the broadcast day. News was "an invaluable builder of prestige," noted Sig Mickelson, who joined CBS as an executive in 1949 and served as head of its news division throughout the 1950s. "It helped create an image that was useful in attracting audiences and stimulating commercial sales, not to mention maintaining favorable government relations. . . . News met the test of 'public service.'"[14] As usual, CBS led the way, inaugurating a fifteen-minute evening news program in 1944. It was broadcast on Thursdays and Fridays at 8:00 PM, the two nights of the week the network was on the air. NBC launched its own short Sunday evening newscast in 1945 as the lead-in to its ninety minutes of programming. Both programs resembled the newsreels that were regularly shown in movie theaters, a mélange of filmed stories with voice-over narration by off-screen announcers.[15]

Considering the limited technology available, this was not surprising. Newsreels offered television news producers the most readily applicable model for a visual presentation of news, and the first people the networks hired to produce news programs were often newsreel veterans. But newsreels relied on 35mm film and were expensive and time-consuming to produce, and they had never been employed for breaking news. Aside from during the war, when they were filled with military stories that employed footage provided by the government, they specialized in fluff, events that were staged and would make the biggest impression on the screen: celebrity weddings, movie premiers, beauty contests, ship launches. In the mid-1940s, recognizing this shortcoming, producers at WCBW, CBS's wholly owned subsidiary in New York, developed a number of innovative techniques for "visualizing" stories for which they had no film and established the precedent of sending a reporter to cover local stories.[16]

These conventions were well established when the networks, in response to booming sales of television sets, expanded their evening schedules to seven days a week and launched regular weeknight newscasts. NBC's premiered first, in February 1948. Sponsored by R. J. Reynolds, the makers of Camel cigarettes, it was produced for the network by the Fox Movietone newsreel company and had no on-screen newsreaders. CBS soon followed suit, with the CBS *Evening News*, in April 1948. Relying on film provided by another newsreel outfit, Telenews, it featured a rotating cast of announcers, including Douglas Edwards, who had only reluctantly agreed to work in television after failing to break into the top tier of the network's radio correspondents. In the late summer, after CBS president Frank Stanton convinced Edwards of television's potential, Edwards was installed as the program's regular on-screen newsreader, its recognizable "face." DuMont created an evening newscast as well. But its *News from Washington*, which reached only the handful of stations that were owned by or affiliated with the network, was canceled in less than a year, and DuMont's subsequent attempt, *Camera Headlines*, suffered the same fate and was off the air by 1950. ABC's experience with news was similarly frustrating. Its first newscast, *News and Views*, began airing in August 1948 and was soon canceled. It didn't try to broadcast another one until 1952, when it launched an ambitious prime-time news program called ABC *All Star News*, which combined filmed news reports with man-on-the-street interviews, a technique popularized by local stations. By this time, however, the prime-time schedules of all the networks were full of popular entertainment programs, and *All Star News*, which failed to attract viewers, was pulled from the air after less than three months.[17]

In February 1949, NBC, eager to make up ground lost to CBS, transformed its weeknight evening newscast into the *Camel News Caravan*, with John Cameron Swayze, a veteran of NBC's radio division, as sole on-camera newsreader. Film for the program was acquired from a variety of sources, including foreign and domestic newsreel agencies and freelance stringers. But Swayze's narration and on-screen presence distinguished the broadcast from its earlier incarnation. He sat at a desk that prominently displayed the Camel logo and presented an overview of the day's major headlines, sometimes accompanied by film and still photos, but sometimes in the form of a "tell-story"— Swayze on camera reading from a script. In between, he would plug Camels and even occasionally light up, much to his sponsor's delight. One of the show's highlights was a whirlwind review of stories for which producers had no visuals, which Swayze would introduce by announcing, "Now let's go hopscotching the news for headlines!" Swayze was popular with viewers and hosted the broadcast for seven years. He became well known to the public, especially for this nightly sign off, "That's the story, folks. Glad we could get together."

The *Camel News Caravan* was superficial, and Swayze's tone undeniably glib, as critics at the time noted. But the assumption that guided its production did not set particularly high standards. As Reuven Frank, who joined the show as its main writer in 1950 and soon became its producer, recalled, "We assumed that almost everyone who watched us had read a newspaper . . . that our contribution . . . would be pictures. The people at home, knowing what the news was, could see it happen."[18] Yet over the next few years, especially after William McAndrew became head of NBC's news division and Frank was installed as the program's producer, the *News Caravan* steadily improved. Making good use of the largesse provided by R. J. Reynolds, which more than covered the news department's rapidly expanding budget, the show increased its use of filmed reports, acquired from foreign sources like the BBC and other European news agencies, the US government and military, and the network's growing corps of in-house cameramen and technicians. It also came to rely more and more on the network's staff of reporters, including a young North Carolinian named David Brinkley, and reporters at NBC's "O-and-Os," the five television stations that the network owned and operated. In the days before network bureaus, journalists at network O-and-Os were responsible for combing their cities for stories of potential national interest. NBC also employed stringers on whom it relied for material from cities or regions where it had no O-and-Os. Airing at 7:45 PM, right before the network's lineup of prime-time entertainment programs, the *News Caravan* became the first widely viewed news program of the television age. Its success gave McAndrew and his staff greater leverage in their efforts to command network resources and put added pressure on their main rival.

The CBS *Evening News*, broadcast at 7:30, was also very much a work-in-progress. Influenced by the experiments in "visualizing" news that CBS producers had conducted at the network's flagship New York City O-and-O in the mid-1940s, it was produced by a mix of radio people like Edwards and newcomers from other fields. Most of the radio people, however, were second-stringers. The network's leading radio personnel, including Murrow and his comrades, had little interest in moving to television. Though this disturbed Paley and his second-in-command, CBS president Frank Stanton, it allowed CBS's fledgling television news unit to escape from the long shadow of the network's radio news operation, and it increased the influence of staff committed to the tradition of "visualizing." With few radio people willing to work on the program, the network was forced to hire new staff from outside the network. These newcomers from the wire services, photojournalism, and news and photographic syndicates brought a lively spirit of innovation to CBS's nascent television news division. They were impressed by the notion of "visualizing," and they resolved that TV news ought to be different from radio news, "an amalgam of existing news media, with a substantial infusion of showmanship from the stage and motion pictures."[19]

The most important new hire was Don Hewitt, an ambitious, energetic twenty-five-year-old who joined the small staff of the CBS *Evening News* in 1948 and soon become its producer. Despite his age, Hewitt was already an experienced print journalist, and his resume included a stint at ACME News Pictures, a syndicate that provided newspapers with photographs. He was well aware of the power of pictures, and when he joined CBS, he brought a new sensibility and willingness to experiment. Under Hewitt, the Edwards program made rapid strides. Eager to find ways of compensating for television's technical limitations, Hewitt made extensive use of still photos and created a graphic

During the 1950s, Don Hewitt (left) was perhaps the most influential producer of television news. He was responsible not only for CBS's successful evening newscast, but also worked on *See It Now* and other network programs. Douglas Edwards (right) anchored the broadcast from the late 1940s to 1962, when he was replaced by Walter Cronkite. Photo courtesy of CBS/Photofest.

arts department to produce charts, maps, and captions to illustrate tell-stories. To make Edwards's delivery more natural and smooth, he introduced a new machine called a TelePrompTer, which replaced the heavy cue cards on which his script had been written. Expanding on the experiments of CBS's early "visualizers," Hewitt devised a number of clever devices to provide visuals for stories — for example, using toy soldiers to illustrate battles during the Korean War. He was the principal figure behind the shift to 16mm film, which was easier and less expensive to produce, and the network's decision to establish its own in-house camera crews. His most significant innovation, however, was the double-projector system that he developed to mix narration and film. This technique, which was copied throughout the industry, made possible a new kind of filmed report that would become the archetypal television news package: a reporter on camera, often at the scene of a story, beginning with a "stand-upper" that introduces the story; then film of other scenes, while the reporter's words, recorded sepa-

rately, serve as voice-over narration; finally, at the end, a "wrap-up,"
where the reporter appears on camera again. By the early 1950s, the
CBS newscast, now titled *Douglas Edwards with the News*, was adding
viewers and winning plaudits from critics. And it had gained the respect of many of the network's radio journalists, who now agreed to
contribute to the program and other television news shows.[20]

The big networks were not the only innovators. In the late 1940s,
with network growth limited and many stations still independent,
local stations developed many different kinds of programs, including news shows. WPIX, a New York City station owned by the *Daily
News*, the city's most popular tabloid, established a daily news program in June 1948. The *Telepix Newsreel* aired twice a day, at 7:30 PM
and 11:00 PM, and specialized in coverage of big local events like fires
and plane crashes. Its staff went to great lengths to acquire film of
these stories, which it hyped with what would become a standard
teaser, "film at eleven." Like its print cousin, it also featured lots of
human-interest stories and man-on-the-street interviews. A Chicago
station, WGN, developed a similar program, the *Chicagoland Newsreel*,
which was also successful. The real pioneer was KTLA in Los Angeles.
Run by Klaus Landsberg, a brilliant engineer, KTLA established the
most technologically sophisticated news program of the era. Employing relatively small, portable cameras and mobile live transmitters,
its reporters excelled in covering breaking news stories, and it would
remain a trailblazer in the delivery of breaking news throughout the
1950s and 1960s. It was Landsberg, for example, who first conceived
of putting a TV camera in a helicopter.

But such programs were the exception. Most local stations offered
little more than brief summaries of wire-service headlines, and the
expense of film technology led most to emphasize live entertainment programs instead of news. Believing that viewers got their news
from local papers and radio stations, television stations saw no need
to duplicate their efforts. Not until the 1960s, when new, inexpensive
video and microwave technology made local newsgathering economically feasible, did local stations, including network affiliates, expand
their news programming.[21]

The television news industry's first big opportunity to display its
potential occurred in 1948, when the networks descended on Philadelphia for the political conventions. The major parties had selected
Philadelphia with an eye on the emerging medium of television. Sales

were booming, and Philadelphia was on the coaxial cable, which was reaching more and more cities as the weeks and months passed. By the time the Republicans convened in July, it extended from Boston to Richmond, Virginia, with the potential for reaching millions of viewers. Radio journalists had been covering the conventions for two decades, but with lucrative entertainment programs on network schedules, it hadn't paid to produce "gavel-to-gavel" coverage—just bulletins, wrap-ups, and the acceptance speeches of the nominees. In 1948, however, television was a wide-open field, and with much of the broadcast day open—or devoted to unsponsored programming that cost nothing to preempt—the conventions were a great showcase. In cities where they were broadcast, friends and neighbors gathered in the homes of early adopters, in bars and taverns, even in front of department store display windows, where store managers had carefully arranged TVs to draw the attention of passers-by. Crowds on the sidewalk sometimes overflowed into the street, blocking traffic. "No more effective way could have been found to stimulate receiver sales than these impromptu TV set demonstrations," suggested Sig Mickelson.[22]

Because of the enormous technical difficulties and a lack of experience, the networks collaborated extensively. All four networks used the same pictures, provided by a common pool of cameras set up to focus on the podium and surrounding area. NBC's coverage was produced by *Life* magazine and featured journalists from Henry Luce's media empire as well as Swayze and network radio stars H. V. Kaltenborn and Richard Harkness. CBS's starred Murrow, Quincy Howe, and Douglas Edwards, newly installed on the *Evening News* and soon to be its sole newsreader. ABC relied on the gossip columnist and radio personality Walter Winchell. Lacking its own news staff, DuMont hired the Washington-based political columnist Drew Pearson to provide commentary. Many of these announcers did double duty, providing radio bulletins, too. With cameras still heavy and bulky, there were no roving floor reporters conducting interviews with delegates and candidates; instead, interviews occurred in makeshift studios set up in adjacent rooms off the main convention floor. Accordingly, there was little coverage of anything other than events occurring on the podium, and it was print journalists who provided Americans with the behind-the-scenes drama, particularly at the Democrats' convention, where Southern delegates, angered by the party's growing commitment to civil rights, walked out in protest and chose Strom Thurmond to run as the nominee of the hastily organized "Dixiecrats." The conventions were a hit with viewers. Though there were only about 300,000 sets in the entire US, industry research suggested that as many as 10 million Americans saw at least some convention coverage thanks to group viewing and department store advertising and special events.[23]

Four years later, when the Republicans and Democrats again gathered for their conventions, this time in Chicago, the networks were better prepared. Besides experience, they brought more nimble and sophisticated equipment. And, thanks to the spread of the coaxial cable, there were in a position to reach a nationwide audience. Excited by the geometric increase in receiver sales, and inspired by access to new markets that seemed to make it possible to double or even triple the number of television households, major manufacturers signed up as sponsors, and advertisements in newspapers urged consumers to buy sets to "see the conventions." Coverage was much wider and more complete than in 1948. Several main pool cameras with improved zoom capabilities focused on the podium, while each network deployed between twenty and twenty-five cameras on the periphery and at downtown hotels and in mobile units. "Never before," noted Mickelson, the CBS executive responsible for the event, "had so many television cameras been massed at one event."[24]

Meanwhile, announcers from each of the networks explained what was occurring and provided analysis and commentary. NBC's main announcer was Bill Henry, a Los Angeles print journalist. He was assisted by Kaltenborn and Harkness. Henry sat in a tiny studio and watched the proceedings through monitors, and did not appear on camera. CBS's coverage differed and established a new precedent. Its main announcer, Walter Cronkite, provided essentially the same narration, explanation, and commentary as Henry. But his face appeared on-screen, in a tiny window in the corner of the screen; when there was a lull on the convention floor, the window expanded to fill the entire screen. Cronkite, an experienced wire service correspondent, had just joined CBS after a successful stint at WTOP, its Washington affiliate. Mickelson had been impressed with his ability to explain and ad lib, and he insisted that CBS use Cronkite rather than the far more experienced and well-known Robert Trout. Mickelson conceded that, from his years of radio work, Trout excelled at "creating word pictures." But, with television, this was a superfluous gift. The cameras delivered the pictures. "What we needed was interpretation of the pictures on the screen. That was Cronkite's forte."

When print journalists asked Mickelson on the eve of the conventions what exact role Cronkite would play, he responded by suggesting that his new hire would be the "anchorman," a term that soon came to refer to newsreaders like Swayze and Edwards as well. Yet in coining this term, Mickelson was referring to the complex process that Don Hewitt had conceived to provide more detailed and up-to-the-minute coverage of the convention. Recognizing that the action was on the floor, and that if TV journalists were to match the efforts of print reporters they needed to be able to report from there as quickly as possible, Hewitt mounted a second camera that could pan the floor and zoom in on floor reporters armed with walkie-talkies and flashlights, which they used to inform Hewitt when they had an interview or report ready to deliver. It worked like clockwork: "They combed through the delegations, talked to both leaders and members, queried them on motivations and prospective actions, and kept relaying information to the editorial desk."[25] It was then filtered and collated and passed on to Cronkite, who served as the "anchor" of the relay, delivering the latest news and ad-libbing with the poise and self-assurance that he would display at subsequent conventions and during live coverage of space flights and major breaking news. Cronkite's seemingly effortless ability to provide viewers with useful and interesting information about the proceedings won praise from television critics and boosted CBS's reputation with viewers.[26]

NBC was not so successful. In keeping with the network's—and RCA's—infatuation with technology, it sought to cover events on the convention floor with a new gadget, a small, hand-held, live-television camera that could transmit pictures and needn't be connected by wire. As Frank recalled, "It could roam the floor . . . showing delegates reacting to speakers and even join a wireless microphone for interviews." But it regularly malfunctioned and contributed little to NBC's coverage. More effective and popular were a series of programs that Bill McAndrew developed to provide background. *Convention Call* was broadcast twice a day during the conventions, before sessions and when they adjourned for breaks. Its hosts encouraged viewers to call in and ask NBC reporters to explain what was occurring, especially rules of procedure. The show sparked a flood of calls that overwhelmed telephone company switchboards and forced NBC to switch to telegrams instead.[27]

Ratings for network coverage of the conventions exceeded expectations. Approximately 60 million viewers saw at least some of the conventions on television, with an estimated audience of 55 million tuning in at their peak. And the conventions inspired viewers to begin watching the evening newscasts and contributed to an increase in their popularity. Television critics praised the networks for their contributions to civic enlightenment. Jack Gould of the *New York Times* suggested that television had "won its spurs" and was "a welcome addition to the Fourth Estate."[28]

Conventions, planned in advance at locations well-suited for television's limited technology, were ideal events for the networks to cover. These were the days before front-loaded primaries made them little more than coronations of nominees determined months beforehand, and the parties were undergoing important changes that were often revealed in angry debates and frantic back-room deliberations. And while print journalists remained the most complete source for such information, television allowed viewers to see it in real time, and its stable of experienced reporters and analysts proved remarkably adept at conveying the drama and explaining the stakes.

Conventions were not the only events that were suitable for TV news coverage. So, too, were congressional hearings. Their appeal to viewers was revealed in 1951, when local stations began to broadcast the fact-finding hearings of the Senate Crime Committee. With a cast of characters right out of a film noir, the hearings attracted increasing press and public attention as they moved from city to city. Public interest peaked in March, when the committee, chaired by senator Estes Kefauver, arrived in New York, hoping to expose the activities of its notorious crime syndicates. Eager to provide a public service, networks decided to broadcast the hearings live. Millions of Americans tuned in, much to the surprise of network officials, who hadn't yet recognized that people would watch television during the day. The hearings were a riveting spectacle, sparking widespread discussion at workplaces and dinner tables around the country. But they attracted viewers because during daytime hours there were no other options; many stations without a network affiliation didn't broadcast any programs in the morning or early afternoon. When a nighttime session was held, NBC and CBS elected not to preempt its already profitable prime-time programming to cover it. With few affiliates and the least popular shows, ABC and DuMont stuck with the hearings. They had a lot less to lose.

Television coverage of congressional hearings was an anomaly. They were feasible for the networks to broadcast only because there wasn't much sponsored daytime programming. By 1954, when the Army-McCarthy hearings began, the daytime schedules of most stations—both independent and network affiliates—were filled with sponsored programs, and electing to preempt them for news had potentially serious economic consequences. The hearings, instigated by senator Joseph McCarthy to determine the extent of alleged Communist influence in the military, were one of the big news stories of the year. Nevertheless, only ABC and the few stations still affiliated with DuMont broadcast them, while NBC and CBS provided viewers with late-night summaries that would not impinge on sponsored programming—especially the advertiser-supported entertainment programs that were drawing the largest audiences in prime time.[29] In short, as TV expanded its reach, and as the networks, individual stations, and advertisers developed programs that were most likely to attract large numbers of viewers and make their investments pay off, news personnel came to recognize that they would occupy no more than a small niche on network schedules. Holding onto that niche would depend on their ability to make their programming compatible with the entertainment shows and advertising that had become the medium's staples.

By the early 1950s, that niche was shrinking. With both prime-time and weekday daytime hours devoted to sponsored programs, most news and public-affairs shows on the networks were relegated to the Sunday afternoon "intellectual ghetto." A holdover from radio, this tradition of airing highbrow programs on Sundays made sense to programmers and fulfilled the expectations of most viewers. This, for example, was where the pioneering interview show *Meet the Press* made its debut in 1947. Created by Lawrence Spivak and Martha Rountree, two well-known journalists, *Meet the Press* began as a radio program on the Mutual network. NBC picked up the television version, which was structured as a press conference, with a single guest answering questions posed by a panel of journalists and Rountree serving as moderator. It wasn't very popular, but attracted attention among politicians, journalists, and viewers who enjoyed its regular diet of political inside dope. Its modest success led CBS to create a similar program, *Face the Nation*, hosted by Ted Koop, the network's well-connected Washington bureau chief, which debuted in November 1954. Both programs relied on the willingness of politicians and public officials to appear as guests, and the revelations they elicited were regularly noted in newspapers, boosting the visibility of television journalism and of the major networks in particular.[30]

By the mid-1950s, the news divisions at NBC and CBS had expanded, and network journalists had grown more ambitious. NBC's expansion was overseen by Bill McAndrew. An ex-print journalist, McAndrew was committed to improving NBC's news offerings, and he pressed network officials for additional airtime, especially in the evenings. But his plans were regularly shot down by Sylvester "Pat" Weaver, NBC's brilliant yet eccentric head of programming. Weaver's background was in advertising, but he ardently believed that television could serve as a tool for cultural enlightenment, and he was unhappy with the *Camel News Caravan* and the state of TV news in general. He took it out on McAndrew and Frank, rejecting their ideas for programs and additional airtime. Looking back on their conflict, Weaver conceded that he had been hard on them and perhaps unrealistic in his expectations. Lacking the technology to provide the "spot" news at which radio excelled, Weaver thought NBC's television journalists should do something quite different, "develop real world coverage—a wide view of trends and developments, national and global, that would have greater significance than any one day's events."[31] He was especially disdainful of John Cameron Swayze, the most readily identifiable NBC television newsman, and he pressured McAndrew to find a more dignified and credentialed replacement. When *Douglas Edwards and the News* surpassed NBC's *News Caravan* in the ratings, the pressured mounted. In October 1956, after a successful trial run as the coanchors of NBC's coverage of the 1956 conventions, Chet Huntley and David Brinkley were installed as the anchors of a substantially revamped NBC newscast, *The Huntley-Brinkley Report*, produced by Frank. Their pairing worked, and it gave the network a more serious and professional showcase. Critics, in particular, raved about the new team, with the articulate and acidly witty Brinkley attracting special notice.[32]

The revamping of NBC's newscast was a direct response to CBS's remarkable success in attracting viewers and winning praise from television critics. With the blessing of Bill Paley and Frank Stanton, Sig Mickelson ended the network's relationship with Telenews and CBS established its own in-house film-production unit. The network also established a film archive that would prove invaluable as a source of background "file footage" to illustrate stories. As the reputation of the network's television news division improved, more of its radio correspondents—including some of the legendary "Murrow Boys"—agreed to move over to TV news, increasing the size and caliber of the staff on which Hewitt could rely for spots on the evening newscast. Increasingly, they served not as newsreaders but as reporters, assigned to bureaus from which they were sent to the location of breaking stories, where they conducted interviews and, with the assistance of cameramen and technicians, amassed the film and audio that served as the raw material of their stories. With its own film production staff, the program shifted to more political and international news—though film from Europe still had to be flown to New York before it could be broadcast.

By 1957, the CBS *Evening News* no longer resembled a newsreel. Routinely relying on the talents of well-known correspondents such as Eric Sevareid, Charles Collingwood, and Howard K. Smith, it was a more serious and informative program. Mickelson, Hewitt, and their staff recognized that they were engaged in an entirely new enterprise, the production of a "full, daily news report." Not a comprehensive report, as one might find in a serious daily newspaper, but "a smattering of the most significant stories," including some that could not be visualized with film and had to be reported as tell-stories. This required determining which stories were truly significant, and balancing that against a natural temptation to favor stories for which they had film. To make this easier, they chose visuals, both stills and film, with an eye toward how they might "aid in understanding" and make stories more comprehensible to viewers. Having visuals, especially film, at their disposal was a revelation; it exerted a growing influence on how they covered the news, allowing them to "tell stories in a new way."[33]

These trends were influential and soon affected the other networks. NBC's evening newscast continued to improve, as Reuven Frank increased its use of visuals and learned "how to discipline . . . pictures the way editors discipline written words."[34] And ABC finally committed itself to news programming, after several false starts. The financially beleaguered network had tried to develop several evening news shows in the late 1940s and early 1950s. All had failed, and the network chose instead to focus on developing prime-time entertainment programs. But realizing that at least some news was essential if ABC wanted to be regarded as a credible network, its president, Robert Kintner, hired veteran radio correspondent John Daly to run ABC's small news unit. Daly had a long track record with CBS and was familiar to the public as host of the game show *What's My Line?* Surprisingly, he continued to host the CBS program after taking charge of news, sports, special events, and religious programming at ABC. Rather than hire an Edwards or a Swayze, he installed himself as the anchor of *John Daly and the News*, a conventional fifteen-minute evening newscast that debuted in October 1953. Lacking network support for an in-house film production team, the Daly program continued to rely on newsreel syndicates for film footage. It also employed the fewest correspondents and had trouble attracting talented journalists. Part of the problem was Daly himself, who enjoyed the spotlight and assumed anchor chores whenever any special event—like the Army-McCarthy hearings—warranted news coverage. Despite meager resources, the program stayed on the network's schedule. For the rest of the 1950s, however, news programming languished at ABC. "We put development of our news department on the back burner," Leonard Goldenson, the company's chairman, conceded in his memoirs.[35]

Television's potential as a medium for news and public affairs was exemplified by *See It Now*, the most innovative program of the era. *See It Now* was conceived by Fred Friendly, an ambitious radio producer whose credits included a successful quiz show, a highly praised radio documentary on atomic power, and a series of record albums, narrated by Ed Murrow, that allowed listeners to experience key moments in recent history through audio recordings of speeches, news bulletins, and special events. A large, imposing man whose energy and brilliance would make him enormously successful but also resented by many of his peers and coworkers, Friendly understood show business as well as journalism, and he shared Pat Weaver's belief in television's capacity for enlightenment and cultural improvement. His success and penchant for innovation impressed Bill Paley and Frank Stanton, and they instructed Sig Mickelson to hire him to produce radio documentaries. But Friendly saw his new job at CBS as a stepping stone into the new field of television and told Mickelson of his interest in producing a "*Life* magazine of the air." Mickelson thought the idea a bit far-fetched, but he appreciated Friendly's enthusiasm and ingenuity and set him to work on his first network project, a weekly radio news program that mixed taped recordings of actual events with live interviews. Hosted by Murrow, *Hear It Now* first aired in December 1950.[36]

Impressed with developments in television, especially coverage of the Kefauver hearings, Murrow was persuaded by Friendly to end their radio show after only half a year and recreate it for TV. Though Murrow continued to have reservations about television's emphasis on the visual, Friendly was excited about the new program and plunged into its development, familiarizing himself with the techniques of documentary filmmaking, photojournalism, and newsreel production, and writing a stirring article in *Variety* on the potential of television journalism.[37] Exploiting Murrow's close personal relationship with Paley, Friendly was also able to establish *See It Now* as an independent unit outside of Mickelson's control. Coproducers Friendly and Murrow reported directly to Paley and Stanton, an arrangement that gave them substantial autonomy and ample funds for story development and the very best equipment—and relieved Mickelson of responsibility for the program's regularly going over budget. These funds came from the aluminum manufacturer Alcoa, which had offered to sponsor *Hear It Now* and was happy to support its migration to television.[38]

Eager to draw as much as possible from the documentary tradition, Friendly's production unit included people with considerable experience in the field, including Palmer Williams, who had worked on documentaries with Frank Capra and John Houseman. To ensure that his program looked professional, Friendly recruited cameramen and film editors from newsreel companies and insisted that the program use high-grade 35mm stock for its filmed reports. He also drew from the staff at CBS News, hiring several seasoned reporters and making Don Hewitt the program's director. Friendly oversaw this motley group, with Williams as his right-hand man, and Murrow as the show's host and commentator.

See It Now debuted on November 18, 1951, with a caveat: "This is an old team learning a new trade," Murrow announced from the show's unusual set, a control room where its technical staff, including Hewitt, were visible to viewers. Murrow's modesty was understandable; they were essentially making things up as they went along. But with the irrepressible Friendly at the helm, *See It Now* had an experimental edge

Edward R. Murrow was the host of the legendary program *See It Now* as well as *Person to Person*, a celebrity chat show that was one of CBS's most popular programs. His two assignments were a testament to the nature of television broadcasting in the 1950s. Photo of Murrow on *See It Now* courtesy of the Museum of Broadcast Communications.

that would bring out the best in Murrow and revolutionize broadcast journalism.

The program's innovations were myriad. Some of them were in the areas of newsgathering and story production. With complete control over their own staff, Friendly and Murrow created a new system that relied on field producers to oversee location filming and reporting, and they used their own film, rather than newsreel or file footage, to illustrate their reports. The field producers worked in tandem with talented reporters like Joseph Wershba, David Schoenbrun, and

Murrow on set of *Person to Person*. Photo courtesy of CBS/Photofest.

Charles Collingwood to craft carefully edited stories. Most of them relied heavily on unscripted interviews and effective use of "crosscuts,"
fragments of much longer interviews that were arranged throughout
stories to encourage narrative flow and a sharper focus. This would
become a standard feature of television journalism. Determined to
make the most of television's capacity for displaying arresting images,
Friendly and Williams created stories that relied on the juxtaposition

of filmed sequences, with a minimum of narration or explanation. The film itself conveyed the point, often more poignantly than words.[39]

The range of subjects covered on *See It Now* was also unusual. Long known for its exposé of senator Joseph McCarthy, an episode recounted in George Clooney's film *Good Night, and Good Luck*, the program is sometimes assumed to have been all hard news and deadly serious investigative features. But from the start it ranged widely, in keeping with Friendly's original source of inspiration, Henry Luce's fantastically successful *Life*. Most broadcasts had multiple segments, and in nearly every show at least one or two of them were reported live from remote locations. A substantial number were human-interest features, some pegged to ongoing news like the Korean War, but others were included because of their potential interest to viewers—a story from Cleveland on a driver's education class for high school students; a report from Florida on spring training with the Brooklyn Dodgers; a filmed story on the Grand Coulee Dam. Some stories were followed over time, with periodic updates and "revisits" to remote locations. Many were reports from abroad that introduced viewers to complex social and political issues like decolonization, the Arab-Israeli conflict, and the prospects for European unification. There were plenty of interviews with newsmakers, both foreign and American, and extensive coverage of events like Queen Elizabeth's coronation and the presidential primary campaigns. Perhaps the most compelling broadcasts were two special hour-long programs on US servicemen in Korea, which aired at Christmastime in 1952 and 1953. To produce the shows, Murrow and a crew of twenty, including five reporters, traveled to Korea and shot hundreds of hours of film. The resulting broadcasts provided viewers with a detailed look at the daily lives of military personnel and the overall progress of the war. They were penetrating and evocative and won the show enormous praise.[40]

As the broadcast progressed and gained the respect of critics and CBS officials, Friendly and Murrow became increasingly bold in their choice of subjects. The programs critical of McCarthy were the most audacious, but their place in *See It Now*'s legacy has overshadowed other stories that tackled controversial issues. Some examined the wider repercussions of the Cold War and anti-Communism—for example, the efforts of the American Legion to prevent a chapter of the American Civil Liberties Union from being established in Indianapolis, or the travails of the scientist and suspected "security risk" J. Robert

Oppenheimer, whom Murrow interviewed at his office at the Institute for Advanced Study in Princeton, New Jersey. Others addressed new issues like the links between cigarettes and lung cancer, the illness that would eventually kill Murrow, and the desegregation of Southern schools in the wake of the *Brown v. Board of Education* decision. And some were new-style television exposés. The most controversial was a story on a small-town newspaper in Texas that ran afoul of the state government and powerful corporate interests for exposing corruption in a program intended to help veterans purchase land.

When *See It Now* debuted in November 1951 it occupied a marginal time slot, Sunday afternoons at 3:30. Before the end of its first season, it was moved to Sundays at 6:30, where it remained for the entirety of its second season. In September 1953, it was placed in prime time, at 10:30 PM on Tuesdays. It held this time slot for the next two seasons. Throughout this period Alcoa remained its sponsor, providing funds for the production and promotion of the show, although on a couple of occasions—most notably, the McCarthy broadcasts—the company refused to be publicly associated with the program and Friendly and Murrow had to publicize it out of their own pockets. At the end of the 1954–1955 season, Alcoa withdrew its support. The company claimed no political motive for this, but many observers were skeptical, suggesting, for example, that the Oppenheimer interview or the story on the Texas land fraud, where Alcoa was expanding its business, had pushed the company to end its sponsorship. Looking back on the decision, Friendly agreed that political pressure was at least partly to blame. "Aluminum salesmen had difficulty explaining to irate customers why their company felt it necessary to sponsor programs *against* McCarthy and *for* Oppenheimer, *against* cigarettes and *for* 'socialized medicine'—which is what some doctors thought our program on the Salk vaccine advocated." He also noted, however, that the program had served Alcoa's purpose, boosting its public image, and that with aluminum sales booming, it didn't need to sponsor *See It Now* anymore. "The job that *See It Now* had been purchased to achieve had been done; for many the name Alcoa had become a symbol of enlightened corporate leadership."[41]

Alcoa executives were not the only ones concerned about *See It Now*; so, too, were Paley, Stanton, and Mickelson. By and large, the CBS executives were supportive of the show, especially considering its expense and the fact that it never attracted a large audience, even when it was moved to prime time. Paley liked the prestige it brought to CBS, and Stanton and Mickelson were impressed with the program's production values and high journalistic standards. Paley and Stanton never interfered with the program's production, and Paley himself phoned Murrow on the eve of the first McCarthy broadcast to affirm his—and the network's—full support. Yet, over time, the particular ways Friendly and Murrow employed documentary techniques raised problems, especially when covering controversial subjects. In the tradition of film documentarians, many of the reports on *See It Now* expressed a point of view. At times, this was unconscious and a result of conventions of which the staff was more than likely unaware—the placement of cameras and selection of film footage, the larger framing of stories, and the arrangement of segments within the program's "flow." But at other times, as in the case of the McCarthy broadcasts, the point of view was consciously chosen and presented in a manner that made it explicit. The March 1954 report on McCarthy was an especially egregious example of this. By knitting together unflattering footage of McCarthy in action, and interspersing these segments with pointed, well-researched rejoinders by Murrow, the program not only undermined the senator's credibility but made him appear dangerously unhinged. *See It Now* provided Murrow in particular with a new venue for the sort of commentary that he had specialized in on radio. And with the aid of visuals and other innovative production techniques, the program established a new standard for probing, often pointed exposés.[42]

This would not have posed a problem for a newspaper publisher. But Bill Paley ran a television network, an organization comprised of dozens of affiliates—independent stations run by conservative businesspeople with licenses granted by the FCC. In 1949, the FCC had issued the Fairness Doctrine, which allowed stations and networks to editorialize but also required them to present a "reasonably balanced presentation" of issues. In practice, this encouraged parties upset by their treatment by broadcasters to demand "equal time" to present their own views—as McCarthy did after his rough treatment by *See It Now*. This opportunity was seized regularly by politicians and other public figures in the early 1950s, and it made the airing of controversial programs with a point of view unattractive from a commercial as well as legal perspective. Time devoted to rebuttals by aggrieved parties preempted profitable network programs and exposed affiliates to potential problems when they went up for relicensing. In a widely cited speech to the National Association of Broadcasters shortly after the McCarthy broadcasts, Paley reaffirmed CBS's commitment to the Fairness Doctrine and reiterated that the network would continue to grant equal time. He also announced that its news programming would be guided by a new principle, the "will and intent to be objective." This speech, which was published as a pamphlet and distributed throughout CBS, made it clear that the documentary-inspired approach developed by Friendly and Murrow would not be the path that the network would follow, and it set the stage for *See It Now*'s demise and a falling out between Paley and Murrow.[43]

After their program was dropped by Alcoa, Friendly and Murrow hustled to find other sponsors, but their efforts were complicated by a related development. Without a regular sponsor, an expensive program like *See It Now* was a financial drain on the network. The show lost its Tuesday night time slot and became an unscheduled floating program, "See It Now and Then," in the words of a television critic. To mollify Friendly and Murrow, the program was expanded to an hour, allowing for more detailed stories. Lacking a regular place on the schedule, however, Friendly and Murrow were forced to negotiate with the programming and sales departments to secure airtime. And with ratings low, the program was often relegated to Sunday afternoons, a painful and embarrassing demotion. To make matters worse, its reports continued to spark demands for equal time, and management's eagerness to give in to them embittered Murrow. In 1958, after a right-wing congressman received equal time to claim that statehood for Hawaii, the subject of an episode in March 1958, was a Communist conspiracy, Murrow wrote a furious letter of protest to Paley. Paley was unimpressed, and when he met with Friendly and Murrow at the end of the season, he informed them that *See It Now* would be canceled. Murrow couldn't believe it. Paley knew that it was the network's most prestigious program, but the costs now outweighed the benefits. The show's predilection for controversial subjects, he confessed, had given him "a constant stomach ache."[44]

Despite its low ratings and penchant for controversy, *See It Now* was enormously influential. It inspired other television journalists to adopt many of the same production methods and storytelling techniques. And its appeal to upscale viewers and what executives and ad agency personnel called "influentials"—consumers whose tastes were supposed to trickle down among their less educated and well-off neighbors—put pressure on NBC to match its success. Reuven Frank recalled, "The people who ran NBC enjoyed telling us that although our news programs were successful enough in ratings, revenue, and other crass criteria, they had no stature, that what we were doing was far short of television's noble potentials." NBC's response was *Background*, which first aired in prime time in August 1954 but was then moved to Sunday afternoons when the new fall season began. A half hour long, like the original incarnation of *See It Now*, each episode covered a single subject in detail through filmed reports, interviews, and occasional live remote broadcasts. Hosted by Joseph C. Harsch, it emphasized foreign policy and national politics, relying in large part on the rapidly improving reportorial skills of NBC's small yet growing corps of correspondents. Early programs focused on nationalist movements in Asia, the fortunes of the American auto industry, and the experiences of a young American draftee as he left his home in Pennsylvania and was inducted into the military. It lasted only one season. "NBC did not believe in us," argued Frank, who served as producer of the program for its final episodes. There was little or no effort to promote the show, and, in the end, it just didn't fit Pat Weaver's nebulous ideas about what constituted a news program.[45]

The network tried again in 1956, with another late Sunday afternoon offering, *Outlook*. Produced by Frank and hosted by new hire Chet Huntley, it offered viewers live and filmed reports on a much wider variety of subjects, very much in the spirit of *See It Now*. The live remotes were especially exciting to Weaver, who was certain that the show would be a hit. It wasn't, but NBC kept it on the air, and Frank and his staff produced some distinguished programs on subjects such as the disposal of nuclear waste, Southern opposition to desegregation, and changes in the USSR after Joseph Stalin's death. The show specialized in in-depth coverage of recent and breaking news stories and became a training ground for reporters like David Brinkley, Edwin Newman, and John Chancellor. Under various names, it lasted seven years and burnished NBC's reputation for high-quality journalism.

News and public-affairs programs that aired on Sunday afternoons shared the "ghetto" with a variety of other cultural programming, including documentaries on history and science that were often produced by network news personnel. The most successful of these programs was NBC's *Victory at Sea*, which first aired in 1952. Drawn from military and newsreel footage, it was a masterfully edited twenty-six-part documentary on US naval operations in World War II and was a big hit for the network. NBC's most ambitious cultural program was *Wide, Wide World*, a project conceived by Weaver that was launched with great fanfare in 1955. Ninety minutes long and broadcast from assorted remote locations, it exposed viewers to an unusually wide range of sights and events—from majestic natural and constructed wonders to glimpses of ordinary people going about their daily lives. It attracted considerable publicity and affirmed Weaver's belief in television's capacity to transport viewers to distant locales.

CBS developed several public-affairs programs for Sunday afternoons as well. The most distinguished was *Omnibus*, a program produced by the Ford Foundation that debuted in 1952. It was a "variety show for intellectuals," showcasing developments in drama, dance, and music. Featuring live and filmed reports, and hosted by the British journalist Alistair Cooke, it won a small yet devoted following. After four years on CBS, it was picked up by ABC for a season before winding up on NBC until its run ended in 1961. Another CBS program, *Adventure*, sought to expose children and teenagers to science. It first aired in 1953 and lasted three seasons. More ambitious was *The Search*, a documentary series on cutting-edge research being conducted at leading American universities that ran for four years beginning in 1954. Seeking to emulate NBC's *Victory at Sea*, CBS also developed multipart historical documentaries. The most successful was *The Twentieth Century*, a sweeping account of the century's most significant events, developments, and personalities that debuted in 1957. Utilizing footage from CBS's growing news film archive as well as newsreels and narrated by Walter Cronkite, it ran until 1966.[46]

By this time, the networks had begun to fill weekend afternoons with sports. This wasn't feasible during television's early years, when primitive camera technology made boxing and wrestling the only sports that looked good on the small screen. But cameras soon improved, and by the early 1950s, major league baseball and college and professional football began to be broadcast by individual stations and informal regional networks. Most of these broadcasts aired on Saturdays, but they began to spill over into Sundays as well, imperiling programs in the "ghetto." The appeal of televised sports, especially pro football, led increasing numbers of stations to sign up with these regional networks and eschew the cultural programming that NBC and

CBS provided them on Sunday afternoons. To prevent massive defections, the major networks were compelled to sign contracts that gave pro sports a secure place on their Sunday schedules. As Sig Mickelson, who led the CBS effort to acquire the broadcast rights to National Football League games, recalled, "it was time to give in and swim with the tide."[47] Televised sports became even more popular in the early 1960s with the introduction of videotape, which made it possible to show "instant replays" in real time and then in slow motion. These developments not only made many more sports, including golf and tennis, suitable for presentation on television; they encouraged the executives who ran leagues and franchises to change rules and adopt other features to make their sports more attractive to television viewers. In short order, Sunday afternoons became a cash cow, and public-affairs and cultural programs were pushed off network schedules altogether.[48]

The evening newscasts also began to feel additional pressure. Surprisingly, it came from ABC. Now led by Leonard Goldenson, a Harvard-educated lawyer and savvy dealmaker who had rescued the network from near bankruptcy, ABC made an aggressive bid to attract families. It launched programs like *The Lone Ranger*, *The Adventures of Rin Tin Tin*, and *Disneyland*, and broadcast them at 7:30 in the evening, upsetting the conventions of prime time. The latter, which debuted in the fall of 1954, was the fruit of a shrewd partnership between Goldenson and Walt Disney and was an especially formidable competitor. These programs aired opposite the *Camel News Caravan* and CBS's *Douglas Edwards* program and quickly began to attract viewers. To compete with such family fare, NBC and CBS were compelled to provide their affiliates with programs that might appeal to families with children. In 1955, to accommodate this shift, CBS moved its newscast out of its 7:30 slot and offered it to its affiliates at 6:45 or 7:15, the choice being up to individual stations. NBC did the same two years later. Gradually, news and public-affairs programs were being shuffled out of the hours when most people watched television.

At the same time, however, novel forms of news-and-information programming were flourishing, often at the most unexpected times. By the mid-1950s, the most successful of these broadcasts was NBC's *Today*. Overshadowed in most histories of TV news by *See It Now*, it was nearly as innovative as its storied competitor and more influential, particularly in the long run. In 1951, when Pat Weaver began thinking about creating a television version of the "rise-and-shine" programs that were successful in radio, there was very little morning programming on either local or network TV. Most stations began broadcasting at 10:00 AM, and until the late afternoon the majority of daytime programs were locally produced, unsponsored filler. There were some exceptions. The most suggestive was in Philadelphia, where a 7:00 AM show hosted by the comedian Ernie Kovacs had become very popular. But Weaver had more grandiose aspirations. His show would be more "newsy" and "tell early risers all kinds of things they should know as they faced the day."[49]

In a memo to his staff and the special production unit that had begun developing the program, Weaver outlined his ambitious plan for the show. *Today* would be broadcast from a street-level studio in the heart of Radio City, enabling the program to connect with the crowds and energy of midtown Manhattan. The studio would include the control room, allowing viewers to see how the program "worked." Like a magazine, it would cover a wide range of subjects, with news bulletins, interviews, live remotes, stories on books and music, musical performances, and comedy—"a bird's eye view of the world and its happenings." The news would be first-rate, "the finest news presentation in history." Most important of all, the program would "change the listening habits of the nation." Drawing on his vast experience in both radio and advertising, Weaver carefully considered how the show might fit into the morning routine of a typical middle-class family. He warned that it should not distract them from their preparation for the day, so that much of the burden had to be carried by audio. He also recognized that, as with radio morning programs, the audience for *Today* would regularly turn over, with some viewers watching no more than fifteen minutes. The most important and useful information, then, would need to be rebroadcast at regular intervals.[50]

Dave Garroway, a popular Chicago television and radio personality, was selected as the program's host. He would be joined by two sidekicks. One would deliver short news reports; the other would interview guests, introduce features, and assist Garroway. All three men would routinely appear together on camera and help give the program a lively, informal tone—one that was quite different from conventional news programs and essential to its appeal. *Today*'s producers were Mort Werner and Richard Pinkham. Werner was especially important in retooling the program after its debut, creating new features

Dave Garroway was the host of NBC's trailblazing morning news-and-features program, *Today*, which debuted in 1952. Garroway hosted the program until 1961, but it remained successful, despite numerous personnel changes, for decades, demonstrating the viability of programs that mixed hard and soft news. Photo courtesy of NBC/Photofest.

and continually adjusting the mix between news and other material to strike the right balance. And it was Werner who conceived the idea of including young women in the show's on-screen "family." Assorted "*Today* Girls" added a feminine presence and made it easier for the program to cover stories on fashion, decorating, and childrearing that viewers considered "women's domain." To beef up the show's presentation of news, Gerald Green, a print journalist, was hired as its news editor. At first, McAndrew and the NBC news staff, resenting *Today*'s massive $40,000 per episode budget and its status as Weaver's pet project, sometimes refused to provide the program with film until it had aired on the *Camel News Caravan*, forcing Green to send his own camera units and reporters to cover big stories. It took several years and Weaver's departure from NBC before the producers of *Today* were able to develop a good relationship with the news division.[51]

The show made its debut in January 1952. Despite massive promotion by NBC, it had only a single sponsor and failed to impress viewers or television critics. A particularly silly feature, "Today in Two Minutes," had Garroway review the headlines of assorted metropolitan newspapers that were tacked to a bulletin board. When the program's cameras were not ogling the technology in the studio control room, they offered live shots from a variety of remote locations like the Pentagon, Grand Central Station, and downtown Chicago—regardless of their connection to the day's news. Newspaper reviews were terrible. One critic quipped, "Do yourself a favor, NBC, roll over and go back to sleep."[52] But Weaver was undaunted. He and the program's staff set to work revising and streamlining the program's diverse features, and within a few weeks the resulting adjustments began to bear fruit. More viewers were tuning in, critical notices had improved, and, one by one, sponsors began signing up for the many "spots" that Weaver had made available to advertisers. Many of the commercials were delivered by Garroway himself, in the same easygoing style that he displayed throughout the two-hour show. Werner, Pinkham, and Green also found the right mix between news and features, and Green, conscious that the program's competition was radio, devised a clever formula for determining how frequently news stories would be repeated. When surveys soon revealed that the typical viewer was watching for nearly an hour, Green made additional adjustments, and the program acquired a more leisurely pace, particularly during the show's second hour.

A year after *Today*'s debut, it had a small yet dedicated audience and forty-four sponsors. But real success didn't come until January 1953, when its "family" gained another member: J. Fred Muggs, a chimpanzee owned by two former NBC pages. Muggs provided comic relief, cavorting with the cast and the program's guests. His arrival sparked a wave of new publicity and a huge increase in viewership. And while Muggs's addition to *Today* elicited snickers among critics and disturbed some of the news staff, the program's producers recognized that his presence encouraged children to pressure their parents to tune in. Muggs lasted four and a half years before his increasingly erratic behavior led to his removal from the show. During this period *Today* became a huge hit and moneymaker for NBC, confirming Weaver's faith that people could be induced to watch TV in the morning and that spot advertising could be more lucrative than relying on single sponsors. In September 1953, a mere eight months after Muggs's arrival, *Variety* reported that *Today* was the most profitable show on television. Advertisers were clamoring for spots on the program, which by then cost almost $4,000 per minute.[53]

Building on the success of *Today*, Weaver and NBC launched another innovative news-and-features program in March 1954. It was called *Home*, and it aired on weekdays at 11:00 AM. Hosted by veteran actress and radio personality Arlene Francis, it was targeted at middle-class housewives and offered a mix of news and features likely to be interesting to women, including segments on fashion, cooking, decorating, childrearing, and travel. Francis, a regular panelist on *What's My Line?*, was a poised and dignified "femcee," and she also served as the program's managing editor. She was assisted by Hugh Downs, a talented young announcer. Like other Weaver-inspired projects, *Home* had an enormous budget and boasted an innovative set, a rotating stage that provided viewers with regular glimpses of the program's cameras and audio equipment. And, like *Today*, it specialized in remotes and filmed reports of stories told through interesting angles. It was also a ratings success, despite Francis's persistent interest in covering serious issues such as divorce and juvenile delinquency. Francis, Downs, and the program's staff were shocked when it was canceled in the summer of 1957 as part of a more general housecleaning after Weaver's dismissal. Though its life was brief, *Home* established the template that virtually every subsequent daytime news-and-features program would follow: a blend of hard and soft news, with an emphasis on the latter.[54]

Both *Today* and *Home* relied extensively on interviews with newsmakers, celebrities, and ordinary people who possessed some element of human interest. This had worked well on radio, and its adaptation to television was perfectly logical. Seeking to fill airtime during the first few years of television broadcasting, the networks and local stations offered numerous interview programs, especially during the empty afternoon hours. And interviews were an essential ingredient of another Weaver-initiated project that debuted in 1954, *Tonight*, a late-night program hosted by the comedian Steve Allen. But most interview programs were casual and superficial and rarely touched on serious subjects. An exception was *Night Beat*, a show produced by Ted Yates that was broadcast on an independent station in New York at 11:00 PM. It was hosted by Mike Wallace, a veteran radio announcer and game-show emcee who had gotten into television in the early 1950s as the costar of a successful afternoon talk show. *Night Beat* was sharp and cynical, offering viewers accustomed to the gentle questioning of most television interview programs an arresting spectacle. Wallace and his staff would conduct extensive research before each interview. And once in front of the camera, Wallace would grill his guests, who included politicians and important public figures. "If they appeared to be hiding behind evasive answers," Wallace later recalled, "I'd press them—or cajole them—to knock it off, to come clean. If, in response to pressure, they became embarrassed or irritated or sullen, I'd try to exploit that mood instead of retreating into amiable reassurance."[55] The program's set provided a perfect setting for his aggressive questioning. Eschewing the comfy surroundings of other chat shows, Wallace conducted his interviews in a bare, darkened studio, with a single, powerful klieg light poised over Wallace's shoulder at his guest. To add drama, Yates and his staff regularly employed close-ups, especially after Wallace posed an especially probing question. It was often riveting television, and it earned Wallace good press and the nickname "The Grand Inquisitor."

The show's success sparked a bidding war among the networks for Wallace's services. ABC eventually won, with Leonard Goldenson assuring Wallace that he would enjoy free reign. But Wallace's stint at ABC was deeply frustrating. A big reason for this was that *The Mike Wallace Interview* was a weekly program that aired in prime time, not late at night, and ABC lawyers and executives were fearful of revelations that might expose the network to lawsuits. "Each night we went on the air, a lawyer would sit in the studio where, facing me, he would hold up cue cards at sensitive moments warning me to BE CAREFUL or STOP or RETREAT."[56] After a single season, the show was dropped by ABC, and though it continued for two more years in syndication, its demise marked the end of Mike Wallace's initial effort to break into the journalistic side of the television business.

The fate of *The Mike Wallace Interview* says a lot about the evolution of television from the late 1940s to the late 1950s. There was, without question, an audience for "The Grand Inquisitor" and for the hardhitting interviewing for which Wallace would become well-known on *60 Minutes*. But it was a niche audience, and programs like *See It Now* or *The Mike Wallace Interview* were out of place on prime-time television by the late 1950s. By this time, well over two-thirds of American households owned a TV, and the television audience included increasing numbers of lower-middle-class and working-class Americans—

small businessmen, office workers and salespeople, factory hands and manual laborers. These were people who hadn't been able to afford sets in the early years. But now, on account of lower prices and rising incomes, they could. More important, they could afford many of the new consumer goods that were being peddled by advertisers, and so came to be seen as a desirable and potentially lucrative *mass* audience. Their emergence as consumers prompted important changes in the marketing strategies of American business. More than ever, the big money was in catering to the mass market, appealing to demographic groups that, because of a lack of disposal income and inconsistent employment, often had been neglected in the past.[57] By the late 1950s, the television audience had grown in another sense as well. It was truly national. The networks, through their affiliates, now reached parts of the country that had been outside the loop in the early 1950s. The new mass audience, then, was not only diverse in terms of social class; it included Americans from a far wider range of backgrounds, including people from the South, rural Midwest, and the Rocky Mountain states whose values and sensibilities were often quite different from those of Americans who lived in the cities and suburbs of the Northeast, the Great Lakes region, or coastal California.

The addition of these groups to the viewing public had a profound effect on the television industry. As the numbers generated by ratings agencies like the Nielsen Corporation revealed, a large majority of viewers—people from all classes—preferred entertainment shows. This encouraged network executives to broadcast more of them and shun programs that were unlikely to appeal to the emerging majority—especially in prime time, when the viewing audience was at its peak. The new logic of mass marketing favored the broadcasting of programs with potential mass appeal. And it discriminated against any program that could not measure up to this standard, including some previously successful entertainment programs that were unpopular with viewers outside the urban Northeast and Midwest. This trend was reinforced by ABC's determined effort to reach parity with NBC and CBS. By shifting their focus to filmed programs designed to appeal to families and children, Leonard Goldenson and his associates put additional pressure on their rivals, who responded by copying many of his innovations and following much the same course.[58]

As network television became more competitive and entertainment-oriented, the kinds of news and public-affairs programs that fared best were early forms of "infotainment" that occupied a specialized time slot or fit comfortably within network schedules then dominated by the likes of *Wagon Train*, *The Adventures of Ozzie and Harriet*, and *The $64,000 Question*. Aside from *Today*, the most successful network infotainment program was CBS's *Person to Person*, which debuted in October 1953 and ran in prime time until 1961. *Person to Person* was conceived by Jesse Zousmer and John Aaron, two producers who were part of Fred Friendly and Ed Murrow's *See It Now* production unit. After quarreling with Friendly, they left the program and enlisted Murrow to serve as host and coproducer of their new venture, an independent production overseen by CBS's entertainment division. This peeved Friendly, who didn't like seeing Murrow's energies devoted to something other than *See It Now*, especially something as lightweight as *Person to Person*. But Zousmer and Aaron were certain their program would be a hit. Seeking to mimic the chatty celebrity profiles in mass-circulation magazines, *Person to Person* would feature live interviews of celebrities broadcast from their homes. At first, Murrow raised the possibility of interviewing ordinary citizens, too, but Zousmer and Aaron convinced him that this would be impractical and disappoint viewers. Instead, they mixed subjects from "serious" fields like politics with ones from entertainment and sports, giving most episodes a nice balance. Murrow's stature enabled them secure distinguished guests, who appeared in fifteen-minute segments, two per episode. *Person to Person*'s first episode, for example, featured the conductor Leopold Stokowski and the baseball star Roy Campanella. Such pairings were typical, and over the years Murrow and Charles Collingwood, who took over as host in October 1959, interviewed a wide range of figures—from the evangelist Billy Graham, Supreme Court justice William O. Douglas, and UN secretary general Dag Hammarskjöld to the pianist Liberace, the prizefighter Rocky Graziano, and the actress Marilyn Monroe.[59]

Broadcast at 10:30 on Friday nights, *Person to Person* was extremely successful for CBS and made its producers, including Murrow, quite rich. Producing the show was not easy. Murrow conducted the interviews from a specially appointed studio in New York, while teams of engineers and technicians provided the audio and video from the homes of his subjects, sometimes three thousand miles away. This required setting up at remote locations several days in advance, where crews worked frantically, installing the cameras, microphones, lights, monitors, and microwave relay equipment that would allow them to "feed" the program back to New York and allow Murrow's subjects to interact with him as if they were in the same room. To ensure a smooth and efficient broadcast, subjects were often provided with questions in advance and went through rudimentary rehearsals before airtime, a practice in keeping with the conventions of live television but a far cry from those employed on *See It Now*.

Person to Person was derided by critics, including Gilbert Seldes, who wryly suggested that the Murrow of *Person to Person* "is not to be confused with the man of the same name who is the star and co-producer of *See It Now*." Another critic, John Lardner, argued that they were the same man but presented two very different sides of him— the "Higher Murrow" and the "Lower Murrow."[60] Murrow was embarrassed by *Person to Person*, and sensitive to criticism of the program— which came not just from critics but from Friendly and others on *See It Now*. But it also served a larger purpose. Hosting the program enabled him to cultivate a less threatening and controversial television persona, and the fame of his guests reaffirmed his stature as CBS's most celebrated and well-connected newsman. It is conceivable that the trust and goodwill he gained from *Person to Person* may have given him more leeway on *See It Now*, particularly when it tackled sensitive subjects.[61] Regardless, he wasn't happy when *See It Now* became an irregularly scheduled "floater" while *Person to Person* retained its place on Friday nights. As Murrow no doubt recognized, television's pioneering, wide-open phase was over. In the future, news and public-affairs programming like *See It Now* would struggle to find a place on network TV. Ironically, its best chance of doing so would be by aping *Person to Person*.

This dismal scenario was perhaps on Murrow's mind when he spoke at a convention of radio and television news directors in October 1958. In a tone at once bitter and inspiring, Murrow argued that network programming, aside from during the Sunday afternoon ghetto, was a depressing spectacle of "decadence, escapism, and insulation from the realities of the world in which we live." The shows that aired in prime time were especially bad. He blamed this on commercialism and the eagerness of the networks to pad their bottom line, and pointed to a feature of American broadcasting that made things especially difficult for journalists. With his quarrels with Paley and Stanton clearly in mind, Murrow observed that radio and television news were part of an industry that sought to combine show business, advertising, and news. It was show business and advertising, however, that ran the show and determined what would appear on-screen. "The top management of the networks, with a few notable exceptions, has been trained in advertising, research, sales, or show business. But by the nature of the corporate structure, they also make the final and crucial decisions having to do with news and public affairs. Frequently they have neither the time nor the competence to do this." This problem was compounded by the eagerness of advertisers to sponsor programs that would garner the largest possible audience. Murrow proposed that big corporations voluntarily donate valuable airtime during the evening hours for the networks to produce programs on issues that the public ought to know about, a policy that anticipated the corporate underwriting that would support public television. But he wasn't very optimistic about this occurring and concluded his address with a call to arms. "This instrument can teach. It can illuminate; yes, it can even inspire. But it can do so only to the extent that human beings are determined to use it to those ends. Otherwise, it's nothing but wires and lights in a box."[62]

2

THE VOICE OF GOD

It would be easy to conclude that Ed Murrow was a naïve idealist

who refused to adapt to the realities of the American television industry. This is certainly the belief of many contemporary critics and academics. They are embarrassed by his frank talk about television serving as a means of "enlightening" the public and have established a vibrant cottage industry devoted to revealing the previously unappreciated complexity and artistic merit of programs that Murrow would have dismissed as drivel. Yet in 1958, when Murrow railed against the state of American television, there were quite a few Americans who agreed with him. And, over the next few years, their influence would increase, encouraging important changes in the industry and in the content of television news.

Most of the people who shared Murrow's dim view of television were members of the professional, upper-middle class. College-educated, with comfortable incomes and often prestigious occupations, they had been among the first Americans to purchase televisions in the late 1940s and early 1950s. And much early programming, including public-affairs shows like *See It Now*, had been designed to appeal to them. Pat Weaver's entire project at NBC had rested on creating programs that would appeal to this class, on the assumption that they were what advertisers called "influentials," and that their tastes and preferences would filter down to the lower-middle class, the working class, and various "provincials" as living standards and educational levels increased.[1]

Like Murrow, many of them were disturbed by trends in the television industry in the second half of the 1950s. They were unhappy about the decline of live drama and the relegation of "intellectual" programs, including public affairs, to the Sunday afternoon ghetto. And they deplored the lack of diversity during prime time, which was now dominated by quiz shows and filmed action-adventure programs, especially Westerns. They had never expected all—or even most— programs on TV to appeal to their tastes. By the late 1950s, however, it seemed as if the networks, led by ABC, were moving "downscale."[2]

Such critics of network television were a distinct minority—even among the educated, upper-middle class, who enjoyed network enter-tainment programs as much as any other Americans. But in certain parts of the country—affluent cosmopolitan suburbs, college towns, and cities with a vibrant arts scene—they enjoyed considerable influ-ence, and at their soirees and club meetings, disdain for the networks was the starting point of many a conversation. Their influence ex-tended into the media and many colleges and schools and was particu-larly great among upwardly mobile "strivers," young men and women from lower-middle-class and working-class backgrounds who were eager to acquire "cultural capital." Often the first in their families to attend college, now accessible thanks to the GI Bill and increased gov-ernment support for higher education, they were keenly interested in learning about the arts, politics, and current events, and their career and cultural aspirations led them to look to television critics, maga-zine journalists, and their high school teachers and college professors for guidance about what to patronize and consume.[3]

By 1960, then, a considerable number of Americans were ambiva-lent about television and receptive to critiques of it that regularly ap-peared in middlebrow magazines like *Time*, *Harper's*, and the *New Yorker*. Most of them watched television, and sometimes enjoyed it, but it was, at best, a guilty pleasure. Others had stopped watching or confined their viewing to selected programs that had been vetted by influential critics. For many, television was emblematic of a new "mass culture" that had arisen after the war, a manipulative opiate that dulled the senses and provided an evanescent high, like so many of the sugar-laded junk foods that lined the shelves of the nation's supermarkets.[4]

These connections, between television and the materialism of the new consumer culture that had emerged in the US in the 1950s, were underscored by a chorus of intellectuals who wrote books and magazine articles on the new problems of an "affluent society." They attracted widespread attention with their claims that postwar abundance had the potential to make the nation "soft," a concern that was often explicitly tied to America's competition with the Soviet Union in the Cold War. Because of its enormous popularity and reliance on advertising, television figured prominently in such critiques. By the end of the decade, it was in approximately 90 percent of American homes and had become the venue for massive, highly sophisticated ad campaigns. Influenced by analyses of German and Russian "totalitarianism," which emphasized the role of mass media in disseminating propaganda and shoring up public support for dictatorial regimes, intellectuals like Arthur M. Schlesinger Jr. and John Kenneth Galbraith argued that commercial television encouraged public ignorance and indifference. Emphasizing escapist entertainment, it distracted viewers from the problems of the day. They called for its reform so that the nation might regain its vigor, solve its domestic problems, and maintain its advantage over the Soviets in the Cold War.[5]

Criticism of television mounted in the fall of 1958, on the eve of Murrow's speech at the RTDNA (Radio-Television Directors News Association), when it was revealed that several popular quiz shows had been "fixed" in order to increase their drama or ensure that popular contestants remain on the air. The resulting scandal sent powerful shock waves throughout the industry. The networks claimed, with some justification, that fault lay with producers and the ad agencies that were responsible for the programs. But as numerous critics noted, the manipulation of quiz shows stemmed directly from a growing network obsession with ratings, advertising revenues, and profits. The quiz show scandal led the networks to cancel many of these programs, and it reinforced their commitment to filmed action-adventure and comedy shows produced in Los Angeles. It spurred them to move away from sole sponsorship and embrace the spot-advertising formula Pat Weaver had developed for *Today* and other NBC programs. By assuming control of program production, the networks hoped to limit the influence of advertisers and develop a new source of revenue. The scandal also made the networks interested in improving their public image, and at a secret meeting in New York in December 1959, they agreed to increase their news and public-affairs offerings and schedule them so that no single network would be hurt by this gesture of goodwill.[6]

Concern about the state of American television remained an undercurrent in the presidential campaign of 1960 and gained political traction after John F. Kennedy's election. Kennedy was determined to strengthen the regulatory muscle of the FCC, which had been plagued by scandal during the Eisenhower administration.[7] Convinced that the commission needed vigorous new leadership, he appointed a Chicago lawyer, Newton Minow, as its new head. In May 1961, in a speech to the National Association of Broadcasters, Minow expressed his unhappiness with network television and suggested that there would be changes in FCC policy. In front of network potentates like David Sarnoff, Frank Stanton, and Leonard Goldenson, he argued that television in the US had become a "vast wasteland," an endless cycle of sensational and formulaic entertainment programs punctuated by "screaming, cajoling, and offending" commercials. You can do better, he told them in an ominous tone that sparked fears of increased regulation. It was a devastating attack that cheered critics. But it alarmed the networks and their affiliates, who feared it would become more difficult to secure license renewals.[8]

For several years, the networks had responded to critics by arguing that viewers were happy with the shows on TV and that public tastes were reflected in the ratings. "People like what we're giving them," Goldenson explained to a reporter for *Forbes* in 1959.[9] Minow's speech suggested that merely giving the people what they liked might no longer be enough. The FCC chair's initial aim was to prod the networks to return to the varied offerings they had provided in the early 1950s, when television serviced a smaller, regionally specific audience. By the early 1960s, however, its audience had not only grown but become more diverse. The networks now reached blue-collar workers, a wide range of ethnic groups, and people from every region of the country, including rural areas. And, following ABC's lead, all three networks had invested in film-production facilities to produce the new-style programs that had proven so popular with viewers. As FCC officials soon realized, there was no going back. There was, however, another alternative: increase news and public-affairs programs, particularly in prime time. By 1962, Minow was urging the networks to follow this path. When they did, their affiliates were compelled to go along, despite reservations about the appeal of news to viewers. Quite expectedly, then, the political and regulatory environment changed in ways that were beneficial and pleasantly surprising to network journalists.

Nervous about running afoul of the FCC, affiliates became more will-ing to broadcast—or "clear," in industry parlance—news and public-affairs shows they had been unwilling to air in previous years. Equally important, with news programs now more likely to reach an audi-ence, advertisers displayed more interest in sponsoring them.[10]

These developments sparked big changes at the networks. Sensing a shift in the political winds, the news divisions agitated for more re-sources and airtime for their programs, and network executives con-ceded to these requests. News budgets expanded. By the early 1960s, NBC and CBS were each spending around $20 million per year on news and public-affairs shows. Even ABC, which under Goldenson had starved its news division to pay for expensive entertainment pro-grams, joined the rush. Between 1959 and 1961, it doubled its spending on news and public affairs to nearly $8 million per year.[11]

This trend of continually expanding budgets accelerated during the 1960s and 1970s as the networks poured revenues earned from their lucrative entertainment divisions into news, and as certain news pro-grams attracted viewers and commercial sponsors and became profit centers in their own right. By the end of 1970s each of the network news divisions had annual budgets nearing $100 million and em-ployed hundreds of employees. They had become powerful institu-tions, the main source of news for a majority of the public and the most visible representatives of a national media establishment that in-cluded prestigious newspapers like the *New York Times*, the *Wall Street Journal*, and the *Washington Post*; national newsmagazines like *Time* and *Newsweek*; and the major wire services that provided local papers with national and international news.[12]

These new resources greatly enhanced the networks' ability to produce news. They hired additional staff, including camera opera-tors, sound crews, and technicians. And they increased the number of reporters and producers on their payrolls—not just at their head-quarters in New York, where programs continued to be produced and broadcast, but at scores of bureaus that were established in the United States and abroad. Large domestic bureaus in cities like Chi-cago, Atlanta, Dallas, and Los Angeles allowed the networks to expand their coverage of events in the US and provide viewers with something approaching a national news service.

The networks also bought new equipment and routinely upgraded it. Among the most important were lightweight cameras and high-speed film-processing machines, which made it easier for correspondents and field producers to edit film and produce stories for quick broadcast. Armed with such equipment, the networks were now able to compete with newspapers as sources of breaking news. They leased additional landlines from AT&T, allowing them to feed more domestic stories from affiliates to the networks and shortening the time it took for stories to get on the air. And they invested in a groundbreaking new technology, videotape. First employed in the late 1950s to record the evening newscasts for rebroadcast on the West Coast, video cameras and editing equipment became increasing important during the 1960s and especially the 1970s as the technology improved and correspondents and field producers were encouraged to use it instead of 16mm film. The networks also purchased time on commercial satellites that began to be launched in the early 1960s. Synchronous satellites like Early Bird, which became available to broadcasters in 1965, were especially valuable. Orbiting at the same speed as the earth's rotation, they allowed for instant live transmission from remote locations. By the early 1970s, the networks had also begun to invest in small, mobile satellite units. Installed in vans, they enabled reporters in the field to send live reports directly to the networks rather than return to bureaus or affiliates to uplink and transmit the feed. It was nothing less than a technological revolution.[13]

Nowhere was the push for more news greater than at NBC. Buoyed by the arrival of Robert Kintner, an ex-journalist and former president of ABC who replaced Pat Weaver as president, the network embarked on an ambitious campaign to overtake CBS and become the nation's premier television news organization. Kintner's strategy was simple: produce more news programs than CBS, and when an important event occurred, stay with it longer. "We couldn't get on the air under Pat Weaver," noted Reuven Frank. "Under Bob Kintner, we were on the air so much we couldn't write the stuff fast enough." Overseen by Bill McAndrew, who served as head of NBC News until 1968, Kintner's plan relied in part on the growing appeal of his news anchors, Chet Huntley and David Brinkley. They became hosts of magazine-style public-affairs shows while continuing to appear on the increasingly popular *Huntley-Brinkley Report*. To increase NBC's output of documentaries, Kintner hired Irving Gitlin and Fred Freed away from CBS, where they had languished in Fred Friendly's shadow. Kintner carved out airtime for all sorts of news-related programs and even got Gulf Oil to become the sponsor of prime-time "instant specials" that Frank and the other producers were encouraged to prepare whenever any event of significance occurred. Looking back at the Kintner era, Frank concluded, "He made possible some of our greatest work."[14]

NBC's growing commitment to news programming and the steady rise of *The Huntley-Brinkley Report* in the ratings alarmed executives at CBS and soon led to Sig Mickelson's firing in 1961. His replacement, Richard Salant, was a protégé of Frank Stanton. A Harvard-educated lawyer with good political instincts and a deep respect for serious journalism, Salant soon won the affection and loyalty of virtually the entire staff. "He was the best thing that ever happened to CBS News," Mike Wallace suggested in an interview in 1998.[15] Salant made particularly good use of CBS's deep pool of talent, finding suitable vehicles for anchors and correspondents like Wallace, Charles Collingwood, Harry Reasoner, and Roger Mudd. Specifically charged with dethroning Huntley and Brinkley from their place atop the ratings, Salant lavished resources on CBS's evening newscast, and in early 1968, against his instincts, he gave Don Hewitt the green light to develop *60 Minutes*. More than anyone else, it was Salant who reestablished the reputation for journalistic excellence CBS had acquired during Ed Murrow's twenty-five years at the network. And his close relationship with Stanton gave the news division favored status within the company as a whole.[16]

ABC's real plunge into the news business began in the early 1960s, when Goldenson hired a new president of ABC News, James Hagerty, an ex-journalist and President Eisenhower's former press secretary. Under Hagerty, ABC finally began building its own in-house newsgathering operation. Lacking staff, the network continued to outsource documentaries and other public-affairs shows. Slowly, however, it also began hiring journalists and producers and establishing bureaus, and it was soon able to dispense with the syndicated service on which it had relied for film. In 1963, when Hagerty grew tired of the job, Goldenson brought Elmer Lower, McAndrew's top lieutenant at NBC, over to ABC to run the news division. Lower increased the size of the news staff and added additional in-house film crews and technical personnel. He did his best to attract "top people," but ABC often had to settle for "promising newcomers who could be developed, over time, into first raters."[17] Early hires included Frank Reynolds, Peter Jennings, Sam Donaldson, and Ted Koppel. Only twenty-three when he joined the network, Koppel benefited enormously from the fact that ABC had such a small staff and was forced to give him major responsibilities. By the late 1960s, Lower had created a small yet capable unit, and while ABC News still lagged behind its rivals in the ratings and expenditures on news programs, its staff had become more professional and committed. As Koppel later noted, "We took a perverse kind of pride in being the youngest, the poorest, and in many instances the hardest working of the news divisions."[18]

The presidential election of 1960 presented the networks with the first big opportunity to display their journalistic bona fides. Together, they spent between $20 million and $30 million covering the primaries and caucuses, the conventions, and the general election. Their fifteen-minute evening newscasts were dominated by election-related news, and they produced numerous politically oriented documentaries and prime-time specials, especially in the run-up to the conventions. Convention coverage was more extensive than ever, with the networks making good use of new technologies that allowed producers to communicate instantly with anchors, commentators, and floor reporters.[19]

The conventions were a big ratings victory for NBC. Expertly produced by Frank, its coverage was enhanced by Huntley and Brinkley's professionalism and easygoing rapport and by the superb floor reporting of Sander Vanocur and Edwin Newman. By contrast, the CBS anchor team of Walter Cronkite and Ed Murrow was poorly matched. A mediocre ad-libber, Murrow was visibly awkward and resentful of Cronkite's seemingly effortless ability to riff on any morsel of news provided by floor reporters. The conventions solidified NBC's popularity with viewers and gave *The Huntley-Brinkley Report* a huge advantage over CBS's *Douglas Edwards with the News*.

The biggest novelty of the election was an idea of Frank Stanton's: televised debates between the major candidates, Richard Nixon and John F. Kennedy. To make these possible, Stanton successfully lobbied Congress for suspension of a provision of the Federal Communications Act that required that all candidates, even those representing the most obscure parties, participate in any broadcast debate. This allowed Nixon and Kennedy to battle head-to-head without any of the other minor candidates present. Eager to take advantage of television's staggering reach, Nixon and Kennedy agreed to four debates. The networks took turns producing them, and they were simultaneously broadcast on all three networks over a four-week period in September and October. The debates attracted an enormous audience. An estimated 77 million Americans watched the first, on September 26, when an ailing and haggard Nixon famously refused the makeup that Don Hewitt suggested he wear and looked terrible next to the tanned and fit Kennedy. Stanton's hope was that televised debates would spur interest in politics and increase electoral participation, and public-opinion polls and scholarly studies have confirmed that the Nixon-Kennedy debates had such an effect. By arousing the public's curiosity, they contributed to the election's high turnout, over 63 percent. They also made candidates more aware of the power of television and mindful of the need to tailor their pronouncements and appearance in order to come across well on the small screen. Though, for legal reasons, presidential debates would not be broadcast again until 1976, the lessons of 1960 were quickly absorbed and soon affected political advertising and the design of public appearances and photo opportunities.[20]

Eager to please the more vigilant FCC, the networks increased the number of special reports and documentaries they broadcast in prime time. They were especially plentiful in the early 1960s, when the three networks each offered at least two weekly series showcasing documentaries, and the news divisions were allowed to preempt poorly performing entertainment shows to present special reports at least two or three times per month—and even more often during the summers, when the networks showed only reruns. In 1961, for example, NBC broadcast over thirty half-hour and one-hour programs on a wide range of subjects, from the Adolf Eichmann trial to a revealing account of the multimillion-dollar US beauty parlor industry; another thirty half-hour episodes of Chet Huntley's magazine program; eleven episodes of *David Brinkley's Journal*; and six big-budget documentaries as part of its floating *White Paper* series. While Kintner's NBC led the way, producing over twice as many special reports and documentaries as its rivals, the other networks also increased their commitment to such programs and displayed a similar variety in their choice of subjects.[21]

Special reports were the easiest to produce and get on the air. They could be prepared with little advance time and slotted in whenever was most convenient—often at 10 or 10:30 PM. Many were tied to breaking news stories and were essentially more detailed reports that could not be accommodated on the evening news. They were made by the teams of producers and correspondents who put together the evening news—or by special-reports units that worked alongside them and shared film and on-air personnel. Cold War conflicts, civil rights protests, urban riots, space launches and splashdowns, campus upheavals, the death of prominent statesmen, elections and important political developments, impromptu interviews with newsmakers—all of these and more were presented to viewers through prime-time special reports.

Documentaries were trickier propositions. They were far more expensive and time-consuming to produce. And as news division chiefs consistently reminded their bosses, they needed a regular spot on the schedule and considerable promotion to build an audience. The prospect of giving up valuable hours of prime time to the news divisions for documentaries upset the heads of the entertainment and sales divisions, and everybody knew that even a massively promoted documentary series would never produce the ratings of an entertainment program. Yet in the early 1960s, with the networks eager to improve their image and curry favor with the FCC, the news divisions briefly gained leverage in these conflicts and were able to secure regular time slots for documentaries.[22]

Producing documentaries was very appealing to television journalists. Frustrated by the limits imposed by the fifteen-minute newscast, TV news people argued that they were necessary to compensate for the brevity and superficiality of reports on the evening news. Documentaries were particularly well suited for a task that the networks had thus far neglected, providing interpretation and analysis. As ABC's James Hagerty explained to the FCC in 1962, documentaries allowed broadcast journalists to present "the how and whys of news occurrences," essential background so that viewers might understand the connection among seemingly random events.[23] Remembering the controversies that Fred Friendly and Ed Murrow had gotten themselves into with *See It Now*, television journalists in the early 1960s rejected the traditional approach of cinematic documentarians. Rather than expose injustice or promote left-wing or humanistic points of view, they were determined to make their documentaries objective and nonpartisan—programs that "explored" and "analyzed" issues. When they arrived at conclusions, as they often did, they were convinced it was a result of a careful appraisal of the facts and a process of deliberate reasoning. Television journalists defended their right to engage in interpretation and analysis by emphasizing their expertise—that they were seasoned professionals who possessed vast knowledge of politics, domestic affairs, and foreign policy. This was hardly unusual. Many journalists, especially ones working for the "prestige press," held similar views about their capacity for objective analysis. They were products of a culture of expertise that had become extraordinarily influential, and network journalists would retain their faith in objectivity for far longer than many other Americans.[24]

At NBC, documentaries were produced by a special Creative Projects unit overseen by Irving Gitlin. Many of them appeared as part of the network's flagship *White Paper* series, but others aired as stand-alone special programs. Produced by a talented team of producers, they employed NBC's most accomplished correspondents, including Huntley and Brinkley, and covered a wide range of topics. In its first season, for example, the *White Paper* series aired programs on the diplomatic controversy sparked by the Soviet capture of American pilot Francis Gary Powers, the sit-in movement organized by black college students, and the decline of the American railway system. In later seasons, it aired documentaries on the workings of the welfare system, varieties of international Communism, and the problems afflicting US cities. NBC's most acclaimed documentary was Frank's two-hour saga "The Tunnel," which told the story of the excavation of a hundred-yard-long tunnel under the Berlin Wall that enabled fifty-nine East Berliners to escape to West Berlin in September 1962. Broadcast in December against the objections of the State Department and after a delay caused by the Cuban missile crisis, it won the Emmy for program of the year.[25]

CBS's flagship documentary series was *CBS Reports*. Overseen by Fred Friendly until 1964, when he briefly replaced Salant as news division president, it was designed to provide a showcase for the network's large pool of correspondents and field producers. Ed Murrow was a producer and narrator of several episodes, including "Biography of a Missile," an engrossing account of the conception, manufacture, and testing of an intermediate-range ICBM, and "Harvest of Shame," an acclaimed examination of the plight of migrant farm workers that aired on Thanksgiving in 1960. Murrow's involvement ended when he was appointed director of the US Information Agency in 1961, and the series employed a rotating cast of producers and reporters. Notable programs in the early 1960s included a profile of Dominican dictator Rafael Trujillo; a controversial examination of racial tensions in Birmingham, Alabama; and "Biography of a Bookie Joint," a street-level exposé of gambling and organized crime that employed hidden cameras and anticipated techniques that Don Hewitt and Mike Wallace would perfect on *60 Minutes*.

Even ABC broadcast documentaries. Lacking resources and in-house film crews and field producers, network executives hired an independent production company, Robert Drew and Associates, to produce a prime-time documentary series. Sponsored by Bell and Howell, a well-known manufacturer of movie cameras, the series, *Bell and Howell Close-Up*, debuted in the fall of 1960. Drew produced some compelling reports, including "Yanki, No," a thoughtful and even-handed examination of the appeal of Communism in Latin America. ABC commissioned documentaries from other independent producers, too, including David L. Wolper. By 1962, however, the network was relying increasingly on its own in-house production team. For a network that was only beginning to get into the news business, ABC broadcast some distinguished programs. One of the most impressive was "Walk in My Shoes," a sensitive report on being African American in the US that aired in 1961. Jack Gould of the *New York Times* hailed it as "a stunning achievement."[26]

A seemingly perfect antidote to unfavorable publicity, prime-time documentaries never caught on with viewers. Despite considerable publicity and determined efforts to create evocative and viewer-friendly programs, they earned terrible ratings. Many Americans simply weren't interested in the subjects they covered. And when people did tune in out of curiosity, they were often alienated by their length, complexity, and heavy reliance on "talking heads." Documentaries were also controversial and deeply worried sponsors. Though producers struggled to be objective, this was difficult, and their commitment to interpretation and analysis often led them to clear-cut conclusions—that, for example, white supremacy in the American South was a national disgrace—that angered some viewers and created precisely the kind of negative publicity sponsors most feared. By 1964, with the Johnson administration occupied by its ambitious new domestic agenda and liberals interested in establishing a new system of public television as an alternative to the "wasteland" of commercial TV, FCC pressure on the networks decreased. Chagrined by their rejection by viewers, all three networks cut back their broadcast of documentaries and shifted resources to other kinds of news programs.

These included news specials, which often attracted large numbers of viewers. The most popular were live and filmed reports on the "space race" between the US and USSR. At first, military officials refused to allow the networks to cover satellite and missile launches, fearing that publicity might compromise national security. But when NASA was established in 1958 it was required by law to provide the public with information about its activities. NASA officials quickly recognized that media coverage of its exploits could ensure public support and congressional appropriations, and they went to great lengths to cultivate the goodwill of the networks by helping them cover the space program. Public interest in the US space program intensified when President Kennedy stepped up his support for the program and announced an ambitious goal, placing a man on the moon by the end of the 1960s. The networks began covering manned space flights and assigning anchors and correspondents to broadcast from Cape Canaveral, where spacecraft were launched, and Houston, the site of NASA's mission control, which oversaw the flights and communicated with astronauts. By 1966, the networks were also providing live coverage of the ocean splashdowns of returning spacecraft, and by the time the Apollo program began, television cameras had been installed inside spacecraft, providing vivid pictures from space as well as footage of astronauts performing their daily activities. Television was vital in transforming astronauts like John Glenn into national celebrities and providing a nation increasingly wracked by internal conflict with a story that was upbeat and potentially unifying. Its coverage culminated in July 1969, when the Apollo 11 astronauts achieved Kennedy's goal and walked on the moon's surface, accompanied by television cameras that provided a worldwide audience with live pictures. Though the networks shared a pooled video feed provided by NASA, they supplemented it with commentary and analysis by their own personnel, often correspondents with a special interest in the space program who became in-house "experts." The most informed, by far, was CBS's Walter Cronkite. On one occasion, watching a successful launch, he exclaimed excitedly, "Go, baby, go!" Cronkite's enthusiasm was mocked by many of his fellow TV journalists, but it struck a chord with much of the public and contributed to his popularity.[27]

The networks also stepped up their coverage of the presidency, and

Presidents Kennedy, Johnson, and Nixon developed new strategies for dealing with television journalists. Kennedy was particularly good at using television to his advantage. To the delight of the networks, he held regular televised press conferences and asked for airtime to address the nation, a practice continued by his successors. He also consented to special televised interviews and encouraged the networks to send correspondents to cover his trips abroad. As satellite and videotape technology improved, the networks were able to expand coverage of presidential trips and overseas summits with foreign leaders. These offered presidents a wonderful stage for advancing their political and diplomatic interests. Nixon's expertly orchestrated trip to China in 1972, for example, was a dazzling spectacle that enabled him to play the role of world statesman and distracted journalists from continued American involvement in Vietnam.[28]

Network interest in the presidency also allowed Kennedy, Johnson, and Nixon to publicize the activities of their families and encouraged the networks to produce features and human-interest stories about them. Kennedy was again the trailblazer, granting network journalists unprecedented access to his wife and young children. "His whole family was made for television," recalled Reuven Frank.[29] First Lady Jacqueline Kennedy was a particularly attractive subject for TV journalists. They accompanied her on several overseas trips, and in February 1962 she led CBS's Charles Collingwood on a tour of the newly redecorated White House. Broadcast simultaneously on CBS and NBC — and four days later on ABC — Kennedy's "Tour of the White House" was viewed by over 46 million viewers and was the most highly rated program of the year. Though the Johnsons and Nixons could hardly compete with the youthful, glamorous Kennedys, they were the subjects of network news coverage, too. Lady Bird Johnson invited reporters to interview her at the White House, and LBJ himself led NBC's Fred Freed and Ray Scherer on a nostalgic tour of the Texas hill country where he had been raised. The Nixons were less accessible to the networks, but they consented to occasional interviews, and their daughters' weddings — like those of LBJ's daughters — prompted special reports.[30]

Keen to attract viewers, the networks also produced special reports on social and cultural trends. NBC, for example, broadcast prime-time special reports on Parisian fashions, the James Bond craze, and "The Pursuit of Pleasure," a 1967 program on the "new morality" that fea-

CBS correspondent Charles Collingwood being given a tour of the White House by First Lady Jacqueline Kennedy in 1962. This prime-time special was one of the most watched programs in television history. Photo courtesy of CBS/Photofest.

tured an interview with LSD guru Timothy Leary and a debate between *Playboy* publisher Hugh Hefner and conservative writer William F. Buckley. CBS offered a profile of Frank Sinatra, a detailed account of a sniper's murderous spree at the University of Texas, and a series of viewer-participation quizzes, conceived by Fred Friendly, on driver's safety, current affairs, and consumer health. ABC was the most innovative of all. In keeping with the network's continued interest in the youth market, it sought to broadcast programs that were more "relevant." These included "The Teenage Revolution" in 1964, several reports on developments in pop and rock music that included film footage of popular rock bands, and a heavily promoted 1967 documentary on a notable trend in women's fashions, "The Mini-Skirt Rebellion."

Stories of this kind were also a staple on NBC's *Today*, which remained the highest rated and most profitable daytime program, despite Dave Garroway's departure in 1961. Former *Home* alumnus Hugh Downs replaced Garroway as the program's host, while one of the show's writers, Barbara Walters, gradually assumed more on-air responsibilities as an interviewer and reporter of both news and feature stories. Now a part of Bill McAndrew's news division, *Today* developed a pitch-perfect blend of hard news and soft features, and in the early 1960s, taking full advantage of new technologies, it stepped up its practice of broadcasting from remote locations, including Europe. Downs was a superb host, engaging in heavily publicized stunts like attending astronaut training camp and getting a pilot's license. But the show also became more "newsy," particularly during election years and when covering the decade's most tumultuous developments, including the Democratic National Convention in 1968, where its reporters were teargassed. Its staff excelled at covering breaking news, and Walters landed numerous interviews with high-profile newsmakers. Deftly mixing seriousness with frivolity, *Today*'s formula for attracting viewers was widely noted by industry figures.[31]

No one was more aware of its success than Bill Paley, a habitual viewer of morning television programs and the chief booster of his network's futile efforts to compete with NBC's big hit. CBS had tried to emulate *Today* as early as 1954, when it launched *The Morning Show*. But every incarnation of the program failed to put a dent in its rival's ratings, despite employing, at various times, Walter Cronkite, Jack Paar, and Dick Van Dyke as hosts. By the early 1960s, CBS was reduced to airing a fifteen-minute news bulletin at 7:00 AM and devoting the rest of the hour to a children's show, *Captain Kangaroo*. The network's next attempt was a strategic retreat. Rather than go head-to-head with *Today*, CBS executives elected to broadcast a live half-hour news-and-features program at 10:00 AM. Hosted by Harry Reasoner and a young actress, Mary Fickett, *Calendar* was conceived as a more literary version of *Today*. It was an ideal vehicle for Reasoner, who had emerged as one of the news division's new stars. Working with the writer Andy Rooney, Reasoner and Fickett covered some hard news, and even brought heavy hitters like Eric Sevareid into the studio to discuss pressing issues. The program was mostly devoted to interviews and "female-oriented" features on subjects like women's rights, birth control, and childrearing. Despite glowing reviews — Jack Gould called

Barbara Walters, Hugh Downs, and Joe Garagiola on the set of *Today* in the late 1960s, a period when the program was unrivaled in the ratings. Photo courtesy of Museum of Broadcast Communications.

it "a delightful oasis of fun and intelligence"—the program was canceled on account of poor ratings after only two years.[32]

It was replaced by a more conventional hard-news program, *The CBS Morning News*, which debuted in September 1963. Like *Calendar*, it also focused on stories of interest to educated stay-at-home mothers, but producer Av Westin, another rising star at the network, added a new wrinkle. Intrigued by the prospect of connecting and cross-promoting the network's news offerings, Westin began producing "backgrounders," seven- or eight-minute reports anticipating stories that would be covered later on the evening news. It was a promising notion, and the program held its own in the ratings, thanks in part to the poise and viewer appeal of its anchor, Mike Wallace. It suffered a fatal blow in August 1965, however, when the network, eager to air reruns of hits like *I Love Lucy*, moved it to 7:00 AM, where it languished for many years, despite numerous changes in format and personnel. In the end, CBS could never compete with *Today*, which retained its dominant position in the early morning well into the 1970s.[33]

Today was not the only bright spot for NBC. So was *The Huntley-Brinkley Report*, which dominated the ratings during the first half of the 1960s. This was a pleasant surprise, even among the executives and producers who conceived of pairing the two men back in 1956. "Everyone thought the program was going to fail," Frank admitted years later.[34] An important turning point occurred in 1958, when Texaco signed on as its sponsor. This relieved NBC News' money problems and increased many affiliates' willingness to clear the broadcast. "Full sponsorship . . . was so attractive," noted Frank, "that almost all the NBC affiliates who had shunned us, whether for ideology or economics, now rushed to jump aboard."[35] More stations meant a bigger audience, and the program's ratings improved. It pulled even with CBS's newscast in 1958, and after two years of fierce competition, *Huntley-Brinkley* moved into the lead, a position it did not relinquish until 1967. Ratings success allowed Kintner and the sales staff to jack up the price of advertising, forcing Texaco to become one of several regular sponsors and giving the broadcast even firmer financial footing.

TV critics often suggested that it was the chemistry between the anchors that was responsible for the broadcast's ratings success. But Frank thought it was something more mundane: each man had a well-defined role that provided balance and became part of the program's flow. When viewers tuned into *The Huntley-Brinkley Report*, they knew exactly what they were going to get. Huntley, a ruggedly handsome former radio announcer, reported or introduced all foreign news and domestic stories about subjects other than national politics and was on the air for least two-thirds of every program. Broadcasting from NBC studios in New York, he exuded masculine authority and gravitas; on his own, he might have been too serious and self-important for many viewers to stomach. Brinkley provided a nice contrast. Reporting from the network's remote studio in Washington, he provided all the political news, relying heavily on the network's excellent Washington-based correspondents. But it wasn't what he covered that made Brinkley such a distinctive presence. It was how. By delivering political news—ostensibly, material of high importance—with wry humor and a notable sense of bemusement, he complemented Huntley's stolidity and routinely punctured the aura of deadly seriousness that pervaded Washington, often with no more than a well-placed quip. An expert writer, he produced his own scripts and per-

Chet Huntley and David Brinkley were the anchors of NBC's hugely successful evening newscast, *The Huntley-Brinkley Report*, which was the most watched network news program in the late 1950s and first half of the 1960s. Brinkley later went on to achieve great success as a broadcaster for ABC. Photo courtesy of NBC/Photofest.

fected a voice ideally suited for television—eloquent yet spare and concise. And, when covering breaking news, "he knew when to shut up" and allow the pictures to do the work.[36]

The Huntley-Brinkley Report's success was deeply humiliating to CBS and led to a major shakeup. In April 1962, Douglas Edwards was sacked and Walter Cronkite became the network's new anchor and managing editor of the evening newscast, a position that gave him considerable authority over the broadcast. In the view of CBS executives, it was something that Cronkite had earned. After a successful career as a reporter and editor for United Press, Cronkite had joined CBS in 1950, hoping for an assignment covering the Korean War. But he wound up working for WTOP, the network's television affiliate in Washington, DC, where he delivered reports explaining developments in Korea. His gift for explanation and pleasing on-air manner were noticed by Sig Mickelson, and he was soon transferred to network headquarters in New York, where he became CBS's jack-of-all-trades. During the 1950s, he served as anchor of its convention coverage; host of its lamentable morning show, where one of his costars was a lion puppet named Charlamagne; and the star of a popular Sunday afternoon program called *You Are There*, which purported to cover history-making events like the Battle of Waterloo as if they were contemporary news. By the end of the decade, Cronkite had also become the network's preferred anchor for coverage of the space program, an assignment he relished and at which he excelled. Mickelson began suggesting him to Paley and Stanton as a replacement for Edwards in the late 1950s. By the time he finally got the job, he was well prepared and already familiar to viewers. Cronkite brought experience, varied skills, and a distinctive wire-service sensibility that would make the program more serious, sober, and Washington-centric.[37]

In the summer of 1963, frustrated by their inability to close what had become a sizeable gap between their broadcast and *The Huntley-Brinkley Report*, Salant and his deputies decided to expand *The CBS Evening News with Walter Cronkite* to half an hour. The news divisions at both CBS and NBC had long pushed for longer newscasts, but affiliates had refused to give up the additional airtime. Circumstances, however, had changed. Surveys and market research now revealed that large numbers of Americans were turning to television for much, if not all, of their news. And with the FCC under the leadership of liberal reformers, it had become more risky for local affiliates to ignore their responsibility to provide a modicum of news for local viewers. With the audience for network news on the rise, and networks now better able to deliver both national and international news, giving up fifteen minutes so that the networks could broadcast a half-hour news report no longer seemed like such a bad proposition to most affiliates. Bowing to pressure from New York, they fell into line.

Expansion was a tantalizing prospect for television journalists, and when word leaked of CBS's plans, NBC announced it would do the same. ABC, still hamstrung by a shortage of film crews and field producers, waited until 1967 to expand its newscast. It called for a re-thinking of many issues. Salant noted, "The broadcast could not have just twice as many stories as there were in the fifteen-minute news, nor could it have the same number of stories, each twice as long."[38] Weeks before the change, small groups at CBS and NBC began planning the new broadcast. At CBS, this effort was led by Salant's assistant, Ernest Leiser, who would soon replace Don Hewitt as the program's executive producer. Leiser saw expansion as an opportunity for more long filmed reports and in-depth magazine-style features. Reuven Frank oversaw expansion at NBC and came to a similar conclusion. But, in a lengthy memo that he wrote and distributed to his staff, he went further, arguing that because television journalism was essentially a "narrative," it was important that "every news story, without sacrifice of probity or responsibility, display attributes of fiction." As he explained, "It should have structure and conflict, problem and denouement, rising action and falling action, a beginning, middle, and an end."[39]

Frank's recommendations were perceptive and reflected the accumulated wisdom of roughly a dozen years in network news, a period when the television audience had become larger and more diverse. Throughout the 1950s, as Frank himself later confessed, network news people hardly thought about their audience. Rather than conduct market research, Frank tried to program for an archetypal viewer: "a woman not yet forty, one college degree, two children, a husband in the professions, busy with PTA and either politics or do-goodery, wistful about being stuck in the home. . . ." If they created programs for her, he figured, "the rest would follow." Though Frank was contemptuous of Pat Weaver's elitism, this was essentially the same thing, a blithe confidence that the masses would follow respectable upper-middle-class "influentials."[40]

For a while, this strategy worked. Millions of Americans, less educated and secure economically than Frank's archetype, tuned into the network newscasts—in part, because in most markets there were no alternatives, and all the networks, in classic oligopolistic fashion, scheduled them at the same time. By the early 1960s, however, as Frank's memo suggested, a tipping point had been reached. The audience for television news had grown so diverse that changes were necessary—not just about what to cover but how. A mass audience meant having to think about the techniques that print journalists had developed to reach readers across lines of class and ethnicity. It meant creating a brand of television news that could serve the variety of needs that the mass-circulation press had learned to serve—to inform consumers about important national and international developments, but also to entertain them and tell about them things that were useful and pertinent to everyday life. Frank warned his colleagues about the temptations of pandering. "There will be no tricks to gain or hold audiences we do not want," he insisted in his memo. And he reiterated his belief that, as before, "if we speak to our equals others will follow." Yet a threshold was about to be crossed. Television news for a mass audience would have to be different, just as newspapers catering to a mass audience differed from the prestige press. In 1963, however, few network journalists realized *how* different, and they were reluctant to consider the full implications of their mission. Indeed, for nearly two decades, they remained convinced that they could have it both ways— reach a majority of the American public yet produce a broadcast that was serious, eschewing the imperative to entertain that was a hallmark of mass-circulation journalism.[41]

On September 2, 1963, after weeks of planning and rehearsals, *The CBS Evening News with Walter Cronkite* began half-hour broadcasts. The change was preceded by an enormous publicity campaign designed to attract the curious, including fans of Huntley and Brinkley. The program wasn't just longer. It boasted a new set, promised an array of new features, and marked its debut with a Cronkite interview with President Kennedy. The expanded *Huntley-Brinkley Report* was launched a week later, to similar fanfare, and with a Kennedy interview as its main attraction. By the time ABC finally expanded its newscast, in January 1967, Elmer Lower and his aides had learned from the successes and failures of their rivals, and ABC's broadcast copied many of their most popular features. But ABC still lacked a solid anchor. The network experimented with so many of them that when it announced a change, hardly anyone noticed. Lower's riskiest move occurred in 1965, when, at the urging of superiors eager to appeal to the "youth market," he hired Peter Jennings, a handsome, twenty-six-year-old Canadian. As Jennings himself conceded, he was ill prepared to be a network anchor and happy to be reassigned as a "roving correspondent" in 1967. ABC's problem wasn't resolved until May 1968, when its seasoned and capable Washington correspondent, Frank Reynolds, was persuaded to become the program's anchor, with former CBS correspondent Howard K. Smith providing commentary.[42]

The expansion of the evening newscasts was a milestone. It inspired bureau chiefs, correspondents, and field producers to look for new stories, and they began badgering producers in New York for airtime. The crush of stories was so great that Leiser and Frank were unable to find very much time for the longer in-depth reports they had hoped would diversify the broadcast. Yet even during their heyday, the networks did little original "enterprise" reporting, and mostly followed the lead of newspapers like the *New York Times* in deciding what constituted the day's news.[43] From our perspective today, the most striking feature of the expanded newscasts of the 1960s was the preponderance of hard news, especially domestic stories produced by reporters and film crews assigned to new bureaus. In part, this was because the 1960s were an unusually dynamic period, and many of the events that occurred were well-suited for television coverage. But there was another reason: network eagerness to provide viewers with a public service and their belief that this meant serious news. The networks took it as their mission to provide viewers with the essential information they needed in order to have a reasonable grasp of the issues of the day—information that would enable them to follow and understand the debates and compromises that shaped policy making. Journalists recognized, of course, that their programs provided only a small fraction of the news, and to be really informed, viewers needed to consult a good newspaper. Early in his career as anchor, Cronkite even toyed with the idea of suggesting this as his "closer." But, inspired by the size of their audience and survey data that revealed that many viewers were rejecting newspapers for television, they were caught up in the importance of their task, and they presented the news with an air of self-confidence that would elicit snickers today.[44]

The networks were confronted with their first big test less than three months after expanding their newscasts. On Friday, November 22, while waving to bystanders from an open limousine in Dallas, President Kennedy was shot and killed by a sniper. When the first wire-service reports arrived, the networks interrupted their regular programming with bulletins informing viewers. Within minutes, the news divisions had commandeered the air and were issuing regular updates on the president's condition. At 2:30 EST, less than an hour after the first bulletins, the networks announced that Kennedy was dead. Now they faced a quandary. In the past, when covering an event that warranted the preemption of regular programming, they had had weeks if not months to prepare. In this instance, however, there was no precedent, and network officials had no idea where or when Kennedy would be buried. There was also the growing mystery surrounding his suspected assailant, an ex-marine named Lee Harvey Oswald. Wishing to keep their options open, and eager to provide a service that differed from the print press, the networks suspended all regular programs and commercials for the next four days, until after Kennedy's state funeral and burial in Washington, DC, a decision that cost them over $30 million in lost advertising revenue. News personnel remained on the air continuously during regular broadcast hours, providing updates and relying extensively on Washington-based correspondents. "We thought . . . it was our responsibility to calm the public," David Brinkley later recalled.[45] Disconcerted by Kennedy's death, millions of Americans turned to television for the latest information about the tragedy, and the networks were praised for the sobriety and tastefulness of their coverage. Even former FCC chair Newton Minow was impressed, calling it "sensitive, mature, and dignified."[46]

Two days after the assassination, while the networks were covering a memorial service for the slain president in Washington, NBC briefly cut away for a live report from Dallas. Police officials had announced that Oswald would be transferred to another jail, and a group of reporters and onlookers, including film crews from all three networks, were waiting in hopes of catching a glimpse of him. When Oswald emerged into view, however, only NBC's cameras were live, and the network was able to capture a startling event: a Dallas nightclub owner, Jack Ruby, approached Oswald and fatally shot him. Though CBS and ABC missed it, they were able to air footage of the murder within minutes thanks to videotape and a new technology that had been developed for television sports, instant replay. It was a surreal moment, the first murder captured live and replayed again and again on television. Yet the networks resisted the temptation to blow it out of proportion, and even this macabre event did not upset the somber tone of their coverage. The Kennedy assassination and its aftermath revealed television's ability to create a national audience for compelling events, a feat that would be repeated on several occasions during the next few decades.[47] There was no guarantee, however, that this would encourage unity and national cohesion, as it seemed to have done in this instance. It could just as easily produce discord—and lead viewers to start blaming the messenger.

Buoyed by critical praise and heightened public visibility, the producers of the evening newscasts redoubled their commitment to informing viewers about national and international affairs. Slowly, *The CBS News with Walter Cronkite* began rising in the ratings, particularly after 1964, when Ernie Leiser replaced Don Hewitt as executive producer. Leiser and Cronkite worked well together, and under their leadership the broadcast became more polished. Employing a talented stable of writers led by Sanford Socolow and a new generation of correspondents, including Roger Mudd and a young Texan named Dan Rather, Leiser and Cronkite developed an effective mix of filmed reports and tell-stories. Over Cronkite's objections, Leiser and his successor, Les Midgley, were also able to include features. The most popular were a recurring series of reports by correspondent Charles Kuralt, *On the Road*. They focused on offbeat subjects and provided a welcome contrast to the often distressing hard news of the era. Launched in 1967, Kuralt's segments were so popular that CBS eventually turned them into prime-time specials. Features like *On the Road* contributed to the Cronkite program's steadily increasing ratings. So did Eric Sevareid's erudite commentaries, which came near the end of most broadcasts. Leiser and Cronkite saw them as the television equivalent of editorials, and neither they nor Salant exercised any authority over their content. Socolow recalled that Salant in particular was committed to the idea of including commentaries. "Salant felt very strongly that one of the distinguishing characteristics . . . of the half-hour evening news broadcast . . . was that we gave the news of the day some context, some meaning, that you wouldn't otherwise get."[48]

By the mid-1960s, *The CBS Evening News* had pulled even in the ratings with *Huntley-Brinkley*, and in 1967 it pulled ahead, deeply perplexing NBC officials. By any measure, including the acclaim of critics, their program was better than ever, yet viewers were defecting to CBS. NBC's problems mounted in May 1969 when Elmer Lower recruited Av Westin to produce ABC's nightly newscast. Westin proceeded to remake the broadcast from top to bottom, promoting Howard K. Smith to coanchor and increasing opportunities for ABC's reporters to get on the air. Lower also expanded the network's foreign and domestic bureaus, and found useful assignments for Tom Jarriel, Sam Donaldson, and Peter Jennings. Serving as the network's London correspondent, for example, Jennings was given free rein to cover the Middle East, which was becoming a news hot spot. The turning point for ABC occurred in 1970, when Lower persuaded CBS's Harry Reasoner to join Smith as coanchor of the ABC *Evening News*. Reasoner had become popular and well-known as Cronkite's regular substitute and as the anchor of CBS's excellent Sunday evening news broadcast, and in 1968, he had become the cohost of Don Hewitt's newest project, an hour-long magazine show called *60 Minutes*. But with the latter near the bottom of the ratings and Cronkite showing no signs of wanting to retire, Reasoner accepted Lower's offer. His arrival sparked an almost immediate increase in ABC's ratings, largely at the expense of NBC's. By this time, Huntley had retired from NBC, and Frank, now president of NBC News, had elevated John Chancellor and Frank McGee to Huntley's former position, creating a new rotating trio of anchors. The new arrangement confused viewers and led to a further decline in the show's ratings. Before Reasoner joined ABC and Huntley retired, ABC's share of the evening news audience had been a paltry 15 percent, while CBS enjoyed a 31 and NBC a respectable 28. By the spring of 1973, CBS was still on top, but the ABC newscast had increased its share to 22, and there were some weeks when ABC and NBC, now with Chancellor as sole anchor, finished in a dead heat.[49]

The years between the Kennedy assassination and President Nixon's resignation in 1974 were a heady period for the network news divisions. While they found it more difficult to get airtime for prime-time documentaries, their evening newscasts were avidly watched by millions of Americans. In the mid-1960s, Nielsen Corporation research revealed that 90 percent of televisions in use at the dinner hour were tuned to one of the three network newscasts. By the mid-1970s, their combined share would fall to 75 percent; because of population growth, however, their cumulative audience was even larger, close to 50 million viewers. This made them attractive to sponsors and profitable for the networks, and gave the news divisions more influence with network executives.

Reaching such a large audience was inspiring to many television news people, reinforcing their pride and sense of self-importance. And because they competed among themselves for a captive audience—before cable, there were few if any viewing options in a majority of television markets—the temptation to sensationalize, to engage in the tricks Reuven Frank suggested were necessary to appeal to the hoi polloi, wasn't as powerful as it would become in later years. Throughout the 1960s and 1970s, the network newscasts clung stubbornly to the aspirational model that Frank and Leiser had developed at NBC and CBS, a program pitched to the educated middle class that, thanks to the benefits of oligopoly, had a considerably larger and more diverse audience. Indeed, the audience the networks most cared about was print journalists and other members of the media establishment. To gain their respect, the network news divisions continued to expand and produce more hard news. Some print journalists and die-hard newspaper readers never fully accepted television as a purveyor of news. But by the mid-1970s, the network news divisions had come a long way, and the size of their audience made their journalism potentially influential. Specializing in subjects that were traditionally the domain of publications catering to the well-educated, the networks saw themselves as paragons of enlightenment, beacons in the "wasteland."

Yet as network producers soon recognized, providing even a perfunctory broadcast to such a large audience was a complicated business. It required them to communicate to viewers with different levels of interest and education, and deliver the news through affiliate stations that were, at best, grudging accomplices. Like Henry Luce's successful magazines, the networks sought to do this by adopting a "national" perspective. In practical terms, this meant identifying stories that they deemed sufficiently important to include in a short, twenty-three-minute program, then reporting them in ways that allowed viewers to see how they were connected to larger, ongoing stories that comprised the drama of our national life. By design, this meant making some viewers aware of things they might not know about. But television journalists assumed that if viewers were better informed about these subjects, they were more likely to be engaged and responsible citizens.[50]

Establishing a national perspective seemed like a perfect job for the networks. No other medium reached so many Americans or had the technological resources to encourage a truly national point of view—to suggest that faraway, seemingly random events were related to wider problems that directly affected their well-being. In doing so, however, the networks were doing more than reporting the news.

They were engaged in what political scientists call "agenda-setting": legitimizing certain issues and concerns, helping to construct the boundaries of public debate. Along with the major political parties and a host of other institutions in postwar America, their programs sought to foster consensus, to encourage viewers to identify with particular ideas and positions within those boundaries and regard any that fell outside them as suspicious and potentially illegitimate. This mission was reinforced by their overwhelming reliance on "official" sources: politicians and diplomats, spokesmen for important organizations, and individuals who were newsworthy because of their affiliation with notable institutions. Their voices and opinions dominated network news coverage, and contributed to the illusion that seemingly everybody of importance held views that ranged along a relatively narrow continuum.[51]

A national perspective was the logical starting point for network coverage of foreign affairs, which in the 1960s continued to be dominated by the Cold War. In the 1950s, the networks had sought to make viewers aware of important overseas events, particularly those that involved the US and its principal Cold War adversary, the USSR. This was important, since journalists were fearful that public ignorance would encourage a revival of isolationism and result in the US pulling back from its overseas commitments as defender of the "free world." In his famous speech lamenting the state of television programming, Ed Murrow had said as much, and his internationalism was widely shared among television journalists and network executives. In the 1960s, with public support for the containment of Communism extremely high, covering international affairs through a Cold War lens that divided the world into "us" and "them" was a surefire formula for engaging viewers. Television journalists, like their counterparts in the print press, also tried to cover developments—like the vogue of "neutralism" in Europe and the Third World—that complicated this Manichaean worldview. But their unstinting belief in American benevolence and the evils of Communism made this difficult, particularly in the relatively short two- to five-minute segments that were common on the evening newscasts; their best work along these lines invariably occurred in documentaries. Most reports on foreign affairs depicted nations and peoples as "up for grabs" and ended on a note of apprehensive optimism—in which concern about the seemingly inexorable "forward march" of Communism gave way to hope that the US and the values of freedom and democracy would ultimately prevail.[52]

Transforming domestic news into national stories was more difficult. Usually, it involved highlighting national trends that provided a context for individual stories. For example, a filmed story about a lack of municipal services in the slums of big cities might focus on problems in, say, Cleveland, from which a correspondent and camera crew would file a detailed report. But producers in New York would add snippets of film from other bureaus or the archives to underscore the story's larger point, that this problem was national in scope. "Nationalizing" stories made them relevant to a wider audience and reinforced the impression that the networks were providing a unique service that distinguished them from newspapers. But as the networks slowly came to realize, many viewers were not happy to be informed about some these developments, and this growing problem underscored an important difference between newspapers and network television. Newspaper readers could skip over stories about subjects they weren't interested in or that might bother them. This wasn't the case with television—the stories progressed, one after the after, in an order conceived by producers, without much, if any, advance warning. And in most markets, if you didn't like what Huntley and Brinkley were reporting and changed the channel, you were likely to encounter Walter Cronkite or Howard K. Smith reporting on the same thing. To make matters worse, the networks made viewers aware of these things through vivid moving pictures, a medium that was especially powerful and could be disturbing. The visceral power of televised images was hard to contain, and they often defied journalists' efforts to embed them within stories that sought to explain events in a detached and rational way. The medium, in short, made the sober, analytic style favored by the prestige press very difficult for television journalists to emulate.[53]

Most stories about both foreign and domestic events also emphasized conflict. This was not just to make them more dramatic. It was in keeping with the venerable journalistic practice of allowing both sides of any question to be heard, an imperative for broadcasters compelled to abide by the FCC's Fairness Doctrine. Network journalists had hoped that expanding the newscast to a half hour would allow them to probe more deeply into complex issues. But with only twenty-three minutes for news and a glut of potential stories, they still lacked for time, forcing them to avoid detail and complexity. Many stories that deserved nuanced treatment were flattened and simplified, made to fit a rigid point-counterpoint format that included the requisite "contrasting viewpoints." This might not have posed a problem if network news conventions allowed journalists to evaluate and comment on the contrasting perspectives presented in their stories, a common practice among journalists in Canada and Europe. The networks, however, expressly forbade this practice. And in their hiring and promotion they openly discriminated against job candidates who evinced strong political commitments of any stripe. Accordingly, the conclusions offered by correspondents in their closing remarks were purposely vague, designed to encourage viewers to make up their own minds or suggest that the truth lay somewhere in between the views expressed by sources.

This problem was compounded by another convention of television news production, a powerful impetus, encouraged by viewer preference and development of new technologies, to emphasize dramatic pictures. During the 1950s, out of necessity, the networks had relied extensively on talking heads—film of speeches and snippets of interviews—and they continued this practice throughout the 1960s. But as they expanded their newsgathering infrastructure and were able to acquire film footage of most of the events they covered, the time allotted to talking heads gradually decreased. Now able to broadcast a wide range of pictures, including reels and reels of film and videotape in network archives available for repurposing as background footage, producers could visualize stories more thoroughly than in the past. This ensured that the conflicts covered by television would be increasingly visual and affect viewers in ways that journalists could scarcely comprehend.

The first signs of trouble were sparked by network coverage of the civil rights movement. Civil rights leaders in the 1950s recognized that the persistence of white supremacy in the South rested on widespread ignorance about its workings outside the region. And one of their aims in launching their campaign of nonviolent protest was to encourage the national media to expose these conditions and put Southern whites in a no-win situation: either capitulate to African Americans demands for integration, political rights, and economic opportunity or resist and risk looking bad in the eyes of the rest of the country. Many Southern whites chose to resist, and the determined effort of self-styled "moderates" to cloak their resistance in the garb of respectability was sabotaged by their more impulsive and shortsighted neighbors, who resorted to violence and were regularly filmed, faces twisted in rage, hurling profane-filled epithets at African Americans. By openly challenging white supremacy—sometimes by violating local law and putting themselves at risk of arrest or mob violence—civil rights activists forced whites outside the South, including television journalists, to confront the racial injustice that lay at the heart of the postwar consensus.[54]

Network journalists did their best to be objective. Indeed, their coverage of the civil rights struggle was notable for its celebration of "moderates" and focus on individual African Americans who did not belong to protest groups and could be depicted as respectable, dignified "victims" deserving of equal rights.[55] Fired from CBS in 1961 for seeking to editorialize at the end of a documentary on Birmingham, Howard K. Smith recalled that Paley and Stanton, fearful of alienating Southern affiliates, had told him, "This is not the kind of stuff we allow on our network." Within two years, however, as segregationists resorted to increasingly desperate measures while civil rights activists retained their stoical commitment to nonviolence, CBS and the other networks found the "center" to be untenable. Their reports continued to provide a platform for white supremacists, including a small number of polished and seemingly sensible figures like the newspaper editor James J. Kilpatrick. To the dismay of Southern affiliates, however, most reports implicitly sympathized with the movement and encouraged white viewers to identify with its aims. "They had to," suggested Smith. "Paley's position was unrealistic. You could not somehow find a position equidistant between right and wrong." In most cases, it wasn't even necessary to editorialize. The facts—and especially the pictures—spoke for themselves.[56]

Television coverage of the struggle for civil rights made many whites in the North aware of the state of race relations in the South and increased public and congressional support for the landmark civil rights legislation passed in the mid-1960s. But many Southern whites, including some who were disdainful of extremist groups like the Ku Klux Klan, resented network news reports that made their region appear benighted. They liked to believe that Southern blacks were largely happy with their lot and were being manipulated by "outside agitators" from the North. And they were convinced that, by lavishing so much coverage on the movement, the networks were encouraging African Americans to engage in more assertive forms of protest. These aggrieved Southern whites included some of the owners and managers of TV stations affiliated with the networks, and they sometimes sought to hamper network efforts to feed stories from their stations to New York for national broadcast. A few refused to broadcast the network news, and when the specter of FCC punishment made this impossible, they hired articulate young men like the future senator Jesse Helms to go on the air and rebut the "lies" broadcast by Walter Cronkite and Huntley and Brinkley. Like many reporters from Northern newspapers, network journalists were routinely harassed and threatened while covering the civil rights beat, and even native Southerners like Howard K. Smith and Dan Rather were made to feel as though they were part of an invading "Yankee" army. "When we were covering a story," Rather wrote in his autobiography, "I was on edge, all day, every day. . . . Only when we were finally airborne on the way out of town did I feel like I could exhale."[57]

Television coverage of the civil rights struggle had other, unexpected consequences. The scenes of violence and disorder that routinely appeared on the evening news were wearying and unsettling to many viewers. They were especially disconcerting to whites who sympathized in the abstract with the goals of the movement but were uncomfortable with forms of protest that involved breaking the law and seemed to invite confrontation and chaos. And in the mid-1960s, despite civil rights legislation and the creation of new social programs designed to end poverty and empower the disfranchised, violence and disorder increased, creating even more dramatic spectacles for the networks to cover. More disturbingly, they began to flare up outside the South and soon revealed that there were racial problems nationwide.

The most dramatic occurred in Los Angeles in the summer of 1965, shortly after president Lyndon B. Johnson signed the Voting Rights Act, when angry and frustrated African Americans in the impoverished Watts district rioted. Sparked by years of police harassment and dismal job prospects, issues that had begun to attract the attention of civil rights leaders, the rioters looted, vandalized, and set fire to local businesses, and they fought pitched battles against the Los Angeles police. The uprising lasted six days and resulted in thirty-four

deaths and over three thousand arrests.[58] It was followed, in subsequent years, by riots in the African American ghettos of other large
Northern cities, including Cleveland, Chicago, Detroit, and Newark.
The riots usually occurred at the height of summer, and they terri-
fied white Americans more than any other event in the 1960s. Large-
scale riots hadn't broken out in the US since the Second World War,
and their eruption at a time of unprecedented prosperity and in the
wake of civil rights legislation that had seemed to have resolved the
race issue perplexed and alarmed most whites. Their fears were ex-
acerbated by the fact that the urban riots of the 1960s were covered in
great detail by the networks and local television stations, which recognized them as big news events tailor-made for TV.[59]

The Watts riot set the pattern. Making use of live shots provided
by a camera filming from a helicopter owned by independent station
KTLA, the networks were able to provide viewers with extraordinary
scenes of mayhem and destruction. Yet as television reporters and
cameramen quickly came to realize, their presence on the scene could
contribute to the spread of the rioting. And their style of coverage created additional problems that sabotaged their efforts to be objective.
They were eager to exploit their biggest advantage over newspapers,
the capacity to broadcast moving pictures, but their reports emphasized the conflict between the rioters and police, an approach that implicitly encouraged viewer identification with the forces of "law and
order." And though the networks tried at times to consider the causes
of the riots, this proved difficult, particularly while they were occurring. Not surprisingly, the networks were condemned by civil rights
leaders and their liberal allies for their superficial treatment of the
riots. A bipartisan commission appointed by President Johnson urged
the networks to explore the "roots" of the nation's urban crisis, and
the networks responded with earnest special reports that sought to
explain why some African Americans had become so frustrated and
angry.[60] To some whites, however, this new interest in trying to explain the reasons why blacks were rioting was deeply perplexing. It
seemed like the networks were apologizing for criminal behavior.

This confusion was encouraged by politicians and activists who
knew how to play to TV cameras and exploit the networks' penchant
for framing stories around conflict. They included a new generation
of civil rights activists who resented the news media's fawning treatment of Martin Luther King Jr. For figures like Stokely Carmichael

and H. Rap Brown, the riots were a rebuke to King's emphasis on nonviolence and an opportunity for them to promote a more radical agenda. Eager for sources willing to explain or even defend the rioting, the networks hung on their every word. Even more compelling to the networks were the Black Panthers, a group of urban-based militants who gained a substantial following the late 1960s. Clad in black leather and berets, and, when possible, brandishing weapons, the Panthers relished the attention—in spite of their professed disdain for "honky" institutions. Insisting that the riots were an extension of civil rights protests and a sign of the "black revolution" to come, militants like Carmichael, Brown, and the Panthers provided television journalists with wonderful sound bites and became the most visible spokesmen for "black rage."

Their doppelgangers were the increasingly strident spokesmen of the political right, men like George Wallace, Ronald Reagan, Los Angeles mayor Sam Yorty, and a host of big-city police officials. Appalled by the riots, but also sensing political opportunity, they skillfully harnessed the growing fears of whites and rode them to political power. As public officials—sources that the routines of newsgathering had long favored—these champions of "law and order" had no trouble getting on TV. And, no less than their radical counterparts, they cultivated a rhetorical style that was tough, uncompromising, and purposely inflammatory. In statements broadcast on the evening news, they issued apocalyptic warnings suggesting that marauding blacks, inspired by agitators like Carmichael and Brown, would soon be invading white neighborhoods. To prevent this, states and municipalities needed new laws that increased police power and reversed recent court rulings that "coddled" criminals. Dismissing the legitimate grievances that had sparked the riots and made many law-abiding African Americans angry and bitter, they blamed them on civil rights activists. By engaging in civil disobedience and winning concessions from feckless white liberals, the movement was encouraging ordinary blacks to lose their respect for authority.[61]

With great visuals and the two sides expressing such polarized views, it was an unusually dramatic story, commanding lots of airtime and drawing the attention of viewers. It is arguable, however, that television made it more dramatic than it need have been. While attempting to be objective, the networks packaged the story of urban unrest in ways that highlighted its most spectacular features. And the presence of television cameras affected the behavior of many of the story's protagonists, inspiring them to say and do things they knew were more likely to get them on TV and advance their political objectives. In some cases, these views and objectives were outside the boundaries of what the networks regarded as legitimate opinion, and their proponents employed rhetoric expressly designed to whip up support among their followers and strike fear into the hearts of their foes—to produce emotional responses that would increase conflict and polarization. In short, network journalists' efforts to produce news reports that would encourage a sober and detached understanding of the problem of urban unrest were undone by the nature of the medium and their attraction to newsmakers whose views and grandstanding made for great television but were more extreme than the reasonable figures that most journalists favored.

Ironically, the story that proved most damaging to the networks was one that, at first, seemed the least problematic, America's involvement in Vietnam. From 1954, when Vietnam gained its independence from France and was partitioned, to the early 1960s, when the corrupt and unpopular South Vietnamese government was beleaguered by insurgents and survived on a lifeline of massive US aid, the networks rarely strayed from what was, in essence, a media party line: America's valiant effort to protect non-Communist South Vietnam from Communist aggressors inspired by the Kremlin. In late 1964, when President Johnson, with a congressional carte blanche provided by the Gulf of Tonkin Resolution, began dramatically increasing American military involvement in Vietnam, he was confident of continued media support. They had, after all, enthusiastically supported the foreign policy initiatives of his predecessors. And given their attachment to the Cold War as an organizing frame for coverage of foreign affairs, there seemed no reason why they wouldn't support this one. Accordingly, the Johnson administration and military officials placed virtually no limits on reporters, expecting them to provide news about the conflict that would sustain public support. But when the war dragged on, and the enemy showed no signs of giving up the fight, the media were confronted with a dilemma. Revealing such "bad news" would surely anger the government and military officials, and it could undermine public support for the war. Yet if they downplayed it, as the Johnson administration and military leaders were suggesting, they would be fully complicit in the escalating tragedy—and lose their credibility with the public.[62]

These problems didn't become visible right away. In the early stages of the US escalation, the networks continued to depict the situation through conventional Cold War lenses, and many reports from Vietnam parroted the daily reports issued by the military. Even when network reporters and film crews accompanied US troops on combat missions, they rarely addressed overall strategy or America's larger objectives. In 1965, eager to provide more interpretation and background, the networks produced numerous special programs on Vietnam—accounts of its history and of the roots of the conflict, coverage of the April "teach-ins" on university campuses, and debates between supporters and opponents of US involvement, the latter represented by foreign diplomats and journalists or, in a CBS broadcast, senator George McGovern. These special reports were inspired by a belief that a full accounting of the situation in Vietnam would invariably support US policy. Occasionally, however, they struck discordant notes, revealing, for example, the difficulties that Americans were having winning the trust of South Vietnamese civilians. Those discordant notes became louder and more frequent in 1966 and 1967, as the number of American troops rose into the hundreds of thousands and the networks stepped up their coverage. Perhaps the most ambitious programs on the war were a series of "Vietnam Reports" that ABC produced for broadcast during prime time. Generally supportive of the war, they examined it from a variety of perspectives and focused in particular on the experiences of American troops. Unfortunately, virtually nobody watched these programs, not least because many affiliates chose to air them at odd hours. Lack of viewer interest in special reports on the war gave network executives the perfect excuse to scuttle them and consign Vietnam coverage to the evening news.

Given the nature of the Vietnam War—that it was a civil war in which the "enemy" included a fair number of South Vietnamese citizens—even reports on the evening news could be problematic. This was clear as early as August 1965, when Morley Safer, recently hired from the Canadian Broadcasting Corporation, filed a report that was broadcast on the CBS *Evening News*. It documented the razing of a South Vietnamese village, Cam Ne, by American marines. While the bedraggled and hysterical residents of the village begged for mercy, the servicemen roused them from their huts and then used flame-throwers and cigarette lighters to burn the structures to the ground. Though Safer's report dutifully noted that the village was suspected of being a Vietcong stronghold, the film provided no evidence of this, and US troops displayed a ruthlessness that conflicted with oft-repeated claims that the US was winning the "hearts and minds" of the South Vietnamese peasantry. Notably, it was the film footage that was most devastating—and not anything that Safer said on camera or in his voice-over. Safer's report enraged President Johnson and led military officials to plead with network correspondents to consider the potential consequences of their Vietnam coverage. Johnson himself called Frank Stanton and delivered a profanity-filled tirade in which he questioned Safer's patriotism and suggested that coverage critical of the American war effort was akin to treason.[63]

By the summer of 1967, reports like Safer's, revealing the serious problems that plagued US forces in Vietnam, had become depressingly common. It was clear to many journalists that the US was losing, and their reports began to display a tone of weary resignation. Alarmed by this trend, the Johnson administration launched an aggressive campaign to generate a better "story" about Vietnam, encouraging the view that the US was making progress and, as general William Westmoreland put it, there was "light at the end of the tunnel."[64] These claims were shattered in January 1968, when Vietcong guerillas and North Vietnamese troops launched a massive assault throughout South Vietnam, demonstrating that they were much stronger than Westmoreland and other military officials had suggested. Emerging from hiding places where they had mixed among sympathetic local peasants, they easily overran and occupied towns and cities American officials had listed as pacified. They even appeared in the capital of Saigon and besieged the US embassy. And though the US and the South Vietnamese army beat them back, inflicting massive casualties, it was a huge diplomatic and public relations triumph for the Vietcong and an utter disaster for the Johnson administration. The networks covered the action in engrossing detail, with vivid film clips of the fighting. Revealing that the government's claims about the war were dubious, the so-called Tet offensive inspired a rush of more complete and objective reporting by print journalists and the networks, including special reports with titles like "Saigon under Fire" and, more ominously for Johnson, "Vietnam and After: What Should We Do?"[65]

The postmortems were devastating. Traveling again to South Vietnam, from where he had issued glowing reports in 1965 about American resolve and the inevitability of victory, Walter Cronkite was shocked by what he witnessed—US troops engaged in fierce combat to reclaim places that he had been told, hours before, were secure. A chastened Cronkite returned, and in special segments on *The CBS Evening News*, he examined the Vietnam situation with a new honesty. And in a prime-time special report summarizing his findings, he concluded with something extraordinary—a clearly labeled commentary in which he stepped out of his role as objective reporter and expressed his personal opinion. The Vietnam War, he announced, had become a bloody stalemate. "It is increasingly clear to this reporter that the only rational way out . . . will be to negotiate, not as victors, but as an honorable people who lived up to their pledge to defend democracy, and did the best they could."[66] Cronkite was not alone. Similarly somber assessments issued from NBC and ABC, and in the wake of Tet, network coverage became more assertive and skeptical of government claims. Yet the networks adopted this stance only when the alternative, reaffirming the government's Vietnam policy, was journalistically untenable, and when they sensed that public sentiment had shifted, too. Rather than leading the public, the networks followed it—or, more precisely, they followed the plurality who shared Cronkite's assumptions, that the American cause was essentially just, but that Vietnam was, as one critic later put it, "the wrong war, in the wrong place, at the wrong time."

Over the next few years, network journalists offered viewers a frank and at times harrowing look at the war's tragic endgame. At ABC, Av Westin ordered producers and reporters to develop stories that focused on US efforts to withdraw from Vietnam, and all the networks explored the war's often unseemly fallout: drug abuse and declining morale among American servicemen; the dysfunction in Saigon, where the US presence had produced a host of distressing social, economic, and political problems; and the Nixon administration's cynical efforts to improve its position at the Paris peace negotiations by launching savage bombing attacks against North Vietnam, reducing much of it to rubble. In early 1973, in the wake of the peace agreement that finally brought the war to an end, the networks broadcast programs summarizing the history of US involvement. They often ended on a note of wistful optimism—expressing hope that the settlement, which preserved the independence of South Vietnam, might prove enduring.[67] But in April 1975, when the South Vietnamese government finally fell and the networks were compelled to broadcast another round of retrospectives, there was no longer any room for optimism. America's campaign to create a viable anti-Communist nation in Indochina had failed.[68]

In breaking ranks with the government and reporting on the war in a more objective vein, network journalists thought they were fulfilling their professional responsibilities and providing viewers with the facts about the war. Vaguely embarrassed by their role in abetting the government's deception, they hoped this would enable viewers to assess US policy and participate in public debate about whether American involvement should continue. When Cronkite proclaimed the conflict a stalemate and suggested a negotiated settlement, he made it clear that this was his opinion—and might not be shared by others who were privy to the same facts. Even in their new more independent and assertive mode, then, the networks sought to remain in the middle of the road. By 1968, however, this was more difficult. Public opinion on the war and many other issues had begun to fragment and become more polarized, increasingly the likelihood that some viewers would object to network efforts to offer a platform to people with very different views. And, much to their surprise and dismay, the networks soon found themselves under attack for *causing* America's defeat in Vietnam.

Criticism of network reporting in Vietnam was inspired in part by the new tone of its post-Tet coverage. From 1969 on, a recurrent theme was not whether the US should get out but *how*, and for many viewers, this was excessively defeatist. But criticism was also sparked by a new interest that all three networks began to show in domestic opposition to the war. Before 1968, network coverage of the anti-war movement was hostile and patronizing. This was because it was dominated by fringe groups like Students for a Democratic Society and included elements that were seemingly anti-American. News reports on anti-war marches and demonstrations often focused on activists carrying incendiary placards or waving Vietcong flags, and correspondents flocked to spokesmen who specialized in fiery rhetoric—and who, in turn, exploited their media connections to become movement "celebrities." Like the Johnson administration, network correspondents often suggested that radical anti-war activists were providing comfort to the enemy. And by depicting them as kooks whose views were beyond the pale, journalists discouraged viewers from taking them seriously.[69]

By 1968, however, the anti-war movement had grown. It now included a much wider range of Americans and was coming to be dominated by liberals and moderates, including mainstream politicians like McGovern and Eugene McCarthy. The emergence of a popular anti-war wing of the Democratic Party was a particularly important milestone. Now there were many more "official" sources willing to criticize the war, widening the range of views that network journalists could cover through their patented point-counterpoint technique. Emphasizing the conflict between pro-war "hawks" and anti-war "doves" enabled the networks to increase their coverage of the anti-war movement and connect it to more conventional subjects like party politics.[70]

These connections were clear at the Democratic National Convention in Chicago, where anti-war delegates, seeking to insert a statement opposing the war into the party's platform, were thwarted by party hawks backing the candidacy of vice president Hubert Humphrey. Humphrey had become the administration candidate after Johnson decided not to run for reelection, and he had pledged to continue LBJ's Vietnam policies, much to the dismay of doves. The acrimony and bitterness inside the conventional hall was intense, at times erupting into name-calling and fisticuffs. And network cameras captured it all in grotesque and often mesmerizing detail. On August 26, the networks interrupted their coverage of the convention to broadcast something even more spectacular—news film reports of violent clashes between angry protesters and the Chicago police. The protesters, determined to march to the convention site to express their hatred of the war, were all considerably to the left of the anti-war delegates who were seeking to work through the Democratic Party. Some of them were diehard radicals, and the whole point of their presence in Chicago was to spark a confrontation that would reveal the US to be a fascist state. They got what they wished for. With television cameras whirring, the Chicago police set upon them with a fury that shocked many onlookers, including the press and anti-war delegates at the convention, who denounced the "Gestapo tactics" of mayor Richard Daley's police.[71]

The Chicago convention was a searing experience for television journalists. They left deeply concerned about the polarization and upsurge in violence that had swept the nation. The months before the convention had seen the assassinations of Martin Luther King Jr. and Robert F. Kennedy, and a new wave of urban riots. After Chicago, they increased their coverage of the anti-war movement, emphasizing its growing appeal among ordinary Americans, and they made a concerted effort to provide a forum for public discussion. They hoped to encourage understanding and compromise, to heal the rift that had split the nation. Among many viewers, however, network efforts to find a middle ground had the opposite effect. Some were disturbed by the publicity the networks provided anti-war activists, whom they regarded as little better than traitors. And others were disconcerted by the scenes of conflict and violence that continued to dominate the evening news. As in the case of the urban riots, network efforts to explain the alienation of anti-war activists backfired. Rather than encouraging a rapprochement, they led many Americans to believe that the networks were on the side of the anti-war movement—and that, by exposing divisions in the US, they were inspiring North Vietnam and the Vietcong to fight on, confident that public opinion would force the American government to withdraw. Nor were many viewers appalled by the "police riot" in Chicago or other evidence of domestic repression. Public opinion polls revealed that a substantial majority sided with Mayor Daley and the police and believed that the networks had neglected to show how Chicago's finest had been provoked by demonstrators. That filthy, foul-mouthed horde had it coming.

Richard M. Nixon, elected president in 1968, was acutely aware of the contempt many Americans were coming to feel toward the network news divisions. Like Johnson, he was disturbed by the media's more assertive reporting about Vietnam and its sympathetic coverage of the anti-war movement. But, unlike LBJ, who owned a Texas TV station and was comfortable with broadcasters and network executives, Nixon had long felt persecuted by the press. He had staged his "comeback" by limiting contact with journalists, and as president, he took measures to prevent them from derailing his agenda. Seizing the initiative, he and his aides launched an aggressive and carefully planned campaign to discredit the major media and the television news divisions in particular. Led by vice president Spiro Agnew, it raised a politically potent charge: that "a small group of men, numbering no more than a dozen anchormen, commentators, and executive producers," decided what was broadcast on the network news programs. This small cabal, an "effete corps of impudent snobs," was part of a larger, more sinister "Eastern liberal establishment" that was out of step with the "silent majority" of Americans who supported President Nixon.[72]

Nixon's campaign tapped into a powerful well of conservative hatred for the media that had been growing throughout the 1960s, as the networks struggled to cover the conflicts of the era and were compelled to provide a forum for a much wider range of views. And it employed language that appealed to blue-collar Democrats who were coming to despise civil rights and anti-war activists and many of the other forces that were challenging the Democratic old guard represented by Humphrey and Daley. But the campaign was also directed at the owners and managers of television stations affiliated with the networks, who were in a position to pressure the networks to dampen their critical coverage of the war. Often conservative businessmen, they shared many of Nixon's views and were alarmed by the new tone of network news coverage. Incensed, they bombarded network executives with complaints about "bias" and fiercely cross-examined news division presidents at annual affiliate meetings. By mobilizing affiliates, Nixon hoped to put the news divisions on the defensive. And, in the short run, he was at least partially successful. The networks sharply curtailed their coverage of the anti-war movement, and executives and producers breathed a sigh of relief when, after a flare-up sparked by the US invasion of Cambodia in the spring of 1970, public protests against the war declined.

But Nixon's campaign against the media had other consequences, and when the Watergate scandal forced him to resign, the press and the television networks reasserted themselves. Alarmed by this bald-faced effort to muzzle the press, many print and television journalists redoubled their commitment to aggressive, hard-hitting reporting.[73] At the networks, it inspired a more powerful esprit de corps and encouraged journalists to produce programs and stories that reaffirmed their independence from the government, the military, and its corporate allies. Caught between affiliates, who often hated this new, more adversarial programming, and their news divisions, network executives usually sided with the latter, a brave rebuke to the Nixon administration's arrogance that won them the admiration of many print journalists. Documentaries and special reports in the early 1970s became more critical and confrontational, often eschewing the conventional emphasis on "balance" to present an explicit point of view. The most famous was CBS's "The Selling of the Pentagon," a penetrating account of the Defense Department's public-relations activities that sparked enormous controversy and almost resulted in Frank Stanton being jailed for his refusal to turn over the producers' outtakes to a congressional committee. But there were other equally distinguished examples, produced by all three networks, and they set a new standard for excellence that enhanced the networks' reputation for serious journalism. Perhaps the most remarkable was "You and the Commercial," a CBS exposé of how television commercials, the very lifeblood of the industry, were designed to influence consumer behavior. The broadcast of such a program would have been unthinkable in the mid-1960s.

By the mid-1970s, the networks had grown in stature and influence. They were the principal source of news for a majority of Americans and had developed a broadcast style well suited for their commitment to journalistic respectability. Confident of their status as objective, impartial professionals and self-appointed watchdogs looking out for the public interest, they saw it as their job to provide viewers with what they ought to know in order to be informed, engaged citizens. It was the news from Olympus, presented in a tone that suggested the voice of God.

This mission neatly echoed the professional ideals of the prestige press. Unlike the *New York Times* or the *Washington Post*, however, the networks delivered news to a broad, diverse audience. And by the mid-1970s, many viewers were not very happy with their performance. Some were disconcerted by all the "bad news" they delivered, while others thought they were disrespectful of authority. Even worse, a growing number of Americans viewed the networks as biased propagandists for an arrogant elite. Many Americans were equally suspicious of the prestige press, but in the days before widely available national editions or the Internet, newspapers like the *Times* or the *Post* were easy to avoid. Network news, by contrast, was a ubiquitous presence, and the fact that it reached so many people made its putative influence a more disturbing prospect.

Thus at the very moment of their assimilation into the journalistic establishment, the network news divisions were losing their credibility with viewers. They were losing it in part because they were

3

PUBLIC ALTERNATIVES

Fred Friendly was apoplectic. As his coworkers well knew, he was prone to fits of manic enthusiasm and titanic rage. But this time was different, and foreboding and anxiety soon pervaded the news department. Since becoming president of CBS News in March 1964, Friendly had pushed his superiors for more airtime for news and documentaries. Exploiting his access to Frank Stanton and Bill Paley, he had secured their approval for an increase in the frequency of news bulletins—short interruptions of regular programming—and for extended coverage of civil rights protests and the congressional debate that preceded passage of the Civil Rights Act. And, for the past few months, he had been demanding, and mostly getting, additional airtime for special reports on America's growing involvement in Vietnam.

Now, in February 1966, he wanted even more—to preempt CBS's daytime programs to broadcast hearings of the Senate Foreign Relations Committee. Chaired by J. William Fulbright, a skeptic of President Johnson's escalation, the committee had called several witnesses who were also known to have doubts about the war. Friendly was convinced that, if enough people heard their testimony, the hearings could trigger a wider public debate about US policy in Vietnam. He was relieved when his superiors agreed to let him begin broadcasting them, and by their willingness to give him a half hour of prime time for a special report summarizing their highlights. But when Friendly pushed for continued coverage over the next few days, Jack Schneider, the newly appointed executive to whom he now reported, refused, arguing that summaries provided on *The CBS Evening News* and in prime time were sufficient. So while NBC continued its live coverage, CBS returned to its regular programming, reruns of *I Love Lucy*, *The Andy Griffith Show*, and *The Real McCoys*.

Enraged, Friendly complained to Stanton, threatening to resign. He was counting on Stanton and Paley to overrule Schneider and reaffirm their oft-quoted claims that news was the network's highest priority. But they called his bluff and accepted his resignation. In a typically grandiloquent gesture, Friendly went public with his criticism of Schneider and CBS's new "bottom line" mentality. The network that had led the way in expanding news and public-affairs programming, he noted portentously, had surrendered to the commercial logic that dominated network television—an obsession with ratings and profits. CBS News had been "emasculated."[1]

In the aftermath of Friendly's resignation, rumors circulated about job offers from NBC and ABC. The one he accepted, as a professor of journalism at Columbia University and "television advisor" for the Ford Foundation, surprised many people in the industry. Friendly was a producer, not an academic, and he had no formal training as a journalist. Nor had he had much contact with the rarified world of private foundations. The Ford Foundation, however, was under new leadership, and its president, former Kennedy and Johnson advisor McGeorge Bundy, thought Friendly was just the man to help the foundation transform the scattered, one hundred or so educational television stations in the US into a powerful "fourth network" that could provide viewers with a real alternative to the "vast wasteland" of commercial television. In 1962, FCC chair Newton Minow had suggested that educational television—or ETV—required an injection of "showmanship" to attract more viewers and fulfill its potential.[2] By hiring Friendly, the most celebrated and respected showman in the television news business, Bundy and the Ford Foundation were betting that the visionary who had created *See It Now* and *CBS Reports* could raise ETV's profile and turn it into a something that would rival the commercial networks.

ETV, the poor, neglected stepchild of the television industry, desperately needed Friendly's vision. In the mid-1940s, when the TV industry began to grow and the FCC started issuing station licenses, few Americans considered the possibility of reserving frequencies for noncommercial uses. It was expected that television would follow the same path as the radio industry and rely on advertising to pay for programming and provide station owners with their principal source of revenue. Most of the people who felt otherwise were educators, particularly faculty and administrators at public universities. They had struggled to establish a small foothold in radio, and they were determined to ensure that at least some television frequencies were set aside for uses other than entertainment and the hawking of consumer goods. In the late 1940s, when the FCC instituted its freeze in issuing station licenses, they began lobbying the FCC and making their case to the public. When the freeze ended in 1952, the FCC allocated 242 channels for noncommercial purposes. Only 80, however, were in the standard VHF band; the remaining 162 were in the UHF band, which most televisions were not equipped to receive. Still, it was a significant triumph, and proponents of educational television were determined to ensure that universities, nonprofits, and community groups took full advantage of the opportunity by securing licenses and setting up stations on the allotted frequencies.[3]

One of ETV's most fervent champions was the Ford Foundation. A relative newcomer to the world of big-time philanthropy, it was flush with money and looking for worthy causes to promote. C. Scott Fletcher, the director of the foundation's Fund for Adult Education (FAE), was especially interested in television's potential. He thought a loosely configured network of noncommercial stations might be an effective medium for popularizing the liberal arts and making the essentials of a college education accessible to the general public. The FAE provided grants to groups that had secured noncommercial licenses from the FCC, enabling them to buy equipment and begin broadcasting. The first was KHUT in Houston, which went on the air in 1953. Thanks to the FAE's largesse and local sources of financial support, the number of noncommercial television stations slowly increased. By 1956, sixteen were on the air, including KQED in San Francisco and WGBH in Boston; by 1962, seventy-six were operating in cities around the country.

From the start, Fletcher and the FAE recognized that noncommercial stations would need programming. They expected local stations to produce the majority of their own programs, catering to local needs. But they also conceived the idea of a "program exchange" that would allow stations to share certain programs, enabling them to be seen in more than one market. In 1952, the FAE established the Educational Television and Radio Center (ETRC). Located in Ann Arbor,

Michigan, it became a kind of lending library for noncommercial stations, providing affiliates with programs in the humanities and national, international, and economic affairs. Stations would send kinescopes—single filmed copies—of programs they produced in these areas to the ETRC; from there, they would be sent through the mail to other stations for broadcast, one after the other. Lacking access to one of AT&T's coaxial cables, which would have made it possible for the ETRC to feed programs to individual stations, as the networks did, this laborious process of "bicycling" was the only way programs could be seen in more than one community. By 1955, despite this logistical hurdle, the ETRC was supplying noncommercial stations with five hours of programming per week. And the prospect of gaining access to this material was an important incentive for groups interested in establishing new educational television stations, contributing to the system's growth.

The Ford Foundation also experimented with television production. It established a Radio-TV Workshop that produced a cultural affairs program called *Omnibus*. Hosted by the British journalist Alistair Cooke, its aim was to introduce "high culture" to the curious and uninitiated. Segments included excerpts from Shakespearean plays and contemporary drama and performances of classical music, and it profiled many writers and artists. Though Cooke described the program as a high-culture "vaudeville show," it kept its educational mission front and center. Rather than merely broadcast classical music, for example, producers allowed renowned composer Leonard Bernstein to explain a particular composition's origins and significance. Over the years, *Omnibus* expanded its horizons to include occasional segments on science and technology, particularly when they overlapped with the arts. The musicians Les Paul and Mary Ford, for example, demonstrated the novel technique of multitrack recording, and the program allowed Americans their first opportunity to view oceanographer Jacques Cousteau's cinematic "undersea adventures." The ETRC offered *Omnibus* to the commercial networks, and it was picked up by CBS in 1952 and scheduled in the Sunday afternoon "intellectual ghetto." In subsequent years, it bounced from network to network, without much promotion or network support, until it was finally canceled in 1961. The networks' lack of commitment to the program redoubled Fletcher's belief in the necessity of expanding noncommercial television and increasing the responsibilities of the ETRC.[4]

The ETRC's profile rose in 1958, when John F. White, a former university administrator and general manager of WQED-Pittsburgh, became head of the organization. Ambitious and media savvy, White moved the ETRC to New York City and added "National" to its name. It became NET, the nucleus of an alternative to commercial television that White began calling "America's Fourth Network." Under White, the weekly package of programs NET offered to affiliates expanded to ten hours, and it stepped up its assistance to groups seeking to establish new noncommercial stations. At first, the programs in NET's weekly package continued to be produced by affiliates or independent producers, and stations could air them whenever they wished—or not at all if they didn't seem appealing to local audiences. As a result, most programs on educational stations in the early 1960s were dry, pedantic lectures on academic subjects, particularly foreign languages and the humanities. Targeted at viewers eager for self-improvement, they were amateurishly produced and looked terrible next to the slick fare broadcast by commercial stations.[5]

White recognized this problem and shifted NET's emphasis. To make noncommercial television more enticing to viewers, NET would seek to acquire and distribute higher-quality programs. He invited the largest, most well-financed stations to increase their production of programs for NET, and he and his associates went abroad, to the BBC and the Canadian Broadcasting Corporation, for programming as well. This alarmed the managers at many stations. They preferred a local and educational approach and feared that White wanted to turn NET into a centralized network that would force stations to broadcast a more uniform and "professional" program package. For many stations, noncommercial television meant decentralized television produced by local stations with local audiences uppermost in mind, a commitment that would constrain White and continue to pose problems for his successors.[6]

White was also committed to finding new sources of financial support and weaning ETV off its dependence on the Ford Foundation. Foundation officials welcomed this, and joined him in the search for more permanent funding. They were pleased when FCC chairman Minow expressed his support for ETV, and when Congress, at Minow's and President Kennedy's urging, passed the Educational Television and Facilities Act in 1962, which provided station owners with federal matching funds to purchase broadcast equipment. With liberals gaining influence in Washington, White and the Ford Foundation were hopeful that federal support for ETV might increase. The prospects for ETV improved further when Congress mandated that all new televisions sold in the US be equipped to receive UHF signals. This spurred many more local groups to establish noncommercial stations on the UHF band and contributed greatly to the system's growth. By the mid-1960s, there were 115 noncommercial stations in the US, with many more on the way. But ETV's growth increased NET's distribution costs and made the lack of an interconnection even more frustrating.

Meanwhile, Ford Foundation officials encouraged White to transform NET into a production center, promising more money on the condition that NET focus largely on providing "a high-quality informational and cultural program service."[7] They pressured NET to reduce the programs in its weekly package to five hours, on the assumption that fewer programs would mean ones of higher quality, and they stipulated that half of all Ford money go to programs about public affairs and international issues. To oversee NET's public-affairs programs, White hired William Kobin, a young producer who had worked at ABC News. Relying on NET's small staff and several talented refugees from commercial television, Kobin began assembling production teams. NET officials also expanded existing programs produced by affiliates, including *News in Perspective*, a monthly roundtable discussion among *New York Times* journalists hosted by Lester Markel, the *Times*' Sunday editor. NET's reliance on bicycling programs to affiliates, however, made programs focusing on news and late-breaking events ill suited for ETV stations. By the time NET's few copies made the rounds, many days or even weeks had elapsed.

Advances in technology gradually made news-oriented programs more feasible. NET and ETV stations, for example, were quick to recognize the usefulness of videotape as a means of creating multiple copies of programs. With multiples, the time it took for programs to reach NET's growing number of affiliates was greatly reduced. Producers at NET were also intrigued by the possibilities for simultaneous broadcast created by the launching of synchronous satellites. In January 1967, NET made a bid to compete with the networks when it purchased satellite time to broadcast President Johnson's State of the Union address. It was NET's first attempt at an interconnected broadcast, and it was followed by two hours of analysis and commentary by scholars and journalists. The experiment was praised by TV critics like

Jack Gould. "The absence of commercial deadlines and the caliber and distinction of the guest commentators," Gould wrote, "enabled NET to offer a much more extended, searching and diversified analysis than the advertising supported networks."[8]

The push for quality had mixed results, and programming on ETV stations varied widely. Local stations, particularly in provincial cities and university towns, continued to broadcast low-budget educational programs and cultural shows that catered to local or regional tastes. They were supplemented by the evolving package distributed by NET. Most of the programs in the package were produced by the biggest stations. WGBH-Boston, for example, was responsible for several programs, including *The French Chef*, Julia Child's cooking show. A Denver-based station, KRMA, produced *Ragtime Era*, an enormously popular music program. Others programs were commissioned by NET producers and executives. They included NET *Playhouse*, an anthology of high-quality drama, and programs featuring classical music and dance. NET's package also included material produced by the BBC. Its first British acquisition was a dramatic series, *An Age of Kings*, which NET broadcast in 1961. The first noncommercial series underwritten by a corporate sponsor, Humble Oil, it presented performances of all of Shakespeare's historical plays. It was a big hit with viewers and encouraged NET officials to look to the BBC and Britain's Granada TV for programs that were "classy" and could match the production values of commercial television. The most successful of these imports was *The Forsyte Saga*, a twenty-six-episode serial that NET began broadcasting in October 1969. Much discussed among the educated upper-middle class, it drew even more viewers to noncommercial TV and moved NET even further from its original mission as a purveyor of "educational" television.

Though NET's lack of an interconnection made broadcasting time-sensitive news shows a problem, it didn't stop William Kobin's production teams from making documentaries. Along with films made by independent producers and big stations like KQED and acquisitions from the BBC and the CBC, they appeared as part of a regular series, NET *Journal*. Kobin's producers were game to tackle difficult, controversial subjects, and they had the full support of NET officials, including John White. They were especially interested in examining race relations and the civil rights movement, and they produced probing reports on the political hurdles that confronted movement activists and the persistent, often subtle discrimination that blacks experienced in their everyday lives. Far more than the commercial networks, NET producers delved into the complex roots of race relations in the US, and their documentaries were notable for the airtime they provided their black subjects. In 1967, NET broadcast a nine-part *History of the Negro People*, and later that year it began a new monthly series called *Black Journal*, a magazine-style program expressly aimed at black audiences. Produced by African Americans, it featured musical performances, poetry, discussions of current affairs, and filmed reports that expressed the "black perspective." Under the direction of Tony Brown, who became host and producer in 1969, it became a fixture on public television, despite complaints by some affiliates that its focus on racism was too negative and confrontational.

NET *Journal* examined other issues, too. Jack Willis produced searing exposés of poverty in Appalachia and the poor quality of New York City's parochial schools, while his colleagues at NET made documentaries about drug abuse, student rebellion on college campuses, and inequities in the distribution of welfare payments to the poor. Inspired by the new skepticism of officialdom that spread through the country in the late 1960s, NET documentaries were often controversial. But with the Ford Foundation as NET's principal source of support and NET officials, including White and his successor, James Day, committed to producing programs that were bold and challenged the conventional wisdom, producers enjoyed far greater latitude than their counterparts at CBS or NBC. As White told affiliates, NET's job was display leadership and courage, "to depart from the safe and sterile, to buck strong pockets of opinion," and address issues in ways that were eye-opening and could not be done by the commercial networks: "If we don't have that courage, we don't belong in this business."[9]

Perhaps the most controversial NET documentary was an independent production that aired in 1968, *Inside North Vietnam*. Produced by Felix Greene, a former BBC producer, it was originally slated to appear on CBS. But when CBS officials saw the completed film—a "tour" of North Vietnam that Greene was allowed to produce with the cooperation of the North Vietnamese government—they refused to broadcast it, arguing that it was irreparably biased. Greene then offered it to NET. At Kobin's behest, Greene shortened the film to an hour and eliminated its most inflammatory footage, and NET produced a panel discussion that was added at the end to provide "balance." But these measures did little to mollify the program's many critics. The attacks began even before the program aired, when word of its impending broadcast reached the Johnson administration and Congress. A letter to White signed by forty-four members of Congress denounced Greene's film as "communist propaganda" and called on White not to distribute it to affiliates. But White went ahead with the broadcast, which Jack Gould commended as "a useful and thoroughly defensible exercise in television journalism."[10]

By this time, Fred Friendly had become the Ford Foundation's television advisor, and he and Mac Bundy had set in motion their plan to turn NET and its affiliates into the fourth network. Bundy was deeply implicated in the US buildup in Vietnam, and like other chastened New Frontiersmen, he had left public office concerned about the splintering of the consensus that had united much of the country in the 1950s and early 1960s. At once intrigued and frightened by the rebellious ferment that was sweeping the nation, he thought a new public television system might be able to provide an outlet for some of these new political and cultural currents—and perhaps direct them back toward the mainstream.[11]

Friendly shared his optimism, and together they developed an audacious plan to provide NET and its affiliates with a permanent interconnection and source of funding. It called for the creation of a nonprofit corporation to oversee the operation of four synchronous satellites—one for each of the three commercial networks and a fourth for a new public television network. Rather than pay AT&T to lease the coaxial cables that enabled them to feed their programs to affiliates, the commercial networks would instead pay a smaller fee to the nonprofit for use of its satellites, which would beam their signal directly to local stations. The profits that the nonprofit satellite operator earned from this business, in turn, would be used to pay for program production, distribution, and promotion for the fourth network. That network would have its own satellite to provide its affiliates with a live interconnection, replacing the inefficient bicycling system NET had employed since the 1950s. The plan attracted quite a bit of press and sparked a lively public discussion, but AT&T and COMSAT, the government-regulated private corporation created by Congress to oversee domestic satellite service, were staunchly opposed. So were the commercial networks. They refused to consider any plan in which they would subsidize a potential competitor.[12]

Though the Bundy-Friendly proposal died, it inspired others to consider how the nation's educational television stations might be transformed into "public television," including a commission established by the Carnegie Corporation, which developed a competing plan. It was revealed in a report published in January 1967. Unlike Bundy and Friendly, who sought the creation of a true network that would openly compete with NBC, CBS, and ABC, the Carnegie Commission favored a decentralized, government-subsidized public television system. Financing would come from revenues raised by an excise tax on the sale of new televisions, a method other nations used to fund their public broadcasting systems. The plan was more palatable to many interests who were likely to be affected, and it won the support of the Johnson administration. Instead of the excise tax, however, President Johnson and the plan's supporters in Congress decided to fund public television through congressional appropriations, an idea that deeply worried Bundy and Friendly and even concerned some members of the Carnegie Commission. Testifying before the Senate Subcommittee on Communications, Friendly sounded a warning about making public television dependent on government funds and potentially vulnerable to political influence. Public television will "rock the boat," he insisted. "There will be—there should be—times when every man in politics—including you—will wish that it had never been created. But public television should not have to stand the test of political popularity at any point in time. Its most precious right will be the right to rock the boat."[13]

Despite his warning, a funding scheme reliant on congressional appropriations was included in the Public Broadcasting Act, which was passed by Congress and signed by President Johnson in November 1967. To appease critics concerned about the potential for government control of public television, the legislation insisted that money earmarked for public television by Congress go to an independent organization, a newly established Corporation for Public Broadcasting. The CPB, in turn, would distribute the funds to local stations and serve as a buffer between them and Congress. The CPB's board was supposed to include representatives from diverse constituencies. Yet in the bill's final incarnation, responsibility for appointing its fifteen members was entrusted to the president, with the stipulation that no more than eight be from the same political party. To the dismay of NET officials, the legislation also allowed the CPB wide authority over the system's

Fred Friendly was the creator of *See It Now* and *CBS Reports* and inspired many other television news programs. He also served as president of CBS News in the mid-1960s and was a founding father of public television, which he hoped would become a legitimate "fourth network." Photo courtesy of Photofest.

interconnection, which was secured through congressional pressure on AT&T to provide it with limited access to a coaxial cable at a reduced rate. In 1969, the newly formed CPB created a new organization to operate the interconnection and distribute programs to individual stations: PBS, or the Public Broadcasting Service. In line with the Carnegie Commission's interest in decentralization, it was conceived as a member organization, not a network. And its membership agreement gave affiliates extensive authority over what they broadcast, including the right to air PBS programs at odd hours or refuse them altogether.[14]

Conceived at the high tide of postwar liberalism, America's new

public television system reflected the diverse and conflicting impera-
tives of the era. In the spirit of the New Frontier and Great Society,
it was envisioned by its architects as an agent of cultural uplift—as
an oasis in the wasteland that would spark an improvement in public
taste and put pressure on the commercial networks to pay more attention to the quality of their programming. Many of its creators also
thought it could foster appreciation of American diversity, providing
programs for specific communities and offering underrepresented
groups opportunities to share their cultures and traditions with other
citizens. They hoped it could become a venue for unrecognized talents
and unorthodox forms of cultural expression, where artists and performers who were not welcome on commercial media could reach a
wider audience. And they were confident that public television could
provide viewers with *real* news and public-affairs programming and
become the place where Americans turned for sober and sophisticated treatment of the nation's problems and for "understanding of
the world, of other nations and cultures, of the whole commonwealth
of man."[15]

It was an ambitious mission, and it papered over some tensions and
conflicting agendas that would deepen over the next few years. First,
it obscured the fault line between NET and most member stations
outside of big cities who were committed to programming for viewers who were, on the whole, more conservative and less sophisticated
than those in New York, Boston, Los Angeles, or San Francisco. And it
downplayed the growing gulf between stations interested in professional programming and other stations interested in what one might
call "people's television," locally oriented and more amateur productions, often inspired by alternative media, that might provide a voice
for the marginalized by giving them access to production facilities—
not just by producing programs about their plight. It also, in its promotion of "uplift," cavalierly assumed a single, progressive ideal of
cultivation and education and failed to anticipate how new notions,
inspired by the civil rights movement and already in circulation in
the late 1960s, would challenge this ideal and inspire some station
managers, producers, and viewers to celebrate the vernacular cultures of ethnic groups and politicized communities and demand programs reflecting this vision. Most important, the new system's potential for providing sophisticated news and public-affairs programming
was jeopardized by its reliance on congressional appropriations, and

by the tension between the progressive emphasis on objectivity, empirical analysis, and Olympian detachment, and a belief that, with the commercial networks committed to a cautious, establishment-oriented centrism, public television should side with the underdog.[16]

While the Johnson administration and its allies were drafting the Public Broadcasting Act, Bundy and Friendly began work on their other notable initiative, the development of a new program that would distinguish public television from its commercial rivals and revolutionize the medium as *See It Now* had done in the early 1950s. It was a live, two-and-a-half hour magazine-style program called PBL (short for *Public Broadcasting Laboratory*), and it debuted in November 1967. Created by a separate production unit within NET and supported by a $10 million grant from the Ford Foundation, PBL was overseen by Av Westin, a young, award-winning producer Friendly had lured away from CBS. It featured news reports, short filmed documentaries, discussions, and a range of artistic performances, many of them by figures associated with the avant-garde. Eschewing the quasi-academic tone of much NET programming, PBL boasted well-known journalists and commentators recruited from the major networks and employed the full array of professional production techniques commonly used by its commercial rivals. Its host was the respected ABC anchorman Edward P. Morgan, and among the correspondents who provided filmed reports were NBC vets Tom Petit and Robert MacNeil.[17]

More than any other television program at the time, PBL provided a platform for dissenting political views and controversial artistic projects. Its maiden broadcast, focusing on race relations, included an Off-Broadway play that imagined a town deserted by its black inhabitants where the remaining whites, played by black actors in whiteface, are incapable of getting along without their "inferiors." And at appointed times when network programs might cut to a commercial, PBL offered ingenious and cynical "anti-commercials" mocking the claims of advertisers and consumer culture more generally. Its frequent news and public-affairs segments were hard-hitting and often came to unequivocal conclusions, in pointed contrast to commercial television's obsession with balance. Not surprisingly, Westin and his fellow producers were assailed by conservatives. They were also condemned by many station managers, who were uncomfortable broadcasting a program so clearly informed by the political and cultural radicalism of the era; a number of stations, mostly in the South, refused to air several controversial episodes. Even *PBL*'s own advisory board complained about the heavy-handedness of many segments. But Friendly stood behind Westin, and the program was renewed for a second season. In a concession to critics, the broadcast was cut to ninety minutes. And in place of the at times anarchic variety that characterized many episodes during its first season, Westin and his staff developed weekly themes. They also began producing segments profiling notable conservatives, including California governor Ronald Reagan and the journalist Brent Bozell Jr. PBL was also placed more firmly under NET's control, a development that disappointed Westin and ultimately led to his departure for ABC News in March 1969.

The new format was well received by critics, and in its second season *PBL* aired some insightful and challenging segments, including a detailed examination of how the commercial television networks put together the evening news. Yet the program failed to attract very many viewers, and it was broadcast for the last time in April 1969. Part of the reason for its failure was its novelty. Unlike *See It Now*, which was launched in television's early pioneering days, PBL appeared when television formats were well established and viewers had clear expectations. For most viewers, even the educated upper-middle class, television was not a place for such wild experimentation, especially the mix of genres that was the show's hallmark. And because it aired shortly after passage of the Public Broadcasting Act and could be interpreted as a harbinger of what "national" programming on public television might look like, it alarmed the managers and boards at many individual stations and redoubled their interest in keeping the newly created PBS a decentralized membership organization and severely limiting the power of the self-styled "sophisticates" at NET. NET officials got the message. Among the programs they chose to replace PBL on Sunday nights was the far more conventional—and successful— BBC import, *The Forsyte Saga*.[18]

Friendly's news background resulted in Ford Foundation support for other news and public-affairs programs produced by NET and its affiliates. In the early 1960s, before Friendly's arrival, the most common news-oriented programs were weekly or monthly discussion-format shows like Lester Markel's *News in Perspective* and *World Press*, a thoughtful analysis of international affairs by academics produced by San Francisco's KQED that was picked up by NET and popular with many affiliates. But when a strike halted publication of San Francisco's two major newspapers in 1968, KQED created a daily news program to fill the breach. Conceived by print journalists who feared that San Francisco's commercial stations could never compensate for the absence of newspapers, *Newspaper of the Air* was improvisational and decidedly low-tech. Lacking resources, aside from a short-term grant from the Ford Foundation, or the ability to produce filmed reports, it was hosted by the *Chronicle*'s managing editor, who was seated at the head of a rectangular table. Arrayed to his right and left were other striking reporters, who had been assigned stories and reported them from notes, without the benefit of film or rehearsal. Each report was followed by questions from the moderator and other reporters. The show was popular with viewers, but when the strike ended after nine weeks and its staff returned to their jobs, it went off the air.[19]

Excited by the program's possibilities, Friendly and the Ford Foundation began soliciting grant applications from stations interested in developing similar news offerings. KQED was among the first to respond. A $750,000 grant enabled the station to revive the program, now called *Newsroom*, hire its own reporters and support staff and, over time, even produce filmed reports. But the format remained essentially the same—emphasizing discussion and in-depth analysis. Not surprisingly, the program frequently sparked controversy. Former KQED manager James Day noted, "Objective reporting was its aim, but not always its result: a reporter's lifted eyebrow, tone of voice, unplanned flippancy, or ad-libbed response to another's question could occasionally tilt the show in one direction or another."[20] Its sensitive and thorough coverage of the student rebellions of the late 1960s was especially controversial, inspiring negative mail and impeding the station's ability to raise money from private donors. Other viewers, however, were more appreciative. Despite steadily rising costs, the program lasted for more than a decade. Versions of *Newsroom* were launched by stations in other markets, giving public television a distinctive profile in local news.[21]

Perhaps the most innovative local news show was *The 51st State*, a program produced by a prominent Newark-based station that covered the New York metropolitan area. Producer Jack Willis sought to make it challenging and provocative, with reports that conveyed the news "from the bottom up." To anchor the program, Willis chose Patrick Watson, an experienced Canadian journalist. He was joined by a regular cast of correspondents, most of them former print journalists.

Their stories emphasized injustice, sympathizing with society's "victims" and expressing an unapologetically liberal, at times even radical, point of view. During its first year, the program wasn't even constrained by time or format. It went as long as Willis and his associates thought that the day's news warranted. *The 51st State* was regularly denounced for being biased, even by former public TV producers like Av Westin. And its overtly antiestablishment tone made it a special target for conservatives seeking to limit news and public-affairs programming on public television. But it also attracted a passionate audience. And unlike the networks or commercial stations, who usually responded to such attacks by pulling punches and beating a hasty retreat, Willis and Watson defended their unique approach. Willis argued that the whole issue of objectivity was a red herring; his sole concern was whether his reporters were conveying the facts. Watson went further, suggesting that balance was an "old-fashioned concept" that in many instances made little sense: "You don't balance out the astronauts with the Flat Earth Society," he quipped in a television interview. Though the program gradually become more conventional, and Willis and Watson left after conflicts with WNET officials, it was a notable departure from the mold and offered viewers a real alternative—just as Friendly has hoped.[22]

National news programs were slower to come to public television. The autonomy enjoyed by member stations after the establishment of PBS in 1970, and their increasing reliance on auctions, pledge drives, and other forms of viewer support, encouraged the broadcasting of "high culture" and British imports—the kinds of programs member stations were certain to clear and that burnished PBS's reputation with critics. Public television's biggest hit, however, was a show for children. *Sesame Street* debuted in November 1969. It was extremely popular and inspired many viewers to sample other public TV programs, boosting viewership on the eve of PBS's launch in 1970. Thanks to such hits, PBS quickly became far more visible than NET had ever been, enhancing member stations' ability to fundraise.[23] With PBS operating the interconnection and negotiating with member stations to air the programs it sought to distribute nationally, NET was reduced to a production center and folded into WNDT, the Newark-based station serving the New York metropolitan area that was rechristened WNET. Meanwhile, the system continued to grow. By 1972 there were well over two hundred public television stations in the US; a decade later, there would be more than three hundred.

The preference for high-toned cultural fare was also a result of a shift in the political winds. With Richard M. Nixon as president, the CPB and PBS found themselves under a new degree of official scrutiny, and many individual stations were determined to avoid the public flaps that were sparked by provocative programs like *PBL*. When the Ford Foundation and the CPB decided to fund another public-affairs show, they quite purposely chose one that was less likely to ruffle feathers, the debate program *The Advocates*. Conceived by Roger Fisher, a professor at Harvard Law School, and coproduced by stations in Boston and Los Angeles, it debuted in the fall of 1969 right after *The Forsyte Saga* on Sunday evenings. *The Advocates* was an earnest attempt to encourage public enlightenment. It was broadcast live from real courtrooms, and featured mock debates between actual lawyers representing liberal and conservative positions on some of the most contentious issues of the day—from no-fault divorce and the legalization of drugs to the Vietnam War and the Arab-Israeli conflict. By limiting the parameters of debate to two options within the mainstream and relying on credentialed experts who would not express excessively radical views, the program was able to attract viewers and appease public television's conservative critics. PBS officials even sought to promote the program on college campuses in hopes that its willingness to tackle issues of interest to youth might encourage civic engagement rather than radical protest or cynicism. Heavily promoted, *The Advocates* attracted a small regular audience and lasted five years before cancelation. Its obsession with balance marked a retreat from the pointedly antiestablishment perspectives that had often appeared on *PBL* and anticipated the emphasis of *The MacNeil/Lehrer Report*.[24]

But other public television programs continued to raise hackles and create problems for PBS officials. One of the biggest controversies was sparked by a NET-produced documentary, *Banks and the Poor*, which was broadcast in November 1970. Produced by Morton Silverstein, it exposed the ways prominent banks financed slumlords and engaged in discriminatory lending practices. The documentary received positive reviews in several prominent newspapers, and Silverstein was commended by the critic John Leonard in *Life* for his innovative technique and courage in taking on such a powerful interest group. The film was brutally candid in its condemnation of major banks and suggested that their policies were attributable to influence peddling and a lack of regulation. In the film's closing minutes, the names of nearly a hundred congressmen and senators with "bank connections" scrolled by. After previewing *Banks and the Poor*, PBS officials were wary of distributing it to member stations, knowing it would incite a firestorm of protest and place PBS firmly in the Nixon administration's crosshairs. But Leonard's advance review had already been published, and they knew they risked angering many viewers if they appeared to be avoiding controversy. So they went ahead and distributed it, and most stations put it on the air. In response to the uproar, PBS officials assembled a panel of professional journalists to develop guidelines for public-affairs programs to ensure they met what PBS president Hartford Gunn called "the highest quality of journalism and professionalism." The guidelines gave PBS new powers as a gatekeeper, and PBS officials were hopeful that their new authority to reject "one-sided" programs would prevent similar incidents.[25]

The demise of *PBL* did not extinguish the impulse to develop original programming that blurred generic lines and addressed controversial issues. In 1971, producers and executives at NET created a new program called *The Great American Dream Machine*. Mixing satire, comedy, short documentary films and one-act plays, music, and animation, it sought to appeal to viewers who were disdainful of commercial television and consumer culture. Produced by Jack Willis and Al Perlmutter, it was risky and irreverent. Virtually all the program's segments, even those conceived as entertainment, addressed significant social and political issues. And when strung together into whole episodes, its disparate parts combined to produce a sharp critique of mainstream America. The program's short documentaries were especially acerbic and heavy-handed, echoing the antiestablishment views of Americans committed to the fashionable "New Politics" liberalism of the period. The program also provided a regular platform for Andy Rooney's ruminations on subjects like the Vietnam War and the sexual revolution, and drew on the talents of some of America's most talented young comedians and actors, including Marshall Efron, who specialized in lampooning the claims of advertisers. The program's most unpredictable feature was a weekly live "conversation" among ordinary people in a Chicago tavern moderated by author Studs Terkel. Participants ranged widely in age, background, and political views, and their spontaneous discussions of subjects like President Nixon, Vietnam, the counterculture, and the economy were spirited and combative.[26]

The Great American Dream Machine was popular with many viewers. Yet its unapologetic leftism disturbed others, and some stations refused to broadcast it. It was also expensive, costing approximately $100,000 per hour to produce. Concerned about costs, the program's producers cut it to an hour for its second season and began rerunning segments. Debuting two months after *Banks and the Poor*, the show also provided conservatives with ammunition in their campaign to draw attention to PBS's left-wing bias. News reports featuring the activist and investigative reporter Paul Jacobs were particularly controversial. Newly empowered to serve as a gatekeeper, PBS officials deleted a Jacobs report on the FBI's infiltration and harassment of New Left groups. This angered the program's producers and sparked newspaper stories and editorials decrying the new "censorship" at PBS.[27] But as former NET president James Day later observed, "What the press saw as censorship the PBS stations saw as an exercise in prudent editorial judgment." From the latter's point of view, Jacobs's piece was one-sided and inflammatory, and they were grateful that PBS had used its new powers to prevent its dissemination to member stations, relieving them of having to censor at their end.[28] The controversy underscored the gulf that separated NET-based producers from member stations, who were keen to please local viewers. If the fourth network was going to broadcast public-affairs programs, they would have to pass muster with the most conservative local stations, fit in with the British imports and more conventional high-culture shows, and accommodate public television's increasing reliance on viewer donations and corporate underwriting. In the end, *The Great American Dream Machine* failed on all three of these counts and was canceled, despite consistently positive reviews, after its second season.

PBS was more successful with conventional public-affairs programs featuring talking heads. Inspired by *Meet the Press*, *Washington Week in Review* began airing in early 1967. It was produced by WETA, the NET station in Washington, DC, and starred prominent print journalists, who discussed politics and national and international affairs. Its focus on developments within the political mainstream—as opposed to the fringes—made it attractive to member stations, complementing their own locally oriented news and public-affairs shows.[29] PBS enjoyed similar success with *Firing Line*, William F. Buckley's often lively debate and discussion program. Buckley, the most widely known conservative intellectual of the era, had launched the show in 1966, offering it to commercial stations through syndication. He brought it to PBS in 1971, at the urging of Henry Cauthen, the head of South Carolina Educational Television. Cauthen, a conservative Democrat, was concerned about NET's reputation for leftist bias, and he was convinced that PBS could broaden its base of support if it included more conservative voices. Given *Firing Line*'s success as a syndicated program, bringing Buckley to PBS was a smart move. It diversified PBS's offerings and underscored the new system's commitment to relying on prominent member stations as production units, reducing its dependence on NET. With initial support from Fred Friendly and the Ford Foundation and the CPB, Buckley's program was widely distributed and proved popular, even among liberal viewers. Compared to latter-day debate programs like *Crossfire*, *Firing Line* was exceedingly genteel. Participants were allowed to say their piece without having to worry about being cut off for taking too much time, and Buckley was a gregarious and sportsmanlike host who respected his liberal guests and cherished the principle of civilized discourse.[30]

Another talking-heads program—*Wall Street Week*—was even more popular. It featured in-depth business and economics news, including detailed reports on trends in the stock market and investment advice. Hosted by Louis Rukeyser, an engaging, telegenic former print journalist and correspondent for ABC, it was first broadcast in 1970 by a consortium of mid-Atlantic public television stations. PBS picked it up for national distribution in 1972. A rotating cast of panelists appeared with Rukeyser to discuss the week's events; later, they joined him in questioning a high-profile guest, often an important government policymaker or the head of an influential company. As Rukeyser told a reporter for the *New York Times* in 1980, "What we've really been doing is a weekly economics show. But if you called it "Economics Week," no one would watch."[31] The program was an instant hit. By the early 1980s, it was PBS's most popular regularly scheduled show. Its success proved that business and economic news could attract a substantial audience, particularly of upscale, more conservative viewers, and it reinforced public television's retreat from controversial left-wing programming. Indeed, *Wall Street Wall* was essentially right-wing, offering a view of the economy that privileged the perspective of investors.[32]

Bill Moyers was another newcomer to television who found a place on PBS. As President Johnson's chief of staff and press secretary, Moyers had been near the center of power during the mid-1960s. But he and Johnson had a falling out over the Vietnam War, and in 1971, after several years as publisher of the Long Island newspaper *Newsday*, Moyers was recruited by NET to host *This Week*, a public-affairs discussion program designed to place news stories in "broader perspective." It included filmed interviews with prominent newsmakers, and though Moyers was initially uncomfortable in front of the camera, he demonstrated a gift for establishing a rapport with his guests. In 1972, the program was revamped and rechristened *Bill Moyers Journal*. It still relied in large part on interviews, however, and some episodes allowed Moyers to engage in long, often lively conservations with intellectuals, policy makers, and political activists. Moyers's program was praised by critics, and his earnestness and idealism were appealing to many viewers, including CBS chairman William Paley, who sought to bring him to CBS. And though conservatives complained about Moyers's liberal sympathies, which were unambiguous, his views were far more moderate than those of Paul Jacobs or some of the other journalists who had produced documentaries for NET or segments for PBL or *The Great American Dream Machine*.[33]

Though PBS executives were cheered by the popularity and upscale demographics of talking-heads shows, some producers sought to continue making the kinds of original, more challenging material for which NET had become well known in the late 1960s. Among them was Craig Gilbert, one of NET's more experienced documentarians. Recently divorced and intrigued by the cultural upheavals of the era, Gilbert became interested in producing a program that would examine the nation's changing social mores and their impact on marriage and family life. Believing the subject was too complex for a conventional documentary, he convinced his superiors at NET to finance a multipart cinema vérité film that would focus on a single family. To the chagrin of other producers, virtually all the money earmarked for public-affairs documentaries on issues like marital relations, the generation gap, and recreational drug use—$1.2 million—went to Gilbert's project, which was envisioned as a blockbuster that would draw new viewers to PBS. After interviewing dozens of families, Gilbert selected his subjects, the Louds, an attractive, upper-middle-class family living in Santa Barbara, California. On the surface, they resembled the sitcom families portrayed on commercial television. Bill Loud was a successful entrepreneur; Pat, a homemaker; their five children ranged in age from thirteen to twenty. They had moved to California in the early 1960s, like so many other families chasing the latest version of the American Dream. Gilbert hired Alan and Susan Raymond, a husband-and-wife production team, to film the Louds over the course of seven months, from late May 1971 to the end of the year. Coincidentally, during this period Bill and Pat's marriage fell apart, a development the Raymonds were able to capture in engrossing detail. While they filmed in Santa Barbara, Gilbert spent most of his time in New York, editing the raw footage into discrete hour-long episodes. He had hoped to produce fifteen, but he was able to gain approval for only twelve. He called it *An American Family*.[34]

The resulting series, which began airing in January 1973, was unlike anything ever seen on American television. In some respects, it resembled some of the more innovative documentaries NET had produced or distributed during the 1960s, which used a similar observational style to reveal the subtle drama in otherwise ordinary situations, with few voice-overs and no formal interviews. But Gilbert structured it as serial narrative—like an afternoon soap opera—and the opening credits featured music and a montage introducing the Louds that resembled the introductory sequence of the ABC hit *The Brady Bunch*. He was careful to devote lots of attention to the Loud children, and went out of his way to include eldest son Lance, who lived in New York City, a decision that dramatically increased production costs. Remarkably, the family proved superb performers, adjusting to the Raymonds' almost continual presence and rarely breaking frame to remind viewers they were watching a film and not real life. The lone exception was Lance, a gay bohemian familiar with the conventions of camp. His often flamboyant presence—and regular jokes and knowing remarks to the camera—enlivened the series and increased its impact on the nation's consciousness. In one way or another, however, all the Loud children were quite different from their parents, especially Bill, who epitomized the conservative values of Richard Nixon's "silent majority." And footage of Bill and Pat in the earliest episodes made it very clear their marriage was on the rocks. As numerous critics noted, Gilbert's aim wasn't merely to observe. It was to condemn middle-class family life and the materialistic postwar American Dream, and he edited the footage in ways that underscored this message. Not surprisingly, the Louds were unhappy with some of Gilbert's editing, especially the way he exploited Bill and Pat's breakup to make his larger point.

PBS's broadcast of *An American Family* was the biggest event in public television's short history. The series was massively hyped, with full-page advertisements in newspapers and magazines, and a feature story in *TV Guide*. The press kit and advertising played up the program's sensational features, including Lance's flamboyance, noting that he had adopted a lifestyle that "might shock a lot of people back home in California."[35] Reviews were largely favorable, and in subsequent weeks, PBS drew from them in ads for the show. But while Gilbert and the Raymonds were mostly praised, the Louds were routinely condemned for being shallow and self-absorbed. The columnist Shana Alexander called them "affluent zombies." The criticism inspired the Louds to appear on television talk shows, where they answered their critics and argued that the film had misrepresented them. The ads, reviews, and attendant publicity sparked extraordinary public interest. The series attracted an estimated 10 million viewers per week, some of them merely to see what all the fuss was about. Like *The Forsyte Saga* and *Sesame Street*, *An American Family* raised PBS's profile, making it easier for individual stations to solicit viewer donations and promote its other programs.[36]

PBS's higher profile was a welcome boost that directed attention away from another development that threatened public television's mission—its deteriorating relationship with the Nixon administration. As the pet project of New Frontiersmen and the Johnson administration, the public television community expected an awkward period of transition when Nixon took office in January 1969. Nixon had run as centrist, however, and early in his first term he supported a number of liberal initiatives that suggested he would not seek a wholesale dismantling of programs established by his Democratic predecessors.[37] So they were surprised when he singled out public television for attack and especially disconcerted by his efforts to control its news and public-affairs programming. Convinced that public television was dominated by radical leftists intent on undermining his agenda, Nixon and his aides devised an ingenious strategy to pressure the CPB and PBS to scuttle any programs likely to offend the president and his political allies. Clay T. Whitehead, Nixon's director of telecommunications policy, was aware of the gulf that separated local stations from

NET, and he did his best to widen it and foment mistrust of PBS and the Ford Foundation as well. Claiming that PBS was seeking to become a powerful, centralized network with the power to dictate the kinds of programs that local stations broadcast—an exaggeration of even Bundy and Friendly's more robust view of public TV and the opposite of the loose system favored by PBS officials—Whitehead made it clear that the Nixon administration was committed to "localism" and a public television system that was "decentralized." More ominously, he suggested that its support for continued federal funding was contingent on reforms that would enhance these features. And by early 1972, he was openly questioning the propriety of federal support for public-affairs programs that "express controversial points of view."[38]

Though the CPB and PBS protested, they had little choice but to comply. In July 1971, aware that NET was the Nixon administration's prime target, the CPB established a new production center for news and public-affairs programs, the National Public Affairs Center for Television (NPACT). Based in Washington, close to the federal government and to the kinds of official sources that had long given the commercial networks' news programs a centrist, establishment-oriented bent, NPACT seemed like the perfect solution to public television's growing political problems. Its founding allowed the CPB to continue to fund public-affairs programs yet reduce its support for the rabble-rousers at NET, and CPB and PBS officials hoped that NPACT-produced programs would be more palatable to member stations. The new organization's board chose James Karayn, a former writer and producer for NBC News who had served as NET's Washington bureau chief, to run the new unit. He announced that NPACT's offerings would be "courageous" and "intelligent," exactly what viewers expected from public television. He also noted, however, that its producers and journalists would display "self-restraint, common sense, and fairness."[39] NPACT, in short, would shift PBS's news and public-affairs programs to the political center, and make them look more like those on the commercial networks.

To compete effectively with the networks, Karayn knew he needed well-known, highly professional anchors. In September 1971, he selected two former colleagues from NBC, Robert MacNeil and Sander Vanocur. MacNeil, a native of Canada, had worked for the CBC and the BBC as well NBC, and had most recently been seen on NET programs on foreign affairs that borrowed from the BBC's acclaimed

documentary series *Panorama*. Vanocur had been one of Bob Kintner's star reporters in the late 1950s and early 1960s, and had served
as White House correspondent during the Kennedy administration.
Karayn's appointments appalled Nixon. The president was especially
upset about Vanocur; he regarded the veteran correspondent as a
"well-known Kennedy sympathizer" and still resented him for his aggressive questioning in the 1960 election campaign. Whitehead began
a nefarious campaign to arouse resentment of Vanocur's and Mac-
Neil's salaries, which, at $85,000 and $65,000, respectively, were well
below the norm for anchors at the commercial networks but lavish
in the niggardly world of public television. Whitehead's skullduggery
sparked congressional hearings to examine pay scales at PBS and the
CPB, and alienated local stations from NPACT. Chastened by the negative publicity and Whitehead's remarks questioning the legitimacy of
using taxpayer dollars to fund a controversial public-affairs show,
NPACT and its new anchors approached the 1972 elections gingerly,
producing a weekly series, *A Public Affair: Election 72*, that was notably
inoffensive. To make matters worse, the CPB, concerned about the fate
of a five-year appropriation that was working its way through Congress, reduced NPACT's budget by 25 percent, forcing Karayn to scale
back coverage of the summer's political conventions.[40]

CPB officials were hopeful about congressional funding, and their
optimism was justified when a bill providing a two-year, $155 million
appropriation was passed by large majorities in both houses of Congress. The Nixon administration had proposed only a one-year appropriation of $45 million and had insisted on "reforms" that would
have increased the power of local stations. With an eye on the White
House, public television's supporters in Congress had included a provision in their more generous bill that mandated that 30 percent of the
$155 million go to local stations. Yet their belief that this would placate
Nixon was shattered when, at the end of June, the president vetoed
the two-year appropriation, noting the "serious and widespread concern" in Congress and among local stations about PBS's emergence as
"the center of power and the focal point of control for the entire public
broadcasting system."[41] In the wake of the veto, several high-ranking
CPB executives resigned, and the Nixon administration began to fill
vacancies on the CPB's board with loyal supporters—at least to the degree that the law allowed.

To ensure even greater control over public television, the now

Nixon-influenced CPB began developing a plan to cut PBS out of national programming and create a new committee that would decide which programs would be funded, produced, and distributed to individual stations. In early 1973, the CPB produced a list of programs it had approved and would continue funding. Conspicuously missing from the list were PBS's nationally oriented public-affairs shows, including *Bill Moyers Journal*, all of NPACT's programs, and, more surprisingly, the steadfastly middle-of-the-road *Washington Week in Review* and William F. Buckley's *Firing Line*. Only the debate program *The Advocates* and Tony Brown's *Black Journal* were spared—the latter as a result of Brown's heroic lobbying. Inspired by Whitehead's broadside against "controversial programming," CPB officials insisted that this opened the way for public television to offer viewers more balanced programs. Most critics and commentators, however, saw it for what it actually was—a bold attempt to eviscerate public television and, as a White House aide put it in a secret memo, "get the left-wing commentators who are cutting us up off public television at once."[42] Disconcerted by the attack on NPACT, Vanocur quit.

Fortunately, a group of powerful licensees, led by the Texas industrialist and philanthropist Ralph Rogers, intervened. Rogers brokered a compromise between the CPB and PBS that allowed member stations influence over the CPB's funding of programs and the creation of a national schedule, and he succeeded in convincing the CPB to restore funding for *Washington Week in Review* and *Firing Line*. He won the trust of moderates on the CPB board, who agreed that the Nixon administration's efforts to muzzle public-affairs programming on PBS had been unseemly. And Rogers and his allies at the CPB pushed for an increase in funding from Congress. With the Nixon administration distracted by the escalating Watergate scandal, it was forced to accept a two-year funding bill that provided the CPB with $120 million, which Nixon signed in August 1973.[43]

By this time, PBS had gained ever greater visibility and prestige—and, ironically, it had Nixon to thank for this. As the details about Watergate began to emerge, linking Nixon and his lieutenants to the break-in at the headquarters of the Democratic National Committee in Washington, the Senate established a special committee to investigate. Chaired by Sam Ervin, it scheduled public hearings for the late spring and summer of 1973. The commercial networks, concerned about the potential impact on ad revenue, agreed among themselves to rotate coverage, ensuring that at any time interested viewers could see them on one of the networks, while those who weren't interested could find the usual entertainment programs on the other two—and no single network would incur the losses resulting from continuous coverage. This discouraged PBS officials from covering them, too. But James Karayn saw the hearings as a chance to reassert public television's independence and boost his beleaguered staff's morale, and he begged PBS president Hartford Gunn to allow NPACT to provide live gavel-to-gavel coverage. Gunn was hesitant, but as Rogers and his allies gained the advantage over Nixon's allies on the CPB, Gunn relented and allowed member stations to vote on the proposal. It passed by a narrow margin, and Karayn and his staff immediately began preparing. Besides live coverage, they would produce detailed evening recaps, with extensive replays of the most riveting testimony. Karayn hoped the Watergate hearings would give PBS the sort of boost ABC had gained from its coverage of the Army-McCarthy hearings in 1954.[44]

The gamble paid off. Anchored by MacNeil and Jim Lehrer, a former print journalist who had worked for Rogers and had been brought to NPACT to help craft PBS's journalistic standards in the wake of the dustup sparked by NET's *Banks and the Poor*, the hearings attracted viewers from the start. And over the course of the summer, as more Americans became aware of the hearings and the seriousness of the charges being leveled against the Nixon administration, PBS's audience grew, earning ratings that rivaled commercial programs. Stations that had voted against broadcasting the hearings now reveled in the attention and accolades, while the big-city stations that had been most supportive of Karayn's plan were emboldened. Ratings for other PBS programs increased, and many stations experienced an increase in donations. More important, MacNeil recalled, "the coverage served another, deeper purpose: it revealed to doubters that public television journalism could be vital, fair, and trenchant when dealing with the most sensitive political material. Perhaps the most important people to discover that were the managers of local stations who had long doubted that we should be in the news business at all."[45] Coverage of the Watergate hearings made stars of MacNeil and Lehrer and boosted NPACT's image in the eyes of member stations and the general public. And, in a final act of poetic justice, in early August 1974, two days before his resignation, President Nixon signed a bill providing a five-year authorization for public television.

But the wounds from the battle with Nixon never entirely healed. The compromise engineered by Rogers "saved" public television, but it left both the CPB and PBS weakened. And it ensured that the system would remain highly decentralized and acutely sensitive to anything that might rock the boat and hurt its reputation. Not only had member stations gained more influence over programming, a development that would reinforce the trend toward safe cultural programs and series like *Nova*, which were most popular with the upper-middle-class viewers who were public television's most important donors; but the charges of left-wing bias strengthened the position of moderates at NPACT and at the big stations that were coming to serve as public television's major production centers, and would have a major influence on the kinds of public-affairs programs that would appear on PBS.

This disappointed many veteran producers and journalists, who had hoped that PBS could retain some of NET's edge. But it is hard to see how it could have been otherwise. Once the system became reliant on congressional appropriations and private donations—for station operating expenses as well as the production and acquisition of programs—the die was cast. The only alternatives it could provide would have to be palatable to these interests. And in an increasingly polarized political environment, where an ascendant right was becoming more critical of the "wasteful" spending of tax revenues, it was inevitable that PBS would resort to safe programming that could be supported by private sources—in anticipation of the day when government support would vanish altogether. It was a system that could accommodate sophisticated news and public-affairs programs, but they had to mirror—or, at the very least, respect—the tastes, preferences, and political views of the educated, upper-middle-class people who comprised most of public television's audience.

Here was the key to public television's gradual gentrification. During the late 1960s, the heyday of edgy programming favored by producers at NET, public television's audience was much smaller. And for a variety of reasons, including the trendiness of left-wing views among the suburban, upper-middle class, a substantial portion of that audience was receptive to antiestablishment muckraking and the left-wing polemics of *The Great American Dream Machine*. By the mid-1970s, thanks to *The Forsyte Saga, Sesame Street,* and *An American Family,* PBS's audience had grown, and the political winds in the nation at large had begun to shift to the right. Drawn to PBS for its cultural programming, many viewers were more conservative, and they complained about egregious examples of left-wing bias. Yet even most of PBS's viewers who still regarded themselves as liberal were no longer committed to the adversarial "New Politics" of the late 1960s. Like many other Americans, they were more suspicious of government—the foundation of liberal solutions since the New Deal—and committed to a brand of expressive individualism that shifted the emphasis of their politics. Increasingly concerned about "rights" and receptive to initiatives that would rely on the market to solve problems and increase individual choice, they were coming to embrace views that were essentially postliberal.[46] By the mid-1970s, then, PBS's audience had grown and changed, with even its liberal core no longer committed to the unapologetic leftism of the late 1960s. Not surprisingly, this encouraged a change in the tone and content of many of its news and public-affairs programs.

The change was evident, for example, in the daily news program that WNET launched in October 1975 and PBS picked up for national distribution several months later. The seeds of *The MacNeil/Lehrer Report* were planted during the Watergate hearings in 1973, when MacNeil and Lehrer performed so ably. After the hearings, they were assigned to separate projects, and MacNeil soon returned to the BBC. In 1975, WNET executives lured MacNeil lured back to the US to serve as host of a nightly half-hour news program, *The Robert MacNeil Report,* and MacNeil and his producers hired Lehrer as their Washington correspondent.[47] The *Report* was conceived as supplement to the nightly newscasts on the commercial networks. Rather than compete with them, it would air immediately afterward and offer an in-depth look at a single story—the sort of examination that the networks, with their mandate to offer a quick summary of the day's most important events, couldn't provide. It would also rely more on interviews and discussion, and less on the expensive filmed reports that were becoming central to network newscasts. The show's set was designed to facilitate discussion and minimize the need for multiple cameras, and its producers were committed to providing guests with lots of time to explain key points and state their case. The aim, as Lehrer noted in his memoirs, was to "help them get their positions or opinions out in a coherent and understandable form," enabling viewers to assess their merit and decide for themselves. The show's emphasis on live, unedited interviews distinguished it from news programs that broadcast heavily edited interviews and sound bites, techniques that had made journalists vulnerable to criticism for quoting out of context. The program also sought to create a civil, supportive atmosphere. "We would not beat up on our guests or embarrass them," Lehrer added, implicitly contrasting their approach with the tactics of notoriously aggressive interviewers like Mike Wallace and Dan Rather. Unlike the nightly news programs on the commercial networks, which, by the mid-1970s, were widely accused of being disrespectful of authority and tainted by liberal bias, PBS's flagship news program would emphasize dispassion, objectivity, and ideological balance.[48]

Rechristened *The MacNeil/Lehrer Report* in early 1976, its centrism and focus on policy and inside dope was appealing to educated, upscale viewers and to corporate underwriters interested in funding a prestige broadcast. Supported at first by the CPB and PBS stations, it soon received a $10 million long-term grant from AT&T, with additional funds for promotion. The program expanded to an hour in 1983, increasing the length of its summary of the day's news and introducing more filmed reports to supplement its trademark interviews and discussions. It became even more deliberate and slow-paced. The reason for this, Lehrer explained, was to focus viewer attention on information and content—and avoid anything that might trivialize it. Like the journalistic mandarins at the networks, MacNeil, Lehrer, and their producers were confident they were providing a public service. "Our approach," producer Al Vecchione explained, "has always been to take on the serious and important issues that we think people need to know about, not the ones that will titillate them."[49] Though this approach turned off some viewers, and the program was condemned by left-wing critics for relying excessively on political insiders, its prestige increased, particularly among upscale news junkies eager for detailed coverage of politics and international affairs. The program was also admired by many conservatives, who regarded it as the most balanced of all the major television news programs. In 1988, the *News-Hour* (the name changed in 1983) gained additional outside support when Pepsi-Co and the MacArthur Foundation joined AT&T as major sponsors, providing the program with a five-year, $57 million grant.

Free from having to address a wide audience, it producers could concentrate on programming for informed viewers who wanted detail
and complexity. Lehrer noted, "We're not in the interesting business;
we're in the importance business."[50] Thanks to such private support
and PBS's transformation into television's first practitioner of niche
programming, it was a luxury he and MacNeil could well afford.

The debut of *The MacNeil/Lehrer Report* in 1976 occurred at a propi-
tious moment in PBS's history. Determined to infuse the system with
more dynamic leadership, Ralph Rogers persuaded the PBS board to
hire a new president. It chose Lawrence K. Grossman, a former advertising executive who had also worked for CBS and NBC. Grossman was
a liberal New Yorker, and many station managers were suspicious of
his background and network experience. But he won them over with
his casual yet effective management style, and under his watch, PBS
continued to grow and attract viewers. Sensitive to the interests of
corporate underwriters and member stations, who had become more
reliant than ever on viewer donations, he continued to encourage the
production centers to produce or acquire programs that would appeal
to PBS's upscale audience. He was also firmly committed to continuing
its tradition of broadcasting news and public-affairs shows, however,
and came up with a plan to air some of them as part of a "public-affairs
block." He argued that this would make it easier for viewers to see
them on a regular basis, and enable PBS to promote them more effectively. Overcoming deeply rooted skepticism, he convinced member
stations to broadcast a core schedule of programs and devote Friday
evenings to a public-affairs lineup that included *Wall Street Week* and
Washington Week in Review. Though Grossman's power was limited, in
his eight years as president PBS made great strides, increasing its financial base among underwriters, including private foundations, and
expanding its roster of public-affairs programs.[51]

The expansion of PBS's public-affairs offerings was encouraged,
too, by the CPB. In the aftermath of the compromise between PBS
and the CPB engineered by Rogers, individual stations gained greater
control over programming, and subsequent congressional appropriations required that nearly a third of federal money go to member stations, enabling them to produce programs. But since an overwhelming majority of PBS stations were not production centers, they
established a cooperative to decide which productions to fund with
their pooled federal resources. When it became clear that the coopera-

tive would do little more than subsidize established hits like *Sesame Street, Masterpiece Theatre,* and *Wall Street Week,* the CPB created its own program fund in 1979 to provide seed money for more innovative projects. An experienced producer, Lewis Freedman, was hired to lead the unit. Freedman had worked for CBS, for Fred Friendly on PBL, and for public stations in New York and Los Angeles. He was extremely ambitious, and proposed expanding programming in public affairs, drama, history, and the arts. Compelled by Congress to steer a "substantial amount" of the CPB's allocation of federal funds to independent producers, a provision inserted by liberals in response to complaints about PBS's lack of diversity, Freedman began looking for producers outside the system's orbit. But in the short run he turned to experienced hands at the big station-based production centers.

One of the most important of these production centers was WGBH in Boston. Its staff was responsible for *Masterpiece Theatre,* the science series *Nova,* and a new program that began airing in 1979, *This Old House.* But it produced public-affairs programs as well, including *World,* a series overseen by David Fanning that broadcast documentaries on international subjects, many of them made by filmmakers overseas. A native South African, Fanning had worked for the BBC and made freelance documentaries. Along with extensive foreign connections, he brought a sensitive, sophisticated eye to the series, which was widely praised for its coverage of often neglected developments, particularly in the Middle East, Africa, and Latin America.[52]

World attracted few viewers and little notice until May 1980, when it scheduled a docudrama entitled *Death of a Princess.* Written by Fanning and a close friend, Antony Thomas, it examined the fate of a nineteen-year-old Saudi princess who rejected her family's arranged marriage and fell in love with a classmate while attending college in Beirut. Unwilling to hide their relationship, they were executed by Saudi authorities for committing adultery. Thomas had hoped to make a conventional documentary about the case, but when important sources corroborating the story refused to appear on film, he and Fanning decided to use actors and produce a script that included their tape-recorded testimony. *Death of a Princess* was structured as a mystery, as the camera followed a journalist in his efforts to uncover the facts. It was financed by WGBH and Britain's ITV, and the completed broadcast aired first in the UK, angering the Saudi government and sparking a diplomatic crisis. The Saudis were outraged by its depiction of the royal family and of the behavior of its bored and sexually frustrated princesses, and they threatened to cut off oil supplies to Britain and any other nations that broadcast the program. These threats were soon directed at the Carter administration and PBS. Already reeling from the Iranian hostage crisis, Carter and his aides advised Grossman to consider the potential consequences. Their concern was echoed by influential members of Congress, who raised the specter of cutting off public television's funding. Mobil, PBS's most generous corporate underwriter, went even further, placing full-page ads in prominent newspapers questioning the veracity of the film and calling on PBS to reconsider its decision in light of the "best interests of the United States." But Grossman refused to buckle, especially in the face of Mobil's opposition; canceling the program would have conveyed the impression that public television was controlled by its corporate contributors. *Death of a Princess* was broadcast as scheduled in May 1980, though PBS added a one-hour panel discussion with Middle East experts in hopes of pacifying the program's critics. It elicited mostly positive reviews and garnered a huge audience, the largest a PBS show had attracted since a heavily promoted National Geographic special in the mid-1970s.[53]

The election of Ronald Reagan made many people in public television nervous. An avowed foe of "wasteful" government spending, Reagan was expected to seek reductions in funding for a wide range of programs, and his new appointees to the FCC and the CPB were committed to the notion that public television should increase its reliance on viewer donations and other private sources of support. Inspired by a congressional committee that made numerous suggestions for alternative financing for PBS, the FCC relaxed its rules governing the underwriting of PBS programs by private corporations. PBS shows were now permitted to credit their underwriters more explicitly by displaying brands and trade names and listing an underwriter's product lines and services—as long as their acknowledgment was "value-neutral" and made no specific claims about a product's quality. PBS referred to the new noncommercial commercials as "enhanced underwriting." To the relief of many station executives, the new political mood alarmed many viewers and encouraged an increase in donations. And underwriters, pleased by the FCC's endorsement of enhanced underwriting, stepped up their support as well. As during the 1970s, however, corporate support went to only certain kinds of programs and accelerated PBS's transformation into a boutique service for the educated, upper-middle class. Though provocative public-affairs documentaries continued to be broadcast, station managers and PBS executives preferred uncontroversial crowd-pleasers like *Masterpiece Theatre* and Carl Sagan's *Cosmos*. And when provocative programs aired, they were keen to offset it with material pleasing to conservatives that demonstrated PBS's commitment to balance.[54]

In 1983, PBS officials carved out a weekly slot in its core schedule for a regular documentary series. That series was *Frontline*, and it became perhaps the most lauded showcase for documentaries in the history of television, a fitting successor to *See It Now*, NBC *White Paper*, and CBS *Reports*. It was Lewis Freedman who came up with the idea. Concerned about the decline of long-form documentaries on the networks, Freedman thought PBS might be able to pick up the slack. He approached David Fanning at WGBH. Fanning had won numerous plaudits for his role in overseeing *World*, and with his extensive foreign connections and track record as a producer, he seemed the perfect candidate to supervise the new series. To prevent it from becoming formulaic or having a single voice, Fanning and his staff solicited proposals from many different producers, including some foreigners, as he had on *World*. He soon came to rely, however, on a rotating repertory of producers and journalists; over the years, they produced most of *Frontline*'s documentaries. Fanning welcomed proposals for programs that challenged powerful institutions and exposed injustices, and *Frontline* was routinely criticized for liberal bias. He dismissed such criticism, arguing that the most powerful documentaries were those that, while faithful to the facts, had a clear point of view. Fanning and his staff were more concerned about maintaining high production values than advancing a political agenda, and their reliance on experienced producers reflected this commitment and, at times, angered independent filmmakers who were unable to get their work on the program or were forced to relinquish control of it to one of Fanning's regulars.[55]

The subjects of *Frontline* documentaries were determined by Fanning and his staff. Proposals most likely to gain approval were those that had compelling characters and could be crafted into an engrossing narrative with a human dimension. To insulate his series from criticism and prebroadcast censorship by PBS, Fanning established a consortium of powerful stations that shared responsibility for *Frontline*. A board composed of representatives of these stations reviewed budgets and other administrative matters but left Fanning and his editorial staff free to determine editorial content. Unwilling to anger the consortium, PBS, too, left Fanning alone, a remarkable arrangement considering the consistently provocative documentaries that appeared as part of the series. To further safeguard his program's independence, Fanning relied only on funds from the CPB and member stations, and he tried hard to keep overall costs low, allowing him to eschew corporate underwriters. He also proved an able diplomat, providing stations with advance copies of potentially controversial programs and helping them develop rebuttals when criticism inevitably arose.[56]

From its inception, *Frontline* broadcast documentaries on an astonishingly wide range of topics, most of them sensitive and important hard-news subjects. In its first season, for example, it aired programs on the political and economic power of the Defense Department, the plight of Palestinians in the West Bank and the Gaza Strip, and an embattled abortion clinic in Pennsylvania. In subsequent years, the program continued in the same vein. It broadcast one of the first accounts of the Iran-Contra scandal and excelled at illuminating complex problems like the conflict between physicians and lawyers over medical malpractice. Some of its most compelling programs were multipart series, like the twelve-part examination of life in the Soviet Union during the Gorbachev era that aired in 1987. Not surprisingly, *Frontline* won every conceivable award for journalistic excellence and enhanced PBS's reputation for public affairs programming.

Frontline's success encouraged PBS to broadcast other documentaries. Some of them aired as stand-alone special programs and were subjected to prebroadcast review by PBS officials. Others were part of *POV*, a new documentary series that PBS launched in 1988. Overseen by Marc Weiss, a veteran producer and advocate for independent documentary filmmakers, *POV* was conceived as a venue for films that were more personal and idiosyncratic than those that appeared on Fanning's program—much to the delight of filmmakers who had failed to get their work on *Frontline*. Weiss and his staff usually selected fully completed films, rather than proposals or rough cuts, and they allowed filmmakers an unusual degree of editorial freedom. *POV*'s format allowed for the broadcast of some remarkably original and compelling works. Less topical than documentaries on *Frontline*, they were more stylistically innovative and at times humorous, harkening back to the experimental flavor of material that had aired on NET in the late 1960s. *POV*'s first season, for example, included Errol Morris's mordant look at pet cemeteries and a moving account of the young Americans who joined the Abraham Lincoln Brigade and fought in the Spanish Civil War in the 1930s. The series regularly aired challenging and controversial works, including *Dark Circle*, an Emmy-winning film on nuclear weapons and nuclear power that PBS had declined to show as a stand-alone film; *Sea of Oil*, a sharp-edged exposé of the environmental destruction wrought by the *Exxon Valdez* oil spill; and Marlon Riggs's *Tongues Untied*, a landmark film about being black and gay that embroiled the series and PBS in controversy when it was broadcast in 1991. *POV* attracted a smaller audience than *Frontline*, but this was expected, considering the nature of the series. And though independent filmmakers remained frustrated with PBS, the addition of *POV* to its schedule demonstrated a willingness to provide a forum for projects that would never otherwise be shown on television.[57]

By the early 1990s, twenty years after PBS's birth and forty years after the establishment of the first educational TV stations, public television had carved out a small yet comfortable niche in the larger television marketplace. To the delight of many viewers, PBS stations offered real alternatives to the programs on commercial television. And while many were upscale cultural offerings or middle-of-the-road news programs popular with donors and corporate underwriters, they also included hard-hitting documentaries and often probing analysis and discussion programs. These were not exactly the alternatives that John White, Fred Friendly, and the producers at NET had envisioned. Nor were they the kinds of programs PBS's left-wing critics clamored for. Few expressed a radical point of view, and virtually never were they targeted at underrepresented segments of the American public. But they were certainly different, and this was reason enough to be thankful for their existence.

News and public-affairs programming on PBS had been cut to suit the preferences of public television's audience. Given the system's difficult birth, lack of federal support, and increasing reliance on viewer donations and corporate and foundation subsidies, this was almost inevitable. Because it was conceived well after the establishment of commercial television, public television began as a niche service catering to Americans who were unhappy with network programming and could support the system through their donations: a subset of the educated, upper-middle class. They became its core audience. Efforts to expand, by individual stations as well as PBS, nearly always sought to build on, rather than reject, this base. This ensured that the alternatives offered by public television were of a particular nature — substantive and sometimes challenging material the commercial networks wouldn't air, but material most appealing to educated, upscale viewers. Some of these viewers, to be sure, enjoyed sophisticated public-affairs programs like *The MacNeil/Lehrer NewsHour* and *Frontline*. But such viewers comprised only a fraction of public television's larger audience. Accordingly, news and public-affairs shows made up only a fraction of PBS's overall programming. At PBS, no less than at the networks, they languished in the shadow of more popular programs. Despite Friendly's efforts, television journalists still lacked a real home.

4

NEWS YOU CAN USE

"Television will never be the same," proclaimed advertisements for *Network*, a biting satire of the industry that arrived in American theaters in late 1976, just as the artificial high inspired by the Bicentennial celebration was wearing off and the nation was sinking back into its post-Watergate doldrums. Written by Paddy Chayefsky and directed by Sidney Lumet, respected veterans of TV's golden age of live drama, it told the story of Howard Beale, an aging network anchor plagued by poor ratings and a worsening mental illness. After being informed that he would be fired, a despondent Beale goes off-script during a broadcast and tells viewers of his plan to commit suicide at the conclusion of his final program. Rather than hasten his retirement, his remarks inspire Diana Christensen, a brilliant and cynical young programming executive, to build an entirely different kind of news program around him. Accompanied by segments featuring celebrity gossip, a fortune teller, and audience-participation polls, Beale is billed as the "Mad Prophet of the Airwaves" and given free rein to "articulate the popular rage." The show is a huge hit, turning Beale into a star—until his rants become boring and predictable and his ratings flag. He then experiences the ultimate "cancelation": he is gunned down during his broadcast by a crypto-Marxist terrorist group hired by the network, a crosspromotion for another Christensen-conceived program, a docudrama chronicling the group's "revolutionary" exploits.[1]

Network was a box-office hit and cultural sensation. A line in one of Beale's rants—"I'm mad as hell and I'm not going to take it anymore!"—became a popular slogan, and viewers appreciated the movie's jaundiced view of television, the radical left, and large corporations. Many television journalists enjoyed the film's send-up of their industry as well. Walter Cronkite, whose daughter had a bit part as a Patty Hearst-like heiress who is kidnapped and brainwashed by terrorists, found it "amusing," noting that it was a satire and bore little relation to the realities of TV news. Most of his colleagues agreed. But his boss at CBS, Richard Salant, was not so amused. Salant refused to see the movie, and his reaction surprised many of his staff and industry observers. Had his long-running battles with the entertainment division, affiliates, and CBS's political foes curdled his sense of humor?

Salant didn't go into detail about his problem with *Network*, but we can now see the reasons for his pique. In the early 1970s, Salant had begun work on a short book of guidelines for CBS journalists. The final product, *CBS News Standards*, completed in 1976, was over sixty pages long. Bound in a loose-leaf binder, it was conceived as a work-in-progress. Some of Salant's associates thought that written guidelines were impractical and the whole project a waste of time. But, sensing that a changing of the guard was occurring in television news, Salant insisted that CBS journalists try to follow the guidelines, and they soon acquired the status of a sacred text. When Salant moved over to NBC in 1979, he produced a similar volume for that network's journalists. Eventually, all three networks would have in-house news guidelines.[2]

Salant's little book exemplified the idealism and high-mindedness at CBS and the other networks during the 1970s. Its most remarkable feature was its long list of prohibitions and restrictions—a list that would have made it impossible for most news programs today to get on the air. For example, it banned dramatic reenactments and the use of music and sound effects in filmed reports. It strictly limited journalists' ability to interview the victims—or their relatives—of accidents and other tragedies, and spelled out the specific circumstances (very few) under which reporters could use hidden cameras and microphones. Sensitive to criticism of CBS's coverage of the upheavals of the 1960s, it established a protocol for reporting on riots and demonstrations, and reiterated the importance of presenting *all* significant facts and viewpoints. And, aside from during clearly labeled "commentaries," it explicitly prohibited editorializing.

Salant insisted that television journalism should not be confused with show business, and that it was vital for TV journalists to draw "the sharpest line possible" between their programs and those produced by their colleagues "on the entertainment side of the business." "This may make us a little less interesting to some—but that is the price we pay for dealing with fact and truth." Decisions about what to put on the air, he argued, should be based on the professional judgments of journalists, not the preferences of viewers. It would be a dereliction of duty for CBS journalists to select stories or shape their presentation based on audience surveys or market research. The purpose of television news was to provide people with what they *ought* to know, so that, as citizens, they could make informed decisions.[3]

Salant's views were firm and uncompromising—more uncompromising perhaps than those of many of his producers and correspondents, who faced the daily challenge of putting on a quality broadcast that would also appeal to viewers. Yet, as abstract principles, they were shared by large numbers of news people at all three networks. They agreed they were in the news business, not show business, and that the line in the sand Salant had drawn should be maintained. Since the late 1960s, the networks had made a strenuous effort to disentangle themselves from their once cozy relationship with officialdom and stake out a more independent and journalistically respectable position. In the process, they had developed sophisticated and probing forms of reportage that sought to reaffirm the distinction between news and entertainment. Now full-fledged members of the journalistic establishment, they were determined to build on these gains and expand their influence. Their budding professionalism was what made the picture painted by *Network* so absurd.

But the ground under their feet was shifting, and it would continue to do so in subsequent years, upsetting their routines and undermining their mission. As someone who routinely traveled between the boardroom and the newsroom, Salant knew that the alternative universe conjured by *Network* wasn't so far-fetched. New currents had appeared and were rising fast, threatening his line in the sand. If they weren't careful, it would disappear, and news programs would be shaped entirely by ratings and the preferences of viewers.

By the mid-1970s, network news was at a crossroads. Since the mid-1960s, the news divisions had carved out a secure niche on network schedules. Unable to attract viewers in prime time with special reports and documentaries, they poured resources into their flagship evening newscasts, which continued to command a large audience and generated considerable advertising revenue. Thanks to population growth, especially the maturation of the enormous baby boom generation, the cumulative audience for network news had increased since the 1960s and would continue to grow in the second half of the 1970s, reaching a peak of 52.1 million in 1980. But their combined audience share—the percentage of households actually watching TV at the dinner hour—had declined from over 90 to 75 percent. A quarter of the television audience was watching something else.

There were several reasons for this. One was network preference for what some Americans regarded as "bad news." Making their broadcasts more substantive turned off some viewers and encouraged them to watch other kinds of programs. To make matters worse, by the mid-1970s, the network news divisions had lost some of the authority they had enjoyed in the 1950s and much of the 1960s. Many viewers were suspicious of them, and during the 1970s these suspicions were fanned by politicians, including President Nixon, who insisted that the networks were part of a sinister "liberal establishment" responsible for virtually everything bad that had happened to America in recent years. Suspicion of network news was encouraged, too, by activists on the political left. They argued that Salant's professed commitment to objectivity was a ruse; in fact, the networks were engaged in the business of "manufacturing consent" for the corporate elite.

In the second half of the 1970s, these arguments, in diluted form, spread from activist circles throughout the culture like a corrosive acid, encouraging cynicism and apathy. They were reinforced by a general alienation from "official" institutions that was even more pervasive. Sparked by the social and political upheavals of the 1960s, it led many Americans to become more skeptical of the authoritative, seemingly objective broadcast style cultivated by the networks. More important, it contributed to a broader skepticism of all professional authority, and discouraged people, especially the young, from believing that it was important to follow the news. If the source was tainted and objectivity was a naïve illusion, what was the point?[4]

But alienation was not the most important reason for the turn away from network news. During the 1960s, when the network newscasts earned a 90 share, many viewers watched them out of habit. It was an evening ritual established in previous years, when there were only a handful of stations in most markets and everybody else seemed to be watching, too.[5] By the end of the 1960s, however, things had already begun to change. Legislation mandating that sets be able to receive

UHF signals had led businessmen to establish new stations on the UHF band. Some of those stations, as we have seen, were part of the growing public television system. Many others specialized in network reruns, old movies, and syndicated programs. Unaffiliated with the networks, they broadcast entertainment programs at the same time the networks were broadcasting news. Viewers now had more options, and during the 1970s and 1980s, thanks to the spread of cable television, those options would increase dramatically.

First established to serve communities in mountainous areas that were beyond the reach of conventional broadcast signals, the cable television industry rapidly expanded in the second half of the 1970s, reaching into suburban and urban areas, and inspiring entrepreneurs like Ted Turner to develop new program services, available only on cable, that were popular with viewers. Though the number of cable-only program services in the 1970s remained limited, a cable hookup offered viewers added benefits. "Must-carry" regulations required cable operators to provide customers with local broadcast stations, including UHF stations that had weaker signals than the VHF stations (channels 2–13) that dominated most markets. This made UHF stations competitive with their VHF counterparts. On cable, there was no discernible difference between the two; coming through a wire rather than over the air, the picture quality was equally clear. Soon new cable-only channels also began to appear, giving viewers even more choices—and inspiring more Americans to sign up for cable. The most ominous was Ted Turner's Cable News Network, which launched in June 1980 and provided viewers with news around the clock.[6]

By the early 1980s, television viewers had many more options from which to choose. And with people tuning into a wider variety of programs, the impression that everybody else was watching network news weakened, inspiring even more Americans to abandon the news for game shows or old episodes of *Star Trek*. Watching TV at the dinner hour remained a ritual in many households. But fewer and fewer television sets were tuned into network news. Meanwhile, for news junkies, the advent of PBS and especially CNN made the network newscasts superfluous. Viewers could get better, more in-depth coverage elsewhere. In short, the networks not only lost many casual viewers who preferred entertainment programs. They lost viewers who were sincerely interested in news and had long yearned for longer, more detailed news programming that the commercial networks could never provide. By 1990, the combined share of the three network newscasts would fall below 50 percent. More important, the appearance of competitors, including CNN, created a new set of pressures at the networks. Competing largely against each other had allowed network journalists to stick mostly to the high road and produce a relatively serious journalism. Competing against entertainment programs would make this considerably more difficult.

The networks were also challenged by changes at the FCC. For two decades, the FCC's "public-interest" requirements had nurtured the aspirational mission of network journalists, creating a climate where the networks were encouraged to devote resources to serious news programs, and affiliates felt compelled to broadcast them. But in the late 1970s, a new vogue of deregulation swept Washington, affecting liberals as well as conservatives and changing many people's views about the proper role of government. In 1981, newly elected president Ronald Reagan appointed a young conservative, Mark Fowler, as head of the FCC. Fowler was openly disdainful of the public-interest requirements imposed on broadcasters, and under his leadership the FCC became more flexible in its interpretation of how stations might serve their local communities. Believing that emerging technologies would end the scarcity of channels and program options, he scoffed at the notion that stations or the networks should do anything more than give the people what they want. Television, he once famously declared, was no different from any other appliance—"a toaster with pictures." Under conservative commissioners like Fowler, the FCC would abolish the Fairness Doctrine and begin to relax the rules that limited the number of radio and television stations individuals or corporations could own, encouraging the growth of large station groups like Group W and Capital Cities Communications. These changes were akin to pulling the rug out from under the feet of network journalists. They emboldened affiliates to demand that the networks make their news programs more entertaining—or allow them to broadcast entertainment programs in their stead. And they brought new players into the industry, particularly at the corporate level, executives who were quite different from the potentates who had presided over the networks since the 1940s, with ideas about serving the public similar to Fowler's.[7]

News programs were not the only network broadcasts that lost viewers in the 1980s. Entertainment programs did, too, even the most popular ones, plunging all three networks into economic crisis. New financial and syndication rules instituted by the FCC in the 1970s had limited their ability to produce their own programs and earn the huge profits that resulted when successful shows were sold to syndicators for broadcast as reruns. So, in effect, the networks had to rent programs from Hollywood studios and independent producers like Aaron Spelling. Deprived of syndication revenues, they became even more dependent on advertising revenues. Yet, as viewers migrated to cable and the total audience for even top-rated network shows declined, the networks found it more difficult to sell ads at premium rates. It was especially hard to sell advertising time on new or untested programs. And in the 1980s, for a variety of reasons, it became even more difficult to predict hits. Advertisers remained eager to buy airtime on the networks, which, despite cable, still attracted a massive audience. They preferred, however, to buy spots on established hits like *The Cosby Show*, which were sure to reach lots of viewers. This, in turn, gave the producers and stars of these programs more leverage, which resulted in a steady increase in the cost of renting them. When coupled with the slump in advertising revenue, this sharply reduced the profit margins of the networks and, in some years, caused them to lose enormous sums.[8]

These financial pressures undermined the firewall that had largely protected the news divisions from the competitive pressures that prevailed in the rest of the television industry. Recognizing the challenge posed by cable, network executives began to look for ways to cut costs and increase efficiency. Almost inevitably, they turned their attention to their news divisions. By the early 1980s, each of them was spending more than $200 million per year—a tenfold increase since the early 1960s. Before cable, when profits were high, competition was limited, and the FCC was looking over their shoulder, this was a luxury the networks could well afford. But no longer. Network executives demanded new economies from their news divisions. And they insisted their programs do something that had been unfathomable in earlier years—make money.

This shocked and alarmed many network news people. Yet there *were* television news programs that made money, and some of the people responsible for producing them were eager to create a more compelling and viewer-friendly variety of television journalism. Long constrained by the Salants of the industry, who sought to turn

TV news into the visual equivalent of the prestige press, they were now able to increase their influence and lead broadcast journalism in new directions. And they were convinced they could do it without forsaking journalistic principles.

A case in point was *60 Minutes*. Created by Don Hewitt, it was perhaps the most inspiring journalistic success story of the 1970s. In the mid-1960s, after being fired as producer of the CBS *Evening News*, Hewitt was reassigned to the network's documentary unit. He enjoyed the work, and produced some interesting and well regarded programs, but he despaired when he thought about how few people ever saw them—particularly compared to the evening news. The only people who tuned in were "documentary freaks," an overeducated minority. He began to wonder if there might be "a better way to move information" than the conventional long-form documentary, and came up with a plan for a magazine-style program that would include a variety of reports and features.[9] There were precedents for such a program, he reminded his superiors, and he argued that a magazine program would complement the network's other news offerings. As he told Salant, "Many stories . . . were too important and complex to be dealt with in the minute and a half or two minutes available on the evening news but still did not need a full hour."[10] Bowing to Hewitt's relentless badgering, Salant agreed, and *60 Minutes* was launched in September 1968 on Tuesday nights at 10:00 as part of the CBS *News Hour*. It was broadcast every two weeks, alternating with other CBS news programs.[11]

Yet *60 Minutes* wasn't an ordinary magazine show with a variety of segments. From the start, Hewitt conceived it as a vehicle for telling stories. And as the program's executive producer and guiding editorial spirit, he thought very carefully about the kinds of segments that could be packaged into a single broadcast and the order in which they appeared. He made a point, for example, of including a soft feature or interview in virtually every program; they were designed to balance the hard investigative reports that were an equally important part of the show's formula. Like his peers at CBS, Hewitt was committed to enlightening viewers. But he was convinced that the best way of doing this was not by discussing and examining issues, the standard approach of documentaries, but through storytelling—crafting eleven-to-fourteen-minute narratives that examined issues along the way.

The protagonists of these narratives were the program's correspon-

In 1968, Mike Wallace and Harry Reasoner were teamed as the hosts of Don Hewitt's trailblazing program *60 Minutes*. Photo courtesy of CBS/Photofest.

dents, who were cast as its stars. When *60 Minutes* was still in its planning stages, Hewitt chose Harry Reasoner to be the host and principal correspondent. At the urging of colleagues, he decided to go with two anchors and picked Mike Wallace to join Reasoner. They made an excellent pair. The wry and laconic Reasoner had an assured, comforting on-air manner, and his superb writing skills gave the program a literary flair that would appeal to upscale viewers. Wallace, the former "Grand Inquisitor" and an accomplished anchor in his own right, gave the program its edge. Not surprisingly, he was assigned mostly interviews and investigative reports. When Reasoner left for ABC in 1970s, the veteran foreign correspondent Morley Safer joined the show. Safer became *60 Minutes'* jack-of-all-trades, reporting on hard as well as soft news, epitomizing the program's hybrid nature. In 1975, Dan Rather, fresh from a stint as the network's White House correspondent, was brought in as a third correspondent, and in the Wallace-Safer-Rather era the show developed an even more distinctive tone. *60 Minutes* acquired a fourth correspondent in 1978 when Reasoner returned to CBS. The writer Andy Rooney joined the show as well, providing humorous commentary at the conclusion of each broadcast. Hewitt and his talented cast of stars attracted a cohort of ambitious younger producers who were eager to work outside the confines of conventional news programs, and their drive and eagerness to innovate inspired the program's correspondents to compete to produce the best stories. Showcasing the talents of its four stars, each possessing a different broadcast style and specializing in different kinds of stories, the program settled into a groove.[12]

Despite its innovations and a chorus of critical praise, *60 Minutes* was anything but an instant success. In its first season it ranked 83rd out of 103 prime-time programs. Ratings for its second season were even worse: matched up against ABC's hit medical drama *Marcus Welby, MD*, it fell to 92nd, and the following season, it plummeted to 101st. During the 1971–1972 season, it was moved around the CBS schedule, and then, after the end of the NFL football season, scheduled as a weekly broadcast on Sundays at 6:00 PM, outside prime time so its poor ratings wouldn't figure into the network's overall numbers. There it remained for the next three seasons—except for short runs in prime time during the summers, when viewership was extremely low. Its cancelation seemed inevitable.[13]

In December 1975, however, Hewitt got a huge break. Forced by an FCC ruling to air a children's or public-affairs program on Sundays at 7:00 PM, CBS moved *60 Minutes* into the time slot after a family-oriented show bombed. Up against *The Wonderful World of Disney* and *The Swiss Family Robinson*, CBS was now the only network with a program appealing to adults, and *60 Minutes* quickly began to build an audience. It finished the season in 52nd place, rose to 18th the next year, and ended the 1977–1978 season in the top 10. In November 1978, it became the top-rated program on television, the first time a regularly scheduled news or public-affairs show ever ranked number one. With the increase in ratings came an increase in the price CBS could charge advertisers. By 1978, a minute of commercial airtime on *60 Minutes* cost $215,000, and since each episode cost less than $200,000 to produce, the program became extremely profitable for the network. Industry experts estimated that it cleared $25 million a year. It finished the 1979–1980 season as the number-one rated show on television, an achievement it would repeat four times over the years. Despite a steady increase in production costs, owing largely to salary increases for Hewitt and its stars, *60 Minutes* remained profitable as well as popular, the jewel in the network's crown.

But *60 Minutes* was not universally loved. In the late 1970s, television critics and some viewers complained about the increasingly aggressive techniques its correspondents had begun to employ in their exposés: using hidden microphones and cameras, selectively editing interviews to make subjects look bad, and staging unscheduled "ambush interviews" designed to catch subjects off their guard. While they made for great drama and were essential to the program's appeal, they aroused perplexing ethical issues and compelled Hewitt to air a special "self-examination" of the show in 1981, in which several of the program's critics were given a prime-time platform to air their complaints.[14] From the beginning, *60 Minutes* was also routinely assailed by conservatives for its liberal bias. Letters from viewers read at the conclusion of each broadcast expressed unhappiness with the program's treatment of business and of the American military in particular. Surprisingly, Hewitt's show was no more popular with the political left. Liberal critics noted that the targets of most exposés were relative "small-fry, not big business, and that Hewitt's emphasis on addressing issues through storytelling and often simple morality plays didn't encourage understanding of structural problems. Liberals were particularly disappointed with the program's gingerly treatment of the Watergate scandal, its reluctance to produce hard-hitting reports on the Reagan administration, and Hewitt's increasingly cozy relationships with the rich and powerful.[15]

There was some truth to these critiques. But critics who assailed the program for its ideological bias failed to appreciate its complexity. Conceived in the late 1960s, when television journalists were becoming more independent and skeptical of powerful institutions, *60 Minutes* exhibited a potent adversarial edge. Hewitt and his producers sensed that much of the public was becoming more cynical, and a news program that sought to uncover corruption and stand up for the little guy against the forces of bureaucracy would captivate many Americans. At times, this meant attacking institutions that were sacred to conservatives—but from a stance that was essentially populist. Rather than expose the workings of the "system," as a traditional leftist critique would, *60 Minutes* emphasized individual or episodic malfeasance— pockets of corruption, seemingly isolated injustices—and made little effort to connect them or develop a more sweeping argument. This was not because Hewitt and his colleagues were corporate lackeys, as their leftist critics suggested. It was because the program's populism worked as television and helped to ensure that *60 Minutes* was appealing to a large audience—one that included more than the documentary freaks or the upper-middle-class influentials who were the usual and most contented viewers of network news programming.[16]

But the program's populism was only the half of it. Hewitt then filtered it through stories that had all the components of classic narrative—heroes, villains, dramatic tension, and resolution. As Hewitt recognized, television favored such an approach far more than it favored the more detached analytic style employed by most documentaries. It was a way of informing that was also compelling and entertaining. His show's populism, then, complemented its emphasis on storytelling and was perfectly attuned to shifts in the public mood in the wake of the 1960s. It was a formula that appealed to a much wider audience than most news programs. Indeed, it allowed the show's stars to descend from the now discredited Olympian heights that Murrow, Huntley and Brinkley, and Cronkite had occupied and reposition themselves as champions of ordinary people. Wallace, Reasoner, Safer, and Rather were perfect heroes for the age—celebrity journalists waging battle on behalf of an alienated and cynical public. And the success they enjoyed by adopting such a guise ensured that other television journalists would adopt it as well.

60 Minutes was not the only innovative magazine show to debut in the late 1960s. In January 1969, NBC launched *First Tuesday*. It aired monthly and was two hours long, and it featured as many as eight different segments. Hosted by Sander Vanocur and Garrick Utley, it also struggled to develop an audience. After a name change and being shifted around NBC's schedule, it was broadcast for the last time in August 1973.[17] NBC tried several other magazine-style programs, particularly after *60 Minutes'* surge in the ratings, but they all failed.[18] One reason for this was NBC's eagerness to copy Hewitt's formula, rather than try to do something different. For fifteen years, CBS had been the trailblazer in television news, and in the late 1970s NBC hired Richard Salant and several other CBS News veterans to revamp its news division and catch up to its longtime rival. By the early 1980s, however, mimicking the high-minded aspirational journalism that had come to define CBS was a dead end. The real action was elsewhere.

At local stations, a very different ethos had taken root, and as the training ground for many young producers and reporters who would later move on to the networks, they became the seedbed for a new kind of television journalism that would eventually remake the entire industry. This was ironic since most local stations had been slow to get into the news business, providing little more than short summaries of wire-service headlines throughout the 1950s. The first to do more were independents like Los Angeles's KTLA and network affiliates on the West Coast, who resented the networks' lack of attention to their region. They recognized that the news fed to them from New York afternoon broadcasts was stale. To make up for this, KNXT, CBS's Los Angeles affiliate, created *The Big News*. An hour-long evening news program produced by Sam Zelman and anchored by Jerry Dunphy, it debuted in October 1961. Like KTLA, KNXT focused on local news and human-interest features. Yet it also reported national and even international news and specialized in updates of stories that had just been covered on the CBS *Evening News*. Thanks in part to Dunphy, a consummate performer who would inspire the Ted Baxter character on *The Mary Tyler Moore Show*, the program was a huge hit. By the mid-1960s, its reporters were traveling across the country and even to Vietnam to cover important stories. It success inspired scores of imitators and helped to spark a revolution in local news. *The Big News* demonstrated that a longer local newscast was feasible if it mixed news and entertaining features and starred anchormen and reporters who were colorful and charismatic. And it suggested that, with enough resources and technology, a local news program could compete with network news and cover many of the same stories.[19]

In the early 1960s, around the same time that Zelman was developing *The Big News*, local stations in other cities were also putting together longer evening news programs. This effort was spurred in part by the FCC, which began to demand that television stations broadcast more news and, as part of the relicensing process, conduct "community ascertainment" surveys to determine whether their programs were meeting local needs. Faced with this new requirement, stations hired consultants, usually ex-ad men or academically trained social scientists, to help with the surveys, and station managers resolved to derive something positive from the exercise by using the data to develop more popular and profitable programming. Consultants like the firm McHugh & Hoffman began producing detailed portraits of local markets, including information about what viewers thought of both local and network news programs.

The results were eye-opening. A majority of viewers—a group that comprised nearly 70 percent of the television audience and consultants identified as the "middle majority"—thought that network newscasts were boring and hard to understand. They were especially unhappy with the emphasis on national politics and foreign affairs, and they objected to the air of detachment cultivated by network broadcasters. For many, watching the evening news was an obligation, like going to church; for others, it was a quick way of getting information that allowed them to chat with friends and was only slightly less tedious than reading a newspaper. What they liked was action—filmed reports of things occurring on-screen, not talking heads—and anchors who appeared human, like Walter Cronkite covering NASA space flights.

This was not what the network news divisions wanted to hear. In the mid-1960s, CBS News executives rejected McHugh & Hoffman's proposal to help them make their news programs more appealing to viewers—as the firm had for several of its affiliates. But local stations, including many network affiliates, were quite happy with the data compiled by consultants, and they were keen to make use of it. Consultants suggested that affiliates turn their local news broadcasts into signature programs that would attract more viewers than other kinds of public-service programming. Signature newscasts would not only make more money; they would encourage viewer loyalty to a particular station's brand. Hired by small chains as well as individual stations, McHugh & Hoffman and a rival firm, Frank Magid Associates, began offering specific advice about how to revamp and expand their clients' local newscasts. By paying close attention to developments in the industry, they soon devised a winning formula.[20]

McHugh & Hoffman's makeover of WABC, ABC's owned station in New York City, was particularly important. Working closely with Al Primo, WABC's new station manager who had developed an innovative local news show in Philadelphia, they borrowed liberally from other programs, added a few ingredients of their own, and created *Eyewitness News*, a name that Primo had conceived in Philadelphia. To deliver the news, they created a four-person anchor team: newsreaders Roger Grimsby and Bill Beutel, weatherman Tex Antoine, and sports reporter Howard Cosell. Inspired by a successful local news program at ABC's station in Chicago, the new team at WABC was encouraged to engage in light banter, an act one critic dubbed "happy talk." They were joined on the set by reporters, who introduced their stories and conversed at length with Grimsby and Beutel. Responding to survey data revealing a lack of public interest in local politics, reporters adroitly shifted their focus, covering the subject through stories on the impact of municipal policies on ordinary people or through investigative exposés. WABC's reporters were young and from diverse backgrounds; some were inspired by the social movements of the era and brought a real passion to their work. Among them was a young lawyer-cum-journalist named Geraldo Rivera, who specialized in aggressive reporting on issues relevant to minorities, the working class, and the poor. The new format was a huge success, vaulting WABC to the top of the ratings.

In response to the success of McHugh & Hoffman's eyewitness news, Magid developed a competing format, *Action News*. Emphasizing short, faced-paced filmed stories—as many as three per minute—and new technology, like mobile vans and hand-held cameras, which allowed for more on-the-spot reporting, *Action News* was launched in 1970s at WFIL, a Philadelphia station owned by the media magnate Walter Annenberg. When Annenberg sold the station to Capital Cities, the action-news format was installed at the company's other stations, enabling them to dominate their markets and overcome the ratings lead enjoyed by stations that had adopted the eyewitness-news format. By the early 1970s, McHugh & Hoffman and Magid were engaged in a fierce competition for clients and influence in the local TV news business. And the success enjoyed by stations that adopted their formats reverberated throughout the industry.

As stations experimented and ratings and market research determined the features most appealing to viewers, the eyewitness-news and action-news formats converged. The resulting hybrid combined features developed by each of them and established a new standard for local news. Like eyewitness news, it included news, weather, and sports, and was at least an hour long; in the 1980s, the huge profits earned by local news led many stations to expand their newscasts to two hours. Most stories were about local events, with a heavy emphasis on violent crime, fires, accidents, and natural disasters—events that lent themselves to vivid film or videotape reports, in the style of action news. Programs were hosted by an anchor team, whose members often wore matching blazers and appeared on eye-catching, space-age sets. In the mid-1970s, in response to survey data and pressure from feminist groups and the FCC, women were added to anchor teams, usually as newsreaders.[21] More often than not, they were young and pretty, and were usually paired with older men. Anchor teams continued to engage in "happy talk," and producers encouraged them to appear down-to-earth and "relatable." When covering big, important stories, they were urged to display, rather than suppress, emotion, reaffirming their kinship with viewers and the community at large. "There was no need to pontificate like the networks," Bill Beutel noted, "because you weren't a thousand miles away."[22] While the networks cultivated a broadcast style that was purposefully Olympian—"news from nowhere," in Edward J. Epstein's phrase—local stations did exactly the opposite, producing a journalism that was rooted in particular communities, featuring anchors and reporters who acted like human beings, not emotionless professionals.[23]

Local news programs covered a lot of stories and presented them at a rapid, almost propulsive pace. Most interviews were reduced to short sound bites of no more than ten seconds. There were regular teasers for upcoming stories, mostly before commercial breaks, and recurring theme music. But there were also long, in-depth investigative reports, often about issues of interest to consumers. Many stations hired special reporters to serve as consumer watchdogs, and they encouraged viewers to write or call in with their complaints about local businesses that engaged in fraud or deceptive advertising. Stories on medicine and health were also very common. So, too, were ones on lifestyle trends. Often prepared especially for airing during "sweeps," the period when ratings were tabulated, these special features were relentlessly promoted, sometimes for days or even weeks in advance. The emphasis on consumer, heath, and lifestyle features was advertised as "news you can use" and was very popular with viewers, enabling local stations to charge advertisers a premium to air commercials during their newscasts. "News you can use" allowed local stations to serve the "public interest" while also boosting ratings. From the point of view of station managers, it was a win-win.

By the early 1980s, the success and enormous profitability of local news broadcasts encouraged many local stations to expand their news operations. Now able to afford the latest technology, including both stationary and mobile satellite dishes, they increased their coverage of more distant breaking news. And they began sending reporters, usually viewer favorites, to cover some national and even international stories, presenting them through angles that were interesting to people in their community. Avidly hyped, these special reports led viewers to think of local stations as providers of more general news — and a potential alternative to the networks. Stations also began to supplement their newscasts with stories on consumer and lifestyle issues produced by syndicators. Distributed via satellite, some of these stories were inserted into newscasts as features. Others aired as stand-along programs in the early evening, often right after the local or network news. The most popular of these syndicated programs was Group W's *Evening Magazine*. First conceived in 1976, at KPIX, Group W's station in San Francisco, a CBS affiliate, it aired five days a week and offered celebrity interviews and assorted features. Its success led Group W executives to distribute it to its stations in other markets and, in 1979, to non-Group W stations as *PM Magazine*. Its popularity encouraged producers of local news programs to increase their focus on consumer, lifestyle, and celebrity-oriented features.[24]

The transformation of local news elicited mixed feelings at the networks. Many veteran journalists and producers were disturbed by the new local news. They regarded it as superficial and sensational, and they blamed consultants for discouraging their comrades at local stations from relying on "professional news judgment" to determine which stories should appear on the air. In a speech to CBS affiliates in May 1976, Walter Cronkite lamented the "pandering to show business values" that consultants had inspired, and he urged his audience to reject their suggestions. Richard Salant, in an interview with the *New York Times*, made it quite clear where he stood: "A journalist doesn't make a survey to find out what people want. You can do that in entertainment but not in news."[25] But there were people at CBS News and the other networks who had worked at local stations and saw some merit in the new approach. Most of them were young, and they were happy to be working in television. Like Cronkite and Salant, they wanted to inform and even enlighten. They knew, however, that they were working in a medium that was notoriously resistant to the sober, analytic journalism practiced by the prestige press. They knew that attempting to follow this model was off-putting to many viewers and a big reason why some people thought the networks were arrogant and elitist. And they knew that the networks could not regain their confidence and loyalty unless they stepped down from Olympus and tried to connect with viewers in new ways. If nothing else, the producers of local news had been able to do this.

Outside of the news divisions, the new local news was viewed more favorably. Aware that a popular local newscast could deliver a large audience to a network's prime-time programming, network executives were happy to see affiliates contributing to the team. And they didn't object when stations opted to broadcast the network news at 6:30 PM, rather than 7:00 PM, in order to schedule an hour of more local news or popular syndicated programs like *PM Magazine* or *Jeopardy!* By the early 1980s, network executives had brought many successful station managers, news directors, and producers to New York to help them deal with the new challenges of the cable era, and network bigwigs, concerned about the ballooning budgets of their news divisions, had become intrigued by the prospect of outsourcing a portion of national newsgathering to local affiliates. With so many viewers watching local news, and local newscasts able to offer them more national news, the time seemed ripe for a makeover of network news—and to reconsider the nostrum that it should strive to tell people what they ought to know.

Change came first to ABC. The perennial third network had long been a programming innovator, pioneering the broadcast of Hollywood-produced filmed programs and shows targeted at teenagers and young adults. It had reached parity with CBS and NBC in the 1960s, and during the mid-1970s, under programming whiz Fred Silverman, its powerful lineup of entertainment programs lifted the network to number one. With hits like *Happy Days, Charlie's Angels,* and *The Six Million Dollar Man,* ABC was awash in ad revenues and in a better position than ever to finally make its news division the equal of its rivals. Under Elmer Lower, who took over in 1963, ABC News had already made progress. With less than half the resources enjoyed by news presidents at the other networks, Lower had built a solid corps of reporters and producers. His most significant achievement was the steady improvement and increasing popularity of the ABC *Evening News.* By the early 1970s, with Av Westin as executive producer and Harry Reasoner as anchor, it had become a well-respected broadcast, at times threatening to surpass NBC in the ratings. Lower's successor, William Sheehan, sought to continue this expansion. At the same time, however, he and Bill Lord, the new producer of the ABC *Evening News*, recognized the need to make their evening news broadcast stand out from the competition. As Lord explained to the television critic Ron Powers, "I want to go into consumer reporting on a regular basis. I want to use specific news features that go into a particular locality. . . . I want the news more involved at the viewer level. Never before have people needed or wanted to understand complex issues more than they do now. I mean long-term inflation, the energy crisis, unemployment."[26] Here was the same interest in informing the public and helping viewers understand important issues that inspired producers and journalists at CBS and NBC. But, as Lord made clear, he was prepared to try to do it in new ways, and his belief in reaching viewers at their level revealed his appreciation of techniques developed by local stations.

There were good reasons for Sheehan and Lord and their colleagues at ABC to look to local news for inspiration. In the late 1960s, the network had hired McHugh & Hoffman to help station managers at its five owned and operated stations (O-and-Os) revamp their newscasts, and the results had been extremely encouraging. They quickly came to dominate their respective markets, and the popularity of their evening news shows had improved the ratings of the ABC *Evening News*. Champions of local news had also moved to network headquarters in New York. Richard O'Leary, the station manager of ABC's Chicago O-and-O, became head of the network's owned-stations division in 1970, and under his leadership, ABC developed an innovative news advisory service that sent executives and news directors from the network's O-and-Os to affiliates around the country. Their assignment was to help affiliates create more appealing news programs that would boost overall ratings—to provide, for free, some of the valuable advice for which other stations were paying consultants. Having learned their lessons well, ABC advisors encouraged local journalists to use conversational language and simple storytelling techniques and emphasize human interest in every story. Here was the key to ratings success, and it would soon shape news broadcasts at all the networks.

The remarkable thing is that it didn't happen right away. In fact, ABC's first big move was an attempt to exploit old-fashioned star power. In October 1976, Barbara Walters joined Harry Reasoner as co-anchor of the ABC *Evening News*. Walters had grown antsy in her role as cohost of NBC's successful *Today* show and yearned for a new challenge. But Richard Wald, the president of NBC News, refused to allow her to become John Chancellor's coanchor, not least because of Chancellor's steadfast opposition. So Walters was receptive when Sheehan and ABC president Fred Pierce approached her about coming over to ABC. Their offer was unprecedented—a salary of $1 million per year, half of it paid by ABC's entertainment division, to coanchor the news and produce six prime-time specials in which she would interview newsmakers and celebrities. Sweetening the deal even further, Sheehan reported that affiliates were willing to allow the network to increase its newscast to least forty-five minutes and potentially an hour in order for Walters to include interviews and other special features on the ABC *Evening News*.[27]

Hiring Walters was quite a gamble, since Reasoner was unhappy with the decision and the network was assailed by critics who unfairly accused Walters of being a journalistic lightweight. And market research conducted by Frank Magid revealed that Walters was unappealing as a potential anchor, and that the network would be better served by employing her strictly as an interviewer. Much of the animus—from critics and fellow TV journalists as well as viewers—stemmed from her enormous salary. Cronkite earned only $650,000 and Sheehan and Pierce were forced to increase Reasoner's salary to $500,000 to equal the news division's portion of Walters's compensation; within a few years, virtually all network anchors and first-string correspondents were earning substantially more than before, a premium attributable in part to the "Walters factor." But resentment of Walters wasn't just a result of her salary. It was also aroused by reports of the perks her agent had been able to finagle. They included a personal assistant, makeup consultant, and wardrobe specialist, guaranteed first-class hotel accommodations, and an office decorated precisely to Walters's liking—the sorts of things more commonly enjoyed by Hollywood stars. Salant, nearing mandatory retirement at CBS, opined, "Is Barbara Walters a journalist or is she Cher?"[28]

The hue and cry might have subsided if the Reasoner-Walters team had clicked. But it was a disaster from day one, when Reasoner gave Walters a lukewarm reception and left it to her to try to dispel the cloud of negative publicity that hung over her appointment. Ever the professional, Walters did her best, reaffirming that she and Reasoner were committed to producing a first-rate news broadcast, and noting that she would make a special effort to highlight why particular news

Having moved to ABC, Barbara Walters became one the biggest stars in television journalism, particularly for her trademark interviews. Here she is interviewing Cuban leader Fidel Castro in 1977. Photo courtesy of ABC/Photofest.

stories—even international ones—were important to viewers, a nod to the "news you can use" formula that must have raised Reasoner's blood pressure. Over the next few months, Reasoner and Walters continued to stumble, and Reasoner's displeasure with their shotgun marriage became more evident by the day. And viewers, after flocking to the program out of novelty, deserted it en masse, sending the *ABC Evening News* back to the ratings cellar. To make matters worse, ABC's affiliates refused to give the network more time for an expanded newscast, and Walters found few opportunities to add interviews and other innovative features to the broadcast. She was reduced to being a newsreader, never her forte, alongside a man who clearly resented her presence. Sheehan and Pierce had bet the house and lost.

The Walters hire wasn't Pierce's only gamble. In November 1975, before her arrival, ABC unveiled *Good Morning, America*, a morning news-and-features program that took direct aim at *Today*. It replaced *A.M. America*, ABC's first effort to produce such a program, which had debuted earlier in the year. Produced by the news division in con-

junction with the consultant Frank Magid, it had been a total failure. Part of the problem was the program's split personality. While
Magid badgered producers to make it entertaining and include lots of
"news you can use," the news division people held back, fearful of tar-
nishing their professional reputations.[29] With *Good Morning, America*,
however, there would be no split personality. It was assigned to ABC's
entertainment division, and its new producers hired two actors, David
Hartman and Nancy Dussault, as hosts. Steve Bell, a veteran ABC correspondent, served as newsreader, but hard news played a minor role
on the show. Though Magid was not involved in the show's development, it bore his influence and made rapid gains in the ratings, particularly after 1980, when Joan Lunden became Hartman's cohost and
the program perfected its blend of celebrity interviews and consumer-
oriented features, a concoction that was considerably more sugary
than *Today*'s.[30] The local news formula, at last, had arrived at a major
network.

Pierce's biggest gamble, however, came in June 1977, when he
named Roone Arledge, the brilliant and mercurial head of ABC Sports,
president of ABC News. Under Arledge, ABC's sports division had become the most innovative and widely imitated broadcasting unit in
network television, the home of *Wide World of Sports*, *Monday Night
Football*, and the network's stellar Olympic coverage, which enlivened
otherwise obscure sports by emphasizing human drama and profiling athletes through techniques that introduced them to viewers "up
close and personal." Eager for a new challenge and sincerely interested in television journalism, Arledge leaped at Pierce's offer to reshape ABC News. But Arledge's appointment was met with dismay by
most people who worked in the news division. While they admired
his skills as a producer, they worried about his lack of experience as a
journalist. Some feared he would make ABC News more "show-biz,"
not unlike the cynical programmers satirized in *Network*. Arledge did
little to calm these fears when he first met with the news division staff
and expressed contempt for their "stodgy" programs and traditions,
or when he brought in a number of his own people from ABC Sports
and demoted seasoned veterans. Sacked from his job as anchor of the
network's Saturday evening newscast, Ted Koppel resigned—until
Arledge convinced him to stay on as ABC's State Department correspondent. Critics outside ABC were equally disdainful, suggesting that

ABC, already notorious for lowbrow and escapist entertainment programming, would now dumb down its news.[31]

Yet Arledge was a true pioneer, and his influence over ABC—and the television news business as a whole—turned out to be far more complex than his critics predicted. He was indeed unhappy with the state of television news and determined to make ABC's news offerings more lively and engaging, as he had done for its sports programs. However, he was also committed to quality, and his interest in developing new forms of television journalism was inspired by a belief that this would enable his staff to cover more news, more completely. At ABC Sports, he had acquired a reputation for profligacy, and once at the helm of ABC News, he began spending enormous sums in order to surpass his rivals. Between 1977 and 1980, the ABC News budget more than doubled to approximately $150 million, which put it at the same level as NBC and CBS. Convinced that the network needed an infusion of new blood, he also began hiring away established correspondents and producers from NBC and especially CBS, offering them huge raises to come work for him. Though he failed to attract some of his most coveted targets, his campaign forced NBC and CBS to raise salaries across the board and reinforced the trend of escalating news division budgets. For example, believing that a CBS radio broadcaster, Charles Osgood, could be a big star, Arledge offered Osgood a $500,000 per year salary to join ABC. At the time, Osgood made a paltry $120,000, and to keep him, CBS was forced to raise it to $400,000. Arledge also spent lavishly on new equipment that enhanced ABC's ability to report breaking news. He was certain that this was the key to success in the future; the network that was best able to take viewers to the scene of a big news story would dominate the ratings. Arledge viewed his spending as an investment that would later pay dividends, and his ultimate goal was a *profitable* news division. He reasoned that if ABC News was profitable, he could protect its independence and acquire more clout in his battle for airtime with the entertainment division.[32]

The first problem that he sought to tackle was ABC's disastrous evening newscast. To help him with it, he brought Av Westin back as the show's producer. Saddled with the Reasoner-Walters anchor team, Westin introduced features that minimized the time the two appeared together on-screen and paved the way for a more varied and faster-paced program. For example, "whip-arounds" strung together reports from several correspondents without returning to an anchor in the main studio. Committed to breaking news and big stories, Arledge implored his producers and correspondents to play up events like the capture of the notorious "Son of Sam" serial killer and the death of Elvis Presley, stories that its rival networks were hesitant to exploit. And with the assistance of Roger Goodman, a talented director he brought with him from ABC Sports, he added technology that enabled the program to display visually arresting charts and graphs and show an interview subject in an on-screen window alongside a reporter or anchor. These were useful and important innovations that enhanced ABC's ability to explain as well as cover the news, and most of them were adopted by its rivals.

The new regime was disconcerting to Harry Reasoner, however, and, taking advantage of an escape clause in his contract, he elected to return to CBS in June 1978. This left Arledge and Westin in a quandary—but also provided them with an opportunity for further innovation. Recognizing that, with Cronkite, CBS possessed the ultimate star, and that Reasoner's departure made it impossible for ABC to compete on the same terms, they developed an entirely new program, *World News Tonight*. Instead of a single anchor or a duo, they organized the broadcast around three subanchors or "deskmen," as Arledge preferred to call them. Based in Washington, Frank Reynolds reported and introduced stories about national politics. Peter Jennings, stationed in London, did the same for international news. And Max Robinson, a successful African American local news anchor, was installed at a studio in Chicago, where he was responsible for reporting other domestic news. Arledge and Westin made Barbara Walters a New York–based special correspondent, a role that allowed her to concentrate on interviews and special reports. Each deskman was expected to go out and report from the field as well as from the studio, and it was hoped that this would give the broadcast an immediacy conventional studio-based newscasts lacked.

Westin made other changes. Inspired by the NBC *Nightly News'* experiment with longer, in-depth reports, which had pleased viewers, he introduced a *Special Assignment* series on subjects like the arms race, the energy crisis, and "stagflation." Making room for these four- and five-minute stories required eliminating or compressing other material, which Westin lumped into a short segment of anchor-read tell-stories and short videotaped reports. And with an eye toward the success of local news, he also developed a new barometer for assessing which stories should be included and receive the most emphasis. Looking over the range of possibilities on a given day, he ordered his staff to think about their viewers and ask these questions: "Is my world safe? Are my city and home safe? If my wife, children and loved ones are safe, what then has happened in the past twenty-four hours to shock them, amuse them or make them better off than they were?" The questions were vague and left plenty of room for exercising "professional news judgment." But they began from premises—the perspective and concerns of the viewer—that were radically different from Richard Salant's.[33]

Orchestrating *World News Tonight* was a challenge, and after helping get it off the ground, Westin was reassigned to another program, and a young producer named Jeff Gralnick took over. Gralnick did his best, and the broadcast attracted more viewers than its predecessor, largely at the expense of the NBC *Nightly News*. But some parts of the show worked better than others, and it became difficult for Gralnick to manage the egos of the deskmen. Reynolds, a longtime ABC vet, sought to become the first among equals, and Robinson expressed little interest in reporting from the field. Jennings was the most impressive, and posting him in London enabled the program to offer more foreign news than its rivals.

Convinced that ABC News still needed a star, Arledge began a protracted courtship of CBS's Dan Rather, hoping to make him the centerpiece of *World News Tonight* and other ABC news programs. When Rather elected to stay at CBS and become Cronkite's successor as anchor and managing editor of the CBS *Evening News*, Arledge turned his attention to Tom Brokaw, the host of *Today*. Again, Arledge failed to get his man. But his aggressive pursuit and the extraordinary money and terms he offered to each of them forced CBS and NBC to increase their salaries and give them unprecedented power. Rather's new deal gave him a minimum of $22 million over ten years; Brokaw's, signed a year later, guaranteed him $18 million over seven years. And Arledge's pursuit of Rather forced CBS news chief Bill Leonard to pressure Cronkite to retire early in order to accommodate Rather's desire to be the network's sole anchor, and led an angry Roger Mudd, Cronkite's presumptive heir, to leave CBS for NBC, where he and Brokaw became coanchors of the NBC *Nightly News* when John Chancellor retired in 1982. Thanks to Arledge, the entire evening news landscape was transformed in a way that undermined CBS's longtime advantage and created an opening for ABC.[34]

In July 1983, with Frank Reynolds fatally ill, Jennings took over as the sole anchor of *World News Tonight* and the tripartite "deskman" system was abolished. But the program floundered, sometimes falling into third place. Though Jennings grew into his job as anchor, and the broadcast continued to provide the most extensive and thoughtful international news, its unpopularity bothered Arledge. Jennings was unhappy, too, and when he signed a new contract, granting him roughly the same authority over the broadcast that Rather and Brokaw had over theirs, he was able to force Arledge to hire a new producer, Paul Friedman. Jennings and Friedman worked well together, and, at Friedman's urging, the program's format changed yet again. *World News Tonight* began to devote more time and attention to the day's big story and include analysis by ABC correspondents, on the assumption that many viewers might already know the facts about it from local news. And it launched a new series in the big hole where the *Special Assignment* reports had long appeared. *American Agenda* explored and proposed solutions to national problems, and it provided a wonderful platform for Jennings to go into the field and report as well as anchor. The new series was expensive and required lots of advance preparation, but it was popular and offset the impression that the cosmopolitan Jennings favored foreign news. It was a winning formula, and by the end of 1989, *World News Tonight* was the nation's most watched evening news program. Arledge and ABC had prevailed.[35]

Arledge and ABC also succeeded in developing a successful prime-time newsmagazine, *20/20*. Occupied with other matters, Arledge at first farmed out the program to Bob Shanks, who had worked on public television's *Great American Dream Machine*. But when the debut broadcast was a disaster, earning some of the worst reviews in television history, Shanks fired the two hosts, art critic Robert Hughes and *Esquire* editor Harold Hayes, and brought former *Today* stalwart Hugh Downs out of retirement to host the program. With Downs presiding, it became a more conventional program, mixing investigative reports with stories on science, health, and popular culture—a lighter, more feature-oriented *60 Minutes*. After a period when it aired irregularly, *20/20* finally got a regular spot on ABC's schedule—Thursdays at 10:00 PM—in May 1979, where it thrived for the next eight years. Barbara Walters was a frequent contributor, and in 1984, at Arledge's urging, she became cohost and her interviews even more frequent features. The show provided a showcase for some ABC veterans as well as the new talent that Arledge brought to the network, including Geraldo Rivera, the flamboyant reporter who had impressed network executives when he was at WABC. Rivera specialized in probing exposés, like his special, hour-long investigation of Elvis Presley's death, which was a huge ratings hit when it aired in September 1979, and his grandstanding style was popular with most viewers.[36]

20/20 was surprisingly successful, regularly garnering a 30 share by 1980. And it was profitable, too, thanks to the efficient system for assigning and producing stories that Av Westin introduced when he became the program's producer in 1981. Far more than at *60 Minutes*, for example, producers and correspondents were forced to consider potential viewer interest in stories before they were approved and funded, and this made for a program that was heavy on pop culture and features resembling those on local news. But Westin was also open to innovation, and when ratings began to flag in the mid-1980s, he conducted audience research and consulted with his producers and correspondents to plot a new approach. For example, eager to produce stories about the fine arts, a potentially esoteric subject, Westin assigned producers to make "process pieces" on celebrated artists explaining how they went about their work. And when one of his producers did a report on depression and it struck a chord with viewers, Westin commissioned other "coping" stories on anxiety, shyness, anger, and jealousy. Westin recognized that there was a good deal of show business in a typical episode of 20/20. But television was show business, he insisted. "As long as show business techniques can be used to transmit information without distorting it, I believe they are perfectly all right."[37] Throughout the 1980s, 20/20 was ABC News' biggest money-maker, and its success provided Arledge with credibility and the resources to develop more substantive fare.

The most substantive, without question, was *Nightline*, a critically acclaimed new program that Arledge and his staff created in 1980. Frozen out of prime time, the networks had long used the 11:30 PM time slot for instant specials on breaking news or obituaries of notable public figures. And in November 1979, when Iranian militants seized the US embassy in Teheran and took its staff hostage, Arledge pressured Fred Pierce to allow him to broadcast a daily news update on the hostage crisis. Hosted by Frank Reynolds and produced by Jeff Gralnick, *The Iran Crisis: American Held Hostage* aired for the first time on November 8 and became a nightly broadcast on November 15. It was an expensive and potentially foolhardy commitment. But Arledge was convinced the public was hankering for information about the hostages, and he thought the story was complex enough to justify more detailed backgrounders that couldn't be accommodated on *World News Tonight*. The grind of doing the new show as well as the evening news soon wore on Reynolds, and he began to be spelled with increasing frequency by Ted Koppel, an expert on foreign affairs who excelled at interviewing and explaining complicated developments. Arledge pressured Gralnick to come up with new angles, yet by February 1980, with no resolution of the crisis in sight, and virtually all the angles covered, the show had reached a seeming dead end.

The prudent course would have been to end the program and relinquish the time slot, but Arledge wanted ABC News to hang on to it. He proposed that the show broaden its focus and become a regularly scheduled broadcast—a shrewd bit of counterprogramming against NBC's *Tonight*, the longtime hit hosted by veteran comedian Johnny Carson. By this time, Koppel had emerged as its star, and when the time came to choose an anchor, he was everybody's first choice. Reluctantly, Pierce agreed, and, thanks in part to the goodwill generated by ABC's news advisory service, most affiliates agreed to clear the new show, now called *Nightline*. When first launched in March 1980, it was only twenty minutes long. But when it caught on among viewers, it was extended to half an hour—and when big stories broke, it routinely ran over, sometimes for a long as ninety minutes. Remarkably, Arledge had done what news chiefs at CBS and NBC had failed to do—get an extra half hour of time for news. And though it was at 11:30, and not an additional thirty minutes for the evening news, it was a big victory for ABC News.[38]

Nightline was a huge hit with critics and attracted a surprisingly large and loyal audience. It regularly bested CBS's late-night programming and sometimes came close to Johnny Carson. Popular among the well heeled and well educated, it became a desirable buy for advertisers, and because it aired late at night, not in prime time, where expectations were greater, its small audience was acceptable to Arledge's superiors. In 1983, they even allowed him to expand the program to an hour, a short-lived and ultimately unsuccessful experiment. Over time, *Nightline* got better and better. Koppel gradually assumed a

Ted Koppel's *Nightline* was the most lauded program launched by ABC during the Roone Arledge era. A longtime correspondent at the network, Koppel turned the program into an innovative and often spontaneous forum for reporting and analyzing a wide range of stories. Photo courtesy of ABC/Photofest.

more important role as managing editor, and producers introduced new features like split-screen technology, allowing him to interview multiple subjects in remote locations simultaneously. They also began the practice of broadcasting from abroad. In 1985, for example, the *Nightline* crew traveled to the apartheid state of South Africa for a series of landmark broadcasts, including a live discussion with a high-ranking South African government official and bishop Desmond Tutu, a spokesman for the oppressed black majority. It was the first time a representative of the South African government had spoken to Tutu — and it occurred on live television, much to Arledge's delight. In this instance, the program was not reporting the news but making it. *Nightline*'s most important feature was its flexibility. It could accommodate interviews as well as detailed investigative reports, and Koppel's extensive knowledge and authoritative style gave the show gravitas and cachet among news junkies and many viewers whose schedules didn't allow them to watch the evening newscasts. Exploiting what television could do best, broadcast unscripted live encounters between news-makers and a highly intelligent journalist, accompanied by filmed reports that offered background and analysis, *Nightline* was a milestone in TV journalism, ranking with *See It Now* and *60 Minutes* as one of the most distinguished and innovative shows in the medium's history.[39]

Arledge was also eager to remake ABC's aging and unpopular Sunday talk show, *Issues and Answers*. To give the new program instant credibility, he hired David Brinkley away from NBC. Brinkley had become uncomfortable at NBC, and he was excited by the proposal that Arledge made to him—serve as host of the Sunday program and play a central role in ABC's election coverage. When Brinkley signed on, Arledge was able to convince affiliates to give up an hour of time, allowing more than one guest and a roundtable discussion. Brinkley then persuaded his friend, the conservative columnist George Will, to join the program. At first, Brinkley and Will were accompanied by a rotating cast of Washington-based print journalists. But the program was dull and didn't attract much notice until ABC correspondent Sam Donaldson became a regular. Donaldson had developed a reputation as an aggressive, at times showboating reporter, and he brought an energy and unpredictability to the broadcast. Viewers were surprised at his outspokenness and penchant for sparring with Will, and his pointed questioning of guests occasionally ruffled feathers. Like Barbara Walters and Geraldo Rivera, Donaldson had an edge that elicited strong feelings, including negative ones, but he was great on television, especially on a program that gave him such leeway. And Brinkley very much enjoyed presiding over the show and ABC's political coverage, adding his considerable star power to the network's growing roster of talent.[40]

By the mid-1980s, Arledge had turned ABC News around. In the process, however, he had raised the stakes in the network news arms race. News division spending, already massive in the 1970s, reached new levels of profligacy as the other networks struggled to keep up with ABC. Much of it was a result of increased salaries. Thanks in large part to Arledge, not only stars but producers, reporters, directors, and technical personnel received big raises in the late 1970s and especially the early 1980s. It was also attributable to the expense of new technology. "Whatever you wanted, he would see that you got it," Brinkley recalled.[41] By emphasizing breaking news and investing in high-tech equipment that made it easier to deliver, Arledge forced his competitors to do the same. In his wake, all the networks were compelled to redesign their news programs. To the dismay of some critics and network journalists, this meant adopting some practices associated with local news. For example, network newscasts became faster-paced, with shorter stories and sound bites and a profusion of dazzling visual effects. But Arledge was also responsible for changes that elevated television journalism. He sought ways to make quality news programs that were interesting and exciting, and he succeeded more than he failed. Some of the visual aids introduced by ABC's producers, for example, enhanced understanding and made it easier to produce stories on subjects like economics. And his interest in covering events as they happened and broadcasting live interviews and discussions with newsmakers gave his programs immediacy and a notable frisson. Under Arledge, journalism was finally adapted to television.

The big loser, at least at first, was NBC. Its news division had lagged behind ratings leader CBS throughout the 1970s, and when Arledge created *World News Tonight*, the *NBC Nightly News* began to lose viewers. Some NBC executives blamed anchor John Chancellor's dry, professorial style. The real problem, however, was that NBC's newscast was so similar to CBS's; the network even hired Roger Mudd as Chancellor's coanchor in November 1980. But the program's ratings remained poor, even after Chancellor retired in 1982 and Tom Brokaw, the network's most impressive young star, joined Mudd as coanchor. In August 1983, NBC officials scrapped the two-anchor format and Brokaw became sole anchor of the *NBC Nightly News*.[42]

This would turn out to be a good move. Initially, however, the broadcast's ratings continued to flag, and removing Brokaw as host of *Today* hurt that program as well. Brokaw had built up a large following in his five and a half years on *Today*. Assisted by Jane Pauley, a young and appealing cohost, he had helped to keep the show popular after Barbara Walters's departure. But the competition with ABC's *Good Morning, America* had begun to make him uncomfortable. Unlike *Today*, which was produced by and accountable to NBC News, *GMA* was produced by ABC's entertainment division and was heavy on features and fawning celebrity interviews. Its budget—approximately $20 million—was 25 percent larger than *Today*'s, and because it was not technically a journalistic enterprise, its bookers could pay for interviews and offer other perks that would have been a breach of ethics for *Today*. To Brokaw's chagrin, competing with *GMA* meant emphasizing the same kinds of features, so his promotion to the *NBC Nightly News* was something of a relief.

When Brokaw left and was replaced by Bryant Gumbel, a former sportscaster, *Today* was surpassed in the ratings by GMA. Inspired by producer Steve Friedman, however, *Today* soon regained its lead. Gumbel developed into a first-rate interviewer, while Pauley, now a mature and versatile on-screen presence, became very popular with viewers. As critics noted, the program's revival was partially attributable to Friedman's willingness to emphasize the high-profile interviews and features that were GMA's stock-in-trade. But he sought to maintain *Today*'s journalistic integrity, and he took risks that paid off, like taking the show to remote locations like the Soviet Union, where Gumbel and Pauley examined US-Soviet relations. The trips were ideally suited for *Today*'s unique mix of hard news, interviews, and features. They became a tradition—not just for *Today* but for other news programs as well—further increasing news division budgets. But at NBC News, the added expense—which increased *Today*'s budget to over $35 million per year—was well worth it, since the show brought in between $150 and $200 million in ad revenues for the network and its affiliates.[43]

Today's revival was also fueled by the astonishing success of NBC's entertainment programs, which were wonderful platforms for promoting NBC News. During the 1980–1981 season, NBC's prime-time ratings were dismal, with one show in the top ten and only three in the top twenty. Seven years later, it had four of the top five rated programs, including *The Cosby Show* and *Cheers*, and eleven in the top twenty. NBC's rise was orchestrated by Grant Tinker, a successful independent producer. In 1984, Tinker hired an old friend and former colleague, Lawrence Grossman, to run NBC News. Grossman had overseen the development of PBS, and like Richard Salant, he was devoted to the television journalism's public-interest mission. But with a background in advertising and programming, he was also flexible and pragmatic. He endorsed Steve Friedman's innovations at *Today* and encouraged the producers of other programs to experiment. Indeed, with the ratings improving and ad revenues on the rise, Grossman was keen to strike out in new directions. He proposed abandoning the traditional half-hour newscast in favor of a ninety-minute "news wheel" that would involve collaboration with the network's affiliates and O-and-Os, and even suggested that NBC's parent company, RCA, buy Ted Turner's CNN and make it possible for the network to provide around-the-clock news.[44]

But Grossman's standing at NBC was undermined when, in June 1986, General Electric purchased RCA — and, with it, NBC. A dynamic conglomerate that had moved beyond its core business into lucrative new fields like finance, GE had been looking for a plum media asset that would enable it to get into cable television. Led by Jack Welch, an aggressive and widely respected chief executive, GE was renowned for its efficiency and relentless obsession with innovation and profits. Its corporate culture was radically different from RCA's, and the takeover immediately raised questions about how NBC, RCA's highly profitable but spoiled "child," would fare under a much stricter "parent." Unwilling to find out, Tinker promptly resigned, and Welch replaced him with Robert Wright, an executive who had risen through the ranks at GE and had most recently run its highly successful financial services division. Wright had no experience in broadcasting, and he was shocked by the industry's lax business practices and especially the cavalier attitude toward spending that prevailed at NBC News. Suddenly, what Grossman regarded as legitimate requests for additional resources — annual rituals at all three networks since the early 1960s — were met with demands that he reduce his spending and prioritize programs most likely to attract viewers. Looking back at his repeated conflicts with Wright and Welch, Grossman noted, "There was a real clash of cultures, a clash of values. . . . It went from being a heavenly job . . . to a real nightmare."[45] In the long run, Wright's plans for NBC would prove successful. In the short run, however, his new regime unsettled Grossman and his staff, and Grossman's often desperate efforts to please his bosses led him to lose credibility and the support of his subordinates, especially newly powerful stars like Brokaw and Gumbel. In the summer of 1988, he was fired and replaced by Michael Gartner, a print journalist and newspaper publisher who had been suggested to Wright by Brokaw.[46]

The network most unsettled by Roone Arledge and ABC, however, was CBS. Arledge's first two or three years at ABC were also years of transition at the perennial ratings leader. In 1978, Salant was compelled to retire, and he was succeeded by Bill Leonard, a longtime deputy who shared his values and priorities. Though Leonard failed to get an extra thirty minutes for the CBS *Evening News*, he oversaw the debut of a highly acclaimed news-and-features program, *Sunday Morning*. Hosted by Charles Kuralt and produced by Robert "Shad" Northshield, a veteran producer who had come over from NBC, it was launched in January 1979 and gained a devoted following. The show was inspired by the example of Sunday newspapers, with their variety of stories and often engrossing features on the arts, travel, and cultural trends, and it was perfect for Kuralt's relaxed and intellectual style. Its success encouraged Leonard to create a version for weekdays, with Kuralt paired with Diane Sawyer, an attractive, intelligent, and uncommonly poised newcomer. But the show's ratings were mediocre. Leonard's biggest coup was hanging on to Dan Rather, and negotiating what insiders called the "Cronkite succession." With the full support of Paley, CBS president Tom Wyman, and network chief Gene Jankowski, Leonard broke the bank to keep Rather. He concluded, however, that the expense was worth it. "He was the right age, had the right credentials, he was well known, he was popular on one of the most popular programs on television. . . . If you were on top, he could keep you there."[47]

But as Wyman adroitly pushed the aging Paley aside and assumed more power at the corporate level, the atmosphere at CBS began to change. Wyman was not a broadcaster; he had come from Pillsbury, and he did not regard the company's television network—or its news division—as the jewels that Paley did. Eager to milk its core divisions to pay for expansion into new fields, he began to pressure Jankowski to control costs and increase profits. Jankowski, a longtime CBS executive whose background was in sales and finance, had long viewed Salant as naïve and profligate, and he was eager to reduce the influence of "Salant people" at CBS News. He looked over at ABC and marveled at the changes that Arledge was making; at CBS, by contrast, the mere mention of changes that might liven up news programming elicited gasps of horror. When the Cronkite succession began to unravel, however, Jankowski got his big chance.[48]

Dan Rather took over for Cronkite in March 1981, and almost immediately, as expected, the ratings for the CBS Evening News declined. But they continued to fall throughout the summer and early fall, and Rather began to appear increasingly uncomfortable. Part of the problem was that, in homage to Cronkite, producer Sandy Socolow had made virtually no changes to the broadcast, ensuring that Cronkite's enormous shadow hung over Rather. And slotting Rather into Cronkite's role didn't exploit his experience as a reporter or his at times passionate style, which had worked so well on 60 Minutes. The decline in the ratings provided Jankowski with the perfect excuse to fire

Leonard and install a more forward-looking person as head of CBS News. "Competition from ABC News was severe and fierce," Jankowski recalled. "The people who were lobbying for the job from the inside came out of the stodgy past. I felt that they didn't have a feeling for what contemporary television was all about."[49] The man he chose was Van Gordon Sauter. A former print journalist, television news director, and local station manager, Sauter had boosted the ratings at CBS's O-and-Os in Chicago and Los Angeles. He had also acquired a reputation as a big spender. To help keep Sauter in line, Jankowski hired another successful local station manager, Ed Joyce, as his assistant. While Sauter provided the vision, Joyce would manage the proverbial store.[50]

Like Arledge, Sauter was critical of Salant-style network news. CBS News was not the *New York Times* or the *Washington Post*, he reminded the staff on numerous occasions. The goal should not be to tell people what they ought to know. Instead, it should be to give them stories that were "pertinent"—that appealed to their interests and satisfied their needs. And they should be conveyed in ways that ordinary people could understand. This, of course, was the gospel of local news, and having succeeded magnificently at stations throughout the nation, it was the closest thing in television to a sure thing. But it was heresy to the many "Salant people" in the news division, and they were aghast when Sauter and Joyce proclaimed it as the new mission of CBS News. Opposition to Sauter, however, was not universal. There were a number of younger producers—including Howard Stringer and Andrew Lack, who would rise to positions of prominence—who were frustrated by the stasis in the news division and eager to innovate. Operating on the margins, often as part of the small CBS *Reports* crew, they had been pushing Leonard to allow them to produce new-style "instant documentaries" more closely tied to breaking news. Young producers working on the evening news had been frustrated, too. They thought the Cronkite broadcast, which relied largely on unimaginative filmed reports from Washington and European capitals, had become pedantic and stale. Recognizing these potential allies, Sauter began cultivating their favor and ostracizing the old guard, whom he derided as "yesterday people."

By devoting most of his time to helping the CBS *Evening News* regain its number-one spot in the ratings, Sauter also won Rather's trust and support. With the assistance of Howard Stringer, who replaced Socolow as producer, Sauter and Rather completely revamped the broadcast. Some of the changes were cosmetic. They incorporated much of the technology that ABC was using to such good effect, and Stringer began shooting Rather from closer than the norm, a change that encouraged Rather to relax and regain his confidence. Rather even began wearing a sweater. But others changes were more substantive. Sauter instructed his producers and reporters to deemphasize Washington-based news and produce more stories about the American heartland. Political stories now had to focus on the impact of national policy on ordinary Americans, ideally through human-interest stories about particular families or communities. And the tenor of the broadcast became softer as Sauter and Stringer increased the frequency of features on consumer affairs, health, and lifestyle trends.[51]

As Rather told a reporter from *Esquire*, the new broadcast's aim was expressly evocative, to produce "moments": flashes of insight beyond the ken of conventional journalism. A moment, Rather explained, was when a viewer watches something and "feels it, smells it, and knows it." Generating moments was essential in order to connect with the audience and ensure that the broadcast was meaningful, and the new interest in eliciting them greatly influenced the selection of stories, which Sauter himself closely monitored. To determine which were most important and how they should be arranged in the line-up, Sauter, Stringer, and Rather relied in part on what Rather called the "back-fence principle," picking the stories that "two neighbor ladies leaning over a back fence" would be most interested in and want to discuss.[52] Sauter and Stringer also began to pressure correspondents to liven up their scripts and delivery and act more like "broadcasters," by which they meant "performers." Soon they began to favor those who were the best at this, leaving others, often longtime contributors, with fewer opportunities to appear on the CBS *Evening News*.

Sauter's makeover of the broadcast sparked howls of outrage from retired CBS people like Salant and Fred Friendly and the increasing number of Salant people who were pushed out or left in the first few months of the new regime. Even Cronkite, still under contract to produce specials and documentaries for the network and a member of the CBS board, was critical of the show-business values that Sauter had imported into the broadcast. But viewers loved it, and the CBS *Evening News* quickly rose in the ratings, reestablishing the comfortable lead that Cronkite's program had enjoyed before the latter's retirement—a lead that it would maintain for over four years.

But Sauter's reforms had other, unintended effects. A by-product of the new emphasis on "moments" and stories reported from the heartland was a recurring focus on the human costs of the economic restructuring the nation was undergoing—stories on plant closures and unemployed factory workers, the decline of once-vibrant blue-collar communities and family farms, and the rise of poverty and homelessness. And the program's interest in the impact of policies emanating from Washington did little to counter the impression that these problems were attributable to the pro-business agenda of the Reagan administration. Conservative intellectuals like George Will criticized the Rather broadcast for seeking to manipulate viewers, and the controversy reinforced the widely held impression that CBS was a bastion of liberal bias.[53]

This impression was strengthened in 1982, when critics blasted a CBS documentary and the network was inundated with negative publicity. Broadcast in January 1982, "The Uncounted Enemy: A Vietnam Deception" was produced by George Crile, one of the network's hot young producers, and narrated by Mike Wallace. It presented evidence that the US military, including general William Westmoreland, had engaged in a conspiracy to misinform the government and the American people about the strength of enemy forces in South Vietnam in the months before the Tet offensive. Enraged, Westmoreland sued the network for libel, and to quell its critics, Sauter ordered an inhouse investigation of the documentary. Led by a respected member of CBS News' old guard, it uncovered numerous problems with Crile's techniques, some of them quite significant—but nothing that contravened the program's conclusions. When its findings were leaked to the press, CBS suffered further embarrassment, not least because, by then, many more people had heard of the scandal through Westmoreland and his allies than had actually watched the program. CBS officials were greatly relieved when, after the case went to trial and it began to go badly for Westmoreland, he and the network reached a settlement that vindicated CBS. But CBS's victory was Pyrrhic. The revelations further tarnished its reputation and inspired conservative activists to mount a quixotic grassroots campaign to buy CBS stock, take over the company, and become "Dan Rather's boss."

While the new "Sauterized" CBS *Evening News* dominated the ratings, his other programming ventures were less successful and more controversial. In January 1982, Sauter fired Charles Kuralt and Shad Northshield from the CBS *Morning Show* and hired a new producer, George Merlis, to reshape the broadcast. Merlis, a former producer of ABC's *Good Morning, America*, kept Diane Sawyer, but he replaced Kuralt with Bill Kurtis, a popular and respected anchor from CBS's Chicago station. The new show moved decisively toward the formula that Merlis had developed at ABC—light banter among the hosts and lots of how-to stories and celebrity interviews—and, not surprisingly, its ratings steadily improved. In August 1983, it passed *Today* and went into second place. The show made Sawyer a star, and she eagerly accepted Don Hewitt's offer to join the cast of *60 Minutes*, in 1984. Instead of replacing her with one of the network's experienced young female correspondents, Sauter hired Phyllis George, a former Miss America and a sideline reporter for CBS Sports, at a salary of $1 million per year. George was totally lacking in relevant experience, but Sauter was certain she would "light up the screen." The experiment was a complete disaster. After eight gaffe-filled months, Ed Joyce, now news division president, removed her from the show—though CBS had to pay her for the remainder of her three-year contract.[54]

Sauter was also determined to reshape CBS's prime-time news programming. Gutting the staff responsible for the network's CBS *Reports* documentaries, Sauter hatched a plan to create an hour-long magazine-style show that would pair Charles Kuralt with newly hired Bill Moyers. The two men had each hosted thoughtful and highly praised half-hour programs during the summer of 1983. But Sauter was keen to put them together and create a program that would tap in to the new wave of Reagan-inspired patriotism that was sweeping the nation. The proposed broadcast, *American Parade*, would be fast paced and include a variety of features, including paeans to the "American spirit," interviews with rock stars, and a comedy news segment. Moyers, not surprisingly, refused to participate, and the program, retooled in the image of Kuralt's successful *On the Road*, aired in the spring of 1984 with Kuralt alone as host. Pitted against NBC's hit *The A-Team*, it was a ratings failure. But it was revived in the summer as *Crossroads*. Produced by Andrew Lack, it now included Moyers, who provided stories on political, religious, and cultural issues, while

Kuralt offered his customary features on off-beat subjects and themes. It brought out the best in its hosts and was praised by many critics. But Lack was eager to cover hipper subjects that interested neither Kuralt nor Moyers, and he persuaded Sauter to let him develop another magazine program. *Crossroads* was canceled after nine broadcasts, and a disgruntled Moyers went back to PBS.[55]

Sauter's willingness to support the creation of a new magazine-style program was disconcerting to Don Hewitt. Sauter respected Hewitt and was impressed with the success he had achieved with *60 Minutes*. By the mid-1980s, however, its audience was getting older, and Sauter and Howard Stringer, who had become Sauter's assistant and would become president of CBS News, wondered how long it could go on. And so they endorsed Lack's plan to create a new show that might appeal to younger viewers and, perhaps, eventually take *60 Minutes'* place. Lack's project, *West 57th*, debuted as a summer replacement in 1985. It starred four young CBS correspondents and employed quick cuts and other technical gimmicks that gave it a distinctly modern look. The program's segments ran the gamut from serious investigative pieces to celebrity profiles, with a heavy emphasis on rock musicians and comedians and subjects that were vaguely salacious—religious cults, drugs, the porn industry. It was panned by critics and unpopular with viewers. Hewitt dismissed it as "light summer fare." But Sauter and Stringer loved it, and they brought it back in the spring of 1986 and again in 1987, when it began a steady run that lasted until 1989. Despite this unprecedented commitment, it failed to attract viewers, and when it was canceled, Hewitt was vindicated.[56]

Under Sauter and Joyce there wasn't just a change in the content of the news. The network's extensive and widely praised newsgathering apparatus also began to be cut back. During the 1970s, news division expenditures had ballooned, and Jankowski and CBS president Tom Wyman were eager to bring them under control. With the cost of talent and new technology increasing, however, this was virtually impossible. Things became more complicated when, in 1985, Ted Turner began putting together financing to buy CBS. Unlike the conservative grassroots campaign to become "Dan Rather's boss," Turner's takeover bid was serious, and it frightened Wyman and Bill Paley. To stave off Turner and any other potential suitors and protect their company's independence, Wyman initiated a stock buy-back program that vastly increased CBS's debt. Paying down this debt became more dif-

ficult when the television network, one of the company's most profitable divisions, suffered a decline in the ratings and the spread of cable
caused a slump in the advertising market. The network's divisions
were ordered to cut their expenses, and with lots of money devoted to
salaries, Sauter and Joyce were forced to cut elsewhere, closing down
news bureaus and firing many longtime employees.[57]

The cuts increased when Wyman was deposed by the CBS board
and, with Paley's support, the investor Laurence Tisch increased his
stake in the company and became its president in September 1986.
Many CBS people, including most of the news division, had hoped
Tisch would be their savior, and they rejoiced when, as one of his first
acts, he fired Sauter and made Howard Stringer the new president of
CBS News. But, typical of the new breed of corporate raiders that were
coming to dominate the American economy, Tisch saw CBS as an investment, and he soon began selling off its pieces and downsizing the
ones he wanted to keep, like the television network and CBS News.
What mattered to Tisch was the company's stock value, and he was
convinced that this depended on controlling costs. Wyman and Jankowski had already forced Sauter and Joyce to make substantial cuts
that had hurt morale; now Stringer was ordered to make even bigger ones. Bureaus in the US and overseas were closed; the ones that
weren't shut down saw their staff cut to the bare minimum. CBS's Paris
bureau was left with a single correspondent. After being "Tisched," the
network was left with a smaller newsgathering infrastructure than its
two rivals.

Tisch's relentless cost-cutting attracted negative publicity—not
least because CBS employees were eager to complain to reporters—
and the network's dirty laundry became a long-running soap opera in
the press. Dan Rather and a CBS producer, Richard Cohen, even published an op-ed in the *New York Times* in March 1987 decrying Tisch's
evisceration of the news division. Interested only in the bottom line,
Tisch was leading the network "from Murrow to mediocrity." Other
ex-CBS journalists, including Walter Cronkite, expressed similar concerns.

To many observers, it seemed as if not just CBS but the entire television news industry was in the midst of an existential crisis. At NBC,
Robert Wright had begun a campaign to cut waste from the news division's bloated budget and make it "lean and mean," the GE way. And
ABC's new owners, the television station group Capital Cities, who ac-

quired the network in 1986, had begun to limit Roone Arledge's free-spending ways. At the time, it was very easy to blame the new owners for all the changes that were occurring in the television news business—the dismantling of bureaus and reduction in newsgathering capacity, the preference for flashy new programming that featured stars and seemed more likely to appeal to viewers and make a profit, the increasing reliance on techniques and talent imported from local news.

But this was unfair. In fact, spending under the old regime was unsustainable and would likely have been cut even if corporate patriarchs like Leonard Goldenson, David Sarnoff, and William Paley had continued at the helm. By the mid-1980s, the three networks were annually spending in excess of $250 million each to produce news programs and maintain their bureaus and infrastructure, with CBS and ABC close to $300 million. This might have been tolerable if the news divisions were big profit centers and could have compensated for the even more extravagant costs of renting entertainment programs. But, despite some programs that earned profits, they were money-losers in an industry in the grips of a growing financial crunch. The financial crunch made developing more popular and profitable programs even more urgent. It reinforced the industry's initial efforts to create different kinds of programming and created a more hospitable environment for the Arledges and Sauters and the many young producers and journalists who had begun their careers in local news and were eager to bring some of its innovations to the networks.

For almost thirty years, the networks had provided viewers with a regular diet of elite-defined news—information that journalists thought people ought to know. Amazingly, they continued to do this after audience research and the success of local news programs clearly revealed that this was not what most viewers wanted. They got away with it because of the FCC's relatively strict interpretation of their "public-interest" requirements and the fact that their colleagues in the entertainment divisions were making tons of money for the networks as a whole and were in a position to subsidize their efforts—and, most important of all, because they were sheltered from competition.

Eventually, however, the growing popularity of cable TV and VCRs, which allowed consumers to watch movies and television programs on tape and, God forbid, fast-forward through commercials, made the industry more competitive and unpredictable. No longer sheltered, the network news divisions were forced to abandon the high-

5

REBIRTH

When, in late 1978, television industry insiders heard that an all-news cable channel was in the works, few of them were surprised. Cable was the next big thing, and scores of new channels were being launched. Rumors had been circulating for months that several groups were sizing up the prospects of an all-news channel, and it seemed inevitable that one or more of them would find a way to turn their plans into reality. But insiders were surprised by the person who emerged from the pack to announce that he would be the first to do so: the cable-TV impresario Ted Turner.

The reckless and entitled son of a wealthy billboard magnate, Turner hadn't seemed destined for much more than a life of exuberant carousing. He was a poor student and perennial discipline problem, and as an adolescent and young man, he devoted most of his energies to competitive sailing. But his father's suicide saddled him with new responsibilities, and in his mid-twenties he began to turn his life around. A congenital risk-taker, he quickly parlayed his father's business into a thriving media empire.[1]

Its centerpiece was an Atlanta-based UHF television station, which he bought in 1970. Specializing in old sitcoms from the 1950s and early 1960s, even older movies, and sports, it had soon gained a large following. Turner shrewdly promoted his station as a wholesome alternative to the turn toward "relevance" at the networks, enabling him to capitalize on the cultural alienation many white Southerners were beginning to feel toward network television and the "East Coast establishment." And he was able to vastly expand its audience by investing in microwave relay towers, which allowed him to reach viewers well beyond his station's original forty-mile radius. By 1975, it had become a regional powerhouse, with fans throughout the South.

News, however, was virtually absent from its schedule. Required by FCC rules to provide at least some of it, Turner offered a no-frills newscast at 3:00 AM. Hosted by Bill Tush, a jocular weatherman, it consisted of little more than a summary of the latest wire-service headlines. The hour of the day brought out the comedian in Tush. He routinely brought his German shepherd, dressed in suit and tie, onto the set to serve as his "coanchor," and on at least one occasion he read the news while wearing a mask bearing the likeness of Walter Cronkite. In the mid-1970s, when Turner was approached at a cable-industry convention by a syndicator interested in selling him a package of news produced by professional broadcast journalists, he dismissed him out of hand. "I hate news," he announced to anyone within earshot. News wasn't what he or his media properties were about. He was a purveyor of escapist entertainment—and proud of it.

So Turner was just about the last person that most insiders expected to establish an all-news cable channel. He had never expressed any interest in journalism, and his other ventures reflected the sensibility of a salesman, someone who understood the public's tastes and was happy to cater to them. But Turner was also an adroit businessman, and he understood far better than others the direction in which the television industry was headed.

Cable was originally conceived to provide Americans in remote, mountainous locations with access to conventional broadcast signals—an adjunct to the larger broadcast industry, the many VHF and UHF stations that beamed their signals from transmitters to the aerial antennas that were perched on the vast majority of American homes. Cable operators built huge mountain-top towers that captured distant broadcast signals and then sent them through wires to the homes of subscribers who lived in places where over-the-air signals could not reach. In the mid-1970s, many cable operators became intrigued by the idea of employing satellites rather than big antennas. Satellite transmission offered viewers a high-quality picture unaffected by the vagaries of the weather. More important, it made it possible for entrepreneurs to develop new sources of programming outside the confines of the broadcasting industry.

The shift to satellite transmission was a momentous development. By the late 1970s, as more and more cable operators opted for satellites and new, satellite-distributed cable channels were launched, the cable industry began to turn into something quite different: a service offering subscribers a growing number of channels that were available only on cable and competed directly with over-the-air broadcasters. Newly established cable channels like Time Warner's HBO beamed their programming from uplinks to commercial satellites on which they leased transponders, devices that allowed them to beam it back down to the earth stations of multiple cable operators, who then sent it through coaxial wires to subscribers. Convinced that satellites were the wave of the future, cable operators, including firms like TelePrompTer and TCI, which owned multiple systems in cities throughout the US, began installing earth stations to pick up the increasing number of channels that were opting for satellite distribution. One of these cable channels was WTBS, Ted Turner's successful UHF station. In 1976, eager to develop a national audience, Turner had purchased an uplink, leased a transponder, and turned it into what he called, with typical bombast, the nation's first "superstation." The cable TV industry was entering a new era.[2]

Its growth was encouraged by a renewed political and cultural interest in diversity and consumer choice. Sensing that new options were appearing on cable, municipalities began granting franchises to cable operators to wire the homes of their residents and establish cable service, even if they already enjoyed easy access to broadcast signals. Meanwhile, cable operators introduced new technology that expanded the number of channels on their menus. The availability of new slots on cable menus, in turn, spurred entrepreneurs and media companies to create new cable channels that were likely to be appealing to viewers and sparked a migration of consumers to cable TV, especially in areas where cable had been slow to develop. Advertisers began to see the potential of the industry and urged their clients to shift some of their advertising dollars to cable. This was vital, particularly for the majority of cable channels, like WTBS, that were available to consumers as part of relatively low-cost basic programming packages; subscribing to premium channels like HBO required paying an additional fee and allowed such channels to forgo advertising. Advertising offered cable operators and the owners of basic cable channels an additional revenue stream, augmenting the sums they earned from subscriber's fees. As cable became more popular in the 1980s, these twin streams would continue to grow, enabling cable operators to increase channel capacity and inspiring the founding of even more cable channels.

The prospect of new cable services reaching a national audience disturbed the networks, which had long relied on the FCC to protect their oligopoly. Throughout the 1960s, the FCC had kept the cable industry under wraps, largely to prevent it from undermining local broadcasters and the networks. Beginning in the late 1960s, however, government officials began to recognize cable television's potential for reaching small, more specialized audiences, complementing rather than duplicating the networks' strategy of programming for a mass audience. In a series of important rulings during the early-to-mid-1970s, the FCC opened the way for the cable industry's expansion—but in a way, it hoped, that would protect the interests of broadcasters. "Must-carry" regulations ensured that the signals of local broadcasters were included in the basic package that cable operators offered consumers; cable operators were also prohibited from importing the signals of distant stations at the expense of local ones. Subsequent rulings were similarly encouraging of the industry's growth—and of its growing reliance on satellite-distributed channels. Portraying themselves as champions of consumer choice, cable operators and programmers were able to gain the support of much of the public, Congress, and the FCC, and they moved aggressively to take full advantage of it.

By 1980, a number of new cable channels had been established, and there were signs suggesting the direction in which the industry would soon move. Turner's "superstation" represented one model. Airing network chestnuts like *Leave It to Beaver* and *Petticoat Junction*, old movies, sports, including all the games played by Turner's Atlanta Braves, and, at 6:00 PM, opposite local and network news, reruns of the science-fiction series *Star Trek*, it relied on a mix of program genres that had long been fixtures on network TV. Its novelty was that it offered them at times when they weren't being broadcast by the networks, giving viewers a real choice. An even more successful strategy, especially in the long run, was specialization: channels like the Reverend Pat Robertson's Christian Broadcast Network (CBN); Warner Amex's Nickelodeon, which produced programs for children; and ESPN, an all-sports channel. At CBN, Nickelodeon, and ESPN particular types of programming became their brands. Viewers came to realize that they could turn to them at any time for the kinds of programs in which they specialized, rather than wait for the particular times or days when they were broadcast by the networks. And the emergence of specialized channels encouraged the development of new programming that would never have appeared on network TV. Advertisers soon recognized that specialized channels were well suited for reaching specific niches of the consumer market, and their interest ensured that specialization would become the cable industry's preferred business model.[3]

Perhaps the most intriguing new cable channel was the Cable-Satellite Public Affairs Network, or C-SPAN. Conceived by Brian Lamb, the editor of a cable-industry trade publication, and financed by cable operators as a public service to viewers, it debuted in 1979, providing continuous coverage of the House of Representatives. When the House wasn't in session, it broadcast special government hearings, press conferences, and related events. In 1986, a sister channel, C-SPAN2, devoted to the US Senate, was established. Thanks to revenues from subscriber fees, C-SPAN's programming continued to expand. By the late 1980s, Lamb and his staff broadcast in-depth interviews with political newsmakers and leading authors. The founding of C-SPAN cheered champions of the cable industry, confirming their hopes that the new technology might be able to do more than provide mindless entertainment. That only a tiny fraction of cable households even watched it didn't matter; its mere existence was cause for celebration. On cable, an unregulated medium, the "public interest" was being served.[4]

With specialization an attractive formula for distinguishing a cable channel from its rivals as well as from the networks, the idea of a cable channel specializing in news made sense—at least in the abstract. But most of the entrepreneurs and cable executives who considered it were discouraged by its anticipated cost. This was because they assumed that any new cable news venture would require the same infrastructure and investment as the networks: expensive technology, a large staff at its headquarters, and a network of bureaus around the country and the world.

Turner recognized the implications of specialization. He understood that, despite WTBS's success, the future would belong not to mixed entertainment channels but to ones that provided viewers with particular types of programming. HBO seemed destined to become the go-to place for recently released movies, and, much to his chagrin, he knew that the founders of ESPN had beat him to sports. No one, however, had yet to claim news. He began to sound out his friends and business associates, even the cab drivers who ferried him around. He would ask, "What if you could turn on your TV any time of the day or night and find out what's happening in the world?" Coming from the man who had given the world Bill Tush, it seemed a bit quixotic and out of character—until the fall of 1978, when he phoned Reese Schonfeld to find out if the idea was feasible.[5]

Schonfeld was the news syndicator who had tried to persuade Turner to put some real news on WTBS. He was a veteran journalist and news executive. As an editor at United Press in the 1960s, he had been responsible for the production of news film for distribution to non-network television stations, an uphill struggle that had made him resentful of the networks. He was especially irked by their ability to get heavily discounted rates from AT&T for their continuous use of its coaxial cables to feed their programs to affiliates. Schonfeld's outfit, UPI Television News, was charged considerably more for its occasional use of the same cables when it sent its package to member stations. This perennial disadvantage inspired Schonfeld's interest in satellites, which promised to cut distribution costs by approximately 90 percent. Here, it seemed, was a real alternative to relying on lines leased from AT&T. It might allow an intrepid news organization to provide news to non-network independent stations and perhaps even satisfy the growing demand for news among network affiliates.[6]

In 1975, Schonfeld established a nonprofit cooperative, the Independent Television News Association (ITNA). Its members were big-city stations unaffiliated with the networks. They had long broadcast successful tabloid-style local news programs but had experienced difficulties acquiring filmed reports of distant national and international events. Schonfeld would provide them with this material. With their seed money, he hired a small staff and opened a few bureaus, allowing ITNA reporters and colleagues in the news departments at member stations to provide some semblance of national coverage. To gain access to international news, he secured agreements with several foreign news organizations; in exchange for ITNA-produced news about the US, they would provide Schonfeld's outfit with news from Europe and beyond. ITNA staffers would then cut and paste this material into packages and send them to member stations via satellite, and stations could use the packages as they saw fit during their 10:00 PM newscasts. By the late 1970s, ITNA was even able to provide live feeds of certain breaking news stories. The new service was popular with member stations, enhancing the scope and quality of their newscasts. And the prospect of gaining access to breaking news from a source other than the "Big Three" intrigued some network affiliates. ITNA's success, Schonfeld later wrote, "proved that a news company could survive on television without an entertainment subsidy. . . . It was the blueprint for CNN."[7]

Schonfeld had heard Turner was interested in establishing an all-news cable outlet. His previous dealings with the Atlanta tycoon, however, hadn't been very inspiring, so he was surprised when Turner called. "Can it be done?" Turner asked. "Yes," Schonfeld replied, but only if its founders adopted the right strategy — relying extensively on computers and videotape technology, maintaining a small, nonunion staff and only a few domestic bureaus, and forging agreements with local stations and foreign news outfits to provide much of the new organization's coverage, as he had done at ITNA. Even then, Schonfeld warned, it would probably require an upfront investment of $20 million and then at least another $1 million per month to keep it going during its first couple of years. All told, it could take as much as $100 million to get it to the point where advertising revenues and subscription fees would match annual expenditures, and any profits would have to be reinvested in the business in order to expand its newsgathering capacity and fend off rivals.

After visiting Turner in Atlanta, Schonfeld was impressed with his commitment and agreed to help him develop the new service, which Turner decided to call the Cable News Network. To raise the necessary money, Turner sold one of his most valuable assets, a TV station he owned in North Carolina. He made Schonfeld CNN's president, and they set out to convince cable operators to add CNN to their basic cable menus. In May 1979, they traveled to Las Vegas to promote CNN at an industry convention. In tow was former CBS correspondent Daniel Schorr, CNN's first hire. Schorr had worked for Schonfeld at ITNA after his firing from CBS in the mid-1970s, and Turner hired him because of his name and the instant credibility he might bring to their venture. In his eagerness to have Schorr on board before their trip to Las Vegas, Turner drafted a contract that allowed the former CBS newsman unprecedented journalistic freedom. "We agreed that I would not be required to perform any assignment that I felt went against my own journalistic standards." Looking back, Schorr noted,

"It was a contract clause I've never had before or since."[8] Indeed, the more time that Schorr spent with Turner, the more impressed he became. He seemed a modern-day Bill Paley.

The Vegas presentation was a smashing success. Turner got commitments from a number of influential cable operators, and their interest sparked others to sign up, too. He offered CNN to them for twenty cents per subscriber—fifteen if they also took WTBS. Turner and Schonfeld returned to Atlanta triumphant. Drawing on Schonfeld's expertise in news production, they found a suitable site for CNN's headquarters, an old country club adjacent to Georgia Tech. Its large former ballrooms were easily converted to offices and a state-of-the-art studio and production facility, where computers and scores of videotape editing machines were installed; in back was more than enough space for the satellite dishes that were needed to acquire footage and completed reports from afar and transmit CNN's feed to cable operators. Basing CNN in Atlanta was crucial. Georgia was a "right-to-work" state where workers had difficulty forming unions, and Schonfeld was adamant that CNN could not succeed unless it was a non-union shop.

To help get CNN off the ground, Schonfeld hired an experienced team of executives and producers. They included Burt Reinhardt, a longtime associate at United Press International Television News, who became Schonfeld's second-in-command; Ted Kavanau, a veteran director of local newscasts, who was put in charge of developing CNN's programming; and Ed Turner, an experienced producer and station-group executive, who became responsible for newsgathering. They were joined by several of Schonfeld's former employees at ITNA and some important hires with extensive network experience. Jim Kitchell, for example, had worked at NBC News for almost thirty years, directing *The Huntley-Brinkley Report* and special events like the Apollo 11 moon landing. Sam Zelman had produced the Los Angeles–based *Big News* for KNXT in the early 1960s and gained a wealth of experience at CBS, establishing foreign bureaus, supervising election coverage, and working with Don Hewitt on *60 Minutes*. But as network vets like Kitchell and Zelman soon came to realize, Turner and Schonfeld weren't interested in replicating the broadcast journalism produced by the networks.[9]

In their initial discussions about what CNN might look like, Turner had proposed a revolving two-hour news "wheel," with recurring half-hour segments devoted to hard news, weather, sports, and entertainment-oriented features. Schonfeld convinced him that, while this format might be effective in the abstract, ensuring that all the bases were covered, it was too rigid. Instead, he argued that CNN should focus on breaking news: when something significant occurred, they should drop everything and "go live." This was a prospect that had long tantalized television news professionals. Before the 1970s, however, producing live reports required extensive planning and costly, cumbersome equipment. Live coverage was best suited for events that were scheduled in advance, like political conventions. And at the networks there was always the problem of preempting lucrative entertainment programs. Going live cost money and ran the risk of angering advertisers, who had paid for spots to appear among sitcoms, dramas, and variety shows—not coverage of airplane hijackings or natural disasters. A story had to be really big for the news divisions to be allowed to get on the air; usually they were only allowed to broadcast a brief bulletin. By the 1970s, this was particularly frustrating, since the networks were investing in portable satellite technology that made unscheduled live coverage more feasible. With such technology and correspondents stationed in bureaus throughout the nation and much of the world, the networks were finally in a position to provide viewers were breaking news. But with airtime so valuable and under the control of network executives, they were prevented from doing so. Their business was broadcasting popular entertainment programs, not supplying viewers with the latest breaking news.

Schonfeld understood this, and his plan was designed to exploit this gap. Devoted to news alone, and with access to cable subscribers' fees lessening its dependence on advertising, CNN could afford to go live as much as possible—and it could stay with developing stories without having to worry about losing viewers or offending advertisers. The key was keeping costs low. Before launch, he and his team established six domestic bureaus—in Washington, New York, Chicago, Dallas, Los Angeles, and San Francisco—and two abroad, in London and Rome. They hired experienced journalists to run them, but they were shoestring operations, with no more than a handful of employees. Most CNN staffers, in Atlanta as well as in the bureaus, were young and inexperienced, some of them right out of college. They were expected to perform several different jobs—filming, writing, editing, and reporting—that at the networks were sharply differentiated and subject to strict union rules. This system minimized costs and ensured that CNN's young staffers gained a wide range of experience and became seasoned professionals far sooner than if they had gone to work for CBS or ABC.

Producing a continuous news service with such a small staff and so few bureaus was impossible. To compensate, Schonfeld resorted to the strategy he had conceived at ITNA—gaining the cooperation of local television stations and foreign news organizations so that CNN could rely on them to cover stories that were beyond the range of its own personnel. An aide, Jane Maxwell, was assigned the task of contacting news directors and persuading them to sign reciprocal agreements with CNN. In exchange for access to their coverage of news in their local areas, CNN would provide them with its coverage of more distant news. The plan was not only practical but ingenious. Because of the popularity of local news programs, many stations had beefed up their news departments and were equipped to provide first-rate reports, and they were eager for material—especially video footage—that would extend the scope of their newscasts. Schonfeld also secured agreements with several foreign news outlets, often the same ones he had worked with while at ITNA. Their cooperation allowed CNN to provide more than a smattering of international news.

Schonfeld was especially determined to avoid the high salaries that the biggest stars at the networks commanded. Even more than unions, they had become a huge drain on the budgets of the networks. At CNN, news would be the star. Instead of the system that prevailed at the networks, in which a small cast of anchors and correspondents hogged the limelight, CNN would downplay its anchors and on-air staff in favor of creating a large, essentially interchangeable ensemble. Schonfeld and his aides wanted competent, attractive anchors who would be good team players, and they went through scores of audition tapes to find people appropriate for CNN. Initially, Schonfeld favored a format with a sole male anchor, and he expected to recruit from the networks. But Sam Zelman convinced him that a dual-anchor system would be better, and he pushed for male-female anchor teams, the format that had become popular in local news.

Regardless of their background, CNN's anchors had to be able to ad lib and interact with reporters in the field as well as read tell-stories, skills that veterans of local newscasts were most likely to have mastered. But Schonfeld and his senior staff were determined to avoid the vacuous "happy talk" that marred so many local news programs, and they crafted a format that sought to ensure that anchors and correspondents restrict their conversations, as much as possible, to the news. It would be delivered quickly, with most reports no more than a minute or two in length, and it would be kept fresh through continuous updates—if possible, with live reports from the scene. Having experience in local news, Schonfeld, Zelman, and Ted Kavanau understood something that the networks had been slow to recognize—that, while CNN had lots of airtime, producers would drive away most viewers if they filled it with long, detailed stories. Stories had to be short. Detail and complexity would be introduced through updates and the development of new angles, an approached that made CNN's news coverage very different from that of its network rivals.

In addition to anchors and reporters, Schonfeld and his staff also hired assorted "experts" to provide commentary and be available for questioning when stories related to their areas of competence arose. Some of them—like the psychic Jeane Dixon, the psychologist and TV personality Dr. Joyce Brothers, consumer advocate Ralph Nader, Senator Barry Goldwater, and the feminist politician Bella Abzug—were well known, and their hiring was intended to raise CNN's profile at relatively little expense. Others were unknown and came to value CNN for the opportunity that it offered them to increase their visibility and professional prestige. CNN's growing reliance on experts led the news channel to create an entire booking department to guarantee that it never lacked knowledgeable talking heads for its anchors to interview. Two experts who appeared regularly during CNN's early years were the newspaper columnists Rowland Evans and Robert Novak. They offered regular political commentary, particularly during election campaigns. When covering political stories, CNN producers were careful to include conservatives as well as liberals. And their ability to devote plenty of time to particular stories created a more fluid and spontaneous environment, where outside experts had the freedom to comment at considerable length. With anchors and reporters—with the exception of Daniel Schorr—prohibited from engaging in commentary, experts came to play an important role, making CNN a place for lively discussion as well as breaking news.

CNN programming was envisioned as a continuous flow. Live reports of breaking news would be followed by regular, continuously updated news summaries composed of anchor-read tell-stories and conventional filmed packages, then more breaking news, and so on. Teams of anchors would put in two-hour shifts, picking up the stories that their predecessors had been covering, as if passing a baton in a never-ending relay race. It was a format that would allow viewers to tune in at any time and quickly find out what was going on. And if they chose to watch for an hour or more, they would end up better informed, about a wider variety of things, than if they had watched the typical two-hour block of local and network news broadcast in the evenings or two hours of *Today* or *Good Morning, America*. Better still, they could tune in at any time—not at the specific time when the networks and their affiliates had chosen. This was a particularly important innovation. Watching TV at the dinner hour would become increasingly inconvenient for many Americans as the nation's economy became postindustrial and service-oriented and the regular rhythms of 9-to-5 employment were replaced by a diversity of work schedules and family activities. With CNN offering news around the clock, there was no longer any need to wait for Walter Cronkite or John Chancellor to know what was happening in the world. As CNN's programming became more professional, there was no longer much need to watch *any* news produced by the networks—unless you were a fan of their big stars, which, of course, gave them even more leverage to bid up their salaries and pull the networks even deeper into the red.

Turner was a master counterprogrammer, and he and Schonfeld concluded that CNN could also benefit from a having a centerpiece during prime time, when the networks aired entertainment programs and it was impossible to find news on TV. That centerpiece was *Prime News 120*, a two-hour newscast they scheduled at 8:00 PM, just as the networks were beginning their three-hour blocks of sitcoms and dramas. It would present a summary of the day's top stories, interspersed with live reports, expert commentary, and interviews with newsmakers, adding "perspective" to the randomness of CNN's continuous news programming. And with two hours at their disposal, they could cover stories in far more detail than the networks.[10]

Prime News would not be the only deviation from CNN's continuous flow. Turner and Schonfeld were also committed to broadcasting programs dedicated to news in specific fields, scheduled to offset the offerings of the networks and local independents. Financial news would be delivered in special segments several times a day, culminating in a half-hour business-news program at 7:00 PM. Sports news would also be a fixture, with detailed, half-hour sports reports, complete with highlights, airing in the evenings and late at night, to include results from the West Coast. And after *Prime News*, CNN would broadcast a news-oriented talk show, and after recaps of business news and sports, a program devoted to entertainment news. Some of this material would be repeated—often in abbreviated slices. Other special segments would cover consumer news, medical news, and fashion. CNN would also broadcast national weather reports, just like the networks did on their morning programs.

CNN's focus on sports and financial news was particularly important and central to its strategy of counterprogramming. The networks had never done much sports reporting, aside from occasional features on the nightly news; even the practice of recapping baseball and football scores fell by the wayside in the 1960s, when hard news become their primary emphasis and sports reporting became the specialty of local news programs—who, understandably, emphasized local teams and competitions at the expense of out-of-town ones. Recognizing this gap in coverage, Turner and Schonfeld resolved to provide a national sports report covering all major sports and all teams equally, despite Turner's ownership of MLB, NBA, and NHL franchises in Atlanta. It quickly became one of the channel's most popular features.

CNN's aggressive move into financial news was even more successful. Here, too, competition from the networks was negligible. Aside from cursory summaries of the stock market, the networks didn't cover much business and economic news. The popularity of PBS's *Wall Street Week*, however, suggested that there might be a substantial audience for it. Schonfeld hired Myron Kandel, a business editor at the *New York Post*, to serve as CNN's financial editor and oversee all business stories on the fledgling news channel. Most of them appeared in clearly identifiable segments in regular intervals throughout the day. They were summarized on *Moneyline*, a half-hour financial-news program hosted by Lou Dobbs, a former local news anchor who had worked in the financial industry. He and former *Wall Street Journal* columnist Dan Dorfman, who provided stock tips and other inside dope, made a good team, and *Moneyline* became a big hit for CNN, attracting advertisers and making a star of Dobbs. He became the program's managing editor and, eventually, a vice president of CNN.

The 10:00 PM talk show was also a success. In Schonfeld's view, it was the natural follow-up to CNN's prime-time newscast, and like many radio interview programs, it allowed viewers to call in and ask questions of the program's guests: "On *Prime News*, we told you what was the most important story of the day. At ten o'clock, we wanted the most important player in the most important story to be on our air, to talk to our journalists, and to be available to take questions from every-body in America."[11] Schonfeld understood that the program needed a good host, someone with wide knowledge who knew how to interview and make guests feel at ease. The problem was money. He didn't have much to offer the candidate he most preferred, David Frost. And so he hired Sandi Freeman, a successful talk-show host from Chicago. Free-man's program was popular and established the precedent of booking celebrities as well as important newsmakers, making it one of CNN's softer shows. The program really took off when Larry King, a popular radio personality who excelled at celebrity interviews, replaced Free-man in 1985.

Throughout the broadcast day, CNN sought to blur the conventions of network and local news, something Turner and Schonfeld regarded as essential if they were going to attract viewers other than confirmed news junkies. That meant covering important national and interna-tional news, as the networks did. Yet it also meant, when possible, covering it in ways that made it relevant to ordinary viewers, in lan-guage they could understand. The luxury of time would allow CNN to go to the scene of news and interview a wide range of people affected by it, not just the big shots and official spokespersons who dominated the stories produced by the networks. And it would enable CNN to turn regularly to the staff at its bureaus and weave their reports—and faces—into the broadcast, allowing them to become as familiar to viewers as the rotating anchor teams based in Atlanta. Ample airtime would also let CNN produce stories on subjects that would never ap-pear on the networks, giving the news channel a more eclectic and at times even humorous tenor. CNN's coverage, in short, pushed in both directions—toward more complete and in-depth stories on hard-news subjects that were the networks' specialty, and toward the soft features and human-interest stories that were a staple of local news.

As the date of CNN's launch approached, Turner's sales team hustled to line up advertisers. Their first big account was Bristol-Myers, a com-pany that specialized in over-the-counter drugs. Interested in buying spots adjacent to medical and consumer-news reports, it made a bold, ten-year commitment. General Mills, Time-Life, and Sears signed up as well, but only short-term. By the end of May 1980, the sales department had acquired seventeen sponsors. After CNN began broadcasting and attracting viewers, many others purchased airtime—though not enough to compensate for the huge losses that Turner was incurring. CNN's operating costs were approximately $2 million per month. And though Turner and Schonfeld anticipated a steady increase in subscribers' fees as more households were wired for cable, they realized that it would take months, maybe even years, for CNN to break even, particularly since Turner was determined to expand its news-gathering capacity by hiring more staff and establishing new bureaus.

CNN went on the air at 6:00 PM on June 1, 1980. After a few introductory remarks by Turner, Dave Walker and Lois Hart began reporting the news. The first hour included reports from New York, Washington, Jerusalem, Key West, and Fort Wayne, Indiana, where Daniel Schorr interviewed President Carter. Additional footage from the Carter interview would be broadcast throughout the evening. There were glitches, including the loss of a feed from the New York bureau, and an atmosphere of high anxiety gripped staffers behind the scenes. Considering the obstacles, however, things began well. At the end of the first hour, Hart told viewers, "Stay with us. We're going to have all kinds of news, sports, weather, and special features, from now on and forever."[12]

Reviews were mostly positive, with a number of commentators expressing surprise that the brash Turner had pulled it off. CNN's tone, Tony Schwartz of the *New York Times* wrote, was "serious, professional, and credible," regardless of the time of the day. Schwartz was especially impressed with *Prime News* anchor Kathleen Sullivan, who exhibited a "well-paced, no-nonsense style." Too many of her colleagues, however, were "eerily interchangeable, uniformly attractive and articulate but bland and one-dimensional." And some people who appeared on its specialty programs, he insisted, were ill suited for TV. Schwartz and other TV critics gave the highest marks to CNN's live coverage of breaking news. They also noted, however, that having so much airtime had a downside: it encouraged producers to include lots of filler and make too much of minor stories. All told, CNN's debut was a boon for viewers interested in news, and if it played to its strengths, it could develop into a news service of "genuine distinction."[13]

By the end of 1980, CNN was available on over six hundred cable systems throughout the US and reached 4.3 million homes, more

The cable television tycoon Ted Turner launched CNN in 1980. Virtually everyone except Turner and his close associate Reese Schonfeld expected it to fail. But it became very successful and helped to transform television journalism. Photo courtesy of Museum of Broadcast Communications.

than twice the number it had reached in June. And Turner and Schonfeld were anticipating a continued increase in subscribers—and in monthly per-subscriber fees that cable operators were compelled to pay CNN. Advertising revenue was also up. But in their eagerness to establish CNN's credibility and make up for holes in its coverage, they were forced to invest money in new bureaus in Miami, Detroit, and Tokyo and add staff at CNN's headquarters in Atlanta. They also had to spend money on legal fees. In May 1981, shut out of the pool that the networks operated, with the cooperation of the White House, to generate video of the president's activities, Turner and Schonfeld filed suit against the networks and President Reagan and his senior staff for denying CNN equal access. The following year, a federal court ruled in CNN's favor, and in a subsequent settlement, the Reagan White House and the networks agreed to accommodate the cable news upstart. A huge moral victory, it came at a price. To be able to provide coverage of the president's travels abroad when it was CNN's turn to produce the feed for the pool, CNN officials had to buy expensive new equipment. And they were expected to share more fully in the expenses of pool coverage, something Turner couldn't really afford. Turner's money problems were so bad he began to consider partnering with one of the major networks. Through Robert Wussler, a former CBS executive who had become his second in command at Turner Broadcasting, he sent word to CBS News chief Bill Leonard about his interest in a possible merger. When Leonard and CBS president Gene Jankowski met with Turner in Atlanta and realized that he wanted to retain control of CNN and would only allow CBS to acquire a minority stake, the potential deal collapsed.[14]

Leonard and Jankowski's interest reflected awareness at the networks that CNN was for real. Executives at CBS, NBC, and ABC were especially concerned about CNN's reciprocal agreements with local stations, including some network affiliates. They struck at the very heart of the relationship between the networks and their affiliates—a relationship forged in the 1950s that many station managers thought had outlived its usefulness. For over two decades, affiliates who wanted to report national and international news on their own programs were restrained by the fact that the networks produced this material and saved the best of it—especially the pictures—for their own evening newscasts. At first, this arrangement was mutually beneficial. Affiliates had neither the resources nor the inclination to produce anything other than local news, and the networks were grateful to have their newscasts cleared by the vast majority of their affiliates. By the 1970s, however, some affiliates had built large, well-equipped news divisions, and they often sent their own people to cover big out-of-town stories. Recognizing the popularity of local newscasts, and that a highly rated local program was a great lead-in for the network news, the networks became more generous about sharing their best footage—but, to many news directors, not generous enough. The bigger stations were especially resentful when the networks sent correspondents and producers to cover breaking stories in their communities, bypassing their own journalists.

When CNN began seeking reciprocal agreements with local stations, network affiliates suddenly had a choice. They could continue to rely on the networks for material to include in their own newscasts and broadcast their particular network's evening newscast when it was fed to them from New York—while also drawing from CNN to enhance their own news programs. Better still, when a big story broke in their community, they could deploy their own reporters to cover it and feed it to CNN for national distribution, giving them an opportunity to perform on a bigger stage. But what was good for local stations was disastrous for the networks. With local stations now able to report national and international news, which they presented as early as 5:00 PM or, in the case of really big stories, even earlier, the networks lost their monopoly over the biggest stories. And viewers had less incentive to watch their signature evening newscasts.

This problem was compounded by the fact that so many network resources were devoted to providing material for these showcase programs. With documentaries out of fashion, newsmagazines other than 60 Minutes a risky proposition and unable to secure spots on prime-time schedules, and the morning news shows dominated by soft news and human-interest features, the evening newscasts were the networks' only platform for the presentation of hard news. Virtually all their time, energy, and resources went into them. This was why network journalists were so eager to expand them to an hour—and why Roone Arledge, when he failed to achieve this, leaped at the chance to appropriate 11:30 PM for Nightline. Having so little airtime amplified their budgetary woes. As the auditors hired by their new owners would soon discover, the networks paid huge overhead costs to maintain bureaus and staff in places that rarely contributed segments to the national newscasts. It was a classic case of excess capacity. When measured against bloated news division budgets, the little news that made it onto the air cost a fortune to produce.

In 1981, Leonard, concerned about these trends, commissioned a group to determine how much it would cost to set up a news service to supply a continuous feed to CBS affiliates—and keep the affiliates out of CNN's clutches. The estimate, based on CBS's regular cost structure, was so high that Leonard suggested to Jankowski that it might be cheaper to buy CNN outright. Jankowski was intrigued, prompting their meeting with Turner. Of course, Turner had his own agenda. He was most interested in CBS's financial resources to tide him over until CNN became profitable. Though he coveted some of CBS News' technology and infrastructure, he was disdainful of their high salaries, deference to TV-industry trade unions, and administrative bloat. Later, Turner would attempt a hostile takeover of CBS—a bid that sparked the massive stock buy-back scheme that would saddle CBS with debt and open the door for Laurence Tisch to take over the company. But it was CBS's entertainment programming and string of affiliates that he coveted, not its wasteful and inefficient news division.[15]

Bill Leonard and CBS were not the only ones concerned about CNN. In August 1981, ABC and Westinghouse, owners of the Group W chain of radio and television stations and a string of cable television systems, announced that they were getting into the cable news business. Two ABC-Westinghouse ventures were planned. The first, scheduled to debut in the spring of 1982, would mimic the all-news format of radio stations like Group W's WINS in New York. It would offer continuous summaries of national and international news in an eighteen-minute news wheel, with five minutes per hour set aside for regional stations to provide local news. Given ABC's resources and the proven track record of the format, it seemed likely to succeed. The second ABC-Westinghouse venture was more audacious and posed a direct challenge to Turner and CNN. It would specialize in breaking news and comprehensive, in-depth reports that couldn't be accommodated on *World News Tonight* or even *Nightline*. "The second channel will give us the opportunity to do all kinds of things we can't on commercial television," Roone Arledge told the *New York Times*.[16] The announcement led many industry observers to predict that CNN's days were numbered. With its deep pockets, state-of-the-art technology and newsgathering apparatus, and clout in both broadcasting and the cable industry, ABC-Westinghouse's new enterprise, called Satellite News Channels, was a potential colossus, and Turner and Schonfeld were enraged when they heard that the first channel would be offered to cable operators for free.

Yet rather than hunker down, they went on the offensive. Back in November 1980, while sharing a meal, Turner and Schonfeld had discussed the likelihood of competitors emerging. Schonfeld had predicted that the most likely challenge would be a channel specializing in headline news. Determined not to allow a competitor to gain a foothold in the industry, Turner instructed him to develop a detailed plan so that CNN could strike first. "If we're gonna have competition, it might as well be us."[17] When Schonfeld delivered his plan, Turner didn't even look it; he slipped it into a desk drawer. In July 1981, however, when he got wind of the ABC-Westinghouse venture, he pulled it out and instructed Schonfeld to proceed. Two days after ABC-Westinghouse officials made their plans for SNC public, Turner announced that CNN would establish its own headline service, and it would launch on January 1, 1982, months before SNC's. CNN2, as it was called at the time, would broadcast news headlines, a business report, weather, and sports in a thirty-minute revolving wheel. At least initially, Turner would offer it to cable operators for free.

Well aware of the dangers involved in establishing a rival to their established brand, Schonfeld and Ted Kavanau went to great lengths to differentiate CNN2 from its parent. First, it was confined to providing headlines and using film footage from reports that had already aired on CNN. CNN would remain the go-to source for live breaking news. And its format would be more rigid and repetitive—with lots of stories and none of the spontaneity that had already become CNN's trademark. This, too, was by design: "Everybody would watch it for a few minutes, but nobody would watch it for very long."[18] Meeting the launch deadline was a heroic undertaking. It required a new building, studio, computer and graphic systems, and a corps of new personnel. And though they could rely on what they had learned the first time around, it called for a huge investment, $18 million to get it off the ground and for operating expenses in the first year, exacerbating Turner's financial problems.

By the time CNN2 went on the air, circumstances favored Turner, and he pressed his advantage to undermine SNC. CNN's success had endeared Turner to cable operators, and he exploited his status as a cable-industry pioneer to foment mistrust of ABC-Westinghouse. Addressing cable operators at a conference in Boston shortly before CNN2's launch, Turner noted that ABC News chief Roone Arledge had recently confessed that ABC would keep its best material and personnel off SNC. In the end, he predicted, ABC would favor its broadcast properties. "A lot of cable operators and their subscribers are very happy with CNN, and aren't going to see much reason to take the ABC-

Westinghouse service," an industry analyst observed.[19] Before CNN2, the only reason would have been because it was free. Now that Turner had created his own free headline service under the well-known CNN brand, however, ABC-Westinghouse would be entering a divided market.

Turner recognized that the more obstacles he could place in front of ABC-Westinghouse before the debut of SNC, the more he could upset its management and spark concern about costs among its shareholders. Unlike Turner Broadcasting, both ABC and Westinghouse were big, publicly held companies, and there were questions about whether they were willing to incur the huge losses that were necessary before the new service could ever break even. Launching CNN2 before SNC's headline service was one obstacle. But there were others, and they had even bigger consequences. In March 1982, as ABC-Westinghouse executives were preparing for SNC to begin broadcasting, Turner invited stations affiliated with the networks to come to Atlanta at his expense, where he announced that he was establishing a syndicated version of CNN2 for sale to broadcast stations. "We're giving them an alternative to the networks now," Ted Kavanau told reporters. "The stations can take our stuff and replace CBS News if they want."[20] Many affiliates were sincerely interested, and Turner's gambit alarmed network executives in New York. As one complained, "Turner not only wants the cable audience, now he wants our over-the-air audience as well."[21] By seeking to move onto their turf, Turner compelled the networks to rethink their relationship with their affiliates and consider expanding the amount of news they broadcast. Finally, after SNC's debut in June 1982, Turner filed suit against SNC and Group W, the Westinghouse subsidiary that managed its cable systems, claiming that they had made secret deals to keep CNN and CNN2 off Westinghouse-owned cable systems. The lawsuit added to the already considerable sum that ABC-Westinghouse had sunk into its first news channel, and analysts were predicting that it would lose between $40 and $60 million in its first year of operation.

Turner's brinksmanship paid off. Though SNC began with 2.6 million subscribers, compared to CNN2's 1.2 million, it encountered myriad problems and its costs soared. Most cable operators remained loyal to Turner, forcing SNC to actually pay them to get its news channel on systems, and ABC and Westinghouse executives became increasingly worried about the effect that SNC's losses might have on investors and the price of their stock. Meanwhile, CNN's ratings and advertising revenue were on the upswing, and it became clear that Turner's pioneering venture would soon become profitable. In October 1983, as SNC's losses mounted, Turner offered to buy SNC from ABC-Westinghouse. Its executives agreed, and Turner paid $25 million for the rival news channel and then shut it down, adding its seven million subscribers to CNN2's subscriber base. He had won the first "cable news war," and CNN2, now called Headline News, became a solid performer, garnering roughly half as many viewers as CNN, just as Schonfeld had envisioned.

CNN was also solidifying its identity. In May 1982, Turner fired Schonfeld and made him a "consultant" to Turner Broadcasting; at Schonfeld's recommendation, Burt Reinhardt became CNN's new president. Turner claimed that Schonfeld's energy and penchant for micromanaging had become liabilities now that CNN had achieved maturity. "Reese wanted to make every decision himself," he insisted. "It just wasn't the kind of management style that was going to make the organization strong in the long run."[22] Schonfeld suggested that Turner had begun to violate the agreement they had reached back in 1979—that Turner would not meddle in the editorial side of the business or try to make "journalistic decisions." Many CNN staffers were concerned when Schonfeld was sacked. Despite his often abrasive management style, he was widely respected, and some of them were fearful that Turner intended to exert more influence over CNN. Their fears was confirmed only days later, when Turner filmed an editorial that aired on CNN and WTBS numerous times over the Memorial Day weekend. A long-time critic of sex and violence in the movies, Turner was enraged when he heard that John Hinckley's attempted assassination of President Reagan had been inspired in part by the movie *Taxi Driver*. In his editorial, he denounced the Hollywood studios for making such films, insisting that they had "absolutely no redeeming social value." "These sorts of movies must be stopped," he concluded. "And if you're concerned, as I am, you should write your congressman and senator . . . and tell him that you want something done about these destructive motion pictures."[23] Turner's editorial outraged many CNN staffers. In his commentary segment on *Prime News*, Daniel Schorr delivered a spirited rebuttal defending the First Amendment rights of moviemakers. But Schorr and others were disturbed when the commentary was not repeated on the news the following morning, as was custom. Many assumed that the decision to kill it had come from Turner himself.[24]

To the relief of his staff and television critics, Turner didn't turn CNN into a personal megaphone. As much as he liked having access to its millions of viewers, and in later years encouraged CNN's documentary unit to produce special programs about issues he was interested in, he was persuaded that editorials risked undermining CNN's growing reputation for objectivity. Turner's partnership with Schonfeld and involvement with CNN had broadened his views of the world and of television journalism. While remaining a fiscal conservative and a populist critic of the East Coast "establishment," Turner became more interested in international affairs and the impact of population growth and development on the environment, and he began expressing increasing respect for the high ideals that inspired journalists. His entry into the TV news business had been something of a lark. By the mid-1980s, however, he had become a true believer, and this shift in his thinking ensured that, despite Schonfeld's departure, CNN would continue along the same path.[25]

That meant relatively straight, objective reporting, and soliciting the opinions of experts from across the political spectrum. CNN producers went to considerable lengths to ensure that conservative voices and views were included in news reports and more detailed, interpretive features. Turner and Schonfeld had founded CNN at the dawn of what historians now call the "Age of Reagan," and Schonfeld's experience in the news business had made him aware of the skepticism and disdain that many ordinary Americans—not just conservatives— felt toward the networks. This is why he had insisted that CNN's news programming avoid the "voice of God" pomposity that prevailed at the networks, and that CNN stories emerge from among its staff in bureaus and the local journalists with whom it had reciprocal agreements, and not from an isolated coterie at its Atlanta headquarters. Its guiding ethos came from local news, and Schonfeld wanted virtually all stories presented in ways that made them accessible and relevant to viewers.

But during CNN's early years, Schonfeld also recognized that the journalistic ideal of objectivity was quixotic. The problem was not with reporters and producers. If they tried, they were perfectly capable of producing news that was faithful to the facts and available evidence and took multiple points of view into account, and producing this became CNN's mission. The problem was with some viewers, who would never accept news stories as objective—even if, by any measure, they were. As Schonfeld later explained, viewer "prejudices" were so deeply rooted that, in the case of a report from the Middle East, for example, "one set of eyes might see a story as Zionist propaganda, and somebody else might call it an Arab handout."[26] Rather than work against this habit, he became intrigued by the possibility of exploiting it, and creating a program in which journalists were open about their opinions and biases. He had heard about a Washington-based radio show in which a liberal and a conservative debated about contemporary issues in an aggressive, bare-knuckle style. The combatants were Tom Braden, a liberal Democrat and successful newspaper columnist, and Patrick Buchanan, Richard Nixon's former communications advisor and a prominent spokesman for the ascendant New Right. Schonfeld hired them for CNN and their show became *Crossfire*. At first, it aired at 11:30 PM, but it did so well that CNN executives moved it to the early evening. Until Larry King's arrival, it was the news channel's top-rated program.[27]

By 1985, it was clear that Turner's gamble had paid off. CNN's coverage of breaking news was unsurpassed, and its handling of diplomatic summits, elections, and the political conventions—the kinds of big events at which the networks had long excelled—was routinely praised by television critics and many viewers. In the wake of its coverage of the Democratic convention in 1984, a writer for the *New York Times* suggested that CNN had joined the journalistic "major leagues."[28] Even former CBS News president Richard Salant had good things to say about Turner's news channel. "I think that for what they spend on it and what they have to work it, it's remarkable what they do," he told a reporter in 1987.[29]

CNN was part of virtually every basic cable package available in the US. And, like other cable TV favorites, it had benefited from a huge spike in cable subscriptions. In 1987, it reached 33 million households, roughly 40 percent of all US homes, while Headline News reached an additional 18 million. Over half a million viewers, on average, watched CNN's evening newscast, while an estimated 2.5 million tuned in at some point during the day. These numbers were well below the 38 million who collectively watched the network evening newscasts. But the economics of the cable industry, and CNN's low operating costs, made it a successful business model. Sponsors were now much easier to find, and both advertising revenues and cable-subscription fees had increased. CNN's syndication service was thriving as well, as broadcast stations signed up to receive news packages from Headline News. And, after five years of losses amounting to nearly $80 million, CNN was finally turning a profit. According to the *Times*, it made $12.5 million in 1985, $38.6 million in 1986, and was projected to make $60 million in 1987. For five years, CNN had been subsidized by profits that Turner made from WTBS. Now CNN was more profitable than WTBS, and it would become the big moneymaker of Turner Broadcasting.[30]

Turner's financial success enabled Burt Reinhardt to expand CNN's budget and newsgathering capabilities. By 1987, it employed fifteen hundred people and spent close to $100 million per year. Its staff was scattered between its Atlanta headquarters and eighteen bureaus, including an increasing number abroad. Yet CNN still spent only a third of what the news divisions at the major networks routinely did, thanks to its unwillingness to hire stars and its reliance on nonunion labor. Everyone from secretaries and gofers to cameramen, producers, and anchors made less than half that of their equivalents at the networks, and the "CNN way" was to get as much as possible out of them, ensuring a high level of efficiency.[31]

The mid-1980s were also the years when CNN began its transformation into a global news service. Early on, Turner and Schonfeld had relied largely on the foreign news agencies with which they had reciprocal agreements for international news. But they also established a few overseas bureaus, and when CNN became profitable, Reinhardt and Ed Turner, his second in command, began setting up more and more of them. The eventual goal, Turner told the *New York Times*, was "to have a bureau in every major capital in the world."[32] Increasingly, CNN correspondents and film crews were equipped with new technology—mobile, "flyaway" satellite uplinks, some no bigger than a suitcase—that allowed them to report live from virtually anywhere. It was expensive, but well worth the investment for a news organization whose reputation now rested on its quick and thorough coverage of breaking news.

But, for Turner, turning CNN into a global operation meant more than providing viewers in the US with stories from abroad. It meant beaming CNN to other countries and building a global audience, a more challenging task. In 1984, Turner and his top executives established CNN International (CNN-I), a new service designed to deliver international news to people outside the US. At first, it offered a simulcast of CNN's Atlanta-based feed, and its viewers were mostly American business travelers staying in foreign hotels. By late 1980s, however, it was aggressively seeking foreign viewers, particularly in Europe, and offering them programming that was at least partially distinct from CNN's US service. CNN's entry into these markets would have been impossible in previous years, when European governments were committed to protecting their state-run broadcasting systems from foreign competition. In the 1980s, however, many governments began to encourage commercial broadcasters to establish new television stations and cable channels, and many of these for-profit broadcasters were eager to partner with CNN so that they might have some international news to complement their local news and entertainment programs. CNN's expansion into Europe was also encouraged by the fact that increasing numbers of Europeans, particularly in the wealthier countries, understood English, and by the willingness of European advertisers to purchase airtime.[33]

Turner's interest in turning CNN into a global news service surprised many observers, particularly those who remembered his early days in the cable industry, when he was a vocal right-winger and often criticized the networks and the media in general for "tearing down America." But Turner was also a farsighted businessman, and his immersion in journalism through CNN had broadened his perspective. Indeed, by the mid-1980s, he was eager to establish reciprocal agreements with news agencies in Communist countries and had become a vocal critic of the Reagan administration's revival of the Cold War. Turner's efforts helped CNN journalists establish a Moscow bureau, and his well-publicized friendship with Cuban dictator Fidel Castro eventually led the Cuban government to allow CNN to open one in Havana. By the early 1990s, Turner had become one of the world's most prominent internationalists—a stance that satisfied his yearning to make a difference and was good for Turner Broadcasting.

Global expansion posed unique problems. While some nations were willing to open up their broadcasting systems to CNN, others were more reluctant. In part, this reluctance was political. Many governments, even some who wanted to provide their citizens with alternatives to state-run media, were responsive to public concerns about American "cultural imperialism." For decades, US syndicators and the Hollywood studios had been exporting American movies and television programs to foreign countries, and by the 1980s this push had reached a new peak, as American media companies sought to recoup the costs of big-budget films and TV programs by maximizing revenues from overseas sales. And though CNN was a news channel, it was still American, and it was an easy target for critics who opposed this trend.[34]

In other countries, government resistance to CNN was inspired by fears that its uncensored news programs might reflect badly on them—or, in the cases of authoritarian regimes like Cuba, provide citizens with information their rulers would prefer they not have. To gain the trust of such nations, CNN established a weekly program called *World Report*. It allowed foreign broadcasters—governments as well as independent commercial ones—to submit completed two-and-a-half-minute news segments in English on things occurring in their countries. Segments that met CNN's minimal production guidelines were then broadcast, without any editing, on the two-hour program. Contributing broadcasters could also air the program—in its entirety or specific segments—in their own nations. In some instances, the segments that aired on *World Report* were little more than propaganda, and the program was criticized for providing a platform for some of the most corrupt and brutal regimes in the world. But it radically expanded the range of perspectives on television. And by providing foreign broadcasters with a venue to air news from their own points of view, it enabled Turner and CNN to build bridges to nations that typically barred or severely restricted the foreign press. As Turner later explained, "We never would have been allowed to stay in Iraq during the [first] Iraqi war if it hadn't been for *World Report*. We've gotten a lot of access as a result of our making a real effort to having people from other countries and other news organizations feel comfortable about us."[35]

Expanding globally required a shift in CNN's voice and perspective. In the beginning, when its audience was entirely domestic, CNN focused largely on US news and reported it from a distinctly American point of view. By 1988, however, thanks to CNN-I, it was available in fifty-eight countries. Sensitive to the diversity of their global audience, executives and producers decided to make CNN's programming less conspicuously "American." They hired more foreigners and assigned them to posts in the US as well as at CNN-I, and they began training their American staff to recognize and respect cultural differences. Turner even banned the use of the word "foreign" in any CNN report. The changes were most apparent to American viewers in CNN's coverage of international affairs, and gave the news channel a distinctly different tone from that of the networks, where Reagan-era patriotism and the appeal of populist reportage had encouraged many journalists to frame international news in ways that unwittingly reminded viewers that it was taking place "over there" or was relevant only when it imperiled "America."[36]

International news soon became CNN's forte. Its journalists excelled at covering terrorist attacks, hostage crises, and plane crashes. And by the late 1980s, many Americans were turning to CNN, and not the networks, for coverage of important overseas developments. On hand, along with CBS, to cover the summit meeting in Beijing between Chinese officials and Soviet leader Mikhail Gorbachev in May 1989, CNN was able to provide the most complete account of the pro-democracy demonstrations that rattled the Chinese government and eventually sparked the bloody crackdown in Tiananmen Square. Sensing that the demonstrations were a big story, CNN's crew of forty smoothly shifted its focus away from the summit, inspiring demonstrators to play to its cameras. Chinese leaders eventually shut down CNN's uplink, forcing CNN reporters to rely on telephone and videotaped reports, shipped to and transmitted from Hong Kong, to inform viewers about developments in the Chinese capital. And though the lack of live video reduced CNN's advantage over its network rivals, its ability to stay with the story around the clock—rather than provide brief bulletins, as the networks did—made it the preferred source for viewers eager for the latest information. An NBC News executive conceded, "The nature of CNN allows it to do things we simply can't do."[37]

A few months later, CNN was similarly well positioned to document the collapse of Communist regimes in Eastern Europe. The drama began in early November in Berlin, and this time all the networks were present. Like CNN, they set up makeshift studios within sight of the infamous Berlin Wall. From here their anchors broadcast the evening news and presided over late-night specials, which included superb reports on the breaching of the wall and the reunion of long-separated family members. But with its ability to stay with a story without interruption—rather than interrupt its regular programming or attempt to shoehorn everything into their newscasts and late-night specials—CNN again became the go-to source for many viewers. And when political upheavals broke out in several other countries, its journalists were able to take advantage of their local connections to provide the most complete coverage.

For many Americans, CNN became the preferred source for breaking domestic news as well. In some cases, it was a beneficiary of blind luck. Needing to fill up the broadcast day, CNN had begun routinely covering the launches of space shuttles; the networks, by contrast, produced short, filmed reports for broadcast on the evening news. Accordingly, only CNN was on the air live on January 28, 1986, when the shuttle *Challenger* exploded seventy-three seconds after liftoff, killing all seven of its astronauts, including an elementary school teacher who had been part of the crew. It wasn't just the fact that CNN was always first on the scene that made it appealing to viewers. It was also its ability to stay with a story and turn it into a compelling narrative. Such a thing occurred in October 1987, when Jessica McClure, an eighteen-month-old toddler, fell into an abandoned well while playing in a backyard in Midland, Texas. Through a local partner, CNN began broadcasting from the scene almost immediately, as rescue workers pondered how to get her out. And it stayed with the story virtually full-time as rescuers used jackhammers to dig a tunnel parallel to the well, and finally pulled her out, almost two and a half days later. CNN's ratings soared, particularly during the drama's climax, as millions of Americans tuned in to learn the fate of "Baby Jessica."

But such events were unusual, and most of the time CNN producers struggled to fill airtime. In the second half of the 1980s, Reinhardt increased CNN's business programs and expanded the length and frequency of special segments on medicine, health, entertainment, and fashion. "This isn't just a news network anymore," he insisted. "It's a news and information network."[38] Beginning in the mid-1980s, CNN also began covering notable criminal trials. When possible, it broadcast them live, thanks to judicial rulings and legislation in many states that overturned bans on cameras in courtrooms. Critics noted that CNN seemed to prefer particularly sensational ones—like the sadistic sexual abuse trial of preschool teachers in Southern California or the murder trial of New York socialite Claus von Bulow—and they feared that trial coverage could crowd out more serious news. There were reasons to be concerned. With lots of time to devote to such cases, and many different "experts" and legal officials willing to talk about them, CNN's coverage could very easily turn into something more closely resembling a television soap opera and crime drama. But covering big trials sharply increased CNN's ratings, making them irresistible. A CNN executive defended its coverage of such events, noting, "We don't sensationalize cases—some of the cases are sensational. We see nothing wrong in reporting about crime. One of the public's main concerns is crime. For every hour of a crime trial, we have tenfold carried dull hearings. We have paid our dues."[39]

Success was gratifying to Turner, Reinhardt, and the CNN staff. They were especially pleased by the results of public opinion surveys conducted in the late 1980s, which revealed that CNN was regarded as the most "believable" television news source. Yet success also changed the news channel's occupational culture and guiding ethos. Gradually, CNN became a more cautious and conventional news organization, and many of its early hires left. With its constantly rotating cast of interchangeable anchors and reporters, CNN was never supposed to be a hothouse of stars. The news was the star, and this priority continued under Reinhardt, a notorious penny-pincher. Regular exposure, however, allowed many CNN anchors and correspondents to shine, prompting offers from the networks. More often than not, Reinhardt let them go and replaced them with less expensive up-and-comers.

If CNN had a star in the late 1980s, it was Bernard Shaw, its Washington-based anchor and most recognized face. A former correspondent for CBS and ABC, Shaw was one of CNN's early hires, becoming its Washington bureau chief in the early 1980s. But he excelled in front of a camera, and his intelligence, self-confidence, and smooth delivery made him exceptionally valuable, particularly during live coverage of breaking news like the Tiananmen demonstrations. He also became CNN's main anchor for political conventions and elections as well as for important events requiring pool coverage, when he served as the news channel's equivalent of Rather, Brokaw, and Jennings. He developed a reputation as a tough interviewer, and was the logical candidate to anchor a new program CNN launched in 1989, *The World Today*, an hour-long evening newscast scheduled directly opposite those on the networks.[40]

CNN also increased its production of documentaries and special reports, which were useful during slow news periods. At first, it didn't produce any documentaries. As the networks had demonstrated, they were expensive and unpopular with viewers, and they clashed

A veteran Washington correspondent, Bernard Shaw was one of CNN's first hires and soon became its most recognizable anchor. Photo courtesy of Photofest.

with CNN's emphasis on breaking news. In the mid-1980s, however, in their never-ending quest to fill airtime, CNN executives gradually added some documentaries to CNN's flow, often at Turner's behest. And Reinhardt created a special Washington-based investigative unit to produce a steady supply of filmed exposés. Finally, in 1989, Turner and Reinhardt hired Pam Hill, the former executive producer of the *ABC Close-Up!* series, to head a brand-new documentary unit. Hill told the press that her move to CNN was inspired by concern about the direction of news programming at the networks. "There's a respect here for the old, fixed ethics of journalism, while the networks are moving in the opposition direction." It was a coup for CNN, and in short order Hill and her team of thirty, recruited largely from the networks, began cranking out probing reports on subjects such as the savings-and-loan crisis and the "business" of college basketball.[41]

By CNN's tenth anniversary, the news channel had become a dominant force in television news. It reached almost 60 million American households and aired in over a hundred countries; in Europe alone, CNN had over 6 million subscribers. Its staff had also grown to nearly two thousand, with bureaus around the world. CNN had also become a huge money-maker, generating annual revenues in excess of $350 million, and over $150 million a year in profits.

CNN's ability to expand yet make money was attributable to efficiency and economies of scale introduced by Reinhardt and Ed Turner. A central assignment desk in Atlanta commissioned stories from reporters and compiled lists of material available to producers of specific programs, including the producers of CNN-I. This system ensured that reporters and film crews were kept busy and that the vast majority of reports they produced were actually used on the air. Many were repurposed, keeping costs per story extremely low. Of course, CNN's financial success was also a result of the economics of cable television, which provided Turner and his staff with a huge revenue stream apart from advertising. Because of this, a specialized channel like CNN could afford low ratings and focus on news. As Turner told the audience at a meeting of the Radio-Television News Directors Association in 1989, "We can live with . . . numbers that would get you fired in five minutes. We can live with it. And we can do well with it. And as a result, we can put on stories that wouldn't even begin to make your newscasts."[42]

CNN's growing respectability and place in the media mainstream was underscored in 1990, when Burt Reinhardt retired and Turner chose Tom Johnson, an experienced news executive from the Times Mirror Company, to be CNN's new president. In choosing Johnson, Turner overlooked a number of internal candidates who had lobbied hard for the job. But to Turner, Johnson seemed like the perfect steward of the impressive organization Schonfeld and Reinhardt had built from scratch, allowing Turner to focus on other parts of his media empire.[43]

Johnson's first task was formidable, to oversee CNN's coverage of the Persian Gulf War. It was shaping up to be the largest US military operation since Vietnam, and reporting on it was certain to be expensive and require the preemption of commercials. The challenges were especially daunting for the networks. Now under the control of cost-conscious owners, they had cut back on foreign correspondents and overseas bureaus, and would have to redeploy staff with fewer local connections. And they were understandably concerned about the war's potential impact on advertising revenues, particularly if it lasted more than a few weeks. CNN executives shared some of these concerns. But, for them, the war was a great opportunity, the kind of big story for which they had been hankering, that would allow them to pull out all the stops and confirm their supremacy. And, being a news channel, they didn't have to worry about its impact on other programs. When Johnson went to Turner with various plans for coverage, with carefully worked out budgets for each, asking how much he could spend, Turner waved him off. "You spend what you think it takes, pal."

With Turner's blessing, Johnson stationed CNN personnel in all the major cities of the Arab world and beefed up its presence at potential news hot spots like the White House and the Pentagon. Using connections to the Iraqi government forged through *World Report*, CNN officials gained permission to use a portable uplink to broadcast live from the Iraqi capital of Baghdad. This would give CNN an unprecedented advantage over its rivals, and enable it to cover the war live, in real time, from behind "enemy" lines. CNN producer Robert Wiener, who supervised the news channel's coverage from Baghdad, called it "the journalistic equivalent of walking on the moon."[44]

Equipped with cameras, the uplink, and satellite telephones, Wiener and a small CNN team, including Bernard Shaw and veteran foreign correspondent Peter Arnett, decamped for Baghdad. On January 16, 1991, after the UN coalition issued its ultimatum to Iraqi dictator Saddam Hussein, and the White House made it clear that an attack was imminent, journalists began to leave Baghdad, and pressure began to mount on CNN to pull their people out, too. Despite enormous pressure from the US government—and a personal call from President Bush—Turner and Johnson decided to let their staff decide whether to stay or get out. To a person, they elected to stay, and when UN-coalition aircraft began bombing the city, on January 17, they were able to get the scoop of a lifetime. With a camera positioned on a balcony of the Al-Rasheed Hotel, where CNN and other journalists had established their makeshift headquarters, and a four-wire satellite telephone offering Wiener and his staff a direct line to Atlanta—the only communication link out of Baghdad once the Iraqis shut down the Al-Rasheed's switchboard and coalition bombers destroyed the Iraqi government's communications system and satellite uplinks—Shaw, Arnett, and John Holliman provided viewers with a blow-by-blow account of the assault. The networks, by contrast, lost their ability to provide pictures, and their phone contact with their correspondents was sporadic at best. Many network affiliates pirated CNN's feed to provide viewers with video.

Pressure from the Iraqi government soon forced CNN to pull out its crew—except for Arnett, who remained in Baghdad and continued to file reports by satellite phone. A week later, the Iraqis relented, and allowed a small CNN crew equipped with a portable uplink to join him; notably, ABC, CBS, and NBC were denied visas that would have allowed them to do the same. Over the next few weeks, Arnett and his crew were the only source of news about developments inside Iraq, though the reports they filed were censored by Iraqi officials. Arnett was taken on "guided tours" of Baghdad and shown the effects of coalition bombing. He was even allowed to interview Saddam Hussein. CNN producers went to great lengths to place Arnett's reports in context and noted on-screen that they had been "approved" by the Iraqis. Arnett, too, offered subtle hints designed to suggest the truth. For example, when the Iraqis took him to a demolished building that they claimed was an infant formula factory—but that Pentagon officials insisted was a site where biological weapons were produced—Arnett noted in passing that a perfectly intact sign identifying the rubble as a former "baby milk factory" appeared in Arabic *and* English, suggesting it was a propaganda ploy. Nonetheless, Arnett was denounced for being an Iraqi dupe and even a traitor, and CNN was deluged with negative feedback from Americans who accused the news channel of aiding the enemy. CNN officials and Arnett's colleagues stuck up for him, noting that, as a reporter, his job was to tell the truth—not take sides, as some of his critics suggested.[45]

Arnett's reports represented a tiny fraction of CNN's coverage of the Persian Gulf War. The overwhelming majority of its reports were conventional stories filed by CNN correspondents and press releases and video footage provided by the Pentagon and other official sources. Television coverage of the Gulf War might have been live, but, compared to the Vietnam War in particular, it was highly censored. US officials and their allies in Saudi Arabia and Israel strictly controlled the information they provided CNN and the networks and other organizations that were part of an accredited pool. Much of it was snazzy video footage showcasing the UN coalition's military dominance and suggesting that the bombing of Iraq had produced virtually no "collateral damage" to the civilian population. The control of information made it hard for television journalists in particular to tell any story other than the one that the Pentagon wanted the public to see. "In effect," a writer for the *New York Times* noted a few weeks after the war's end, "each pool member [was] an unpaid employee of the Department of Defense, on whose behalf he or she prepare[d] the news of the war for the outside world."[46] To fill up airtime and provide context, CNN anchors interviewed scores of "experts," the vast majority of them ex-military figures who expressed views unambiguously supportive of the US and its allies.[47]

In the end, being able to rely on Arnett gave CNN's coverage an extra dimension, and its ability to stay with the story around the clock was once again an important advantage that encouraged viewers to tune in. By contrast, the networks were forced by economic considerations to return to their normal programming after only three days. CNN achieved its highest ratings on the night the bombing began, drawing 10.8 million households, just under the 12.4 million who were watching CBS, the lowest-rated network. And though the ratings declined, they remained much higher than normal. During the war, CNN averaged between 3.8 and 4.2 million daily viewers, a dramatic increase from its prewar average of about 600,000. This enabled the sales staff to boost rates for a thirty-second commercial from $3,500 to $20,000.[48] And the buzz sparked by its war coverage contributed to a spike in cable subscriptions, increasing the revenues CNN would gain from subscriber's fees. Amid the glow from its triumph, CNN officials announced new plans. "We're looking to establish an even larger worldwide presence," Ed Turner told the *New York Times*. "We're going to be opening new bureaus. Now that we've got the world's attention, we're going to spend more money trying to keep them interested."[49]

The Persian Gulf War was CNN's coming of age. It had become the place to turn for breaking news, the equivalent of a "video wire service" that presented news in real time, rather than in edited packages that aired once a day in the early evening. With twenty-four hours a day at its disposal, CNN was able to provide detailed and exhaustive coverage of virtually everything, including a surprising amount of international news, making it something close to the "news network of record" that journalists at the networks had long wished to be. More remarkable still, CNN had become an important source of news for millions of people outside the United States, including many world leaders and opinion shapers. Available in over a hundred countries, it not only served but was helping to forge the "global village" that the Canadian media theorist Marshall McLuhan had prophesied.

CNN's success demonstrated that cable could be a wonderful platform for substantive television journalism, the home for which TV news people had long yearned. On CNN, the news didn't coexist awkwardly with more popular and profitable entertainment programs. There were no fights with entertainment-division executives over airtime—and no pressure to curtail coverage of a big story so that "regular programming" could resume. News was the whole show. It was the reason people tuned in. This made for a very different environment than at the networks or local stations, and it aroused hope that, on cable, news programming might regularly achieve the high standards celebrated by Richard Salant and other industry leaders, offering viewers breadth as well as depth, background and context as well as the riveting immediacy of live shots.

But if cable was a platform on which TV news could thrive, it was also a pathway to cultural irrelevance. CNN emerged in an era of program abundance, when there were many more alternatives available to viewers, including particular channels catering to specific programming genres, subcultures, and consumer tastes. And during 1990s, the number of cable channels continued to multiply, giving viewers even more choice, and allowing them to indulge their desire to watch only particular kinds of programs—and avoid others, including news. In the process, the television audience splintered, and most individual programming outlets, including CNN, became niche services. The good news was that the economics of cable made niche services profitable. The bad news was that this inspired the establishment of even more specialized channels, and further fractured the television audience.[50]

CNN's rise was great for news junkies, who now had a channel of their own. And it was convenient for casual viewers who could turn it on when something big was occurring—the murder trial of an ex-football player, a Washington sex scandal, a ghastly terrorist attack. But, under normal circumstances, CNN would never attract a large audience, or have the reach or potential influence that the networks had enjoyed. It wouldn't even come close. In the multichannel era, there were simply too many things for people to watch instead—and virtually no broader forces suggesting that it was more virtuous to watch CNN than MTV or ESPN. The TV news habit, never very strong to begin with, stood little chance in a culture in thrall to individual consumer choice.

6

THE NEW ENTERTAINMENT

Robert Wright, the GE executive who became president of NBC after
GE's acquisition of the network, expected to encounter some waste
and inefficiency when he assumed his new post in September 1986.
After all, few companies in any industry could match GE's standards
for controlling costs and maximizing profits, and he knew that the
television industry was quite different from the other fields where GE
owned subsidiaries. Having worked his way up the corporate ladder at
GE, Wright was one of the company's most accomplished executives.
He had run several of its most successful divisions and had become a
favorite of the firm's chairman, Jack Welch. Welch had bought NBC as
part of a larger plan to move GE away from its traditional emphasis on
manufacturing and into the more profitable information-and-service
sector, and he had chosen Wright to run the network because he was
confident his protégé could make it a launching pad for new ventures.[1]

By television industry standards, the network that Wright would
run was an exemplary organization. Its entertainment programs
dominated the ratings and enabled the network and its affiliates to
earn huge profits. But Wright was looking beyond the traditional
competition among the "Big Three," and what he saw worried him. He
recognized that cable television had changed the rules of the game,
and that in the future NBC's competitors would be HBO, TBS, ESPN,
and MTV.

Wright's appraisal of what the future had in store for the networks
was spot-on. The television industry had entered a new, multichannel age. In this new age, which dawned in the 1980s and emerged full-
blown in the 1990s, cable channels would become increasingly popu-

lar and lure more and more viewers away from the networks. Network programs would still command the largest audiences. And simply by virtue of the size of those audiences, the networks would continue to air the biggest hits. Given the choices now available to viewers, however, even their biggest hits would not achieve the ratings of blockbusters in the 1970 or early 1980s. This would undermine the leverage the networks had enjoyed over advertisers and make it harder to get top dollar for individual spots, even on the most popular programs. Even worse, to keep successful programs on their schedules, Wright and other network chieftains would be forced to pay staggering sums to their producers and stars, increasing costs and imperiling profit margins.[2]

Wright was especially concerned about the profligacy at NBC News. By the time he arrived at the network, the news division was spending about $275 million per year. Yet, in Wright's view, they had little to show for it. Though *Today* had returned to form and the network's evening newscast was improving in the ratings, Wright couldn't understand the rationale for such massive spending, particularly since market research demonstrated that many viewers were now getting their news from local stations or CNN. The entire project of network news mystified him. What was the point of maintaining an expensive infrastructure of bureaus around the nation and the world if news was essentially a sideline to the network's main business of broadcasting entertainment programs, and other sources could deliver it just as well—or perhaps better?

Wright wasn't alone. The presidents of CBS and ABC had also begun to reconsider the mission of network news. They really had no choice. With the costs of renting entertainment programs on the rise, they could no longer afford to give their news divisions a blank check to produce programs watched by a dwindling number of viewers. Like Wright, they began to pressure their news divisions to reduce spending and develop more appealing and profitable programs. If the pressure at ABC was less than elsewhere, it was only because Roone Arledge had seen the writing on the wall and had already embraced the new formula.

The squeeze was put on all network divisions, not just news. Corporate executives demanded that managers and producers run their units more efficiently and insisted on changes in programming to keep viewers from defecting to cable. They also lobbied hard for additional deregulation, a campaign that bore fruit when the FCC gradually eliminated the Financial Interest and Syndication ("Fin-Syn") Rules instituted in the 1970s that had prevented the networks from producing and owning programs, and Congress passed legislation that increased the number of television stations a single corporation could own. These changes enabled the networks to enter into potentially lucrative partnerships with production companies and Hollywood studios, and created potent new revenue streams. As the "owners" rather than "renters" of programs, for example, the networks would profit when they sold their programs to syndicators. Unshackled from the restraints that had limited their ability to earn revenue from sources other than advertising, ABC and CBS became attractive to big companies that were eager to move into the television industry. In 1995, the Walt Disney Company purchased Capital Cities/ABC. The deal offered Disney, which had already gotten into the cable TV business and owned a major stake in ESPN, a new platform for material produced by its studios. ABC, meanwhile, gained a ready source of programs that could be acquired for less than those produced by other studios. And the entire company stood to profit when Disney-produced programs that were hits on ABC were syndicated. Keen to develop a similar arrangement, Viacom, the media giant that owned Paramount Studios, publishing houses, and the successful cable channels Showtime, Nickelodeon, and MTV, acquired CBS in 1999.[3]

All the networks were now in the hands of large, diversified companies. Eager to achieve "synergies"—opportunities for in-house production and promotion across different media—they would push network executives to develop new, more cost-effective methods of production and distribution. More important, they would insist that the networks offer programs that distinguished their product from material on cable, enabling them to carve out a profitable niche in the new multichannel marketplace. And they would continue to pressure their news divisions, spurring them to develop identities that set them apart from CNN.

The first step was assessing the new state of the marketplace. By the late 1980s, there were several different kinds of informational programming that appealed to viewers and might serve as a source of inspiration for network journalists. The most obvious was local news. Emphasizing crime, natural disasters, weather, sports, consumer and health news, human-interest stories, and investigative exposés, local news programs had become very popular and profitable.[4] Viewers were also flocking to syndicated programs broadcast by local stations in the 7–8:00 PM hole between the evening newscasts and the beginning of prime time. Among the most popular was *Entertainment Tonight*, a daily half-hour entertainment-news report produced by Paramount Television that debuted in September 1981. It covered the latest movies, music, and television shows, and offered show-business celebrities a wonderful venue for flattering interviews and photo opportunities. Like CNN's entertainment-news report, *ET* capitalized on the networks' reluctance to include this material in most of their programs, and its success prompted them to broadcast more of it—and not just on morning news shows like *Today*.[5]

Soon *ET* was joined by a more raffish set of programs also broadcast in the early evening. *A Current Affair* began airing in 1986. Produced by 20th Century Fox, a movie and television studio recently purchased by Rupert Murdoch, it was considerably racier than *ET*, specializing in crime stories, scandals and celebrity gossip, and sensational investigative reports, terrain that became more appealing to producers in the wake of the FCC's repeal of the Fairness Doctrine in 1987. The program's host, Maury Povich, was especially effective, employing facial expressions and a wry, deadpan delivery to express his opinion and mock the subjects of stories—anticipating the affect that Jon Stewart would use on *The Daily Show*. Another tabloid TV show, *Inside Edition*, was launched in 1988, offering a similar mix of stories. After its first anchor, British talk-show king David Frost, was fired, the program's producers hired Bill O'Reilly, a veteran CBS and ABC correspondent, to take his place. A third tabloid program, *Hard Copy*, debuted a later year. It feasted on sensational crime stories and scandals, and its success compelled its rivals to follow suit, resulting in a further lowering of standards. Tabloid TV reporters sometimes covered hard news—like national politics and the fall of the Berlin Wall—and displayed a healthy skepticism of officialdom and the spin conjured by public relations and marketing specialists. But, on the whole, the new programs were heavily tilted toward the most sensational stories, and they introduced techniques and features that were highly controversial, including dramatic "reenactments" of events. They were also vital in whipping up public interest in notorious criminal cases and turning figures like the Menendez brothers, John and Lorena Bobbitt, and Tonya Harding into infamous celebrities.[6]

The new programs were assailed by television critics, intellectuals, and many network journalists. By then retired and reduced to the role of elder statesman, Walter Cronkite became an especially vocal critic, calling the shows "garbage" and arguing that the information they conveyed was "absolutely, totally useless stuff."[7] Former CBS News president Van Gordon Sauter, however, leaped to their defense. In a widely discussed article in *TV Guide* published in 1989, Sauter praised the tabloids for their eagerness to meet viewers at their own level — rather than condescend to them like the networks. He suggested that they were democratizing journalism and welcomed their ability to shake up the "elitists" who inhabited the "Turgid Triangle of Imperial Journalism, a spiritual and geographical locus embracing the District of Columbia, the West Side of Manhattan, and Cambridge, Mass."[8]

By the early 1990s, completely rejecting the lessons provided by tabloid TV was a luxury the networks could no longer afford. Sure, the tabloid programs were crass and routinely engaged in dubious journalistic practices, and most people at the networks agreed that it would be a mistake to slavishly imitate them. Yet the tabloids knew how to reach viewers in the new, more competitive television market-place and suggested approaches the networks might be able to refashion for use in their own programs.

By this time, too, the very idea of pandering was coming under assault in the wider culture, as Sauter's spirited defense of the tabloids suggested. One reason for this was the growing popularity of what the writer Thomas Frank has called "market populism," a belief that consumer choice was a form of democratic empowerment. Long championed by the business community and given additional impetus and a vaguely countercultural edge by the expressive individualism of the 1970s, it spread widely in the Reagan era and especially the 1990s, encouraging public support for the deregulation of industries and other policies that would increase the choices available to consumers. In effect, market populism legitimized FCC chairman Mark Fowler's dictum that the "public interest" was what interested the public, and it created a climate that was far more encouraging of network news programming that openly catered to the preferences of viewers.[9]

In previous decades, most well-educated Americans, including many of the corporate elite, would have rejected market populism as a cynical and potentially dangerous excuse to exploit the public's poor taste and most primitive yearnings. In this view, merely satisfying consumer demand without considering what you were selling was unseemly and amoral. It reflected badly on the business community and was certain to coarsen the tone of American culture. In the 1940s and 1950s in particular, the professional and managerial classes were deeply commitment to cultural "standards" and the virtues of education and "uplift." It was an article of faith shared by liberals and conservatives—even socialists on the far left. These beliefs inspired the dramatic expansion of public colleges and universities, the creation of educational television stations, and a host of other initiatives. Knowledge and "cultural capital" once accessible only to the well-to-do would be made more widely available, and the tastes of the general public would improve.[10]

This faith was shaken in the 1960s when new social movements openly challenged the establishment and called into question the values and assumptions that sustained its cultural authority. And it became increasingly unfashionable in 1970s and 1980s, even among many conservatives, who turned instead to the libertarian-inflected market populism expressed by Sauter.[11] By the early 1990s, increasing numbers of educated Americans viewed standards and cultural uplift as elitist. This wasn't just because they had been discredited in the 1960s or because of the popularity of market populism. It was also, more subtly, a result of the influence of multiculturalism and postmodernism, new theoretical trends in academia that, in diluted and at times bowdlerized form, spread more widely among the general public. Standards and uplift were a form of "cultural imperialism," an effort to impose an elite-defined ideal of cultivation and citizenship on a diverse public whose values, traditions, and perspectives were deserving of recognition and respect.[12]

Market populism, multiculturalism, and postmodernism were particularly crippling to the aspirations and professional ideals of television journalists, who, unlike their colleagues at many newspapers, were expected to reach a broad audience. For one, they raised fundamental questions about the networks' mission to provide viewers with what they ought to know. Was this mission really in the public's interest? Or was it, as many of their critics suggested, merely a rationale for claiming an undeserved position of cultural authority? What gave television journalists the right to decide what was news, especially since so few had gone through formal training and had learned the trade in an industry that had long been influenced by entertainment values? Weren't viewers entitled to at least some influence over programming? Was there a point, a middle ground, where serving the "public interest" and the public's interest might overlap?

While market populism attacked the notion that television journalists should attempt to tell people what they ought to know, multiculturalism and postmodernism cut even deeper. They suggested that truth itself was contested and subjective, determined by the perspective and lived experiences of individuals and groups. People committed to postmodernism were dubious that professional journalists could present an objective account of any event—or that such a thing even existed. Most Americans were unaware of these new theories, but their influence seeped into popular culture and advertising and contributed to the spread of a hip cynicism that celebrated ironic detachment and made the pretentions of network journalists appear hypocritical or absurd.[13]

By the time of the Persian Gulf War, then, the larger cultural environment in which network journalists had to operate had changed profoundly. The attitudes and expectations of the television audience had become more diverse—and powerful forces in the culture were actively encouraging this diversity and inspiring viewers to make new demands of producers and think about television in new ways. Skepticism of journalistic objectivity was widespread. And many viewers were openly disdainful of the notion that the network news divisions—or any other elite source—should decide for others what was important to know. Even the attitudes of loyal viewers were affected by these trends. Though they still looked to the networks for a relatively objective presentation of the news, they expected at least some stories to be "useful" and "interesting," like local news. And now that they had viewing options, they felt no compunction about tuning out if news programs didn't meet these expectations. It was their right as consumers.

The networks responded by fully embracing many of the changes they had begun to make in the 1980s. Increasingly, story selection was determined by the "back-fence" principle developed by Sauter—the stories that were most likely to elicit discussion among viewers. Network programs included more consumer, health, and lifestyle reports. And national and international news was framed in ways that made the distant worlds of politics and diplomacy relevant to viewers.[14]

Giving viewers more of what they wanted—rather than what journalists thought they ought to know—altered the perspective as well as the content of network news programs. Building on the populism they had introduced in the 1970s, the networks continued to look out for the little guy and expose violations of widely shared ideals like fair play and equal opportunity. Committed to serving as public watchdogs, they remained suspicious of many powerful institutions and especially of politicians, who were assumed to be most interested in reelection and maintaining power. This mirrored the cynicism of much of the public and allowed them to advertise their independence from the government and other institutions the networks had closely identified with and had often spoken for before the late 1960s. But chagrined by conservative accusations of liberal bias, and perhaps by a sense of having contributed to the "crisis of authority" that occurred in the 1970s, the networks also displayed a renewed respect for order and an even more powerful commitment to moderation and bipartisanship.[15]

Coverage of policy making was downplayed. In its place, the networks developed a new style of reporting that treated politics as if it were a game: a never-ending campaign in which particular policies were assessed in terms of their potential impact on reelection chances and partisan advantage. Rather than evaluate proposed policies on their merits, a task likely to result in complex, boring stories that would turn off most viewers and perhaps require favoring one side over the other, network journalists offered inside dope on strategy and assessed the success of politicians' efforts to stay "on message." They analyzed the spin that media advisors and campaign consultants produced to package particular initiatives and covered important presidential speeches and other events like theater critics, passing judgment on the quality of the "performance" and its likely effects. In some respects, this was an updating of their public-interest mission. With the assistance of pollsters and consultants, politicians and elected officials had become very skilled at image projection and getting favorable press, especially on TV. Ronald Reagan proved especially good at it, transforming many journalists into his unwitting accomplices. Enabling viewers see what was going on behind the scenes, then, was useful. It made journalists seem courageous and independent, and could prevent the public from being hoodwinked by politicians and their "spin doctors." Yet it could also encourage cynicism, reinforcing the impression that the essence of politics was self-interest, not policy making or public service.[16]

Treatment of international news also changed. Despite their assertiveness during the latter years of the Vietnam War, the networks never wavered in their support for the US in its conflicts with its Communist adversaries. And in the 1970s, they continued to present news from abroad through lenses shaped by the Cold War. But network journalists also expressed concern about developments that might lead the US into another Vietnam-style quagmire, and they made new efforts to explain the interests and perspectives of nations and peoples who would have been dismissed in previous years as America's enemies. This persisted into the early 1980s, complicating the Reagan administration's determination to pursue a more vigorously anti-Communist foreign policy in places like Africa and Central America. By the mid-1980s, despite Reagan's popularity, the networks continued to maintain a semi-independent course, supporting the administration's broader goals but questioning particular initiatives. Unwilling to identify with the US government to the same degree as they had during Vietnam, the networks shifted their focus, reporting on threats to "America"—the nation and its people rather than the government—posed by terrorists and other shadowy elements beyond the pale of legitimate dissent and diplomacy. This approach proved especially useful when the Cold War ended and the old framework became completely obsolete.[17]

The network that was most successful in responding to the new challenges of the late 1980s and early 1990s was ABC. Under Roone Arledge, its news division had become innovative and profitable, enabling Arledge to gain the respect of his superiors at Cap Cities and preventing the severe budget cuts that the owners of the other networks had imposed on their news divisions. *World News Tonight* was the nation's most watched evening newscast, and *Nightline* and *This Week with David Brinkley* had great demographics and were acclaimed by critics. And the newsmagazine *20/20* continued to attract many viewers and advertising dollars, becoming the news division's biggest revenue generator. Now produced by Victor Neufeld, it moved aggressively into territory long dominated by afternoon talk shows like *The Oprah Winfrey Show* and *Donahue* with reports on medical and psychological conditions and inspirational human-interest stories.

The program's most popular features were Barbara Walters's trademark interviews, often of people recently thrust into the news. No one was better at landing these high-profile "gets," and they boosted the program's and ABC's reputation for journalistic intrepidness.[18]

Determined not to lose the initiative, Arledge lured one of CBS's brightest new stars, Diane Sawyer, to ABC. Sawyer had become frustrated as part of the ensemble on *60 Minutes*, and Arledge convinced her that she would have more opportunities at ABC. He paired her with the veteran correspondent Sam Donaldson on an ambitious new program called *Primetime Live*, a live, hour-long broadcast, produced in front of a studio audience, composed of interviews with newsmakers and celebrities, live reports delivered from the scene of big breaking stories, and town-hall-style discussions and debates. It was massively hyped but flopped with viewers and critics when it debuted in August 1989, forcing Arledge and producer Rick Kaplan to change the program's format. Kaplan got rid of the studio audience and added more taped features and interviews, turning it into a more conventional newsmagazine. This suited Sawyer but disappointed Donaldson, who preferred the spontaneity of live interviews and breaking news. By the early 1990s, the program's ratings had improved and it had found a secure place on ABC's schedule.

ABC's most surprising success story was *World News Tonight*. Produced by Paul Friedman, it became the ratings leader in early 1989, a position it held until the mid-1990s. This increased Peter Jennings's influence within ABC News, and prompted Arledge to give him a new contract that raised his salary to $7 million per year. It seemed a good investment. By 1992, advertisers were paying $55,000 for a thirty-second commercial, and the program was generating an annual profit of more than $50 million. The most remarkable thing about *World News Tonight* was that it managed this feat without moving downscale. Though the program included a healthy dose of features, consumer-oriented "news you can use," and weekly profiles of the "Person of the Week," its main emphasis was hard news, and it was widely regarded as the most serious and thoughtful of the network newscasts. Determined to help Americans understand the complexities of the post–Cold War order, Jennings and Friedman increased their coverage of international news and went to great lengths to explain developments in places like the Balkans, the Middle East, and Somalia. Their coverage of domestic news was thorough and often illuminating, and they continued their popular and respected *American Agenda* series on pressing domestic issues. Far more than their rivals, Jennings and Friedman seized the opportunity to make their program interpretive—a venue where viewers could go for a better understanding of the day's most important events, not a headline service or a source of unfiltered breaking news like CNN. The evolution of *World News Tonight* was a sensible response to one of the perplexing realities of the era—that, thanks to CNN and local newscasts, most viewers had already seen reports of the day's big stories. Here was one route toward product differentiation.

As ABC's fortunes rose, CBS's declined. Crippled by budget cuts and nasty infighting that sapped morale and sparked negative publicity, CBS News lost its position as the most watched and respected news division. With Laurence Tisch looking over his shoulder, news chief Howard Stringer imposed stringent new economies and prodded producers to develop new programming. Stringer's biggest problem was arresting the steady decline in the ratings of the CBS *Evening News*. Compared to the urbane Jennings and NBC's Tom Brokaw, a laconic, mild-mannered Midwesterner, Dan Rather was a tense, tightly wound, at times passionate broadcaster. Though many viewers liked this, others were put off by it, and some CBS officials began to worry that Rather had become too polarizing to serve as CBS's most visible face. Their misgivings were reinforced when Rather was involved in a number of incidents that raised questions about his judgment and professionalism, culminating in a testy live interview with vice president George H. W. Bush in February 1988. At a time when all the networks were trying to differentiate themselves from the competition, however, his passion could also be viewed as an asset, and his superiors were impressed with his ability to rebound from setbacks and perform well under pressure. Rather was especially effective during the Persian Gulf War and on occasions when he was able to report from the site of big stories, leading CBS officials to ponder how they could get him out from behind his anchor desk and into the field as much as possible. "Dan in action is pretty hard to beat," noted Stringer. "That helps him. I think we can build on that."[19]

By early 1993, Rather and the CBS *Evening News* had regained the initiative and were a solid number two in the ratings, and Rather had signed a long-term contract extension with the network. In a bid to leap past *World News Tonight* and redefine the evening newscast, he was paired with Connie Chung in a new dual-anchor format that debuted in June. Though they would routinely appear side by side in the same studio, the idea was for Rather to spend a lot more time on the road reporting on big stories.[20] Chung had spent her early career at the network and its Los Angeles station before moving to NBC in the 1980s, where she anchored the weekend news and hosted popular special reports. She had come back to CBS in 1990. She was highly experienced and extremely well liked by viewers, scoring the highest "Q ratings" in the industry, and CBS executives were confident the new format would satisfy Rather and Chung, appeal to viewers, and increase interest in other programs in which Chung appeared. But it failed on all counts, reversing the gains the program had made. Chung could never escape from Rather's shadow, and Rather spent less time in the field than he had hoped, making the atmosphere in the studio increasingly tense. Deploying Chung on new magazine programs and encouraging her to line up interviews with the subjects of tawdry tabloid stories also seemed to cheapen her journalistic credibility and the image of the CBS *Evening News*. By mid-1995 their partnership was over, Chung had left CBS in a huff, accusing the network of sexism, and Rather had resumed his duties as the program's sole anchor. "I worked hard to make it work," Rather insisted in an interview. Chung, not surprisingly, thought otherwise.[21]

CBS's greatest success and most ambitious experiments involved its newsmagazines. Don Hewitt's *60 Minutes* continued its remarkable run, rising to the number-one spot in the ratings during the early 1990s. And with such ratings came even more prodigious advertising revenues, ensuring huge profits for the network. Hewitt hired new correspondents to replace Sawyer and Harry Reasoner, who retired in 1991, and neatly integrated them into the program's ensemble. But CBS executives persisted in their efforts to develop news programs that might appeal to younger viewers. The most successful was *48 Hours*, which debuted in January 1988. Inspired by *48 Hours on Crack Street*, a documentary that aired in 1986, it employed innovative, cinema-vérité techniques to examine subjects from the perspective of real people. In its early years, the program's whole hour was devoted to a single story, which producers followed in engrossing detail over the course of two days, the rationale for the program's title. Hosted by Rather, who sometimes also served as a reporter, and produced by Andrew Heyward, a rising star who eventually became the news division's president, it attracted a growing audience and became a solid hit for CBS by the early 1990s.[22] Wisely, Heyward made it very different from *60 Minutes*. Its use of hand-held cameras and extensive reliance on raw interview footage matched its often gritty subjects and made it well suited for covering crime stories, a popular subject that became the program's main focus by the mid-1990s. Heyward also sought to create prime-time magazine programs for Connie Chung. The most popular was *Eye to Eye with Connie Chung*, which mixed interviews and features in the style of ABC's *20/20*. Chung was expected to do for CBS what Barbara Walters had done for ABC, but she was never able to gain the same level of respect as an interviewer, and her programs, which routinely covered the same subjects as tabloid shows like *A Current Affair*, embarrassed some CBS staffers. Few tears were shed when she decamped for ABC.

By far the most troubled network in early 1990s was NBC. At the behest of Robert Wright, news division chief Michael Gartner had made NBC News more efficient. But many staff were unhappy with the cuts and their implications for newsgathering, and they were frustrated by the poor performance of most NBC programs. Tom Brokaw's evening newscast was a distant third in the ratings, the network continued to struggle in its efforts to produce a successful newsmagazine, and it nearly killed its most successful and consistent money-maker, *Today*, when network officials replaced cohost Jane Pauley with younger, more glamorous Deborah Norville. The transition was handled clumsily, and Norville, a very competent anchor and correspondent, became the target of public criticism for having "stolen" an older woman's job—despite the fact that Pauley had wanted to the leave *Today* for opportunities in prime time. The program's ratings went into free fall, and it soon fell behind *Good Morning, America*, now hosted by the dependable and appealing Joan Lunden and Charles Gibson. Disaster was averted when Norville went on maternity leave and was replaced by Katie Couric, a Washington-based reporter who had begun to contribute segments to the program. Ratings went up instantly, and in April 1991, Norville was dismissed and Couric became Bryant Gumbel's new cohost.[23]

Ironically, NBC's biggest disaster grew out of a welcome and unanticipated success. Since Wright's arrival at the network, he had pressed the news division to come up with inventive prime-time programming. In response, they tried flashy specials on subjects like teenagers "scared sexless" by the AIDS crisis and programs that borrowed features from syndicated tabloid shows. Perhaps the most unusual was *Yesterday, Today, and Tomorrow*, a newsmagazine that mixed nostalgic features with more conventional investigative reports and human-interest stories and routinely employed reenactments. Accompanied by graphics identifying them as "dramatizations," they were ideal for visualizing events for which producers had no film, allowing for a reduction in screen time devoted to talking heads. "It's an idea whose time has come," Sid Feders, the NBC producer in charge of the program, announced."[24] But after a trial run in the summer of 1989, the show impressed neither viewers nor NBC executives and never made it onto the network's regular schedule. A very different program, *Real Life with Jane Pauley*, didn't fare much better. It sought to examine the "changing patterns of American life" through uplifting human-interest stories.[25] After its cancelation, Pauley reemerged as coanchor of a more conventional newsmagazine, *Dateline NBC*. Offering the usual mix of investigative exposés, newsmaker interviewers, and human-interest features, and scheduled at a time, 10:00 PM, when other newsmagazines had become popular, it drew respectable numbers from the start and soon became a hit, ending what Bill Carter of the *New York Times* called "television's longest running exercise in futility."[26]

But NBC's triumph was imperiled when a segment broadcast in November 1992 was revealed to have been faked. It was an exposé claiming that General Motors trucks could explode if involved in a collision. To ensure that producers would have fiery video footage, NBC technicians had affixed incendiary devices to the gas tank of a GM pickup, but investigators hired by GM soon uncovered the deception. GM filed suit against the network, and NBC was forced to settle, with Pauley and her coanchor, Stone Phillips, compelled to read a lengthy, abject apology on the air. The scandal was an acute embarrassment for the network and its parent company, GE, and led Michael Gartner to resign as head of NBC News.

The *Dateline* affair sparked considerable discussion about changes in the television news business. Faced with competition from popular tabloid programs like *A Current Affair* and *Hard Copy*, it was not surprising, critics noted, to see NBC News resort to tricks that would make their program a good show. And it wasn't just a problem at NBC. All the networks were feeling pressure to move in this direction. As

Dan Rather complained in a speech to the Radio-Television News Directors Association in October 1993, "They've got us putting more and more fuzz and wuzz on the air, cop-shop stuff, so as to compete not with other news programs but with entertainment programs, including those posing as news programs."[27]

There were still differences between the syndicated tabloid shows and network news programs. The latter, for example, refused to pay for big interviews and were reluctant to employ reenactments. And they emphasized different subjects. Network newsmagazines preferred investigative exposés and reports on consumer and health news to the crime, scandal, and celebrity stories that dominated the tabloid programs. But critics had identified an important trend: more tabloid-like stories were appearing on network programs, producing ratings that made the temptation to add even more of them irresistible. For example, when ABC's Diane Sawyer interviewed a woman who had accused a Kennedy family member of rape, *Primetime Live* earned its highest ratings. Eager to produce news programs that might connect with viewers, the networks were moving into the terrain of the tabloids. Yet with the tabloids fiercely competing for viewers and continually increasing their emphasis on sensationalism, the networks still lagged well behind, making it easier for network executives and producers to rationalize this departure from tradition. Compared to *Inside Edition* or *Hard Copy*, their programs still appeared staid and respectable.

Even CNN was feeling the pressure. After the Persian Gulf War, CNN officials continued their expansion, adding new overseas bureaus and increasing their menu of specialized programming for international audiences. CNN's astonishing growth as a global news service, however, masked some problems in the US. While profits were robust, providing the revenues that subsidized Ted Turner's other cable ventures, domestic ratings remained inconsistent—high when big, breaking news occurred and viewers flocked to CNN to find out what was going on, but low under normal circumstances. By early 1994, CNN's ratings had declined sharply. It reached an average of 250,000 households per day, its lowest level since 1982, forcing the sales staff to reduce the rates they charged advertisers.[28] This frustrated many CNN executives and producers and encouraged them to look for stories they could build into must-see blockbusters. But there were dangers in resorting to this strategy. It gave producers an incentive to exaggerate a story's importance and could affect the calculus they employed to choose which stories to emphasize. And when hours and hours were devoted to a blockbuster, regardless of its importance, it crowded out other news, especially stories about events overseas.

CNN executives and producers were soon embroiled in a fierce in-house debate. Some argued that CNN should remain true to its long-time mission. Covering breaking news, including blockbusters, was its brand, giving it a clear identity in the crowded cable television marketplace. Others wondered whether serving as a video wire service could ever generate consistently high ratings. Now that CNN had an extensive and talented corps of correspondents and field producers, it was time, they suggested, for CNN to move away from this approach and develop magazine-style programs and increase in-depth, inter-pretive reporting. Then there was the issue of domestic versus for-eign news. Covering the latter had enhanced CNN's reputation and pleased Turner and the producers who worked on CNN-International. But it was a big reason for the news channel's declining popularity. As CNN president Tom Johnson confessed, "Unless there are Americans involved in a big international story, viewers don't seem to have any real interest." It made sense, therefore, to reduce coverage of foreign news and increase CNN's emphasis on domestic stories.[29]

In June 1994, these discussions were put on hold when O. J. Simp-son's ex-wife and a friend were murdered, and the well-known former football star, television pitchman, and movie actor was charged with the killings. CNN and the networks paid massive attention to the case. And, with so much time at their disposal, CNN producers turned it into the ultimate blockbuster. In the months before Simpson's trial began, they reported every morsel of information related to the case, no matter how minor, and provided lots of airtime for "legal ex-perts" to discuss the merits of the evidence and speculate about its outcome. When the trial finally began, in January 1995, CNN and a recently launched cable channel, Court TV, covered it live, and CNN devoted many other hours to Simpson-related programming, includ-ing nightly special reports that offered highlights and commentary on the day's most dramatic moments. The frenzy peaked in early October, when the jury delivered its verdict of not guilty in front of a worldwide audience estimated at 150 million. The Simpson case produced a 500 percent increase in CNN's ratings and the preemption of much of its regular programming. At times, critics suggested, it was "all O. J., all the time." CNN officials justified this by insisting that it was news and the public was deeply interested. And, without a doubt, the public was. But CNN's breathless wall-to-wall coverage of the Simpson case sullied its reputation. For several years, CNN producers had adroitly balanced hard domestic and international news with soft, at times sensational, material, an approach that ensured airtime for stories the networks routinely neglected. Now it began to shift gradually toward the sensational.[30]

The networks also benefited enormously from the Simpson case. It dominated the evening newscasts. By early 1997, when Simpson's civil trial for wrongful death ended, a Simpson-related report had been the lead story on the NBC *Nightly News* seventy-three times. CBS and ABC were not far behind. They led with Simpson stories on sixty-six and fifty-three days, respectively. The case also became a regular subject of segments on prime-time newsmagazines, including the venerable *60 Minutes*. Even *Nightline* covered it extensively. In Ted Koppel's view, it was "the biggest crime story of the decade."[31]

At the networks, too, the balanced shifted, as coverage of complex and "boring" subjects declined, and the line between the tabloid programs and network news broadcasts continued to blur. The Simpson case legitimized the use of reenactments, particularly in coverage of crimes and criminal trials, and of other technical gimmicks designed to make stories more arresting—close-ups, dissolves, and dramatic music and sound effects. With the assistance of these techniques, network news reports increasingly took the form of slickly produced, visually compelling mini-narratives, not unlike entertainment programs on TV.[32] The Simpson case also increased the visibility of on-screen experts who specialized in inside dope and informed speculation. Soon, they began to offer their opinions about subjects like politics and the state of the economy and became nearly as prominent as conventional reporters. Finally, the ratings boost that the Simpson case gave news programs encouraged the networks to increase the hours devoted to news during prime time. With ample evidence of what would sell, producers expanded their newsmagazines into franchises airing several nights a week. Safe, inexpensive alternatives to scripted dramas and comedies, they eventually commanded up to ten hours of prime time and became consistent money-makers for the networks.

NBC's commitment to the Simpson case was a major factor in its mid-decade revival. Under Andrew Lack, the former CBS producer responsible for *West 57th* who replaced Michael Gartner as news chief after the *Dateline* fiasco, NBC News experienced a dramatic turnaround in its fortunes. This was a result in part of the success of NBC's entertainment programs. *ER*, *Friends*, and *Frasier* were the top-rated programs on television, and they provided network officials with a terrific platform for promoting NBC News. But it was also a result of some shrewd decisions to revamp existing programs and allow the winds generated by the Simpson case to propel the network ahead of its rivals.

Working with a new producer, ABC vet Jeff Gralnick, Tom Brokaw redesigned the NBC *Nightly News*. They began to conceive the whole broadcast as a narrative, with a carefully chosen lead story serving as the program's beginning, and heavily promoted special segments resembling the consumer, health, and investigative reports on prime-time newsmagazines as its central features. Often, these features were related in some way to the program's top story, giving the entire broadcast a consistent theme. Critics and their rivals at the other networks accused them of producing "news-lite," but the new format was popular with viewers.[33] And as some of their critics were forced to concede, Gralnick and Brokaw continued to serve up a decent portion of hard news. NBC's mission was not just to deliver the news but, as one producer put it, "make it interesting and relevant to viewers." By the end of the 1990s, this approach had paid off, and the NBC *Nightly News* had become the nation's most watched evening newscast.[34]

Lack also oversaw the rehabilitation and expansion of *Dateline*. Putting the GM scandal behind them, he and the program's executive producer, Neal Shapiro, turned it into a solid hit and big moneymaker. Though it presented stories on serious subjects like welfare reform and the North American Free Trade Agreement and continued with investigative exposés, its forte was celebrity profiles, big newsmaker interviews, and what the critic Walter Goodman called "worry-of-the-week" health and medical stories.[35] By 1995, NBC was broadcasting editions of *Dateline* three nights a week. In 1996, network officials added another edition on Sundays, which would compete head-to-head with CBS's *60 Minutes*. At times in the late 1990s, *Dateline* aired five times a week.

NBC's inventive use of *Dateline* as a franchise inspired the other networks to do the same. ABC created another edition of *20/20*, and in

1998 it folded *Primetime Live* into 20/20, hoping to achieve the economies of scale that Lack and Shapiro had achieved with *Dateline*, where a single staff and anchor team were responsible for every edition of the program and could easily follow big stories over the course of the week.[36] *Dateline*'s success also prompted changes at CBS. Don Hewitt increased the cast of correspondents on *60 Minutes*, added a short-lived segment featuring guest pundits, and began to include more reports on late-breaking news. And, in 1999, he finally allowed CBS to produce another edition of the program, *60 Minutes II*, which was broadcast on Wednesdays. Produced by Jeff Fager, a gifted young producer who had impressed Hewitt, *60 Minutes II* was a veritable clone of its parent, eschewing the sob stories and sensationalism common on *Dateline* and 20/20.[37] Meanwhile, *48 Hours* increased its emphasis on investigative reports and especially crime stories, ensuring little overlap between CBS's two prime-time franchises. By the end of the 1990s, prime-time newsmagazines had colonized much of the turf once dominated by syndicated tabloid programs, contributing to a steep decline in the latter's ratings and the cancelation of *A Current Affair* and *Hard Copy*. This was a vindication of sorts for Maury Povich, who had endured the barbs of network journalists while host of *A Current Affair* and had seen his wife, Connie Chung, assailed for "going tabloid" on her CBS programs in the early 1990s. Shows like *A Current Affair* had lost viewers because network newsmagazines had "co-opted" the genre, he argued. "When our ratings went through the roof, they took notice."[38]

Another one of NBC's perennial underperformers, the Sunday morning talk show *Meet the Press*, also experienced a dramatic revival. It began when NBC's Washington bureau chief, Tim Russert, became the program's host in 1991. Russert, a lawyer who had worked as an aide for several prominent Democratic politicians, joined NBC News in 1984 as an executive. When he was named the host of *Meet the Press*, the program was languishing in third place in the ratings, behind CBS's *Face the Nation* and the long-time leader, *This Week with David Brinkley*. Recognizing the need to shake things up, Russert and his producers developed a new format that emphasized interviews with Washington politicos, whom Russert interrogated in a sharp, prosecutorial style. The show's ratings steadily improved, and *Meet the Press* was the biggest beneficiary when David Brinkley retired and *This Week* began losing viewers. By the end of 1997, Russert's show was the most watched Sunday morning talk show, and Russert had become ubiquitous on the NBC *Nightly News* and NBC's election and political coverage. His knowledge of and enthusiasm for politics and Beltway inside dope enlivened NBC's news programming, and his program's upscale demographics made it appealing to advertisers and profitable for the network, earning an estimated $40 million a year.[39]

NBC News' biggest success was *Today*. With the versatile and appealing Katie Couric as Bryant Gumbel's cohost and a dynamic young producer, Jeff Zucker, at the helm, it rebounded quickly from the decline in popularity it experienced as a result of the Deborah Norville affair. Zucker made the program more lively and spontaneous. He encouraged Couric and Gumbel to continue with interviews beyond the usual two to three minutes if the occasion seemed to warrant it, and he expanded the features and stunts that had been the show's hallmark since the Hugh Downs era. It was Zucker, for example, who instituted the weekly musical concerts in the Rockefeller Center plaza outside the program's street-level studio, a huge hit with viewers. In its first half hour, *Today* also remained the newsiest of the morning programs. NBC correspondents and pundits like Russert appeared regularly, and Couric in particular excelled at virtually every kind of assignment — from interviewing the most important statesmen and politicians to cavorting with celebrity guests and her fellow cast members. Thanks to Couric, the program's popularity was undiminished when Gumbel retired in 1997 and was replaced by Matt Lauer, the program's newsreader. Refining the formula that the program's producers had conceived in the 1960s, Zucker's cast developed a distinctive, easygoing rapport that was crucial to the program's continued success yet extremely hard to replicate, as CBS discovered when it hired Gumbel and his old *Today* producer, Steve Friedman, and they tried — and failed — to revive the perpetually moribund CBS morning show by imitating many of *Today*'s most popular features.

NBC's most audacious gambit was its move into cable television. Robert Wright and GE chairman Jack Welch had been plotting this since GE's purchase of NBC, and in April 1989, NBC established its first cable channel, the Consumer News and Business Channel (CNBC). It was a modest venture, offering stock market updates and other business news a few hours a day, and was available in only 17 million homes. Its fortunes improved when NBC bought out a rival, the Financial News Network, and CNBC absorbed much of its staff and more than doubled its potential audience. Gradually, CNBC broadened its programming and began experimenting with shows other than traditional business news, particularly in prime time, when the markets were closed. In 1993, NBC hired Roger Ailes, a former political consultant and experienced television producer, as CNBC's new president, with a mandate to update its programming to make it appealing to a wider range of viewers. Ailes added programs on personal finance and improved the channel's production values to make it more pleasing to the eye. Its most successful nonbusiness program was *Rivera Live*, a popular talk show hosted by the flamboyant and controversial former ABC correspondent Geraldo Rivera that rode the O. J. Simpson case to the top of the cable TV ratings. When a settlement with cable operators allowed NBC to establish another cable channel, Ailes developed a plan to take some of the programming ideas he had been working on at CNBC and spin them off into a new channel called America's Talking, which would specialize in talk shows and audience-participation programs.[40]

But Ailes quit when NBC decided to do something else with the new cable channel, and CNBC fell under the control of Bill Bolster, an experienced producer of local news. Bolster was talented and a good manager. But he was also the beneficiary of blind luck: a dramatic run-up in the stock market that mesmerized many Americans and drew hordes of new viewers to CNBC. "As the market has gone up, and in some ways become, at its worst, the national lottery, CNBC has grown right along with it," a media-industry analyst observed in 2000. Tapping into the new enthusiasm and drawing on conventions from local news, Bolster turned CNBC into a spectacular showcase for the "new economy." Accompanied by flashy graphics and easy-to-comprehend "stats," his anchors and reporters covered the market as if it were a sporting event, with extensive "pregame" speculation and "postgame" wrap-ups. This format made CBNC an ideal platform for ambitious stock analysts and financial news pundits like the former broker Jim Cramer, as well as for homegrown talent like anchor Maria Bartiromo, whom viewers and industry wags dubbed the "Money Honey." Though CNBC's audience dropped markedly during prime time, by 2000 its average daily ratings briefly exceeded CNN's, making it the most watched news and information channel on cable television.[41]

CNBC was not NBC's only cable venture. In 1995, it entered into a partnership with the software giant Microsoft to create an all-news cable channel and accompanying Internet site. MSNBC launched in July 1996, taking over the production facilities and "shelf space" on cable systems formerly occupied by Ailes's short-lived America's Talking. It was a promising enterprise and, on paper, seemed likely to present CNN with a tough challenge. Rather than build a newsgathering apparatus from scratch, its producers could rely on the experience and resources of NBC News and instantly offer high-quality programming. NBC stars like Tom Brokaw, Jane Pauley, and Katie Couric could be used to draw viewers to MSNBC, and the new channel could serve as a "farm team" for up-and-coming talent before their promotion to NBC. NBC officials envisioned the two channels working in perfect harmony, with viewers turning to MSNBC and its website for more detailed coverage of stories they encountered on the NBC *Nightly News* or *Today*. And when a really big story broke, Brokaw's viewers needn't switch to CNN when NBC returned to its regular programming; they could see him on MSNBC, where he would continue broadcasting. With MSNBC as the network's main site for breaking news, NBC could also reduce costly preemptions and avoid the bitter fights for airtime that news division presidents had waged since the 1960s. Best of all, NBC would collect fees from cable operators that added MSNBC to their programming packages, giving the network an additional revenue stream that could defray the costs of producing news programs for both organizations, a stream that would grow as more cable operators added MSNBC to their systems.

But for several years, despite these advantages and heavy promotion by NBC, MSNBC failed to attract viewers. Part of the problem was that it lacked a clear identity. Ailes dismissed it as "a $500 million launch in search of a format."[42] At times, it sought to mimic CNN by specializing in breaking news, sparking a new competitiveness to be the first to broadcast big stories. At other times, MSNBC producers adopted a different approach, selecting two or three stories that they followed closely over the course of a day. Often, they were the same ones that were featured on NBC's news programs and highlighted MSNBC's ability to provide depth and detail. During prime time, MSNBC appeared even more schizophrenic. Its most lavishly promoted show was *Internight*, an interview program hosted by a rotating cast of NBC News' biggest stars, including Brokaw, Couric, Bryant Gumbel, and sportscaster Bob Costas. Though its bookers were able to secure A-list guests, the rotating cast of hosts was confusing and deprived the program of a consistent voice. It was followed by a conventional hour-long newscast hosted by Brian Williams, a polished correspondent and anchor whom NBC officials were grooming as Brokaw's successor on the NBC *Nightly News*. MSNBC's most unusual prime-time programs were *Time and Again*, a nostalgia program hosted by Jane Pauley, and *The Site*, an ill-fated effort to cover the latest trends in technology. The latter was part of Andrew Lack's bid to make MSNBC appealing to young, tech-savvy viewers. Throughout the day, MSNBC anchors encouraged viewers to contact them through email, which they occasionally read on the air, or visit MSNBC's website. Lack also hired a crop of young commentators to provide expert analysis and serve as regular participants in a freewheeling discussion program that was supposed to evoke the atmosphere of a college bull session. He made a point of choosing figures whose views were out of the ordinary and seemed like they might play well on TV. Among them was an acerbic blond named Ann Coulter.[43]

Nothing seemed to work. Desperate for viewers, MSNBC officials abandoned their interest in appealing to the tech-savvy and increased features on fashion and the entertainment industry. They tried documentaries and repurposed investigative reports that had appeared on *Dateline*. In 1997, they even hired popular ESPN sportscaster Keith Olbermann to host a prime-time "news-oriented talk program." The sardonic Olbermann had gained a following as anchor of ESPN's *SportsCenter*, and Lack hoped that he would add some energy and humor to MSNBC's lineup. Olbermann was excited about branching out and addressing subjects other than sports, but he was disgusted by MSNBC's wall-to-wall coverage of the Clinton-Lewinsky scandal and left in 1998. By the end of the 1990s, MSNBC's ratings were terrible. It had fallen way behind CNBC as well as CNN, and Lack and his staff were at a loss about what to do about it.

The only bright spot was its website. Under Merrill Brown, a former print journalist and media executive, MSNBC.com became the most popular and innovative news site on the Internet. At the time of its launch, it was a relatively modest enterprise, providing visitors with links to items of potential interest, including the web pages of MSNBC's television programs and NBC's thirty owned-and-operated stations. Very quickly, however, it added new features. By 1999, visitors could find lots of original material, even short news clips produced by Brown's staff and stories reported by its many domestic and foreign partners. Much of it was interactive, encouraging the input and engagement of viewers. These features made perusing MSNBC .com quite different from watching the news. As Brown explained, "The goal from the beginning has been to package the experience, instead of giving people endless lists of things—which for many other news sites is the norm." Brown was also keen to "personalize" MSNBC, making it easier for visitors to find exactly the information they wanted, or having particular stories or packages of news sent to them by email. MSNBC.com was a big hit with consumers. In October 1999, it drew over 7 million "unique visitors"—the coin of the realm on the Internet. This was a million more than CNN Interactive, its nearest rival. Its success led CNN and the other two broadcast networks to expand their news websites and encouraged increasing numbers of Americans to look to the Internet, rather than TV, for news and news-related features.[44]

In February 1996, less than two months after NBC and Microsoft had announced the impending launch of MSNBC, the Australian media baron Rupert Murdoch revealed that he, too, was getting into the cable news business. Like Ted Turner, he was not someone to be underestimated. Murdoch had built his father's newspaper business into a global media empire that included a movie studio and the Fox television network. Thanks to Murdoch's deep pockets, extensive support from the FCC, and edgy, offbeat programs that appealed to younger viewers, Fox had managed to become a true fourth network, breaking into the exclusive club long dominated by CBS, NBC, and ABC. Murdoch had defied expectations in making Fox a success. Could he do the same with cable news?[45]

To run the new Fox News Channel, Murdoch hired Roger Ailes. It was a brilliant decision. No one knew more about what worked on the small screen. Ailes's career in television had begun in the early 1960s, when, after graduating from college, he had gone to work for a Westinghouse station in Cleveland. By 1968, he had risen through the ranks to become the executive producer of *The Mike Douglas Show*, a popular syndicated talk show. When, in the run-up to the 1968 election, Richard Nixon appeared on the program, Ailes admonished him for not taking television seriously. Impressed, Nixon hired him as a campaign media advisor, and Ailes helped to conceive the strategy that was so successful in selling Nixon to voters. He stayed on for a couple of years as a TV advisor, but was soon let go and became a freelance media consultant for politicians and businesses. By the mid-1980s, he had become a highly sought hired gun for conservative politicians, including President Reagan and Vice President Bush, helping them prepare for debates and suggesting potent jokes and one-liners they could use when confronted by a hostile press. It was Ailes who orchestrated Bush's vituperative exchange with Dan Rather on the CBS *Evening News*, an incident that is widely regarded as having toughened Bush's public image.[46]

But Ailes soon grew tired of political consulting and leaped at the chance to run CNBC. He was especially excited about its spin-off, America's Talking, and incensed when NBC decided to shut it down and relaunch it as MSNBC. Rather than run the new channel, he quit and signed on with Murdoch. Their backgrounds led many observers to predict that Fox News would tilt to the political right. Murdoch's newspapers were unabashedly conservative, and he had suggested that CNN was "too liberal." But Ailes dismissed the notion, insisting that Fox News would be "fair and balanced." "Our job is to be objective," he insisted in an interview. "We'd like to restore objectivity where we find it lacking."[47]

In the months before FNC's debut, Murdoch and Ailes hustled to get things ready. While Ailes negotiated agreements with foreign broadcasters and Murdoch's UK-based Sky News to provide FNC with international news and began building its in-house newsgathering staff, Murdoch struggled to secure "carriage," a place on the menus cable operators offered consumers. This was not easy, since many cable operators wanted only two news channels on their systems and preferred the seemingly more promising MSNBC. Murdoch found it especially difficult to get on systems owned by Time Warner, which had just acquired CNN and wasn't eager to accommodate yet another rival news channel. To persuade recalcitrant cable operators to add FNC, he offered them an unprecedented one-time bounty of $10 per subscriber. He also enlisted the assistance of politicians like New York mayor Rudolph Giuliani and launched a well-organized lobbying effort to get FNC on Time Warner cable systems. These efforts would eventually pay off. But it took time, and when FNC debuted on October 7, 1996, it was available in only 17 million households compared to MSNBC's 48 million.[48]

By this time, Ailes had assembled a staff of six hundred, many of them ex-CNBC and America's Talking employees. Most were based at

FNC's headquarters in midtown Manhattan. They were also assigned to brand-new FNC bureaus in Washington, Miami, Chicago, Denver, Los Angeles, San Francisco, Hong Kong, Jerusalem, and London. Building FNC's newsgathering infrastructure was extremely expensive. Total start-up costs ran well beyond the $100 million for which Murdoch and Ailes had originally budgeted, and Ailes conceded that Murdoch was likely to spend over $400 million before FNC became profitable, which he expected to be in 2001. But Murdoch never blanched. He kept writing checks, and his boldness was rewarded when FNC achieved the success he and Ailes had prophesied.

Ailes's oft-expressed desire to provide an alternative to CNN went further than most people realized. He knew that, even with Murdoch's ample resources, it would be virtually impossible for FNC to replicate CNN's capacity for covering breaking news wherever and whenever it occurred. But this was never his aim. Instead, Fox News would counterprogram: mix breaking news with in-depth reports on subjects of particular interest to FNC viewers and opinion-oriented talk shows in prime time, as he had planned for America's Talking. A practical solution to CNN's virtual ownership of breaking news, it was a formula that would redefine cable news.

For most of the broadcast day, FNC programming was organized around the classic news wheel format perfected by all-news radio stations and CNN's Headline News. Recaps of the latest headlines aired every half hour, followed by more detailed reports from the field and discussion and analysis by FNC anchors and assorted experts. In between, FNC offered special reports on subjects like religion, health, law, politics, and popular culture. Everything was fast-paced, like local news, with flashy graphics and sound effects. Its signature programs—the ones Ailes was convinced would be central to FNC's success—appeared in the early evening and prime time. They included a business report anchored by CNBC alum Neal Cavuto, a talk show hosted by former *Inside Edition* anchor Bill O'Reilly, and a *Crossfire*-style debate program featuring Sean Hannity and Alan Colmes, two little-known radio personalities. Ailes made a point of ensuring that conservative voices were prominently featured on FNC's prime-time shows as well as its news reports. His highest priority, however, was that FNC be engaging and entertaining, particularly during the evening. Impressed by the popularity of talk radio hosts like Rush Limbaugh and Don Imus, Ailes sought to bring their expressive edginess to cable television.

Ailes's strategy rested on a perceptive understanding of both the television marketplace and American politics and culture. By the mid-1990s, the proliferation of new cable channels had increased consumer choice and altered viewer expectations. Many viewers liked edgy entertainment shows, and they were receptive to news and information programs that diverged from the stolid traditions of the past. They also liked television personalities who seemed "real" and openly expressed their emotions. It was an easy segue from expressing emotions to expressing opinion, particularly if a TV host was honest and consistent—and viewers felt they knew where he was coming from. As Limbaugh had demonstrated, expressing opinion could be very entertaining. And his program attracted people who disagreed with him or tuned in just to hear what outrageous thing he would say next.[49]

Ailes was also aware that many Americans were convinced that the networks and CNN were affected by liberal bias. It was a complaint that conservatives had been making since the late 1950s, and it was revived shortly before FNC's debut when CBS correspondent Bernard Goldberg published a scathing op-ed in the *Wall Street Journal* accusing his colleagues of purposefully slanting news stories in ways that discredited conservative figures and ideas. For the most part, Ailes agreed with the critics, and his decision to promote FNC as "fair and balanced" was a direct pitch for their support. They were a ready-made audience for FNC, the foundation on which Ailes would build the news channel.[50]

Yet he also understood that, for many conservatives, this conviction was part of a larger worldview. FNC's potential viewers were also likely to be listeners of conservative talk radio shows and perhaps even readers of conservative magazines, members of an increasingly well-organized "movement culture" that had gained many members and considerable political influence since the 1980s and especially after the Republican sweep of Congress in the 1994 midterm elections. Tailoring FNC to their interests and political beliefs would make them unusually loyal—more loyal than most viewers were to conventional cable channels. It would kindle devotion to FNC's "brand." The possibility that FNC might also strengthen their identification with conservative politics—and attract new people to the movement—was an added sweetener.[51]

CNN officials greeted their new competitors with the usual swagger. Tom Johnson conceded that they expected "strong competition," particularly from MSNBC, but he was confident that CNN would prevail. "I don't believe the market will support all of those channels," he noted portentously.[52] But Johnson and his superiors at Time Warner, who had just purchased Turner Broadcasting and regarded CNN as its most valuable asset, were concerned. The emergence of rival all-news channels could divide the advertising market and result in fewer revenues and profits for CNN—and, by extension, for Time Warner. Fending them off would not be easy. NBC and Fox had deep pockets and seemed prepared for a long, protracted struggle. And they weren't the only problem; CNN was being threatened on the margins as well. CNBC had made considerable strides, and another business channel, Bloomberg Television, had launched. Cable channels like E! were moving aggressively into entertainment news, and since its gavel-to-gavel coverage of the Simpson trial, Court TV had become increasingly successful. To win the latest round in the "cable news wars" CNN would have to take risks and alter its mission.

CNN's first initiative was a bold and costly attempt to derail CNBC, the creation of a separate business-news channel, CNNfn. Run by Lou Dobbs, the popular host of *Moneyline*, it would cover the stock market and economic trends, like its main rival. But it would do so in a more engaging and professional manner—with better production values and reports drawing on CNN's extensive global resources and access to prominent figures from the business community. In typical CNN fashion, it was launched in December 1995 with only a $50 million investment and boasted economies that promised to keep operating expenses low. Distribution, however, was a significant problem. With CNN and Headline News already on their menus, cable operators were wary of adding CNNfn. As a result, when it began broadcasting, CNNfn could be seen by 5.5 million viewers, compared to CNBC's 56 million. And industry observers openly wondered whether the audience for business news was large enough to accommodate two channels offering essentially the same service.[53]

Competition between them soon became fierce. Led by Bill Bolster, CNBC developed very effective techniques for jazzing up business news and attracting viewers intrigued by the astonishing increase in stock prices, while CNNfn struggled to keep up. CNBC's audience remained minuscule—in 1997, though available in 61 million homes, its average weekly audience was 2.3 million. But its demographics were sterling, allowing its sales staff to charge a premium for commercials, and by 1999 it was making $400 million for NBC. Because of similar demographics, CNNfn was a big money-maker, too, despite its smaller audience and more limited distribution. But in 1999 it suffered a terrible blow when Dobbs quit after a row with superiors, and CNN officials were forced to find new anchors for *Moneyline*, the most popular business-news program on cable television, which was broadcast on both CNN and CNNfn. Both channels were also hurt by the collapse of the stock market and the economic slump of the early 2000s, which reduced the overall audience for business news back to pre–bull market levels. In the end, CNNfn could never come close to its rival, and in 2004 CNN officials shut it down.

CNN's strategy for shoring up its main domestic service was less ambitious—maintaining its commitment to breaking news while expanding its offering of special programs. The O. J. Simpson case inspired *Burden of Proof*, a legal-affairs talk show hosted by Greta Van Susteren, a former lawyer who had impressed CNN executives and many viewers with her performance as an expert analyst. And in a nod to the format Ailes had developed at CBNC and America's Talking, CNN producers created an audience-participation talk show called *Talk Back Live*. Focusing on topics in the news, it was broadcast in the afternoons in front of a live audience and allowed viewers as well as the studio audience to submit questions via email and fax in a partnership with the Internet provider CompuServe.

But the specter of new competition led Turner and Johnson to move more aggressively. In 1997, Johnson hired Rick Kaplan, a former ABC producer, to be the new head of CNN's US broadcasting service. Kaplan had played a key role in Roone Arledge's transformation of ABC News, producing *Nightline*, *World News Tonight*, and *Primetime Live*. Driven and highly combative, he seemed well qualified to help CNN create new programs that would attract viewers and lift it above its rivals. Money flowed into program development, and CNN's production values and on-air look were spruced up to resemble those at the networks. Its large ensemble of anchors and correspondents was cut, increasing the airtime and visibility of stars like Bernard Shaw, Wolf Blitzer, Christiane Amanpour, and political commentator Jeff Greenfield, whom Kaplan had hired away from ABC. At Kaplan's insistence, CNN producers also lessened the repetition of stories to encourage viewers to tune in for longer periods. "We want to have really smart, news-oriented programming that people will make an appointment to see," he told a reporter for the *New York Times*.[54]

Borrowing a page from his broadcast rivals, Kaplan created a series of newsmagazines called *NewsStand*. They would air at 10:00 PM, right after Larry King's popular interview show, and exploit CNN's new relationship with publications in the Time Warner media empire. One would be a partnership with *Time* magazine. Anchored by Bernard Shaw and Jeff Greenfield, it would specialize in exposés and reports on hard news subjects in the vein of *60 Minutes*. Another program, a joint production with *Fortune* magazine, would offer business news. A third version of *NewsStand* would specialize in entertainment news, making use of the resources of Time Warner's popular magazine *Entertainment Weekly*. Some segments would be produced by CNN journalists, while others would be produced by their print partners. Kaplan hoped that partnering with successful magazines would give the programs in the series an instant, clear-cut identity, and that their readers could be lured to CNN. He was confident the *NewsStand* programs would increase CNN's viewership in prime time, and he envisioned expanding them to seven nights a week. "This is a long-term investment," he insisted.[55]

But problems arose from the start. The first broadcast of *NewsStand: CNN and Time* sparked a scandal when it came to light that a segment claiming the US military had used lethal nerve gas during the Vietnam War had relied on unconfirmed and potentially dubious sources. CNN was swamped with criticism and negative press, and an in-house investigation concluded that the story's main thesis was "insupportable." Eager for a scoop that would have launched the series in high style, the segment's producers had been too eager to provide a neat and tidy story, discounting sources that would have complicated their argument or lessened its dramatic impact. A chastened Tom Johnson was forced to issue a public apology and retraction. The incident made people aware of *NewsStand*—but in the wrong way. And it added fuel to the charge that CNN was biased.[56]

Though *NewsStand* recovered from the fiasco, it never gained a substantial audience. Part of the problem was that "appointment viewing" depends on having a regular spot on the schedule and consistent promotion, so that viewers know when to tune in. But unlike the talk shows on FNC, which could easily focus on breaking news and incorporate live reports from the field, *NewsStand* was a taped series. So when breaking news occurred, CNN officials often had little choice but to preempt it. To Kaplan's dismay, CNN executives were also reluctant to promote the program—or any of their programs—in the aggressive manner that the networks plugged *20/20* or *Dateline*. Kaplan and his producers made adjustments, making *NewsStand: CNN and Time* more fluid and accommodating to breaking news, for example. But this was more difficult with the programs devoted to business and entertainment news, and they continued to be routinely preempted, particularly during the Clinton impeachment hearings in the late 1998 and early 1999.

By the end of 1999, *NewsStand* had become little more than a placeholder on CNN's schedule. Its filmed reports appeared amid live reports and updates of breaking news, with no apparent logic or larger purpose. Only a *NewsStand* graphic in the background distinguished it from CNN's usual flow of programming. Producing these filmed reports, however, still required extensive resources, which were diverted from other units. This angered many CNN staffers and undermined their faith in Kaplan's leadership. Becoming *the* source for breaking news had placed Johnson and Kaplan in a bind. It was what viewers expected from CNN—the signature feature that allowed them to stand out in the television marketplace. Efforts to broaden their offerings could very easily conflict with this mission and disappoint the channel's viewers. "CNN is like the Kleenex of cable news," a television news executive observed. "If you're so heavily branded as breaking news, even with [millions] in promotion, can you ever bring people in other than with breaking news?"[57]

The presence of new rivals, however, changed CNN's treatment of breaking news. In previous years, CNN producers routinely included many items of international news, on the assumption that this was responsible journalism and the reason Turner and Burt Reinhardt had established all those foreign bureaus. By the mid-1990s, however, it was clear that, with the end of the Cold War, most Americans, even the confirmed news junkies who regularly watched CNN, were not particularly interested in overseas developments. They preferred news about domestic issues, especially politics, which had become increasing contentious and partisan. When MSNBC and FNC made their debut, CNN lost its freedom to exercise unilateral judgment about what to cover. When it spent too much time on the Middle East peace talks or the Rwandan genocide, and its rivals went with domestic stories, CNN would lose viewers. Rather than encourage a diversity of coverage, competition in the cable news business produced a gradually narrowing in the subjects covered by all three news channels as they tripped over themselves trying to cater to the preferences of viewers. This trend was reinforced by the fact that MSNBC and FNC were not content to merely split the small existing audience for news with CNN—an audience more disposed to be interested in international developments and other hard news stories than the general public. They were determined to enlarge it by attracting new viewers. To do so, however, the news on cable would have to become even more "entertaining."

By early 1998, CNN and other television journalists—and the print press, too—were forced to reckon with another development, the growing prominence of "new media" on the Internet. This didn't just mean MSNBC.com or the websites that the TV networks, local stations, and newspapers had launched to supplement the material they delivered through "old media." There were now hundreds of small, informal, amateurish operations on the World Wide Web that trafficked in news, usually tidbits of gossip gleaned from conventional media and then repackaged and posted with links to the original source. And their numbers were increasing, enlarging the media marketplace and creating yet another source of competition for conventional news providers like CNN. Though some online journalists engaged in old-fashioned reporting, cultivating sources and sifting through evidence to develop stories before posting them on the Internet, the vast majority didn't. They were aggregators, conveyors of information acquired from other sources, much of it unsubstantiated rumors and allegations. In short, the operators of many online media outlets didn't follow conventional journalistic practices, and the "news" they posted didn't meet the standards of professional journalism. Yet to a cynical public suspicious of the pretensions of old media, including CNN and the networks, this was a source of their appeal.[58]

The proliferation of new media, and the willingness of many Americans, especially the young, to turn to them, increased the pressures on print and television journalists. In the past, marginal online operators like Matt Drudge, an aspiring muckraker who operated a website called the Drudge Report, might have been ignored, just as television journalists and the print had long ignored racy supermarket tabloids. But as more and more Americans turned to the web for news, could professional journalists blithely ignore the stories circulating on the Internet? What if they turned out to be true? And what if, while you held fast to professional standards, your competitors began reporting on them and gained the advantage?

This is how the Clinton-Lewinsky sex scandal became the biggest story of the late 1990s, a blockbuster that increased the audience for cable news and boosted the ratings for the networks as well. CNN and the networks had followed the "Whitewater" investigation for several years. Sparked by accusations that Bill and Hillary Clinton had engaged in financial improprieties in the late 1970s and early 1980s, when Clinton was a politician in Arkansas, the case was kept alive by Clinton's Republican critics, who hoped that it might expose unseemly details about Clinton's past that would discredit him and hamper his ability to govern. But investigators, led by special prosecutor Kenneth Starr, were unable to come up with any hard evidence against the Clintons, and the press and public soon lost interest in the case. Undeterred, Starr expanded the scope of his investigation. Rumors of marital infidelities had dogged Clinton throughout his political career. They had been revived by his political critics when he began his presidential campaign, forcing the Clintons to submit to a tough interview with Steve Kroft on *60 Minutes* in January 1992, in which they cryptically acknowledged past marital difficulties but insisted that they were behind them. The charges remained in the news when a former Arkansas state employee named Paula Jones filed a sexual harassment suit against Clinton and claimed that, while he was governor, they had had an affair. Jones's suit offered Starr a new line of inquiry. It required Clinton to make a deposition under oath about his sexual activities with other women, and allowed Starr to investigate rumors that Clinton had engaged in affairs while president and may have lied about it in his deposition. By January 1998, Starr had reason to believe that Clinton had engaged in sexual relations with Monica Lewinsky, a White House intern. More important, he was certain that Clinton had committed perjury, and that the president had persuaded Lewinsky to commit perjury by denying their affair in the affidavit she had been forced to submit in the Jones case.[59]

The case broke when Matt Drudge reported on his website that

Newsweek editors had decided not to publish a story by one of their writers that would have exposed the affair. Not wanting to be scooped, newspapers and the networks picked up the story. The networks actually summoned their anchors back from Cuba, where they had gone to report on Pope John Paul II's historic visit to the Communist-ruled nation and had expected to remain for the week.

It was the perfect story for the new age of infotainment. First, it involved sex and infidelity, the stuff of soap operas, and offered the networks and cable news channels in particular an opportunity to increase their ratings, especially when Lewinsky handed over to Starr a dress stained with semen that matched Clinton's DNA and then revealed grotesque details about their sexual activities in her grand jury testimony. But it wasn't just about sex. To the delight of professional journalists, Clinton was accused of committing a relatively serious offense—lying under oath and pressuring Lewinsky to do the same—that had potentially significant political implications. Right away, before it was clear that he and Lewinsky had had a sexual relationship, reporters and pundits began speculating about whether he would have to resign in disgrace, raising the stakes in ways that turned it into an even bigger story and justified the enormous attention they were paying to it. Perhaps unwittingly, perhaps not, they chose to make it a big deal.[60]

In August 1998, after months of denials and a four-and-a-half-hour closed-door grilling by Starr's legal team, Clinton acknowledged an "inappropriate relationship" with Lewinsky. It was the "gotcha" moment the press had been eagerly waiting for, when all its trafficking in prurience was rewarded. But Clinton denied committing perjury and maintained that the entire scandal had been orchestrated by his Republican critics. His sole offense, he suggested, was adultery, a private matter between himself and his family. This argument failed to impress most reporters and pundits or many of his fellow politicians, and in December the Republican-led House of Representatives voted to impeach him—to force him to stand trial in the Senate, where House prosecutors and Clinton's defense team would present their cases and the full Senate would vote on whether to remove him from office. The decision to launch impeachment proceedings against Clinton lifted to story to an even higher level—and provided the networks and cable news channels with an even more compelling reason to continue to follow it. They insisted that it was history in the making, with only a few naysayers like CNBC's Geraldo Rivera suggesting that it had been blown up beyond all proportion.

By January, when Clinton's Senate trial began, it was clear that a majority of Americans agreed with Rivera. They might have regarded Clinton as a sleazy creep, but they didn't believe that lying to hide his affair justified removal from office—particularly since the affair only came to light because of Starr's extraordinary zealousness and the persistent efforts of Clinton's right-wing critics, who had been conspiring against him for nearly twenty years. By this time, too, many of his critics among the political class—including some Democrats who had once suggested he resign—had regained their senses and come to realize the implications of removing a sitting president for such a minor offense. Accordingly, the trial's outcome was foreordained. Support for removing Clinton from office would never come close to the necessary two-thirds vote. This deprived coverage of the proceedings of its drama, and made media commitment to the story more annoying to viewers who had had enough of the affair. On February 12, voting largely along party lines, the effort to remove Clinton from office failed.

The Clinton-Lewinsky scandal was an important turning point in the history of television news. Eager to draw viewers to their news programs, the networks pulled out all the stops. It was the most reported story on networks' evening newscasts, a regular subject of segments on prime-time newsmagazines and the morning news shows, and fodder for discussion programs like *Nightline* and *Meet the Press*. Even comedians like Jay Leno and David Letterman discussed it, ensuring that it was at the center of the nation's collective consciousness. CNN and the other cable news channels went even further, offering gavel-to-gavel coverage of the impeachment hearings and making the scandal topic number one of their discussion and debate programs. MSNBC and Fox News were particularly zealous in their coverage, since reporting on it was cheap and provided plenty of opportunities for their prime-time pundits to pontificate, the reason many viewers watched Chris Matthews or Bill O'Reilly.

But more coverage didn't necessarily mean better coverage. Much of the "reporting" on the story by television journalists consisted of talk, speculation, and idle gossip, a trend that was especially pronounced on the cable news channels, which had so much time to fill. This reinforced their propensity for emphasizing opinion and argument, which were easier and less expensive to produce than original investigative reporting—and more entertaining to viewers. Rather than ferreting out new information, the networks and cable news channels spent most of their time commenting on information uncovered by others. And when they engaged in conventional reporting, they often relied on single anonymous sources, a standard that would never have passed muster a decade earlier. To make matters worse, thanks to the twenty-four-hour cable news channels and the Internet, the news cycle was continuous and produced a stream of new allegations and evidence that news organizations were compelled to report and discuss, some of them from sources, like the Drudge Report, outside the orbit of the mainstream media. With new material constantly emerging, there was little time to follow up and verify these leads or weigh the significance of new information. The result was a journalism that seemed exhaustive but in fact was less complete, making it more difficult for consumers to separate fact from rumor, innuendo, and spin.[61]

With the Clinton-Lewinsky scandal, the line in the sand Richard Salant had sought to draw between news and entertainment—a line that had begun to blur in the 1980s and early 1990s and was partially erased during coverage of the O. J. Simpson case—was completed obliterated. The networks, cable news channels, and tabloid infotainment programs now covered the same stories, often in very similar ways. Incipient trends in reporting and production dating back to the 1960s and 1970s, once held in check by the scrupulous exercise of "professional news judgment" and the dictates of the FCC, sprouted and blossomed with alarming speed. Television news became storytelling and commentary, with engaging visuals and, on the cable channels, a large dollop of "expressiveness."[62] It was programming that blended perfectly with the entertainment programs that had dominated the medium since its inception. It made few intellectual demands on viewers—demands that most viewers, empowered as consumers to watch only what they liked, now rejected as "work." Instead, it catered largely to their preferences, offering stories that viewers were more likely to regard as interesting and entertaining. TV news had bent to the will of the marketplace. And, as even many critics were forced to concede, it had become really good television. When it was shaped entirely by the market, however, could it also be good journalism?

7

FADE TO BLACK

By the new standards of television journalism, the summer of 2001 was a "slow news period," prompting the networks and the cable news channels to redouble their commitment to the kinds of stories that had become increasingly prominent since the O. J. Simpson case. The big story of the summer was the disappearance and presumed murder of Chandra Levy, a young Washington intern. It had all the makings of a blockbuster: an attractive, middle-class victim; a high-profile, media-rich setting, the world of Washington interns and the temptations of sex and power; and a potential suspect, representative Gary Condit, whose involvement suggested a more dramatic, *Law and Order* version of the Clinton-Lewinsky scandal. By late August, when it became clear that Levy and Condit had been having an affair, television news executives and producers were virtually salivating at the prospect of Condit's arrest and the ratings spike that would occur when his trial began.

Television coverage of the Levy case was extraordinary—not least because Condit was innocent and television journalists eagerly participated in the fervent speculation that encouraged the public to regard him as a suspect. But it was hardly an aberration. Indeed, the Levy case was emblematic of the state of television news in the new millennium. The calculations and exercise of "professional news judgment" that went into determining what constituted a major story had changed, and television journalists had devised arresting new techniques for conveying the news to viewers. Reports on the Levy case drew on the storytelling conventions developed by the prime-time newsmagazines and tabloid programs like *A Current Affair* and were pitched in the same tone as mysteries and police procedurals. It would take little work for Dick Wolf and his team of *Law and Order* writers to turn them into one of their trademark "ripped from the headlines" episodes. Broadcast journalists were finally producing good television, and they were more willing than ever to tailor their programs to audience preferences.[1]

Curiously, however, these adaptations to the marketplace did little to stem the exodus of viewers. Over the next decade, the ratings for network news programs—especially the evening newscasts, which, not coincidentally, were most likely to include hard news stories on the economy and international affairs—continued to decline. And though the cable news channels increased their overall audience, their gains couldn't make up for the loss in viewership experienced by the networks. Fewer Americans were watching television news of any kind; after 2001, even local news programs experienced a decline in ratings. No matter what journalists did, television news seemed to be on the road to extinction.

The problem, in a nutshell, was the Internet. By the early 2000s, Internet usage among Americans was increasing at an astonishing rate. Many people were going online rather than watching TV, and by 2010 they were watching programs that had first aired on the networks or cable on computers through new streaming services. Soon, programs would debut on Internet platforms, not television, making it possible for consumers to eschew cable and satellite TV services and acquire all their entertainment online. In a manner reminiscent of the 1950s, when consumers switched en masse from the movies, radio, and newspapers to television as their main source of entertainment and information, they were now switching from television to devices connected to the Internet—not just computers but smartphones, tablets, and a new generation of high-definition televisions that, through lightning-fast broadband connections, offered the prospect of being able to watch virtually anything, at any time, on demand.[2]

Responding to these trends involved risks and some difficult choices. One option was to hunker down and protect their legacy as television journalists by producing programs that might bring consumers back to TV news, just as their comrades in the entertainment side of the television business were doing. For many executives, producers, and journalists at the networks, this was an appealing strategy that kindled their ambition and professional pride. They had figured out how to make a profit in the more competitive multichannel age, and they were confident they could develop programming that could still command large audiences—ones big enough to make news an attractive buy for advertisers interested in reaching more than a market niche.

The cable news channels faced a different predicament. All they needed to be profitable was a relatively small, loyal audience of regular viewers. But now that there were three of them—more, if you included Headline News, CNBC, and other more specialized news outlets—they ran the risk of competing for a finite market of news junkies and reducing the market share that each of them enjoyed. Somehow or another, they needed to attract new viewers and enlarge the audience for cable news. This meant finding more blockbusters like the Levy case and developing programs that exploited them to maximum advantage.

A more radical option was to abandon the sinking ship of television news and move decisively into online journalism. This would pit them against newspapers and many other purveyors of online news in an uncertain and highly competitive field. It would no doubt require the shuttering of old legacy programs and extinction of whole genres—writing off the huge investment they had made in technology and infrastructure that was specific to television. But it offered real hope for the future, a chance to stake a claim in the new world of online news before other organizations beat them to it and gained reputations as the go-to source for news on the Internet.

Not surprisingly, television journalists decided to hedge their bets. They stepped up efforts to bring viewers back to TV news, shoring up programs with proven track records and investing new resources in those that were losing their appeal. At the same time, they expanded their early online ventures and began developing web-only programming that might provide a fallback should the revival of their legacy business fail.

The risks were particularly great for the networks. They had endured a very painful, decade-long process of retrenchment. Bureaus had been closed, long-time employees had been fired or forced into early retirement, spending on newsgathering and costly "enterprise" reporting had been pared back. Even more than in previous years, reports on network news programs were inspired by stories that had been broken by other news organizations and involved little original reporting. Despite the multimillion-dollar salaries paid to their biggest stars, the network news divisions were now profitable, and their prime-time programs were less expensive and more reliable than most entertainment programs.

By the early 2000s, the networks had also gone to considerable lengths to make their news programs different from those on CNN and its recently launched rivals. Rather than directly compete with the cable news channels to deliver breaking news, the networks had increased their production of slickly edited packages summarizing or contextualizing the biggest stories. This approach made good use of their technological infrastructure, skilled production staff, and cadre of high-profile correspondents. And it was suitable for a variety of different programs. With the proper editing, stories could be altered for airing on morning news programs, the evening news, or even shows like *60 Minutes* or *Nightline*. Producing news packages was a sensible strategy for attracting viewers. While the cable news channels competed for the attention of news junkies, the networks sought to appeal to a larger swath of casual news consumers, people already aware of the headlines, who had probably even seen video of breaking news on cable, who turned to the networks for more information, especially compelling narratives that highlighted the human dimensions of a story or placed the issues at stake in stark relief.[3]

News division executives conceded that they gave short shrift to stories that, in previous years, would have been covered in more detail. But they insisted that the new TV news was no less responsible than that of Walter Cronkite or Huntley and Brinkley. And they had a point. In the Cronkite era, the networks had refused to cover very much consumer or health news, subjects that were particularly interesting to women, and their techniques for delivering hard news had alienated many viewers. The networks now delivered a wider variety of news in ways that were interesting and engaging. As NBC News president Andrew Lack explained, engaging viewers helped them make sense of the news. It was about "organizing information" so that they could "feel," "see," and "understand" its importance.[4]

Meanwhile, the cable channels continued their campaign to increase their popularity by assuming functions once performed by the networks. The most important was serving as the source of breaking news. This, of course, had been CNN's raison d'être from the moment of its birth in 1980. Yet CNN now had rivals, and this increased the pressure to be the first to report big stories—and to stay with them continuously, long after the networks had returned to their regular programming. By the early 2000s, only the biggest stories prompted the networks to interrupt prime-time entertainment programs with news. And the realization that most viewers were likely to turn to the cable news channels led the networks to reduce their coverage to a bare minimum—short bulletins or a crawl of text at the bottom of the screen. Blockbuster stories—the school shootings at Columbine High School in Colorado, John F. Kennedy Jr.'s fatal plane crash, or Chandra Levy's disappearance—were the lifeblood of the cable news channels, producing spikes in the ratings that could last for weeks. "Cable news channels dine on crisis, on major sustained stories," Erik Sorenson, the president of MSNBC, noted in July 2001, when his channel and its competitors were feasting on the Levy story. "We find big stories and interesting stories and we run with them." When authentically big stories were unavailable, they routinely hyped middling ones to make them seem bigger. Despite a wealth of airtime, CNN, MSNBC, and Fox News Channel increasingly emphasized depth over breadth, selecting the two or three stories that seemed most interesting to their viewers and then following them over the course of the day. This kept these particular stories in the news and often compelled the networks to pay more attention to them.[5]

The cable news channels also replaced the networks as a source of political news. Responding to a reduction in network coverage of Washington-based news, they stepped into the breach and made it their specialty. But rather than offer the detailed, potentially boring "process" pieces that the networks had produced in the 1970s and 1980s, which carefully assessed proposed legislation and followed its progress through Congress, or complex stories on vexing domestic problems, as Peter Jennings and Paul Friedman had sought to do with their *American Agenda* series on ABC's *World News Tonight*, CNN and its competitors spent most of their time on the political horse race, the competition for partisan advantage that reached a climax during elections. The reason for this was simple. Campaign coverage was good for business. Ratings for the cable news channels increased substantially during election years, and turning every year into a prelude to the next election seemed a good way of turning casual viewers of campaign coverage into regulars. While the networks scaled back their coverage of the nominating conventions, arguing that they offered virtually no real news—only partisan pageantry—the cable channels turned them into spectacles where they could showcase their talent and whip up excitement for the main event in November. Far more than the networks, the cable news channels treated politics like a spectator sport. They reveled in inside dope and glimpses of behind-the-scenes strategizing, as each side prepared its game plan and anchors and pundits assessed their performance. By 2000, they had even come up with a convenient way of identifying the competing teams: "Red" and "Blue," a shorthand description of the nation's political divide that grossly oversimplified the complex and hard-to-categorize views of the American public.[6]

Breaking news, saturation coverage of compelling blockbusters, and a focus on the political horse race was the formula that enabled the cable news channels to increase their audience in the period between exposure of the Clinton-Lewinsky affair and the terrorist attacks in September 2001. According to Nielsen Media Research, the average daily audience for the three cable news channels rose from less than 500,000 in December 1997 to over 800,000 in August 2001, with large spikes occurring in response to several big stories. For example, the Clinton impeachment hearings lifted daily viewership to well over 1 million. They rose even higher in the wake of the shootings at Columbine High School in Littleton, Colorado, and when John F. Kennedy Jr. was killed. Then, after falling back to around 500,000 to 600,000, they increased in the run-up to the bitterly contested election of 2000, and reached a new peak—nearly 2 million—during the legal drama surrounding the disputed Florida results. The Florida recount story, which culminated in the Supreme Court's controversial *Bush v. Gore* decision, was a tremendous boon for the cable news channels, offering them a meaty story that was perfectly suited for their growing reliance on interviews and analysis by experts, pundits, and prominent guests.[7]

It was particularly helpful to FNC, which emerged as CNN's most formidable rival. Mixing coverage of breaking news with stories of interest to political conservatives and lively talk shows hosted by combative, highly opinionated personalities, FNC vaulted ahead of MSNBC in early 2001 and began closing the gap on first-place CNN. It was particularly strong in prime time, and its lineup of opinion-oriented talk shows, led by *The O'Reilly Factor*, developed large and extremely devoted followings. Stoking viewer outrage over Gore's decision to con-

Bill O'Reilly (left), a former network correspondent and host of the tabloid program *Inside Edition*, became very successful as host of Fox News' *The O'Reilly Factor*. Here he is being interviewed in 2004 by Jon Stewart on Comedy Central's fake news program, *The Daily Show*. Photo courtesy of Comedy Central/Photofest.

test the election results by demanding a recount of the votes cast in Florida, O'Reilly and his fellow conservative firebrands on FNC attracted many new viewers, often people alienated by the story's treatment on CNN or the networks. Liking what they saw, they became regular viewers during the day as well. By the summer of 2001, FNC and CNN were neck-and-neck in prime time, and the average daily prime-time audience for the three cable news channels had increased to approximately 1.6 million viewers.[8]

FNC's extraordinary success was a big blow to CNN and a personal embarrassment to Ted Turner. Back in 1995, during a panel discussion at a cable industry conference, Turner had dismissed Rupert Murdoch's bid to create a rival news channel by announcing, "I'm looking forward to squishing Rupert like a bug." It was also disconcerting to executives at Time Warner and AOL, who were in the midst of an expensive merger of the two companies and were unhappy with the programming failures and decline in morale that had occurred under CNN-US head Rick Kaplan. Kaplan was fired, and Time Warner executives conducted an extensive assessment of CNN's operations and programming. They concluded that there was considerable "waste" and "redundancy" in CNN's vast system of bureaus, and that Kaplan's emphasis on expensive long-form documentaries and newsmagazines had been a mistake. In July 2001, they sacked Tom Johnson, the president of CNN who oversaw all its operations, and replaced him with Walter Isaacson, a former editor of *Time*.

Isaacson had won plaudits for his stewardship of *Time*, but he had no television experience and seemed an odd choice for the job. He began to receive advice from two other newcomers, Jamie Kellner, the new president of Turner Broadcasting, and Garth Ancier, a new executive vice-president. Kellner and Ancier had worked at Murdoch's Fox network and a new youth-oriented network, the WB. Unlike Isaacson, they were TV guys, and they were determined to "spice up" CNN so that it could better fend off its new rivals. As Ancier explained, CNN had good journalists who knew how to produce the news. They just weren't very good at television. "It wasn't part of the culture." It would be now.[9]

Isaacson made it clear that CNN was not abandoning its original mission or devaluing its brand. He and his staff would continue to provide viewers with straight, objective, hard news, especially the breaking news that had become its trademark. But, he added, "good journalism doesn't have to be boring."[10] Over the past decade, he suggested, CNN had become complacent and ceased to be an industry pioneer. The time had now come to regain the initiative and take television journalism to another level. CNN would do this by reemphasizing storytelling. "I want smart people telling interesting tales, not people whose natural instinct is to give you their opinions."[11]

Introduced over a period of several months, the changes instituted by Isaacson and his associates were dramatic. They changed CNN's look, moving away from the dignified network-news aesthetic Kaplan had brought to CNN and adding the flashy graphics and sound effects common on its cable rivals, especially Fox News. They ordered producers to deemphasize filmed news packages in favor of extemporaneous live reports from the field, which Isaacson thought would give CNN more "urgency"—and, not coincidentally, reduce costs. Persuaded by Kellner and Ancier that CNN needed more stars, Isaacson hired Paula Zahn, a former host of CBS's morning news show, to anchor a new morning news program and recruited Aaron Brown and Connie Chung from ABC, installing them in prime time alongside

CNN stalwart Larry King. At first glance, Brown's program was a conventional news show. But he was encouraged to express his feelings and reveal his human side. Chung's was devoted to newsmaker interviews. CNN also hired a raft of younger correspondents and would-be anchors, including Anderson Cooper, who had shown a talent for the kind of emotive reporting that Isaacson wanted to make CNN's hallmark. The changes at CNN's sibling, Headline News, were even more dramatic. They included new telegenic anchors, snazzy graphics that nearly filled the screen, and more stories on pop culture and lifestyle trends. Cable news' dowager was ready for the new millennium.[12]

The routines of television news were soon unsettled, however, by the biggest blockbuster of all, the carefully planned terrorist attacks launched by the radical Islamist group al-Qaeda on September 11, 2001. By targeting the twin towers of New York's World Trade Center, one of the most iconic structures in the media capital of the world, al-Qaeda virtually guaranteed an enormous worldwide audience for its bold strike against the US. It was astonishing television—perhaps the most viscerally powerful images ever conveyed by the medium. And they were delivered in real time. Drawn to the World Trade Center by reports that a plane had crashed into the North Tower, camera crews were on hand when a second plane roared over their heads and plowed into the South Tower, an extraordinary spectacle that was replayed endlessly over the next few hours. The second crash immediately changed the nature of the story—from a bizarre aviation accident to an audacious act of terrorism—and led the networks to cancel their regular programming and turn the story over to their news divisions. Minutes later, another plane crashed into the Pentagon in Washington, DC. The event wasn't captured live, but images of the burning Pentagon soon appeared on television screens as well. Millions of Americans—and people around the world—watched in horror as firefighters and police frantically sought to rescue people trapped in the burning buildings. The spectacle became even more macabre when, in a scene reminiscent of a big-budget movie, the South Tower and then the North Tower collapsed into smoldering heaps of concrete, broken glass, and twisted metal. Thousands of people, including countless rescue workers, were still inside.[13]

The networks stayed with the story for seventy-two straight hours, eschewing not just their regular programming but all commercials, which cost them an estimated $100 million per day. They shared video footage among themselves and with the cable news channels. Cable channels that normally broadcast entertainment programs picked up the feed from the networks or a cable news channel owned by the same company. In the immediate aftermath of the attacks, viewership reached new heights, with the biggest gains experienced by the networks. Seeking reassurance, large numbers of Americans turned to Tom Brokaw, Peter Jennings, and Dan Rather, the veteran anchors who had presided at important events for two decades and offered the perfect combination of emotion and gravitas. Network officials were hopeful that this boost in viewership would persist and arrest the steady decline of their audience. The cable news channels experienced a big spike in their audience, too. Collectively, they drew an average of 2.7 million viewers for the month during the daytime and over 4.5 million in prime time. CNN was the biggest beneficiary, much to Walter Isaacson's relief.

The attacks briefly increased viewer interest in international news, particularly stories that sought to explain why many people in the Middle East were sympathetic to the terrorists and despised the US. "Hard news, even foreign news, is back in vogue," noted a reporter for the *New York Times* in late September. This was a relief for many journalists and producers, who had been vaguely embarrassed by the depths to which they had sunk since the Clinton-Lewinsky scandal. "In retrospect," CNN's Isaacson confessed, "when we had a period of no urgent news, we all . . . probably spent too much time looking for different approaches that could attract higher ratings." The terrorist attacks had been a "wake-up call," inspiring viewers to demand hard news about things that "really matter," something that TV news organizations were happy to supply.[14]

Thanks to budget cuts that had eliminated or reduced the size of overseas bureaus, however, this would be not be as easy as it would have been in years past. For example, in 1989, when the Berlin Wall fell, ABC had seventeen bureaus; in September 2001, it had only seven. Even CNN, now under the control of AOL Time Warner, had reduced its overseas staff and increased its reliance on freelance stringers. The trend at the networks and CNN was to transform bureaus into single-correspondent operations, in which reporters covered a large area and "parachuted" into particular locales when breaking news occurred. Equipped with the latest technology, especially portable, suitcase-size satellite uplinks, staff correspondents or stringers could provide vivid pictures and live reports, enabling viewers to see what was happening in faraway places. But without extensive connections and a wide array of sources, including people on the street, could they provide context or the kind of interpretive reporting that was necessary to really understand what was happening in the Arab world?

The implications of this were significant. The attacks sparked a powerful sense of national unity—that all Americans were potential targets of hostile forces abroad. And though the motives of the hijackers and their sympathizers were complex and were attributable in part to specific American policies in the Middle East—and not just a blinding hatred of the "Great Satan"—this was easily forgotten amid the patriotic fervor of the moment, a fervor the Bush administration, for a variety of reasons, was keen to strengthen and exploit.

Having won election through the surprising and widely disparaged intervention of the Supreme Court, Bush's first few months in office had been inauspicious. After gaining congressional approval for a massive tax cut, his administration's legislative agenda had stalled in the face of determined Democratic opposition. With his approval rating declining, Bush had assumed a low profile during the summer. But in the aftermath of the 9/11 attacks, he rose to the occasion, delivering eloquent remarks in tribute to its victims and vowing to be the "uniter" that he had promised to be in his election campaign.

Behind the scenes, however, Bush and his closest advisors were quick to recognize the unique opportunity now available to them. By consciously framing the terrorist attacks as war on the US, rather than a criminal act, they could mobilize public support for a number of foreign and domestic initiatives that would have been impossible to get through Congress before 9/11. For old-fashioned Cold Warriors like vice president Dick Cheney and secretary of defense Donald Rumsfeld, a "war on terror" could replace the now defunct campaign against Communism that had united Americans during the Cold War and enabled presidents to centralize power in the executive branch. Other members of Bush's foreign policy team thought it might allow the US to topple anti-American regimes and spark a "democratic revival" in the Middle East. Well before the attacks, Bush and his advisors had begun to talk about how they might depose Iraqi dictator Saddam Hussein, who was still in power a decade after the Persian Gulf War. Still others, including Bush's most influential advisor, Karl Rove, were convinced that the Bush administration could exploit the war on terror to break the logjam in Congress and revive the stalled Republican domestic program.[15]

But they couldn't do this by themselves. They needed journalists to adopt the same frame and filter news through it. At first, the media, especially the networks and cable news channels, were happy to oblige. Shocked by the 9/11 attacks and eager to rally Americans behind the government, they rarely questioned the Bush administration's interpretation of events. They didn't object to the military's virtual quarantine of information about its operations in Afghanistan, where US forces were battling the Taliban and searching in vain for al-Qaeda leader Osama bin Laden and the other masterminds of the terrorist attacks. Nor did they raise much of a fuss when Congress passed the USA Patriot Act, which vastly expanded the police powers of the federal government in the interests of "homeland security," nor when, at the slightest sign of cracks in the new consensus, government officials announced a new threat that required elevating its "terror alert," coercing would-be critics back into line. Many anchors wore American flag lapel pins and, in interviews and public appearances, expressed their unqualified support for the Bush administration's efforts to capture and punish bin Laden. In an embarrassing appearance on David Letterman's talk show shortly after September 11, Dan Rather offered to "line up" behind the president. Fox News' Brit Hume suggested that the war on terror justified pro-American coverage because our foes were not a legitimate adversary but "murdering barbarians." Geraldo Rivera, FNC's latest high-profile hire, went further, vowing to kill bin Laden if he encountered the al-Qaeda leader while on assignment in Afghanistan. Suspending the skeptical attitude toward government and politicians that had shaped reporting in the 1990s, television journalists made it clear that they were loyal members of the team. It was as if Vietnam had never happened.[16]

This remarkable development wasn't entirely a result of fear or opportunism, and it might not have occurred if members of the political establishment, especially the opposition Democratic Party, had been more assertive about questioning the Bush administration's initiatives. No less than the media, prominent Democrats were inspired to line up behind President Bush, and in the months after 9/11 they were too intimidated to press the Bush administration to back up its increasingly extravagant claims—that al-Qaeda was in league with Saddam Hussein, that Hussein was amassing "weapons of mass de-

struction" that he intended to supply to al-Qaeda agents bent on ter-
rorizing the West, or that Iraq, Iran, and North Korea comprised an
"Axis of Evil" that required an aggressive new policy of "preemption"
and the sort of military mobilization not seen since the early years of
the Cold War.

The lack of official sources willing to question these claims and dissent from Bush administration foreign policy gave mainstream news
organizations little recourse but to parrot the administration's line.
The conventions of newsgathering privileged such sources. And under
ordinary circumstances, they allowed for competing views and perspectives to appear in the news. Since the Reagan era, the dynamics of
Washington partisanship has ensured lively debate and ample fodder
for the TV news industry's trademark point-counterpoint reportage,
particularly on hot-button issues that sharply divide the major political parties. But these were not ordinary circumstances, and the lack of
official sources contesting administration claims made it much easier
for Bush and his advisors to manage the discourse and compel media
support.[17]

There were critics of the Bush administration's war on terror. The
vast majority, however, were outside of the mainstream, mostly liberals and leftists who had long opposed American militarism and
the hard-line Cold War policies that had led the US into the Vietnam
War—a cabal the administration and their allies could easily dismiss
as whiners and malcontents who hated America. By regularly playing
the patriotism card, Bush administration officials and their surrogates
in Congress and the media were able to prevent the views of these out-
liers from seeping very far into the mainstream.

This became more difficult in the fall of 2002, when it became clear
that Bush and his advisors were determined to invade Iraq and overthrow Saddam Hussein, and many of America's allies began questioning the rationale for this shift in the focus of the war on terror.
Unconvinced that Hussein was in league with al-Qaeda or that he possessed weapons of mass destruction, many nations that had endorsed
the first Persian Gulf War refused to sanction Bush's plan for "regime
change" in Iraq. By early 2003, when Bush failed to get UN support
for military action against Iraq but persisted in seeking to cobble
together a coalition force to give the US mission the appearance of
international support, the disagreement between the US and many of
its major allies had deepened, inspiring more Americans, including

some leading Democrats, to express their skepticism. Undeterred, the Bush administration pressed on, playing up dubious intelligence reports that seemed to confirm that Hussein was hiding biological and nuclear weapons from UN inspectors. By March 2003, on the eve of the American-led invasion, over 70 percent of the American public supported the use of military force in Iraq. And while the media, including the networks and cable news channels, dutifully noted the reasons why some people thought the war was a bad idea, they gave supporters of the war far more airtime than its opponents. And they did little to counter the Bush administration's insidious suggestions that opposing the war was un-American.

It was no accident that the war in Iraq was the quintessential television event. Months before the invasion began, Bush administration and military officials began planning how they would convey it to the American public in the new age of around-the-clock media coverage. They were determined to control the story and encourage media identification with the US-led campaign. And they recognized that the enormous news hole that the cable channels in particular needed to fill required a constant stream of new information. Severely limiting media access, as the military had done in Afghanistan, was unlikely to produce enough news to fill this hole and could inspire independent journalistic inquiry or provide a forum for naysayers. Accordingly, they settled on a more open and seemingly transparent approach, turning "Operation Iraqi Freedom" into an extravagant and compelling reality TV show. Instead of the usual bare and colorless room where military officials issued briefings to reporters and television cameras, they had Hollywood producers create a more visually arresting set, as one might see on *Survivor*. And they supplemented the official military-produced film of airstrikes—a staple of television war coverage since the Persian Gulf War—with a more intimate, ground-level view of the conflict by allowing several hundred credentialed and specially trained reporters, including veterans like Ted Koppel, to accompany American and British troops as "embedded" correspondents.[18]

Launched during prime time on March 19, 2003, and lasting for six weeks, Operation Iraqi Freedom was a dazzling show and produced some great television moments. Perhaps the most dramatic occurred on April 9, when coalition forces and the press entered Baghdad, the Iraqi capital, and television cameras captured a stirring sight, a group of Iraqis, with the assistance of an American tank, toppling a large statue of Saddam Hussein in a public square. It was just as Cheney had predicted — American forces were being greeted as liberators. But as numerous studies of media coverage of the Iraq War later revealed, television reporting from the front lines was far from transparent, and even the famous statue-toppling incident was something of a pseudo-event. In order not to offend tender American sensibilities, the networks and cable channels elected not to broadcast video footage of bloodshed and casualties, and they abided by a Bush administration request not to show any of the coffins or body bags arriving in the US bearing American dead. And while embedding reporters with military units was a terrific way of giving the war a human dimension, it was not a very good way to shed light on the big picture. The parade of experts who offered analysis and commentary were no better. Mostly retired military officers, they were eager to discuss military strategy and tactics, not the political and diplomatic problems that were certain to result if the US had to keep a large occupation force in Iraq. Ironically, the cable news channels, with plenty of airtime that could have been devoted to context, did an especially poor job of explaining the big picture. As usual, ABC's *Nightline* and PBS's *NewsHour* did the best. Ted Koppel's reports from the front lines were particularly cogent and informative.[19]

This was indicative of a larger pattern. By and large, the networks offered viewers a wider array of perspectives than the cable news channels. And they were less likely to express open identification with coalition forces. The most blatantly pro-American coverage came, not surprisingly, from Ailes's Fox News. Predisposed to see things from the Bush administration's point of view, FNC anchors and reporters had trouble containing their enthusiasm at the prospect of expanding the war on terror to "take out" Saddam Hussein and "liberate" Iraq. FNC's talk-show hosts were particularly bellicose, goading their guests to rant about Hussein's malevolence and the benefits that would follow any American-instigated regime change. They denounced nations that refused to join the US-led coalition as cowardly appeasers and routinely suggested that Americans who opposed the war were traitors who had cast their lot with the enemy. And once the war began, FNC became the military's biggest cheerleaders, covering its relentless march to Baghdad with the unabashed enthusiasm of drunken alumni at a football game watching their team roll over a particularly hapless opponent. It was, as numerous industry observers noted, an entirely new kind of TV journalism. Eschewing objectivity and the skepticism of officialdom that had inspired many journalists since the era of Vietnam and Watergate, coverage of the war on FNC came perilously close to propaganda.[20]

Despite its departure from the norm—or perhaps because of it— FNC rose to the top of the ratings in the months after the 9/11 attacks, surpassing CNN in January 2002, and increasing its lead over its rivals during the Iraq War in the spring of 2003. During the war's giddy first week, FNC averaged 5.6 million viewers in prime time, compared to CNN's 4.4 million and MSNBC's paltry 2.2 million. By the end of 2003, the ratings of all three cable news channels had declined, but FNC's lead over CNN had increased, and its prime-time programs drew 50 percent more viewers than CNN's. Clearly, many viewers didn't want objective journalism about US foreign policy. With the nation "at war," they wanted unapologetic pro-American cheerleading.

FNC's success soon produced a widely discussed "Fox effect" among its cable rivals, especially MSNBC. Like FNC, MSNBC producers placed an American flag in the corner of the screen after the 9/11 attacks and moved gingerly toward a more "patriotic" presentation of news about the war on terror in the months before the beginning of Operation Iraqi Freedom. The outbreak of the war—and FNC's staggering ratings success—encouraged MSNBC officials to become even more pro-American. They hired conservative supporters of the war, including Michael Savage, a notorious right-wing radio personality, to host evening talk shows and they presented mawkish stories on American troops in the field. Embattled MSNBC president Erik Sorenson defended the new emphasis by claiming that conservative voices were needed for balance and suggesting that the country wanted more positive reporting that would give the Bush administration and the military the "benefit of the doubt."[21] CNN, as usual, tried to remain in the middle of the road, a necessity for any organization that advertised itself as the "world's news network." By March 2003, however, the pressure to support the US mission became overwhelming, and CNN executives and producers found it virtually impossible to maintain an independent point of view. CNN's professions of internationalism, always a problem for some Americans, had become an acute liability in an atmosphere where, as President Bush put it shortly after 9/11, "you're either with us, or you're with the terrorists."

On May 1, 2003, in an expertly choreographed spectacle aboard an aircraft carrier, Bush announced that the "combat phase" of Operation Iraqi Freedom was over. Hussein was in hiding and would soon be captured by American troops. His government had been overthrown, and American officials expressed confidence that Iraq would soon be a vibrant, functioning democracy. Speaking before television cameras in prime time, under a huge banner reading "Mission Accomplished," Bush praised the military for their efforts, and tried to give the campaign a suitably upbeat Hollywood ending. By attacking the US, he noted, "the terrorists and their supporters declared war on the United States, and war is what they got." Offstage, Karl Rove must have been delighted. Everything had gone according to plan. The war had been won. Iraq had been liberated, and the US had flexed its muscles, sending a message to other nations around the world. And, best of all, the American public had rallied behind the Bush administration, providing it with renewed political capital.

But uncomfortable facts soon ruined the show's happy ending. Substantial numbers of Iraqis expressed unhappiness with the American occupation and organized a spirited and highly effective armed insurgency. The insurgency forced the US to keep a huge military force in Iraq and produced a stream of American casualties. US military and intelligence operatives were unable to find any hidden weapons of mass destruction—the public rationale for the war. Apparently, Hussein, who told UN inspectors before the war that he had shut down his weapons programs, had been telling the truth. Even worse, a number of sources, including former high-ranking Bush administration officials, came forward with claims that Bush and his closest advisors had been planning to overthrow Hussein before the 9/11 attacks and had purposely hyped dubious intelligence in order to convince Congress and the public that Hussein had weapons of mass destruction and had to be deposed. The Bush administration and its surrogates tried to discredit these critics by impugning their motives and even their patriotism. Yet their revelations were impossible to ignore.

Gradually, the networks and the cable news channels, with the notable exception of Fox News, awakened from their torpor. In April 2004, as the Bush team were revving up their reelection machinery, the CBS program *60 Minutes II* broadcast a sensational report, illustrated with eerie digital photographs taken by US servicemen, documenting instances of sadistic torture of Iraqi prisoners at Abu Ghraib, a former prison where Hussein had incarcerated his enemies that was now being used by American forces to detain suspected insurgents. It was followed by additional reports in newspapers and magazines that revealed that the torture of prisoners was widespread and sanctioned by official policy. The Bush administration responded indignantly that the Abu Ghraib case was an isolated incident perpetrated by a few "bad apples," and they successfully changed the tenor of the discussion so that the word *torture* virtually disappeared from media reports. Instead, reports described it as "mistreatment" and "abuse." But charges that US officials had resorted to torture—not just at Abu Ghraib but in their interrogation of suspected terrorists held at Guantanamo Bay—would not go away, and were revived in late 2005 by Senator John McCain, giving the story a new legitimacy and inspiring television journalists to pursue it more aggressively.[22]

Emboldened by their exposure of the Abu Ghraib torture, CBS broadcast another potentially explosive story on *60 Minutes II* in September 2004. Produced by Mary Mapes and narrated by Dan Rather, the same team who had done the report on Abu Ghraib, it revealed that President Bush had received special privileges while serving in the Texas Air National Guard during the Vietnam War. Rumors of this had circulated for years, and Mapes and her crew conducted interviews and examined a cache of documents that seemed to provide confirmation. Heavily promoted by CBS and rushed to be ready for broadcast during the program's season premier, Mapes's report immediately aroused the ire of bloggers on the Internet. They questioned the authenticity of the documents and claimed that Mapes and Rather had a vendetta against Bush. At first, CBS, Mapes, and Rather defended the report's accuracy. But when mainstream news organizations joined the investigation and began examining the documents, their authenticity fell further into doubt. It now seemed likely that they were forgeries, and Mapes and Rather had been duped. Two weeks after the report aired, CBS president Andrew Heyward was forced to issue a retraction and apology. An independent panel hired by CBS exonerated Mapes and Rather of ideological bias. It concluded, however, that they had engaged in sloppy journalism and been too eager to produce a dramatic scoop in time for the season premier. This hardly satisfied CBS's many right-wing critics and provided them with yet more evidence of CBS's liberal bias.[23]

By early 2005, many more Americans had begun to question the wisdom of Operation Iraqi Freedom, and the Bush administration found it more difficult to influence the news media's coverage of its foreign and domestic policies. On the Internet, in the alternative press, and on the websites of foreign news outlets, from newspapers like *Le Monde* and the *Guardian* to the cheeky Qatar-based television network Al Jazeera, stories critical of the American occupation and the war on terror were widely available to Americans. And as they multiplied and began to spark discussion and debate, segments of the American press became more willing to question and criticize the Bush administration. But it was a slow and halting process, and it angered American opponents of the war who were frustrated by the media's reluctance to defect from the "team" that Bush had mobilized after the 9/11 attacks. Not until Hurricane Katrina struck New Orleans at the end of August 2005 did most of the mainstream media reassert themselves and begin to produce journalism that was largely independent of the administration's influence. Caught off guard by the storm and seemingly indifferent to the devastation it was causing, Bush and his advisors lost control of mainstream media discourse and spent the rest of his presidency in a defensive crouch.

Ironically, until Hurricane Katrina, one of the few places on television where American viewers could hear unambiguous criticism of Bush administration policies was the cable channel Comedy Central. Established in the early 1990s and owned by media giant Viacom, it specialized in old sitcoms, movies, standup and sketch comedy, and a smattering of original programming. Among the latter was a satirical news program called *The Daily Show*, which began in 1996. Hosted by Craig Kilborn and focusing mostly on pop culture subjects, it was broadcast at 11:00 PM Eastern Time, opposite local news programs and before the late-night talk shows. The program changed considerably in 1999, when Jon Stewart, an experienced comedian, replaced Kilborn, and a former editor of the satirical newspaper *The Onion*, Ben Karlin, became the program's head writer and executive producer. With Stewart and Karlin at the helm, *The Daily Show* became more news-oriented, particularly during the 2000 election campaign. The show's following increased after 9/11, when Stewart and his "correspondents" became even more topical and began chiding the news media for their unwillingness to question or criticize Bush administration policies. For a number of months after Bush's dramatic "Mission Accomplished" speech, Stewart was one of the few voices on television regularly asking about Iraq's supposed weapons of mass destruction, and his dogged refusal to let the issue die kept it in the spotlight and eventually inspired journalists to begin asking as well.

Not surprisingly, the show was assailed by conservatives and even many professional journalists for criticizing Republicans far more than Democrats. To the right in particular, *The Daily Show* was an appalling example of liberal bias. Stewart and Karlin conceded that their humor often titled to the left, yet they reminded their critics that, unlike Fox News, they made no claims to being journalists. They also noted that the party in power presented an easier target, and that some Republicans said things that were so ignorant or absurd that they invited ridicule. The problem, as Stewart and Karlin saw it, was that the media were too afraid to call them on it, creating an opening for *The Daily Show* to do so. Karlin suggested that the mainstream media were shackled by "weird handcuffs": "They have to present both sides of the argument, even if one side . . . is wrong."[24]

By 2004, the program had become a running critique of the conventions of television journalism, making it very appealing to young viewers unhappy with the state of TV news. Stewart made his own views about the industry's emphasis on punditry and partisan debate quite clear in October 2004, when he appeared on CNN's *Crossfire* and berated hosts Tucker Carlson and Paul Begala for "hurting America" with their verbal food fights. Rather than debunking misinformation to determine truth, as television news programs ought to be doing, they preached to the converted—Carlson to conservatives, Begala to liberals—echoing the partisan attacks of politicians. When pressed by critics for solutions to the crisis of contemporary television journalism, Stewart stopped short of suggesting a return to the conventions of Richard Salant. That would have made him seem old-fashioned, and he may well have been too much of a postmodernist to believe that journalists could reveal the "truth." But his program's critique of TV news conventions implicitly raised viewer awareness of the fact that the networks and cable news channels were not providing it. And, in its own peculiar way, *The Daily Show* undertook the difficult task of doing so.[25]

As *The Daily Show* became more popular, its profile rose. By 2005, the buzz surrounding the program was intense, and its ratings had swelled. Stewart's opening monologues, which summarized and dissected the leading news stories of the day, were widely discussed and circulated on the Internet. Audience research revealed that they were the main source of news for many viewers. Often accompanied by video footage, they routinely exposed hypocrisy and dissembling. Unlike conventional news anchors, Stewart regularly offered his opinion in the course of presenting a story and noted when something seemed top-heavy with spin. His interviews were also noteworthy. *The Daily Show*'s success made it a desirable forum for newsmakers, and Karlin and Stewart were able to land many high-profile guests. Stewart often asked smart, probing questions, mixing humor with seriousness and, at times, palpable outrage. Though, as some critics noted, he was just as likely to pull back and go easy on them. Stewart defended this practice by noting that he was a comedian, not a journalist, and that *The Daily Show* was "fake news." The "reports" delivered by his regular correspondents could also be sharp-edged, exhibiting many features common in *The Onion*. They mercilessly mocked the pretentions of TV journalists and provided producers with opportunities to poke fun at the perversity of "professional news judgment" in the age of info-tainment.

In the fall of 2005, one of the program's longtime "correspondents," the comedian Stephen Colbert, got his own program, *The Colbert Report*. It followed *The Daily Show* and was designed to spoof the opinion-driven talk shows that dominated prime time on the cable news channels, especially Fox News' *The O'Reilly Factor*. It was an instant hit with viewers and critics and increased Comedy Central's reputation for innovative programming. Colbert's character, a blustering, egomaniacal right-winger, displayed many of O'Reilly's signature traits, and the program included features that mimicked those on the *Factor*. For example, mocking O'Reilly's claim that his program constituted a "no-spin zone," Colbert regularly described his own program as a "no-fact zone." *The Colbert Report* was especially derisive of what its producers regarded as the ignorance and cynicism of the American right, which was reflected in the bluster of O'Reilly, Sean Hannity, and other pundits on Fox News. On the program's first broadcast, Colbert coined the word "truthiness"—gut feelings about what ought to be true, regardless of the facts—to describe the delusional mindset of some right-wingers. "Let's face it folks," he noted in mock seriousness, "we are a divided nation . . . between those who think with their head and those who know with their heart."[26] Colbert's character was a big fan of President Bush and regularly bashed liberals for seeking

A *Daily Show* correspondent, Stephen Colbert, became the host of his own Comedy Central program, *The Colbert Report*, a spoof of shows like O'Reilly's. Photo courtesy of Comedy Central/Photofest.

to undermine the Bush administration's achievements. The comedian rarely appeared out of character, even when being interviewed on other programs, and he shocked many journalists when he hosted the White House Correspondents' Association dinner in April 2006 and mocked Bush in the latter's presence. By expressing unbridled support for Bush and his policies, Colbert was able to criticize them far more explicitly than Stewart. For example, at the WHCA dinner, in the course of praising Bush for his commitment to principles, Colbert noted, "The greatest thing about this man is that he's steady, you know where he stands. He believes that same thing Wednesday that he believed on Monday, no matter what happened on Tuesday." It was devastating, and made Colbert, like Stewart, a hero to the growing number of Americans who were unhappy about the continued US presence in Iraq and the Bush administration's policies in general.[27]

The popularity of *The Daily Show* and *The Colbert Report* attracted lots of commentary and news industry attention. In a *Rolling Stone* cover story in November 2006, *New York Times* columnist Maureen Dowd called Stewart and Colbert "America's Anchors."[28] Their appeal among younger viewers was particularly interesting to industry executives and observers and sparked discussion about whether any of their innovations might be transferable to news programs on the networks.

This was a matter of some urgency. After a brief spike in the wake of the 9/11 attacks, the cumulative audience for the networks' evening newscasts had continued to decline. In 2004, the NBC *Nightly News*, ABC's *World News Tonight*, and the CBS *Evening News* attracted an average daily audience of 28.8 million viewers, down from 32.9 in 2001 and nearly 41 million in 1993. And their remaining viewers, with a median age of sixty, were much older than the wider television audience. Though the evening newscasts were still attractive buys for advertisers and were profitable for the news divisions, they were much less attractive than programs that appealed to younger viewers. Network officials worried that, unless they were able to draw an appreciable number of younger viewers, the audience for the evening newscasts might continue to decline and get older, and affiliates would demand that they be replaced with more popular programming. With news readily available on cable and the Internet, there seemed few good reasons, aside from nostalgia, for the networks to produce evening newscasts.[29]

It wasn't just the age of the audience that worried network executives. The three anchors of the evening newscasts were also getting old and had been at their jobs for over two decades, and many feared that their eventual retirements would produce an even steeper ratings plunge. Dan Rather was already in his early seventies, and Brokaw and Jennings in their mid-sixties. Brokaw had begun to contemplate retirement shortly before the 9/11 attacks, but his interest in his job was revived by the prospect of a return to hard news, and he elected to stay on a little longer. To the disappointment of NBC officials, it wasn't long enough.

In May 2002, Brokaw announced that he would retire after the 2004 elections, giving his superiors plenty of time to determine a successor—and, potentially, a new direction for the broadcast. But, in a move that surprised many industry observers, NBC News president Neal Shapiro immediately announced that Brian Williams would take over as anchor of the NBC *Nightly News*. Shapiro's predecessor, Andrew Lack, had lured Williams to NBC with promises that he would eventually inherit Brokaw's job. Since coming over, however, he had spent most of his time marooned at MSNBC and CNBC, where his prime-time newscast had generated poor ratings. To increase his stature, Shapiro named him a roving special correspondent and assigned him important interviews. He also began to fill in when Brokaw was on vacation or took a day off. On December 1, 2004, in a poignant broadcast, Brokaw signed off for the last time, and the next day, Williams assumed his duties.

He hardly missed a beat. Displaying an uncanny professionalism, Williams performed admirably and maintained the program's lead in the ratings. He was especially impressive in his coverage of Hurricane Katrina in August 2005. Reporting from New Orleans, he showed courage, passion, and intelligence. And though he was very much a conventional anchor, he also tried to show a more human side and make the program more interesting to younger viewers. In March 2005, for example, he began writing a blog that appeared on the MSNBC website. It provided a snapshot of stories that would be covered that evening on his broadcast and allowed readers to glimpse the process that Williams and his colleagues went through to decide the order of the report and which stories deserved the most attention. In an interview, Williams suggested that its aim was to "lift the veil" and demonstrate the work—and often difficult decisions—that went into producing the evening news.[30] In his blog, Williams sought to develop a less formal voice, and he often expressed dissatisfaction or remorse about segments broadcast the night before. Williams also became a regular on the talk-show circuit, where he revealed a wicked sense of humor that viewers of the *Nightly News* rarely saw. Comfortable with his celebrity and the demands of being an anchor at a time when serious journalists appeared on entertainment programs, Williams was the first network anchor to try to adapt to the postnetwork age.

Brokaw's retirement was supposed to be ABC's opportunity to pull ahead of the NBC *Nightly News*. Peter Jennings's program had been second in the ratings since the late 1990s, and ABC executives were confident that some of Brokaw's viewers could be induced to defect when Williams took over. Like Brokaw, Jennings's interest in broadcasting was rekindled by 9/11, and he became excited about the prospect of producing more hard news stories about international developments. Throughout the 1990s, he had tried to resist the pressure to include more soft news in order to compete with Brokaw, and he was confident that his longtime interest in the Middle East and complicated foreign issues suited the new zeitgeist and would result in an increase in viewership for *World News Tonight*. But Jennings and ABC were dealt a cruel blow when Jennings contracted lung cancer and was forced to take a medical leave in April 2005. In August, he died at the age of sixty-seven.[31]

Jennings's illness and death threw ABC News into disarray and compelled its president, David Westin, to grapple with an unexpected succession crisis. While several different anchors filled in, Westin examined his options and considered the wisdom of adopting a new course. The safest bet was Charles Gibson, the veteran ABC anchor and correspondent who, with Diane Sawyer, had helped salvage *Good Morning, America* in the late 1990s. But Westin was also intrigued by the prospect of hiring an anchor—or even a duo—who might connect better with younger viewers. After Gibson rejected Westin's offer to take the job for a year, Westin sought to implement his plan B. In January 2006, Elizabeth Vargas and Bob Woodruff, both in their forties, took over as coanchors of *World News Tonight*. The new format would allow both anchors to report from the field as well as the studio, but it was otherwise a conventional broadcast. Sadly, the new team never had an opportunity to gel. Less than a month after their debut, Woodruff was seriously wounded while on assignment in Iraq, and Westin was again forced to rely on a rotating cast of substitutes to accompany Vargas. But with the program losing viewers, and Vargas pregnant and planning to take a maternity leave, Westin went back to plan A. He named Gibson the sole anchor of *World News Tonight*.

Gibson took over on May 29, 2006. At sixty-three, he was in many ways a throwback to an earlier era, but this didn't seem to hurt him in the least. The program's ratings increased, and in 2007, *World News Tonight* briefly pulled ahead of Williams's broadcast in total viewers, before falling back into its familiar spot as number two. Gibson was comfortable with a mix of hard and soft stories, and he owed much of his success to the fact that he was roughly the same age as his viewers. They had seen him in many different roles at ABC—as a White House and Capitol Hill correspondent, cohost of *Good Morning, America*, regular substitute on newscasts and *Nightline*. He was familiar and embodied the tried-and-true virtues of network news, and he had no problem emphasizing the kitchen-table stories most popular with elderly viewers. After flirting with change, ABC had gone old-school. It was a good strategy for the short term. Older viewers were loyal and dependable, and network journalists knew very well what they liked. And, by 2007, it was clear what they didn't like: the new-style CBS *Evening News*.

CBS had long been the most conservative of the networks, and news division president Andrew Heyward had struggled to enliven the place. By the early 2000s, the network's reality and scripted entertainment programs dominated prime time, and Heyward was convinced that ratings for its news programs could be increased. He was particularly concerned about Dan Rather's evening newscast, which had been in third place for many years. Like Peter Jennings, Rather had not been pleased by the eagerness of executives and producers to broadcast soft news. And because of his clout as the program's managing editor, the CBS *Evening News* often ignored or downplayed stories—like the Chandra Levy disappearance—that Rather and his executive producer regarded as excessively salacious or sensational. But Rather was getting old, and his imminent retirement offered Heywood a chance to remake the program along more contemporary lines.

That occurred sooner than Rather would have liked, in the aftermath of the scandal that resulted from Rather's participation in the discredited *60 Minutes II* report claiming that George W. Bush had received special treatment in the National Guard. On March 9, 2005, Rather anchored his last broadcast, and Bob Schieffer, for many years his regular substitute and the host of the interview program *Face the Nation*, took over on a temporary basis, while Heywood and CBS executives decided what to do with the show. In a press conference shortly before Rather's departure, network president Les Moonves suggested that the broadcast could be radically changed. "One of the things we're looking at is having something younger, more relevant," he revealed. "As opposed to that guy, preaching from the mountaintop, about what we should and should not watch."[32]

Over the next year, CBS officials went around and around debating what to do—and how much to change the program's format. They consulted with a wide range of people, including the producers of entertainment and reality programs. Rumors about their deliberations filled the pages of trade publications and major newspapers. Meanwhile, Bob Schieffer was engineering a remarkable revival of Rather's old program. Instituting only minor changes—the most important were more two-way conversations with correspondents at the conclusion of their reports—Schieffer picked up many viewers from ABC, which was in the midst of the succession crisis produced by Jennings's illness and death. Finally, in April, CBS announced that the network's new anchor would be Katie Couric, the cohost of NBC's *Today*. She would preside over a substantially different broadcast designed to appeal to younger viewers. Unlike their rivals, CBS was moving boldly into the future.

In some respects, hiring Couric made a lot of sense. She was an experienced, highly versatile journalist and was extremely popular, despite a spate of bad press in the last years of her tenure on *Today*. She was especially good at interviews and establishing a personal rapport with viewers, exactly the opposite of the "preaching from the mountaintop" Moonves had derided. With producer Rome Hartman, Couric began developing plans for the new broadcast and spent part of the summer on a highly publicized "listening tour" to find out what Americans wanted from a news program, a development that no doubt made Richard Salant roll in his grave. CBS also convened focus groups to provide more concrete data, and, in the months before her debut, it launched a massive promotional campaign for the show. To kindle additional interest, Couric regularly dropped hints about its format, suggesting, for example, that its tone would be more conversational and that it would try to offer more positive, uplifting stories, which Couric and Hartman believed the public was hankering for. These were all ideas that had been floated by CBS executives and some of the outside people they had contracted to advise them. And, in other kinds of programs, they were effective techniques for reaching younger viewers. But what if the problem wasn't presentation? What if younger viewers simply didn't want to watch news on TV? Would a new-style broadcast still appeal to the program's core audience—the viewers who had stuck with Rather and Schieffer? Would it enable Couric to draw viewers away from Brian Williams and Charlie Gibson? Was CBS, in its manic desire to be contemporary, barking up the wrong tree?

The new CBS *Evening News* made its debut on September 5, 2006. Opening with a startlingly informal greeting, "Hi, everyone," Couric delivered the news from a glitzy, space-age set. She was cool and professional, and the broadcast went off without a hitch. It included taped reports and interviews, but very little breaking news—except for an "exclusive" look at photos of Tom Cruise and Katie Holmes's new baby that would shortly appear in *Vanity Fair*. Its most unusual segment, "Free Speech," allowed a guest to express his opinion; the first installment was a complaint about media polarization by Morgan Spurlock, the director of the documentary *Supersize Me*. At the end, after showing a montage of anchor sign-offs, including the one used by the protagonist of the film comedy *Anchorman*, Couric asked viewers to submit suggestions about how she should close the program. "Thank you so much for watching," she exclaimed, her legs dangling in front of her as she sat at the edge of her desk.

Reviews of the program were largely negative, with most of the criticism directed not at Couric but the new program's overemphasis on soft news. The highlight, for virtually all reviewers, was the program's lead story, Lara Logan's report from Afghanistan, in which the intrepid young South African, wearing local dress to disguise her identity, interviewed members of the Taliban. It was revealing and great television. But it was also ten days old, and its placement in the lineup suggested that the program would prioritize *60 Minutes*–style features. The segment on Suri Cruise was pilloried. "If this is the new direction of the CBS *Evening News*, you might want to start watching *Entertainment Tonight*," opined the critic for the *Miami Herald*.[33] The hostile reviews were attributable in part to CBS's relentless promotion of the program in the weeks and months before its debut, which kindled unrealistic expectations. But Couric and Hartman were also to blame. They had been more concerned with the appearance of the show than its content, and its reliance on gimmicks and fluff were guaranteed to rile critics. In the months that followed, they persisted in broadcasting the kinds of feature stories that worked on *Today* and allowed Couric to display her winning personality. Many were quite consciously pitched to female baby boomers like Couric herself, and their prominence, critics noted, resulted in many big, important stories getting short shrift.

Had viewers responded positively, the negative press wouldn't have mattered. But, after an initial spike in the ratings, they fled in droves. Over 13 million people watched Couric's debut. By May 2007, her audience was down to 5.5 million viewers, almost 2 million fewer than Schieffer had drawn before Couric took over. Hartman was fired and Rick Kaplan, the journeyman producer who had begun his career at CBS, took his place. The "Free Speech" segment was canned, feature stories and other gimmicks were cut back, and the broadcast slowly increased its emphasis on more conventional hard news. In a magazine interview, Couric confessed to being unhappy with her new job, and rumors spread that she and CBS were trying to negotiate an exit strategy. But she soldiered on, despite continued low ratings. Her ratings improved slightly during the 2008 election campaign, especially after her well-publicized interview with Republican vice-presidential nominee Sarah Palin. But they sank again in 2009. CBS's great experiment was a monumental bust. The CBS *Evening News* remained a distant third in the ratings, and there seemed nothing that the network could do about it—except, like ABC, go old-school.

This was the big lesson the networks learned from CBS's failure. The 20–25 million Americans who were still willing to watch network news at 6:30 PM wanted a relatively traditional broadcast. If a network moved away from this, many of its viewers would defect to another network. Bob Schieffer's and especially Charlie Gibson's success—at Couric's expense—was proof of this. As a result, when Gibson retired at the end of 2009, and Diane Sawyer took his place, ABC didn't change the nature of the broadcast. It remained a blend of hard and consumer-oriented soft news, with the carefully crafted packages that viewers had come to expect from the networks, the classic formula that had worked so well since the 1980s.

As market research revealed, this formula, so appealing to older viewers, was one reason that younger viewers weren't watching network news. But it wasn't the only reason. By the early 2000s, young Americans were overwhelmed with entertainment options—not just TV programs but movies, video games, and a wealth of diversions on the Internet. If they wanted to find out what was going on, they went online or watched *The Daily Show*. And unless they were part of peer groups that regarded being informed as important, they were more likely to spend their time seeking information about their favorite actors or musicians, watching "viral" videos on YouTube, or avidly following sports. Regardless of what the networks tried to do to attract them, they weren't going to watch network news.[34]

It wasn't just young people who were unwilling to watch. Even the baby boomer moms who seemed most likely to appreciate Couric's rebranded CBS *Evening News* were abandoning the networks. During the era of Cronkite and Huntley and Brinkley, Americans worked fewer hours, and many more were home at 6:30 PM. But in the intervening years American life had changed. Commutes were longer, and most Americans were required to spend more hours on the job, making it impossible to be home when the networks broadcast their newscasts.

In many households, both parents worked full time and used much of their precious time off to attend to family and household responsibilities. Especially among the middle class, childrearing was more labor-intensive, and shuttling children to and from sports, ballet, music lessons, and other activities could be enormously time-consuming and often reached into the early evening hours. Many Americans who were still interested in following the news were unable to watch the network newscasts; the new rhythms of daily life forced them to turn instead to cable or the Internet. And even those who were at home when the network newscasts aired were not always in the mood. As a Couric fan from her *Today* show days explained: "I have Bloomberg, CNN and all of the information coming at me over the Internet every day [at work]. By the time I get home, I pretty much know what I need to know and could use a little peace and quiet."[35]

The network newscasts were a fading franchise. In 2010, the three of them drew, on average, a combined audience of 21.6 million viewers, down from 22.9 million in 2008 and 28.8 in 2004. The evening news habit was confined largely to older Americans, and it seemed likely that when they passed from the scene, so, too, would the NBC *Nightly News*, ABC's *World News*, and the CBS *Evening News*.

They weren't the only network news programs losing viewers. So were the prime-time newsmagazines, even CBS's *60 Minutes*. In 2005, for example, *60 Minutes* averaged over 15 million viewers per week; by 2009, it was averaging less than 12 million. The numbers generated by NBC's *Dateline* and ABC's *20/20* were worse, leading network officials to scale back the nights on which they aired. They usually replaced them with reality shows, which, like news programs, were inexpensive to produce but generated better ratings and more desirable demographics. Even the morning news programs, the most successful franchise in television news history, were attracting smaller audiences. In 2004, the three morning news programs—*Today, Good Morning, America*, and CBS's *The Early Show*—drew a combined average audience of 14.6 million viewers. In 2009, it was down to 12.8 million. Their viewers were also older. The only bright spot for the networks was ABC's *Nightline*. After the show was revamped in 2005, after Ted Koppel's retirement, into a fast-paced, multisegment interview and live-report program, its audience increased, at times beating Jay Leno and David Letterman. In short, if there was a time of the day when news could hold its own on network television, it was 11:30 PM, when many more people were home and in the mood to watch news on TV, particularly a program that emphasized big, pertinent stories and made good use of ABC's resources and high production standards.

Considering the widespread availability of the cable news channels, it was remarkable that network news programs still attracted so many viewers. This was a testament to network efforts to distinguish their programs from those that were broadcast by the cable news channels, and their renewed commitment to the tried and true. While the networks were unable to reverse the decline in the popularity of their programs, they were able slow it down and hang on to far more viewers than many observers had predicted. And they did it by retreating in part from the fluff and sensationalism that had dominated news programming before 9/11.

By 2006, network executives recognized that their hoped-for revival of conventional television news programs wasn't going to happen. And so they stepped up their presence on the Internet. Capitalizing on the increased accessibility of high-speed Internet connections, the networks moved away from text-based stories and began to include more video reports, including some that never made it onto any conventional TV programs. They added video blogs and other features designed to make viewers feel more connected to the network. Katie Couric's video blog, launched shortly after her debut on the CBS *Evening News*, was particularly novel and engaging, enabling viewers to eavesdrop on Couric and her staff as they prepared their program for broadcast. The networks made their websites more interactive, with links allowing visitors to comment on both televised and web-only reports and to follow their favorite network journalists on social media like Facebook. They streamed their evening newscasts and posted outtakes and additional footage from interviews that had aired on newsmagazines and the morning news programs. They also created web-only programs that were ideally suited for experimentation. Charles Gibson's web version of *World News*, for example, covered the same stories as his television broadcast—but presented them through techniques that made them appear "raw and personal, as if they were made for MTV rather than ABC."[36] There were more two-ways and in-depth discussions, and more occasions for anchors and reporters to present first-person essays and commentary. Increasingly, stories were available for sampling as bits rather than as part of programs that had to be watched in their entirety, and they were accompanied by related materials—maps, charts, full transcripts of interviews, links to stories in other media—that were potentially interesting to viewers. To draw visitors, the networks established programs that sent news alerts to consumers' computers and mobile devices and made it possible for these services to be personalized according to a particular consumer's interests or needs.

By 2010, all three networks had elaborate, full-service websites. No longer supplements to their television programming, they were stand-alone operations that could serve as their hub long after the demise of conventional television news. Here they provided many of the same kinds of things they had long broadcast on television—which would be quite familiar to viewers of their regular broadcast TV programs. Yet the websites also were places where innovations in storytelling and delivery were actively encouraged, and where entirely new kinds of programming were certain to emerge, just as new kinds of programming had resulted from journalism's migration from print and radio to television.[37]

But there were still some unanswered questions. Could advertising adequately support this shift from television to online news? The good news was that viewers were far more accepting of "preroll" commercials than industry observers had thought they would be. But even if the network news divisions moved entirely onto the web, they still needed a lot of money to produce news. Despite the reduction of overhead and the move to single-person mobile bureaus, newsgathering was expensive. More ominously, the networks had huge sums invested in their broadcast stars. Would stars even be necessary in the new world of online news? Nobody knew for sure.

The decline in viewership of network news programs was accompanied by an increase in the number of Americans watching cable news. The increase was most dramatic during and immediately after the Iraq War in 2003. Yet even when viewership dipped in the second half of 2003, it remained higher than it had been previously—a new "sea level" of approximately 1.5 million people during the day and 2.5 million in prime time. The audience for cable news increased again during the 2004 election campaign and reached another peak in 2008—1.8 million and 3.5 million, respectively—when the economic crisis and a historic presidential election drew large numbers of Americans to their televisions. On election night, the three cable news channels attracted over 26 million viewers, compared to 34 million for the networks, and more viewers watched CNN (12.3 million) and Fox News (9 million) than CBS (7.8 million).[38]

Riding the wave of patriotism sparked by the 9/11 attacks, Fox News became the most successful and influential cable news channel of the decade. Though CNN boasted a larger "cume"—industry-speak for casual viewers who tuned in for a few minutes to catch up with the latest headlines—and experienced spikes in viewership on election nights and when blockbuster stories broke, FNC's daytime audience steadily increased, and it established a huge lead over its rivals in prime time. Ratings supremacy allowed Murdoch and Ailes to demand top dollar in subscriber's fees from cable operators and in the price they charged advertisers. By 2010, it was estimated that Fox News was producing $700 million a year in profits, more than its cable news competitors and the news divisions of the three networks combined.[39]

As many industry observers noted, FNC's success was a result in part of its popularity among conservatives and its place at the center of a powerful conservative media echo chamber that included talk radio programs, magazines, blogs, and websites.[40] But as Ailes regularly reminded his critics, merely putting conservatives on the air wasn't enough. They had to be interesting and entertaining—and, most important, relatable to viewers who were suspicious of cultural elites and the media establishment. The real key to Fox News' appeal was its populism: its identification with Americans distrustful of distant institutions and of the authority and seeming arrogance of government bureaucrats, credentialed experts, and self-styled cultural sophisticates. Its prime-time hosts were particularly skilled at channeling the alienation felt by many of its viewers and appearing to be ordinary, down-to-earth Americans, despite their multimillion-dollar salaries and status as media celebrities.[41]

After the 2008 election, FNC shrewdly exploited conservative fears about the new Obama presidency to increase the audience for its daytime programming. It provided a platform for a wide array of cynical and mendacious conspiracy-mongers and emphasized stories that conjured a growing sense of apocalyptic doom. Ailes also hired a former radio shock jock named Glenn Beck to host a talk show in the early evening. Beck had been successful on Headline News, and when he came over to Fox, he was given free rein to rant about Obama's "hatred of white people" and march toward "socialism." His program became a big hit, giving FNC an even more formidable evening lineup, and making it a magnet for viewers frightened by the economic crisis and willing to listen to Beck's absurd and historically inaccurate "lectures" on monetary policy and the Constitution. Eager to consolidate FNC's position at the top of the ratings, Ailes re-signed his biggest stars, including Bill O'Reilly and Sean Hannity, to lucrative long-term contracts, though Beck left, by mutual consent, in 2011, when his ratings dipped and his rants became extreme even by FNC's standards. By the summer of 2011, Ailes was in the midst of what he called a "course correction," moving FNC's daytime news reports in particular away from the obsessively anti-Obama themes that had dominated coverage since the election. Though this may have upset some of the news channel's most conservative viewers, it was a good business decision and revealed that Ailes remained at the top of his game. With its consistent brand, Fox News had carved out an influential and profitable niche, and its example was not lost on its competitors.

Its most aggressive imitator was MSNBC. It had floundered since its birth in 1996, moving from one programming strategy to another, with little to show for it. For several years, it sought to compete with CNN as a source of live, breaking news. After 9/11, MSNBC executives decided to change course and specialize in prime-time talk shows. They tried to hire comedian Bill Maher, flirted with the idea of creating a program for the outspoken former pro wrestler and Minnesota governor Jesse Ventura, and commissioned *Daily Show* co-creator Lizz Winstead to develop an unorthodox news discussion program hosted by Connie Chung and Maury Povich. Designed to appeal to fans of *The Daily Show*, it fizzled when given a trial run during the daytime on Saturdays and never made it to prime time. MSNBC's only real success was *Scarborough Country*, a news-oriented talk show hosted by Joe Scarborough, a telegenic former Republican congressman. He became an MSNBC regular and, in 2007, the cohost of an influential and respected morning news program, *Morning Joe*.

MSNBC finally hit its stride in 2006, when it sought to capitalize on growing public disaffection with the Bush administration. Its point man in this effort was Keith Olbermann, the host of *Countdown with Keith Olbermann*, which became a big hit for the cable channel and the centerpiece of an increasingly potent—and unapologetically liberal—prime-time lineup. The mercurial Olbermann had spent most of his career as a sports reporter, but he was deeply interested in politics, and his trademark sarcasm and outrage gave him an edginess that was popular with younger viewers. Olbermann's emergence and a more general tilt toward political news during the daytime, which MSNBC officials promoted by calling their channel the "place for politics," helped to revive *Hardball*, Chris Matthews's politically focused talk show. And, in August 2008, as the general election was heating up, MSNBC hired the liberal pundit Rachel Maddow to host a third prime-time talk show. Maddow had appeared as a guest on several MSNBC programs, including Olbermann's, and her stints as a fill-in on *Countdown* convinced MSNBC executives that she could be a success. Openly gay, with an intelligent yet unpretentious broadcast style, Maddow exceeded their expectations. Her addition to MSNBC's prime-time schedule enabled the perpetual also-ran to surpass CNN, and its popularity with younger viewers encouraged MSNBC executives to openly acknowledge the channel's new "progressive" emphasis. After Olbermann's departure in January 2011, Maddow's program became MSNBC's biggest draw, attracting over a million viewers per night.

While MSNBC's tilt leftward was good for ratings and profits, pleasing corporate executives at NBC Universal, the cable channel's parent company, it was not well received at NBC News, where executives, producers, and journalists were concerned that MSNBC's partisanship would contribute to brand confusion and tarnish their own reputation for objectivity. They had been similarly squeamish about MSNBC's hiring of conservatives like Michael Savage and Tucker Carlson. After the 2008 political conventions, NBC News personnel complained when Olbermann and Matthews appeared as part of the network's election coverage team and refused to behave like objective journalists. Bowing to the pressure, NBC executives sent them back to MSNBC, despite market research that suggested that their presence was more likely to attract viewers to NBC.[42]

The tension between MSNBC and NBC News increased in 2010 when MSNBC launched a new marketing campaign that openly advertised its liberal identity—unlike the Orwellian slogan "fair and balanced" that Fox News continued to employ. Microsoft had already sold its stake in MSNBC to NBC in 2006, and the MSNBC website included material related to both news organizations, another potential source of brand confusion that alarmed NBC journalists. Accordingly, in July 2012, NBC News changed the name of its website from MSNBC.com to NBCNews.com. It became the online platform for NBC news programs alone, while Maddow and her liberal comrades were shunted off to their own dedicated website.

The biggest loser of the early 2000s was cable news pioneer CNN. This was not for lacking of trying. After the news channel's short-lived experiment with prime-time talk shows, it returned to its emphasis on breaking news. Its new president, Jim Walton, was a veteran from CNN's days as a start-up, and his hiring was interpreted as a vote of confidence by Time Warner in CNN's founding mission. But the cable news industry had changed, and Walton recognized the necessity of having distinct programming in prime time. In 2004, he hired Jonathan Klein, a former producer of CBS's *48 Hours*, to reshape CNN's domestic service. Klein axed the long-running debate program *Crossfire* and replaced it with a new general-news show, *The Situation Room*, hosted by Wolf Blitzer, which reviewed the big headlines of the day and presented detailed reports about a relatively wide range of subjects. Fast-paced and visually arresting, it incorporated the latest technology and gave CNN the most modern news program on TV. Klein also made Anderson Cooper the anchor of an evening news program. Cooper had worked as a foreign correspondent for a number of news organizations, and he became a CNN star with his impassioned, highly emotional coverage of Hurricane Katrina. Hopeful that Cooper could attract younger viewers to CNN, Klein called him "the anchorperson of the future."[43] Klein's determination to reshape CNN's prime-time offerings in a more news-oriented direction even led him to force Lou Dobbs, one of CNN's most popular personalities, to leave. Dobbs still had a loyal following, but he had become increasingly cranky, veering far from business news to editorialize about illegal immigration. Klein replaced his program with a politically oriented news show hosted by John King, who had impressed during the 2008 elections with technologically enhanced explanations of complex electoral trends.

These changes, designed to ensure that CNN was the "newsiest" of the three cable channels and hewed closely to the middle of the road, failed to reverse its continued slide in the ratings. Though CNN attracted its biggest numbers ever during the 2008 election campaign, the bump in its ratings was short-lived. In 2009 and 2010, its share of the cable news audience continued to decline—particularly in prime time but during the daytime as well. Ratings for Larry King's once popular talk show were so low that he was losing important guests to competitors Sean Hannity and Rachel Maddow. In 2010, CNN's median prime-time audience was 564,000, compared to 747,000 for MSNBC, and a whopping 1.9 million for FNC. The daytime figures were also disappointing. Though CNN attracted over 100,000 more viewers on average than MSNBC, its median audience, 450,000, paled next to FNC's 1.1 million.[44]

Clearly, the relatively small niche audience for cable news preferred commentary and opinion, especially in prime time. They were already aware of the news of the day, probably from the Internet, and didn't need this from a cable news channel. This not only affected what the cable news channels programmed in prime time; during slow news periods, it encouraged them to whittle down the stories they covered to a handful that could be followed throughout the day—and to choose them in light of the interests and the ideological disposition of their viewers, providing ample fodder for discussion on their evening talk shows. A consistent brand pitched to a precisely targeted audience that could be made to identify with an organization's mission and on-air personalities—this was the route to success in the cable news business, the one Roger Ailes had created to make Fox News a hit, and that MSNBC executives were now following to build a loyal audience for their cable channel.[45]

The good news was that CNN was profitable—thanks in large part to the fact that it included CNN-International, Headline News, and its increasingly sophisticated and popular website, which produced news for distribution on several different platforms. It also remained the place to which a majority of American viewers turned when they wanted to see breaking news. With its still extensive system of bureaus, floating foreign correspondents equipped with the most up-to-date mobile uplinks, and the ability to collect and post user-generated content, CNN was well equipped for the post-television age, when consumers would get all their news and entertainment from streaming services that they could watch on a variety of devices.

This post-television age is imminent, and its arrival will mean the end of television news as we have known it for the past fifty years. On the Internet, a new journalism has already begun to emerge, and over the next decade it will likely become our principal source of news. Potentially, it will combine the best features of print and television, and provide us with unprecedented access to information about current events, including links to related content that will make it possible to learn about them in great detail. It will probably incorporate many of the features of television news and be familiar to Americans who have grown up with TV. But it will include new features that will astonish and make us wonder why we ever lamented the passing of television journalism. A web-based journalism can offer the arresting visuals—the pictures of breaking news in particular—that TV has long specialized in. And it can provide a platform for the compelling features and in-depth reporting that were hallmarks of *60 Minutes* and Ted Koppel's *Nightline*. Better still, it can supplement them with all kinds of other material, encouraging a more engaged and interactive form of news consumption. It is conceivable that a web-based journalism will be far better at helping us understand the wider world and, more than any previous medium, allow us to feel that we're really a part of it, rather than impotent bystanders.[46]

There is a danger, of course, that legitimate web-based news providers will be engulfed by an avalanche of more specialized and partisan news outlets, and that many consumers will rely entirely on the latter for their news. Research has revealed that Internet news has increased audience fragmentation and segmentation, and there is little evidence that this trend will soon be reversed.[47] With objectivity and professional authority so widely disdained, it has become easy for people to think that their favorite sources of news—usually the ones that affirm what they already believe—are entirely sufficient to understand what's going on in the world. But relying entirely on a narrow range of sources may make it more difficult to appreciate the perspectives of others. And it may deepen our political impasse and prevent us from solving the serious problems that confront our nation and the world. More important, if Americans confine their news consumption to information about a very narrow range of subjects, the few things they are interested in, they might not acquire the breadth of knowledge necessary to be thoughtful and effective participants in civic affairs.

There is an even greater danger: that the wealth of diversions available on the Internet, particularly as it becomes the platform for virtually all forms of entertainment, will encourage us to neglect online sources of news in favor of more arresting and entertaining alternatives. This is what happened when the scarcity and limited options of the network era gave way to the bounty of cable TV. After all, learning about what's going on in the world can seem like work, and many of us do enough of that simply to earn a living.

But the Internet is different from television in a crucial respect. It is a source of information and a means of connecting with others. People regard it as a resource, and this makes it an ideal platform for news and analysis—and for eliciting interest in things outside the realm of individual experience. We have already witnessed how it can spark engagement and activism. And, when coupled with social media, it has the potential to inspire many more Americans to become better informed about truly important things. Historians a century from now may look back at our era and identify it as a turning point, when new technologies enabled us to create richer political communities and gave us the perspective to grapple successfully with the problems of day. Or they may conclude that we squandered a wonderful resource by turning it into yet another diversion. The choice is ours.

NOTES

Prologue

1   Books on television news that are more sensitive to these complexities include Edward Bliss, *Now the News: The Story of Broadcast Journalism* (New York: Columbia University Press, 1991); and Steve M. Barkin, *American Television News: The Media Marketplace and the Public Interest* (Armonk, NY: M. E. Sharpe, 2003). I found the latter particularly helpful in thinking about the television industry.

Chapter One

1   On Sarnoff, see Robert Bilby, *The General: David Sarnoff and the Rise of the Communications Industry* (New York: HarperCollins, 1986); on the origins of NBC, see Michele Hilmes, "NBC and the Network Idea: Defining the 'American System,'" in Hilmes, ed., *NBC: America's Network* (Berkeley: University of California Press, 2007), 7–24.

2   Quoted in David Sarnoff, *Pioneering in Television: Prophecy and Fulfillment* (New York: Radio Corporation of America, 1948), 74–75.

3   Sarnoff, *Pioneering*, 48, 44–45.

4   See Erik Barnouw, *The Sponsor* (New York: Oxford University Press, 1978).

5   For details, see Susan Smulyan, *Selling Radio: The Commercialization of American Broadcasting, 1920–1934* (Washington: Smithsonian Institution Press, 1994).

6   See Robert W. McChesney, *Telecommunications, Mass Media, and Democracy: The Battle for the Control of US Broadcasting, 1928–1935* (New York: Oxford University Press, 1993).

7   Edward Bliss Jr., *Now the News: The Story of Broadcast Journalism* (New York: Columbia University Press, 1991).

8   On Paley and CBS, see Sally Bedell Smith, *In All His Glory: The Life and Times of William S. Paley and the Birth of Modern Broadcasting* (New York: Simon and Schuster, 1990).

9   Gary Paul Gates, *Airtime: The Inside Story of CBS News* (New York: Harper and Row, 1978).

10   See Gary R. Edgerton, *The Columbia History of American Television* (New York: Columbia University Press, 2007).

11   On the FCC and NBC, see Christopher H. Sterling, "Breaking Chains: NBC and the FCC Network Inquiry, 1938–1943," in Hilmes, ed., *NBC*, 85–97.

12   These statistics are from Kathryn H. Fuller-Seeley, "Learning to Live with Television," in Edgerton, *The Columbia History of American Television*, 91–110.

13   For more on the FCC and its support for NBC and CBS, see J. Fred MacDonald, *One Nation under Television: The Rise and Decline of Network TV* (Chicago: Nelson-Hall, 1994); and especially William Boddy, *Fifties Television: The Industry and Its Critics* (Urbana: University of Illinois Press, 1990). On DuMont, see David Weinstein, *The Forgotten Network: DuMont and the Birth of American Television* (Philadelphia: Temple University Press, 2003).

14   Sig Mickelson, *The Decade That Shaped Television News: CBS in the 1950s* (Westport: Praeger, 1998), 8.

15   NBC's role in developing TV news has been slighted in most of the literature. For a corrective, see Kristine Brunovksa Kamick, "NBC and the Invention of Television News, 1945–1953," *Journalism History* 15 (Spring 1988): 26–34.

16   Mike Conway, *The Origins of Television News in America: The Visualizers of CBS in the 1940s* (New York: Peter Lang, 2009).

17   See Harry Castleman and Walter J. Podrazik, *Watching TV: Six Decades of American Television* (Syracuse: Syracuse University Press, 2010).

18   Reuven Frank, *Out of Thin Air: The Brief, Wonderful Life of Network News* (New York: Simon and Schuster, 1991), 96.

19   Mickelson, *Decade*, 18.

20   See Conway, *The Origins of Television News in America*; and Don Hewitt, *Tell Me a Story: Fifty Years and 60 Minutes in Television* (New York: Public Affairs, 2001).

21   On early developments in local news, see Craig M. Allen, *News Is People: The Rise of Local TV News and the Fall of News from New York* (Ames: Iowa State University Press, 2001).

22   Mickelson, *Decade*, 15.

23   For a detailed account of television coverage of the 1948 conventions, see Frank, *Out of Thin Air*, 7–27.

24   Mickelson, *Decade*, 81. For more on coverage of political conventions in the 1950s, see Sig Mickelson, *From Whistle Stop to Sound Bite: Four Decades of Politics and Television* (Westport: Praeger, 1989).

25   Mickelson, *Decade*, 94.

26   For Cronkite's early career, see Douglas Brinkley, *Cronkite* (New York: Harper-Collins, 2012).

27   Frank, *Out of Thin Air*, 60, 56–57.

28   Quoted in Mickelson, *Decade*, 96.

29   On the Army-McCarthy hearings, see Thomas Doherty, *Cold War, Cool Medium:*

Television, McCarthyism, and American Culture (New York: Columbia University Press, 2003).

30 See Bob Schieffer, *Face the Nation: My Favorite Stories from the First 50 Years of the Award-Winning News Broadcast* (New York: Simon and Schuster, 2004); and Rick Ball, *Meet the Press: Fifty Years of History in the Making* (New York: McGraw-Hill, 1998).

31 Pat Weaver with Thomas M. Coffey, *The Best Seat in the House: The Golden Years of Radio and Television* (New York: Alfred A. Knopf, 1994), 229.

32 Gould quoted in Barbara Matusow, *The Evening Stars: The Making of the Network News Anchor* (Boston: Houghton Mifflin, 1983), 72.

33 Mickelson, *Decade*, 54.

34 Frank, *Out of Thin Air*, 96.

35 Leonard Goldenson with Martin J. Wolf, *Beating the Odds: The Untold Story behind the Rise of ABC* (New York: Charles Scribner's Sons, 1991), 274.

36 On Friendly's career and the genesis of *See It Now*, see Ralph Engelman, *Friendlyvision: Fred Friendly and the Rise and Fall of Television Journalism* (New York: Columbia University Press, 2009).

37 *Variety*, July 11, 1951, 45.

38 See Mickelson, *Decade*, 43–50.

39 See Engelman, *Friendlyvision*; and especially A. William Bluem, *Documentary in American Television* (New York: Hastings House, 1965).

40 See Daniel Einstein, *Special Edition: A Guide to Network Television Documentary Series and Special Reports, 1955–1979* (Metuchen, NJ: Scarecrow Press, 1987), 469–497.

41 Fred W. Friendly, *Due to Circumstances beyond Our Control* (New York: Random House, 1967), 75.

42 See Bluem, *Documentary in American Television*.

43 On Paley's concerns about editorializing, see Mickelson, *Decade*, 44–45; and Smith, *In All His Glory*, 364–365.

44 See Engelman, *Friendlyvision*; and Joseph E. Persico, *Edward R. Murrow: An American Original* (New York: McGraw-Hill, 1988).

45 Frank, *Out of Thin Air*, 46, 84.

46 See Einstein, *Special Edition*, for information on all of these programs.

47 Mickelson, *Decade*, 177. For more on CBS's efforts to meet the challenge posed by regional sports networks in the mid-1950s, see Mickelson, *Decade*, 173–182.

48 See also Benjamin G. Rader, *In Its Own Image: How Television Has Transformed Sports* (New York: Free Press, 1984).

49 Weaver, *The Best Seat in the House*, 230.

50 Quoted in Robert Metz, *The Today Show* (Chicago: Playboy Press, 1977), 28, 30.

51 For details, see Metz, *The Today Show*.

52 Quoted in Metz, *The Today Show*, 39.

53 Metz, *The Today Show*, 94.

54   On *Home*, see Bernard M. Timberg, *Television Talk: A History of the TV Talk Show* (Austin: University of Texas Press, 2002), 39–45; and Inger L. Stole, "There Is No Place like *Home*: NBC's Search for a Daytime Audience, 1954–1957," *Communication Review* 2 (September 1997): 135–161.

55   Wallace quoted in Timberg, *Television Talk*, 52–53.

56   Wallace quoted in Timberg, *Television Talk*, 54.

57   See Richard S. Tedlow, *New and Improved: The Story of Mass Marketing in America* (New York: Basic Books, 1990); Regina S. Blaszczyk, *American Consumer Society, 1865–2005* (Wheeling: Harlan-Davidson, 2009). For the larger implications, see Gary Cross, *All-Consuming Century: Why Commercialism Won in Modern America* (New York: Columbia University Press, 2000); and Lizabeth Cohen, *A Consumer's Republic: The Politics of Mass Consumption in Postwar America* (New York: Knopf, 2003).

58   James L. Baughman, *Same Time, Same Station: Creating American Television, 1948–1961* (Baltimore: Johns Hopkins University Press, 2007). See also Boddy, *Fifties Television*.

59   Timberg, *Television Talk*, 26–27. For a detailed list of interview subjects on *Person to Person*, see Einstein, *Special Edition*, 394–422.

60   For an interesting discussion of this issue, see Jeff Merron, "Murrow on TV: *See It Now*, *Person to Person*, and the Making of a 'Masscult Personality,'" *Journalism Monographs* 106 (July 1988).

61   On Murrow and *Person to Person*, see Persico, *Edward R. Murrow*, 343–354.

62   The full text and streaming audio of Murrow's October 1958 address to the RTDNA is available online: see http://www.rtdna.org/pages/media_items/edward-r.-murrow1106.php.

Chapter Two

1   See Boddy, *Fifties Television*; and Boddy, "Operation Front Lobes versus the Living Room Toy: The Battle over Program Control in Early Television," *Media, Culture, and Society* 9 (June 1987): 347–368. On the high hopes that many social, economic, and political elites had for television, see Anna McCarthy, *The Citizen Machine: Governing by Television in 1950s America* (New York: New Press, 2010). See also Michael Schudson, *The Good Citizen: A History of American Civic Life* (New York: Free Press, 1998).

2   On the class components of popular culture audiences, see Michael Kammen, *American Culture, American Tastes: Social Change and the 20th Century* (New York: Basic Books, 1999); and Herbert Gans, *Popular Culture and High Culture: An Analysis and Evaluation of Taste* (New York: Basic Books, 1974).

3   See Gary A. Steiner, *The People Look at Television: A Study of Audience Attitudes* (New York: Knopf, 1963), 231–235. On "strivers," see Helen Lefkowitz Horowitz, *Campus Life: Undergraduate Cultures from the End of the Eighteenth Century to the Present* (Chicago: University of Chicago Press, 1987); and Lawrence W. Levine, *The Opening of the American Mind: Canons, Culture, and History* (Boston: Beacon Press, 1996).

4   See, for example, the essays in Bernard Rosenberg and David Manning White, *Mass Culture: The Popular Arts in America* (Glencoe: Free Press, 1957).

5   Richard Pells, *The Liberal Mind in a Conservative Age: American Intellectuals in the 1940s and 1950s* (New York: Harper and Row, 1985); and Paul R. Gorman, *Left Intellectuals and Popular Culture in Twentieth-Century America* (Chapel Hill: University of North Carolina Press, 1996).

6   See Boddy, *Fifties Television*, 214–232; and Kent Anderson, *Television Fraud: The History and Implications of the Quiz Show Scandals* (Westport: Greenwood Press, 1978). The meeting in New York City was reported by *Variety*, December 2, 1959, 21.

7   James L. Baughman, *Television's Guardians: The FCC and the Politics of Programming, 1958–1967* (Knoxville: University of Tennessee Press, 1985).

8   The text of Minow's speech is widely available online. For a good account of the political context, see Mary Ann Watson, *The Expanding Vista: Television in the Kennedy Years* (New York: Oxford University Press, 1990).

9   *Forbes*, June 15, 1959, 15.

10   On Minow's shift to promoting news and especially documentaries, see Baughman, *Television's Guardians*; Watson, *The Expanding Vista*; and Michael Curtin, *Redeeming the Wasteland: Television Documentary and Cold War Politics* (New Brunswick: Rutgers University Press, 1995).

11   *Variety*, July 12, 1961, 27. For a succinct account of the expansion of the network news divisions in this period, see Curtin, *Redeeming the Wasteland*, 120–138.

12   See Halberstam, *The Powers That Be*.

13   The best account of these developments is Christopher H. Sterling and John M. Kittross, *Stay Tuned: A History of American Broadcasting* (New York: Routledge, 2001).

14   Reuven Frank interview, Archive of American Television (hereafter AAT), part 4, 24:00; part 10, 6:00. For access, go to http://www.emmytvlegends.org/interviews /people/reuven-frank. For more on Kintner, see the entry on him at the Museum of Broadcasting website: http://www.museum.tv/eotvsection.php?entrycode =kintnerrobe.

15   Mike Wallace interview, AAT, part 6, 15:40. For access, to go to http://www .emmytvlegends.org/interviews/people/mike-wallace.

16   On Salant, see http://www.museum.tv/eotvsection.php?entrycode=salantricha.

17   Goldenson, *Beating the Odds*, 289.

18   Koppel quoted in Marc Gunther, *The House That Roone Built: The Inside Story of ABC News* (Boston: Little, Brown, 1994), 36.

19   See Mickelson, *From Whistle Stop to Sound Bite*.

20   See James N. Druckman, "The Power of Television Images: The First Kennedy-Nixon Debate Revisited," *Journal of Politics* 65 (May 2003): 59–71; Kathleen Hall Jamieson and David S. Birdsell, *Presidential Debates: The Challenge of Creating an Informed Electorate* (New York: Oxford University Press, 1988); and Robert J. Donovan and Ray Scherer, *Unsilent Revolution: Television News and American Public Life* (New York: Cambridge University Press, 1992).

21   See Einstein, *Special Edition*, for a detailed list of such programs.

22   See Curtin, *Redeeming the Wasteland*.

23   Hagerty quoted in Curtin, *Redeeming the Wasteland*, 138.

24   Curtin, *Redeeming the Wasteland*, has a very good discussion of the tension between interpretation and objectivity. On the culture of expertise among journalists, see Herbert J. Gans, *Deciding What's News* (New York: Pantheon, 1979); and Daniel C. Hallin, "The Passing of the 'High Modernism' of American Journalism," *Journal of Communication* 42 (September 1992): 14–25; and Michael Schudson, *The Sociology of News* (New York: Norton, 2003), 64–89.

25   See Einstein, *Special Edition*, for details and airdates of these programs.

26   *New York Times*, September 24, 1961, X23.

27   For more on TV coverage of the space program, see Donovan and Scherer, *Unsilent Revolution*, 47–57; and Watson, *The Expanding Vista*, 112–128. See also Walter A. McDougall, *The Heavens and the Earth: A Political History of the Space Age* (New York: Basic, 1985).

28   See Donovan and Scherer, *Unsilent Revolution*, 163–176.

29   Frank, *Out of Thin Air*, 167.

30   See Einstein, *Special Edition*, for details and airdates.

31   Metz, *The Today Show*.

32   Gould quoted in Douglass K. Daniel, *Harry Reasoner: A Life in the News* (Austin: University of Texas Press, 2007), 75.

33   On CBS's persistent problems developing a morning news show, see Gates, *Airtime*, 269–287.

34   Frank interview, AAT, part 3, 25:30.

35   Frank, *Out of Thin Air*, 122.

36   Frank interview, AAT, part 4, 5:50. For a thoughtful discussion of the Huntley-Brinkley show, see Barbara Matusow, *The Evening Stars*, 70–103.

37   See Brinkley, *Cronkite*, for details about Cronkite's early career. For Cronkite's own view, see Walter Cronkite, *A Reporter's Life* (New York: Knopf, 1996).

38   Salant quoted in Susan and Bill Buzenberg, eds., *Salant, CBS, and the Battle for the Soul of Broadcast Journalism: The Memoirs of Richard S. Salant* (Boulder: Westview Press, 1999), 41.

39   Selections from Frank's memo appear in his memoir *Out of Thin Air*, 181–182.

40   Frank, *Out of Thin Air*, 126.

41   Frank, *Out of Thin Air*, 182.

42   On ABC's anchor problems, see Bliss, *Now the News*, 312–314.

43   See Gans, *Deciding What's News*.

44   See Hallin, "The Passing of the 'High Modernism' of American Journalism."

45   David Brinkley interview, AAT, part 4, 20:20. Go to http://www.emmytvlegends.org/interviews/people/david-brinkley.

46   Minow quoted in Castleman and Podrazik, *Watching TV*, 165. On coverage of the JFK assassination and its role in legitimizing television news, see Barbie Zelizer,

Covering the Body: The Kennedy Assassination, the Media, and the Shaping of Collective Memory (Chicago: University of Chicago Press, 1992).

47   See Daniel Dayan and Elihu Katz, *Media Events: The Live Broadcasting of History* (Cambridge: Harvard University Press, 1992).

48   Sanford Socolow interview, AAT, part 1, 59:00. For access, go to http://www .emmytvlegends.org/interviews/people/sanford-socolow.

49   On Reasoner's move to ABC, see Daniel, *Harry Reasoner*, 127–151.

50   See Edward Jay Epstein, *News from Nowhere: Television and the News* (New York: Random House, 1973).

51   There is a voluminous literature in political science on this subject. For an introduction, see W. Lance Bennett, *News: The Politics of Illusion* (Boston: Longman, 2012); and for a detailed examination of television's agenda-setting function, see Shanto Iyengar and Donald R. Kinder, *News That Matters: Television and American Opinion* (Chicago: University of Chicago Press, 2010).

52   Daniel C. Hallin, *We Keep America on Top of the World: Television Journalism and the Public Sphere* (New York: Routledge, 1993).

53   Epstein, *News from Nowhere*, provides a brilliant discussion of these issues.

54   The literature on the civil rights movement is enormous. See, for example, Harvard Sitkoff, *The Struggle for Black Equality*, rev. ed. (New York: Hill and Wang, 2008).

55   For a detailed examination of network coverage of civil rights issues, see Aniko Bodroghkozy, *Equal Time: Television and the Civil Rights Movement* (Urbana: University of Illinois Press, 2012). For an interesting comparison of coverage in the 1960s and the 1980s and 1990s, see Sasha Torres, *Black, White, and in Color: Television and Black Civil Rights* (Princeton: Princeton University Press, 2003).

56   Howard K. Smith interview, AAT, part 4, 13:00. For access, go to http://www .emmytvlegends.org/interviews/people/howard-k-smith.

57   Dan Rather, *Rather Outspoken: My Life in the News* (New York: Grand Central Publishing, 2012), 107. See also Clive Webb, ed., *Massive Resistance: Southern Opposition to the Second Reconstruction* (New York: Oxford University Press, 2005); and David Greenberg, "The Idea of 'the Liberal Media' and Its Roots in the Civil Rights Movement," *The Sixties: A Journal of History, Politics, and Culture* 1 (December 2008): 167–186.

58   See Gerald Horne, *Fire This Time: The Watts Uprising and the 1960s* (Charlottesville: University of Virginia Press, 1995).

59   For a thoughtful account of the urban riots and their consequences, see Michael W. Flamm, *Law and Order: Street Crime, Civil Unrest, and the Crisis of Liberalism in the 1960s* (New York: Columbia University Press, 2007).

60   Examples include NBC's "Summer 67: What We Learned" (September 1967), CBS's "Remedy for Riot" (March 1968), and "The Cities," a three-hour documentary that CBS aired on consecutive nights in June 1968.

61   For a perceptive account of the 1960s that emphasizes the role of these prophets of polarization, see Rick Perlstein, *Nixonland: The Rise of a President and the Fracturing of America* (New York: Scribner's, 2008).

62   See Daniel C. Hallin, *The "Uncensored War": The Media and Vietnam* (New York: Oxford University Press, 1986): and Chester J. Pach Jr., "And That's the Way It Was:

The Vietnam War on the Network Nightly News," in David Farber, ed., *The Sixties: From Memory to History* (Chapel Hill: University of North Carolina Press, 1994), 90–118.

63   See Hallin, *The "Uncensored War,"* 131–133. See also Morley Safer's reminiscences about it. Morley Safer interview, AAT, part 4, 22:00. For access, go to http://www .emmytvlegends.org/interviews/people/morley-safer.

64   For more on the growing resignation expressed by network journalists and the Johnson administration's efforts to reverse it, see Chester Pach, "'We Need to Get a Better Story to the American People': LBJ, the Progress Campaign, and the Vietnam War on Television," in Kenneth Osgood and Andrew K. Frank, eds., *Selling War in a Media Age: The Presidency and Public Opinion in the American Century* (Gainesville: University Press of Florida, 2010), 170–195.

65   "Saigon under Fire" was broadcast by CBS on January 31, 1968; "Vietnam and After" aired on NBC on February 11, 1968. For more on TV coverage of Tet, see Chester J. Pach Jr., "Tet on TV: US Nightly News Reporting and Presidential Policy Making," in Carole Fink, Philipp Gassert, and Detlef Junker, eds., *1968: The World Transformed* (Cambridge: Cambridge University Press, 1998), 55–81.

66   Cronkite quoted in Gates, *Airtime*, 211.

67   See, for example, CBS's "Peace in Perspective," broadcast on January 24, 1973; and ABC's "Years of Anguish—Day of Peace," which aired on January 27, 1973.

68   These retrospectives, which all aired on April 29, 1975, included "Vietnam: A War That Is Finished" (CBS); "7382 Days in Vietnam" (NBC); and "Vietnam: Lessons Learned, Prices Paid" (ABC).

69   See Todd Gitlin, *The Whole World Is Watching: Mass Media in the Making and Unmaking of the New Left* (Berkeley: University of California Press, 1980).

70   See Hallin, *The "Uncensored War."*

71   On the events in Chicago, see David Farber, *Chicago '68* (Chicago: University of Chicago Press, 1988).

72   The best account of this is Perlstein, *Nixonland*.

73   See Michael Schudson, *The Power of News* (Cambridge: Harvard University Press, 1995), 142–165; and Darrell M. West, *The Rise and Fall of the Media Establishment* (Boston: Bedford/St. Martin's, 2001).

74   On the postwar consensus as a political project, rather than a fact, see Wendy L. Wall, *Inventing the "American Way": The Politics of Consensus from the New Deal to the Civil Rights Movement* (New York: Oxford University Press, 2008).

75   For more on the fragmentation of American society in the 1970s, see Bruce Schulman, *The Seventies: The Great Shift in American Culture, Society, and Politics* (New York: Free Press, 2001); and Thomas J. Borstelmann, *The 1970s: A Global History from Civil Rights to Economic Inequality* (Princeton: Princeton University Press, 2012).

Chapter Three

1   See *New York Times*, February 16, 1966, L86. The controversy is discussed in full in Gates, *Airtime*, 122–128; and Engelman, *Friendlyvision*, 214–233.

2   Minow, "ETV Takes a Giant Step," *New York Times*, September 16, 1962, sec. 6, p. 40.

3   For a concise history of public broadcasting, including the origins of educational television, see Ralph Engelman, *Public Radio and Television in America: A Political History* (Thousand Oaks, CA: Sage, 1996). For a more detailed account focusing on television, see James Day, *The Vanishing Vision: The Inside Story of Public Television* (Berkeley: University of California Press, 1995).

4   On *Omnibus*, see Einstein, *Special Edition*; and "Omnibus," *Encyclopedia of Television* (http://www.museum.tv/eotvsection.php?entrycode=omnibus).

5   For a description of programs on ETV in the early 1960s, see Minow, "ETV Takes a Giant Step."

6   In *Vanishing Vision*, Day, a former station manager and president of NET, provides a very good account of these tensions within ETV.

7   NET memo from 1963 quoted in Day, *Vanishing Vision*, 79.

8   *New York Times*, 11 January 1967, 95.

9   Quoted in Day, *Vanishing Vision*, 86.

10 *New York Times*, January 23, 1968, 79.

11 For more on Bundy, see Kai Bird, *The Color of Truth: McGeorge Bundy and William Bundy, Brothers in Arms* (New York: Simon and Schuster, 1998).

12 For details, see Engelman, *Friendlyvision*, 234–242; and Friendly, *Due to Circumstances beyond Our Control*, 301–325.

13 Quoted in Engelman, *Friendlyvision*, 249.

14 See Engelman, *Public Radio and Television in America*; and James Ledbetter, *Made Possible By . . . The Death of Public Broadcasting in the United States* (New York: Verso, 1997).

15 Carnegie Commission on Educational Television, *Public Television: A Program for Action* (New York: Harper & Row, 1967), 93. For more on the political context, see G. Calvin Mackenzie and Robert Weisbrot, *The Liberal Hour: Washington and the Politics of Change in the 1960s* (New York: Penguin, 2008).

16 The best discussion of these tensions is in Ledbetter, *Made Possible By . . .* ; see also Laurie Oullette, *Viewers like You? How Public TV Failed the People* (New York: Columbia University Press, 2002).

17 On PBL, see Engelman, *Friendlyvision*, 271–298.

18 For more on PBL's cultural pretentions and its vexed relationship to many member stations, see Oullette, *Viewers like You?*, 189–192.

19 On *Newspaper of the Air*, see Day, *Vanishing Vision*, 54–55.

20 Day, *Vanishing Vision*, 56.

21 See Neville Compton, "Spontaneous News: KQED's 'Newsroom,'" *Columbia Journalism Review* 8 (Summer 1969): 48–49.

22 On *The 51st State*, see Day, *Vanishing Vision*, 204–211. Willis and Watson quoted in Day, 206.

23 For accounts that emphasize PBS's reliance on the support of upscale viewers, see Ledbetter, *Made Possible By . . .* ; and Oullette, *Viewers like You?*

24   On *The Advocates*, see Oullette, *Viewers like You?*, 125–131; and Laurence Jarvik, PBS: *Behind the Screen* (Rocklin, CA: Forum, 1997), 164–181.

25   On the controversy surrounding *Banks and the Poor*, see Day, *Vanishing Vision*, 219–220. Gunn quoted in Day, *Vanishing Vision*, 179.

26   See Day, *Vanishing Vision*, 172–176; and Oullette, *Viewers like You?* 195–203.

27   See, for example, *New York Times*, October 17, 1971, D19.

28   Day, *Vanishing Vision*, 183.

29   On *Washington Week*, see Timberg, *Television Talk*, 299.

30   See Jarvik, PBS: *Behind the Screen*, 183–197.

31   *New York Times*, July 20, 1980, F1.

32   For background on this subject as well as information about *Wall Street Week*, see John Quirt, *The Press and the World of Money* (Byron, CA: California-Courier, 1993); and Howard Kurtz, *The Fortune Tellers* (New York: Free Press, 2001).

33   On Moyers, see Timberg, *Television Talk*; and Jarvik, PBS: *Behind the Screen*, 55–94.

34   For details, see Jeffrey Ruoff, *An American Family: A Televised Life* (Minneapolis: University of Minnesota Press, 2002).

35   Quoted in Ruoff, *An American Family*, 100.

36   For a discussion of the broader context that made interest in the program so great, see Natasha Zaretsky, *No Direction Home: The American Family and the Fear of National Decline, 1968–1980* (Chapel Hill: University of North Carolina Press, 2007); and Robert O. Self, *All in the Family: The Realignment of American Democracy since the 1960s* (New York: Hill and Wang, 2012).

37   On the Nixon administration see Perlstein, *Nixonland*; and especially Melvin Small, *The Presidency of Richard Nixon* (Lawrence: University Press of Kansas, 1999).

38   See David M. Stone, *Nixon and the Politics of Public Television* (New York: Garland, 1985). Whitehead quoted in Day, *Vanishing Vision*, 219.

39   Quoted in Day, *Vanishing Vision*, 214.

40   See Stone, *Nixon and the Politics of Public Television*, 80–132; Jarvik, PBS: *Behind the Screen*, 103–106; and Day, *Vanishing Vision*, 214–216.

41   Quoted in Day, *Vanishing Vision*, 228.

42   Quoted in Day, *Vanishing Vision*, 236.

43   For details, see Stone, *Nixon and the Politics of Public Television*, 227–286.

44   On television coverage of the Watergate scandal, see Day, *Vanishing Vision*, 246–249.

45   Robert MacNeil, *The Right Place at the Right Time* (Boston: Little, Brown, 1982), 288.

46   For a brilliant account of the changing political and social views of the educated middle class, see Barbara Ehrenreich, *Fear of Falling: The Inner Life of the Middle Class* (New York: Pantheon, 1989); and for a more general account of changes in the 1970s, Borstelmann, *The 1970s*.

47 On the origins of *The MacNeil/Lehrer Report*, see Jarvik, PBS: *Behind the Screen*, 95–115.

48 James Lehrer, *A Bus of My Own* (New York: G. P. Putnam's Sons, 1992), 132. For a contemporary left-wing critique of *MacNeil/Lehrer*, see Andrew Kopkind, "MacNeil/Lehrer's Class Act," *Columbia Journalism Review* 18 (September/October 1979): 31–38.

49 Quoted in Jarvik, PBS: *Behind the Screen*, 118.

50 Quoted in David Stewart, *The PBS Companion* (New York: TV Books, 1999), 149.

51 On Grossman's appointment and achievements, see Day, *Vanishing Vision*, 255–260.

52 On Fanning, see Arthur Unger, "*Frontline*'s David Fanning: Upholding the Documentary Tradition," *Television Quarterly* 23 (Summer 1991): 27–41.

53 See Engelman, *Public Radio and Television in America*, 174; Day, *Vanishing Vision*, 268–272.

54 On PBS in the Reagan era, see Ledbetter, *Made Possible By . . .* ; and William Hoynes, *Public Television for Sale: Media, the Market, and the Public Sphere* (Boulder, CO: Westview, 1994). For example, in order to balance a documentary series on the history of the world economy that featured the liberal economist John Kenneth Galbraith, PBS aired *Free to Choose*, a multipart series hosted by the conservative economist Milton Friedman, in 1980.

55 See Unger, "*Frontline*'s David Fanning"; and B. J. Bullert, *Public Television: Politics and the Battle over Documentary Film* (New Brunswick, NJ: Rutgers University Press, 1995).

56 Jarvik, PBS: *Behind the Screen*, 121–143.

57 See Bullert, *Public Television*, for a detailed discussion of PBS, POV, and the documentary film community.

Chapter Four

1 On *Network*, see Shaun Considine, *Mad as Hell: The Life and Work of Paddy Chayefsky* (New York: Random House, 1994); and Dave Itzkoff, *Mad as Hell: The Making of "Network" and the Fateful Vision of the Angriest Man in the World* (New York: Times Books, 2014); for an account of the 1970s that emphasizes the cynicism that it expressed, see Dominic Sandbrook, *Mad as Hell: The Crisis of the 1970s and the Rise of the Populist Right* (New York: Knopf, 2011).

2 See Richard J. Schaefer, "The Development of the CBS News Guidelines during the Salant Years," *Journal of Broadcasting and Electronic Media* 42 (Winter 1998): 1–22.

3 Quoted in Susan and Bill Buzenberg, eds., *Salant, CBS, and the Battle for the Soul of Broadcast Journalism*, 192–193.

4 See Schulman, *The Seventies*.

5 For a thoughtful examination of news audiences and the importance of "ritualistic" news consumption, see Michael Schudson, *The Sociology of News*; and Matt Carlson, "Rethinking Journalistic Authority," *Journalism Studies* 13 (August 2012): 483–498.

6   See Megan Mullen, *Television in the Multichannel Age: A Brief History of Cable Television* (Malden, MA: Blackwell, 2008).

7   See Kimberly A. Zarkin and Michael J. Zarkin, *The Federal Communications Commission: Front Line in the Culture and Regulation Wars* (Westport, CT: Greenwood Press, 2006).

8   For a detailed and engrossing account of the financial difficulties that plagued the networks during the 1980s, see Ken Auletta, *Three Blind Mice: How the TV Networks Lost Their Way* (New York: Random House, 1991).

9   Don Hewitt interview, AAT, part 3, 24:30. For access, go to www.emmytvlegends.org/interviews/people/don-hewitt.

10   Quoted in Buzenberg and Buzenberg, *Salant, CBS, and the Battle for the Soul of Broadcast Journalism*, 40.

11   For an account of the program's genesis, see Don Hewitt, *Minute by Minute* (New York: Random House, 1985); Axel Madsen, *60 Minutes: The Power and the Politics of America's Most Popular TV News Show* (New York: Dodd, Mead, 1984); and especially David Blum, *Tick-Tick-Tick: The Long Life and Turbulent Times of 60 Minutes* (New York: Harper, 2005).

12   See Blum, *Tick-Tick-Tick*, in particular, for details about the program's history.

13   See Einstein, *Special Edition*, for exact dates and airtimes as well as information about ratings.

14   It aired on September 27, 1981.

15   See Blum, *Tick-Tick-Tick*, for more on criticism of the broadcast.

16   For a particularly interesting and persuasive analysis of how the program works as television, see Richard Campbell, *60 Minutes and the News* (Urbana: University of Illinois Press, 1991).

17   On *First Tuesday*, see Einstein, *Special Edition*; and Frank, *Out of Thin Air*, 308–314.

18   They included *Weekend*, *Prime Time Sunday*, and the NBC *Magazine with David Brinkley*. For details about these programs, see Einstein, *Special Edition*.

19   My account of the evolution of local news is deeply indebted to Craig M. Allen's pathbreaking research. See Allen, *News Is People*.

20   On consultants, see also Ron Powers, *The Newscasters: The News Business as Show Business* (New York: St. Martin's, 1977).

21   On the addition of women to local anchor teams, see Craig Allen, "Gender Breakthrough Fit for a Focus Group: The First Women Newscasters and Why They Arrived in Local News," *Journalism History* 28 (Winter 2003): 154–162.

22   Quoted in Allen, *News Is People*, 104.

23   For a contemporary account, see Edward W. Barrett, "Folksy TV News," *Columbia Journalism Review* (November–December 1973): 16–20.

24   On *PM Magazine*, see Timberg, *Television Talk*, 271.

25   Quoted in Powers, *The Newscasters*, 91.

26   Quoted in Powers, *The Newscasters*, 60.

27   See Goldenson, *Beating the Odds*, 393–399; Barbara Walters, *Audition: A Memoir* (New York: Knopf, 2008), 281–309.

28   Magid's research is discussed in Matusow, *The Evening Stars*, 187; Salant quoted in Powers, *The Newscasters*, 164.

29   For details about *A.M. America*, see Powers, *The Newscasters*, 134–146.

30   On the spirited competition between *Good Morning, America* and *Today*, see Judy Kessler, *Inside Today: The Battle for the Morning* (New York: Villard Books, 1992).

31   On Arledge's move to ABC News, see Goldenson, *Beating the Odds*, 399–419; and Gunther, *The House That Roone Built*, 24–29.

32   See Gunther, *The House That Roone Built*, 141–142; and Roone Arledge, *Roone: A Memoir* (New York: HarperCollins, 2003), 163–174.

33   Av Westin, *Newswatch: How TV Decides the News* (New York: Simon and Schuster, 1982), 62–63.

34   See Matusow, *The Evening Stars*, for a detailed account of Arledge's courtship of Rather and Brokaw. See also Gunther, *The House That Roone Built*, 142–147.

35   See Gunther, *The House That Roone Built*, for details about the evolution of *World News Tonight*.

36   See Gunther, *The House That Roone Built*, for information about the genesis and history of *20/20*. On Rivera, see Powers, *The Newscasters*; and Geraldo Rivera, *Exposing Myself* (New York: Bantam, 1991).

37   Westin, *Newswatch*, 44.

38   On the origins of *Nightline*, see Gunther, *The House That Roone Built*, 112–118.

39   For details on *Nightline*'s many innovations, see Ted Koppel and Kyle Gibson, *Nightline* (New York: Times Books, 1996).

40   Gunther, *The House That Roone Built*, 155–174.

41   Brinkley interview, AAT, part 5, 10:25.

42   On the travails of the NBC *Nightly News*, see Matusow, *The Evening Stars*, 227–263.

43   See Kessler, *Inside Today*.

44   On Grossman's regime at NBC News, see Auletta, *Three Blind Mice*.

45   Lawrence Grossman interview, TV Oral History Project, Donald McGannon Communications Research Center, Fordham University, 41:00. For access, go to http://libdigcoll2.library.fordham.edu/cdm4/item_viewer.php?CISOROOT =/ORALHIS&CISOPTR=28&CISOBOX=1&REC=14.

46   These machinations are covered in Auletta, *Three Blind Mice*.

47   Quoted in Matusow, *The Evening Stars*, 42.

48   The best account of this is Peter J. Boyer, *Who Killed CBS?* (New York: Random House, 1988).

49   Gene Jankowski interview, TV Oral History Project, Donald McGannon Communications Research Center, Fordham University, 28:35. For access, go to http://libdigcoll2.library.fordham.edu/cdm4/item_viewer.php?CISOROOT =/ORALHIS&CISOPTR=5&CISOBOX=1&REC=19.

50   On Sauter's background, see Boyer, *Who Killed CBS?*, 24–39.

51   For a detailed analysis of the changes produced by Sauter and Stringer, see

Michael Massing, "CBS: Sauterizing the News," *Columbia Journalism Review* (March/April 1986): 27–37.

52 Quoted in Boyer, *Who Killed CBS?*, 140.

53 This was ironic, since Sauter regarded himself as a political conservative. See Nancy Collins, "Van the Man," *New York*, January 23, 1984, 38–49.

54 For details, see Boyer, *Who Killed CBS?*, 211–226.

55 See Einstein, *Special Edition*.

56 For details, see Einstein, *Special Edition*; and William C. Spragens, *Electronic Magazines: Soft News Programs on Network Television* (Westport, CT: Greenwood Press, 1995).

57 See Boyer, *Who Killed CBS?*

Chapter Five

1   The best account of Turner's early life and career is Robert Goldberg and Gerald Jay Goldberg, *Citizen Turner: The Wild Rise of an American Tycoon* (New York: Harcourt Brace, 1995). See also Porter Bibb, *Ted Turner: It Ain't as Easy as It Looks* (New York: Crown Books, 1993).

2   See Mullen, *Television in the Multichannel Age*; and Patrick R. Parsons, *Blue Skies: A History of Cable Television* (Philadelphia: Temple University Press, 2008).

3   For more on the economic logic that inspired the founding of specialized cable channels, see Amanda D. Lotz, *The Television Will Be Revolutionized* (New York: New York University Press, 2007); and Howard J. Blumenthal and Oliver R. Goodenough, *The Business of Television* (New York: Billboard Books, 2006). On the importance of niche markets, see Joseph Turow, *Breaking Up America: Advertisers and the New Media World* (Chicago: University of Chicago Press, 1997).

4   See Stephen Frantzich and John Sullivan, *The C-Span Revolution* (Norman: University of Oklahoma Press, 1996).

5   See Hank Whittemore, *CNN: The Inside Story* (Boston: Little, Brown, 1990), on the origins of CNN. For its place within Turner's career, see Bibb, *Ted Turner*, 151–162.

6   For background on Schonfeld, see Whittemore, *CNN*, 6–9; and Reese Schonfeld, *Me and Ted against the World: The Unauthorized Story of the Founding of CNN* (New York: HarperCollins, 2001).

7   Schonfeld, *Me and Ted against the World*, 43.

8   Schorr quoted in Whittemore, *CNN*, 49.

9   For detailed information about CNN's early management team and their backgrounds, see Whittemore, *CNN*.

10 Schonfeld, *Me and Ted against the World*, 79.

11 Schonfeld, *Me and Ted against the World*, 118.

12 Quoted in Whittemore, *CNN*, 150.

13 *New York Times*, June 29, 1980, D27–8.

14 See Bill Leonard, *In the Storm of the Eye: A Lifetime at CBS* (New York: G. P. Putnam's Sons, 1987), 220–222.

15 On Turner's long-time interest in acquiring a broadcast network, see Goldberg and Goldberg, *Citizen Turner*; and Bibb, *Ted Turner*.

16 *New York Times*, August 13, 1981, C18.

17 Schonfeld, *Me and Ted against the World*, 247.

18 Schonfeld, *Me and Ted against the World*, 249.

19 *New York Times*, January 4, 1982, C17.

20 Quoted in Whittemore, CNN, 243.

21 Quoted in Whittemore, CNN, 242.

22 Quoted in Whittemore, CNN, 241.

23 Quoted in Whittemore, CNN, 244.

24 For Schorr's perspective, see Schorr, *Staying Tuned: A Life in Journalism* (New York: Pocket Books, 2001), 311–312.

25 See Ken Auletta, *Media Man: Ted Turner's Improbable Empire* (New York: W. W. Norton, 2004).

26 Schonfeld, *Me and Ted against the World*, 287.

27 On *Crossfire*, see Ronald N. Jacobs and Eleanor Townsley, *The Space of Opinion: Media Intellectuals and the Public Sphere* (New York: Oxford University Press, 2011), 46–47; and Eric Alterman, *Sound and Fury: The Making of the Punditocracy* (New York: HarperCollins, 1992).

28 *New York Times*, August 19, 1984, H1.

29 Quoted in *New York Times*, April 19, 1987, F1.

30 For information about CNN's financials in the mid-1980s, see *New York Times*, April 19, 1987, F1, F8–9.

31 For details about CNN's newsgathering practices, see John Lancaster, "Inside CNN," *Columbia Journalism Review* 24 (January/February 1986): 44–48; and Ernest Leiser, "The Little Network That Could," *New York Times Magazine*, March 22, 1988, 30–31, 34–35, 38.

32 *New York Times*, April 19, 1987, F9.

33 On CNN's transformation into a global news service, see Don M. Flournoy and Robert K. Steward, *CNN: Making News in the Global Market* (Luton, UK: University of Luton Press, 1997).

34 See John Tomlinson, *Globalization and Culture* (Chicago: University of Chicago Press, 1999); and, for a more positive assessment, Tyler Cowen, *Creative Destruction: How Globalization Is Changing the World's Cultures* (Princeton: Princeton University Press, 2004).

35 Quoted in Flournoy and Stewart, CNN, 34.

36 See Hallin, *We Keep America on Top of the World*, 87–112.

37 *New York Times*, May 25, 1989, C25.

38 Quoted in Whittemore, CNN, 288. For the implications of this see, Edwin Dia-

mond, *The Media Show: The Changing Face of the News, 1985–1990* (Cambridge, MA: MIT Press, 1991), 55–63.

39   Quoted in Whittemore, *CNN*, 270.

40   See Jeff Alan, *Anchoring America: The Changing Face of Network News* (Chicago: Bonus Books, 2003), 337–352.

41   Hill quoted in Whittemore, *CNN*, 299. For more on Hill's unit and its productions, see Steve Weinberg, "CNN Goes for the Gold," *Columbia Journalism Review* 29 (September/October 1990): 21–25.

42   Quoted in Whittemore, *CNN*, 305.

43   For details, see Bibb, *Ted Turner*, 288–302.

44   See Robert Wiener, *Live from Baghdad: Making News at Ground Zero* (New York: Doubleday, 1992).

45   For a thoughtful discussion of the controversy over Arnett, see Walter Goodman, "Arnett," *Columbia Journalism Review* (May/June 1991): 29–31.

46   *New York Times*, March 3, 1991, 230.

47   For more on media coverage of the Persian Gulf War, see Douglas Kellner, *The Persian Gulf TV War* (Boulder, CO: Westview Press, 1992); and John R. MacArthur, *Second Front: Censorship and Propaganda in the Gulf War* (New York: Hill and Wang, 1992).

48   *New York Times*, February 11, 1991, D8.

49   *New York Times*, March 4, 1991. D6.

50   For a details, see Lotz, *The Television Will Be Revolutionized*; and Turow, *Breaking Up America*.

Chapter Six

1   For an account of the logic behind GE's acquisition of NBC, see Christopher Anderson, "Creating the Twenty-First Century Television Network: NBC in the Age of Media Conglomerates," in Hilmes, ed., *NBC*, 275–290.

2   By the end of the 1990s, the industry's top-rated program—NBC's *ER*—was drawing an audience that wouldn't have put in the top ten in 1985, despite the fact that the number of households with television had increased by nearly 15 million. For an informative account of the rise of the multichannel era and its implications for the networks, see Lotz, *The Television Will Be Revolutionized*.

3   Lotz, *The Television Will Be Revolutionized*.

4   See Matthew R. Kerbel, *If It Bleeds, It Leads: An Anatomy of Television News* (Boulder: Westview Press, 2000); and Neil Postman and Steve Powers, *How to Watch TV News* (New York: Penguin, 1992).

5   On *ET* see, Sara C. Magee, "That's Television Entertainment: The History, Development, and Impact of the First Five Seasons of 'Entertainment Tonight,' 1981–86" (PhD diss., Ohio University, 2008).

6   For a thoughtful analysis of tabloid TV, see Kevin Glynn, *Tabloid Culture* (Durham: Duke University Press, 2000).

7   Cronkite quoted in *Gainesville (FL) Sun*, March 8, 1989, 2A.

8   Van Gordon Sauter, "In Defense of Tabloid TV," *TV Guide*, August 5, 1989, 3.

9   Thomas Frank, *One Market under God* (New York: Doubleday, 2000).

10   See Kammen, *American Culture, American Tastes*; and the essays in Steve Fraser and Gary Gerstle, eds., *Ruling America: A History of Wealth and Power in a Democracy* (Cambridge: Harvard University Press, 2005).

11   On the tension between "normative" conservatism and free-market libertarianism, see Godfrey Hodgson, *The World Turned Right Side Up: A History of the Conservative Ascendancy in America* (Boston: Houghton Mifflin, 1996); and David Farber, *The Rise and Fall of Modern American Conservatism: A Short History* (Princeton: Princeton University Press, 2010).

12   See Daniel T. Rodgers, *Age of Fracture* (Cambridge: Harvard University Press, 2011).

13   On television, advertising, and "hip cynicism," see Mark Crispin Miller, *Boxed In: The Culture of TV* (Evanston: Northwestern University Press, 1988); and Frank, *One Market under God*. For a critique of postmodernism and multiculturalism's influence on American intellectual life, see Todd Gitlin, *Twilight of Common Dreams: Why America Is Wracked by Culture Wars* (New York: Holt, 1996).

14   For a perceptive account of these changes, see James T. Hamilton, *All the News That's Fit to Sell: How the Market Transforms Information into News* (Princeton: Princeton University Press, 2004).

15   See Hallin, *We Keep America on Top of the World*, 76–98.

16   See Bruce A. Williams and Michael X. Delli Carpini, *After Broadcast News* (New York: Cambridge University Press, 2011); James M. Fallows, *Breaking the News* (New York: Pantheon, 1996); and Thomas E. Patterson, *Out of Order* (New York: Knopf, 1993).

17   Hallin, *We Keep America on Top of the World*. See also Mark Hertsgaard, *On Bended Knee: The Press and the Reagan Presidency* (New York: Farrar, Straus and Giroux, 1988).

18   See Gunther, *The House That Roone Built*.

19   *New York Times*, September 3, 1990, 31.

20   *New York Times*, May 18, 1993, C18.

21   *New York Times*, September 10, 1995, SM50.

22   *New York Times*, September 26, 1991, C20. See Tom Flynn, "*48 Hours*: The Birth of an Unconventional Magazine Show," *Television Quarterly* 37 (Spring/Summer 2007): 51–55.

23   See Kessler, *Inside Today*, 225–263.

24   *New York Times*, July 27, 1989, C20.

25   *New York Times*, July 17, 1990, C13.

26   *New York Times*, March 31, 1992, C19.

27   *New York Times*, October 1, 1993, A12.

28   *New York Times*, August 22, 1994, D1.

29   *Broadcasting & Cable*, June 13, 1994, 16.

30   *New York Times*, October 2, 1995, D9.

31   *New York Times*, February 6, 1997, 37.

32   For a more detailed discussion of this trend, see Geoffrey Baym, *From Cronkite to Colbert: The Evolution of Broadcast News* (Boulder: Paradigm, 2010).

33   See James McCartney, "News Lite," *American Journalism Review* (June 1997): 18–25.

34   *New York Times*, December 30, 1997, E2.

35   *New York Times*, March 19, 1996, C16.

36   *New York Times*, June 8, 1998, D1.

37   See Blum, *Tick-Tick-Tick*.

38   *New York Times*, January 19, 1999, C1. For analysis of prime-time newsmagazines, see Jack Kuney, "TV's Magazines—Fact or Fiction?," *Television Quarterly* 29 (1997): 76–80.

39   *New York Times*, December 13, 1999, C1.

40   *New York Times*, July 9, 1995, H27. For more on Ailes's tenure at CNBC, see Kerwin Swint, *Dark Genius* (New York: Union Square Press, 2008).

41   *New York Times*, July 10, 2000, C1. See also Kurtz, *The Fortune Tellers*.

42   Quoted in *Broadcasting & Cable*, October 7, 1996, 52.

43   *New York Times*, December 15, 1996, TE4.

44   *New York Times*, December 27, 1999, C1.

45   See Neil Chenoweth, *Rupert Murdoch* (New York: Crown Business, 2001).

46   Swint, *Dark Genius*, 76–98.

47   Quoted in Scott Collins, *Crazy as a Fox: The Inside Story of How Fox Beat CNN* (New York: Portfolio, 2004), 24.

48   See Collins, *Crazy as a Fox*; Zev Chafets, *Roger Ailes: Off Camera* (New York: Sentinel, 2013); and Gabriel Sherman, *The Loudest Voice in the Room: How the Brilliant, Bombastic Roger Ailes Built Fox News—and Divided a Country* (New York: Random House, 2014).

49   On Rush Limbaugh and talk radio, see Howard Kurtz, *Hot Air* (New York: Basic, 1997), 228–255.

50   Goldberg expanded his 1995 op-ed into a book, *Bias: A CBS Insider Exposes How the Media Distort the News* (Washington, DC: Regnery, 2001). On the roots of the liberal-bias complaint, see Greenberg, "The Idea of 'the Liberal Media' and Its Roots in the Civil Rights Movement." For a dispassionate, nonpartisan debunking of the notion of liberal bias, see Everette Dennis, "How "Liberal" Are the Media, Anyway? The Continuing Conflict of Professionalism and Partisanship," *International Journal of Press/Politics* 2 (September 1997): 115–119.

51   See Ken Auletta, *Backstory: Inside the Business of News* (New York: Penguin, 2003), 249–280. For more on the conservative movement and the media, see Kathleen Hall Jamieson and Joseph N. Cappella, *Echo Chamber: Rush Limbaugh and the Conservative Media Establishment* (New York: Oxford University Press, 2008); and Thomas B. Edsall, *Building Red America: The New Conservative Coalition and the Drive for Permanent Power* (New York: Basic, 2006).

52   *Broadcasting & Cable* 126 (June 24, 1996): 46.

53   See Kurtz, *The Fortune Tellers*.

54   *New York Times*, June 8, 1997, D8.

55   *Broadcasting & Cable* 128 (June 1, 1998): 35.

56   See Neil Hickey, "Ten Mistakes That Led to the Great Time-CNN Fiasco," *Columbia Journalism Review* 37 (September/October 1998): 26–32.

57   *Broadcasting & Cable* 129 (December 13, 1999): 48.

58   See Elliot King, *Free for All: The Internet's Transformation of Journalism* (Evanston: Northwestern University Press, 2010); Henry Jenkins, *Convergence Culture: Where Old and New Media Collide* (New York: New York University Press, 2006); and Williams and Delli Carpini, *After Broadcast News*.

59   For a terrific summary of the case, see Jeffrey Toobin, *A Vast Conspiracy* (New York: Random House, 2000).

60   See John B. Thompson, *Political Scandal: Power and Visibility in the Media Age* (Cambridge: Polity, 2000).

61   Bill Kovach and Tom Rosenstiel, *Warp Speed: America in the Age of Mixed Media* (New York: Century Foundation Press, 1999).

62   For a detailed summary of these trends, see Thomas E. Patterson, "Doing Well and Doing Good: How Soft News and Critical Journalism Are Shrinking the News Audience and Weakening Democracy—And What News Outlets Can Do about It," (Cambridge, MA: Shorenstein Center, Kennedy School of Government, Harvard University, 2000), 1–28.

Chapter Seven

1   See Leonard Downie and Robert G. Kaiser, *The News about the News: American Journalism in Peril* (New York: Knopf, 2002), 111–156; and Bonnie M. Anderson, *News Flash: Journalism, Infotainment, and the Bottom-Line Business of Broadcast News* (San Francisco: Jossey-Bass, 2004).

2   See Lotz, *The Television Will Be Revolutionized*; and Jenkins, *Convergence Culture*, for detailed discussion of these trends.

3   For more detail about the growing distinctions between network and cable news, see the Pew Research Center's *State of the Media Report* for 2004, available at www.journalism.org.

4   Quoted in Downie and Kaiser, *The News about the News*, 151. For a good summary of changes in network news, see Marc Gunther, "The Transformation of Network News," *Nieman Reports* (Nieman Foundation for Journalism at Harvard, 1999). For access, go to http://www.nieman.harvard.edu/reports/article/102153/The-Transformation-of-Network-News.aspx.

5   For more on the cable news channels, see Downie and Kaiser, *The News about the News*; and Anderson, *News Flash*.

6   For a quite different and more persuasive analysis of the American electorate in the post-Reagan era, see Nolan McCarty, Keith T. Poole, and Howard Rosenthal, *Polarized America* (Cambridge: MIT Press, 2008); and Larry M. Bartels, *Unequal*

Democracy: The Political Economy of the New Gilded Age (Princeton: Princeton University Press, 2010).

7   Statistics come from the Pew Research Center's *State of the Media: 2004.*

8   See Collins, *Crazy as a Fox.*

9   *New York Times*, July 15, 2001, BU1.

10 *New York Times*, July 10, 2001, C1.

11 *Broadcasting & Cable* 131 (July 16, 2001): 16.

12 See *Broadcasting & Cable* 132 (February 18, 2002): 16–18.

13 The best account of the 9/11 attacks is Lawrence Wright, *The Looming Tower: Al-Qaeda and the Road to 9/11* (New York: Knopf, 2006). See also Terry McDermott, *Perfect Soldiers: The 9/11 Hijackers* (New York: Harper, 2005).

14 *New York Times*, September 24, 2001, C10.

15 See James Mann, *The Rise of the Vulcans: The History of Bush's War Cabinet* (New York: Penguin, 2004); and Edsall, *Building Red America.*

16 Frank Rich, *The Greatest Story Ever Sold: The Decline and Fall of Truth in Bush's America* (New York: Penguin, 2006).

17 For detailed analysis of media coverage of 9/11 and the Iraq War, see W. Lance Bennett, Regina G. Lawrence, and Steven Livingston, *When the Press Fails: Political Power and the News Media from Iraq to Katrina* (Chicago: University of Chicago Press, 2007).

18 See Rich, *The Greatest Story Ever Sold.*

19 See Matthew A. Baum, *Soft News Goes to War: Public Opinion and American Foreign Policy in the New Media Age* (Princeton: Princeton University Press, 2003); and Paul Friedman, "TV: A Missed Opportunity," *Columbia Journalism Review* 42 (May-June 2003): 29–31.

20 See FNC and the Iraq War, see Collins, *Crazy as a Fox*; and Swint, *Dark Genius.*

21 *New York Times*, April 16, 2003, B9.

22 See Bennett, Lawrence, and Livingston, *When the Press Fails*, for more on the significance of McCain's revival of the torture issue.

23 See *New York Times*, January 11, 2005, A1.

24 *New York Times*, October 3, 2004, ST1.

25 On *The Daily Show*'s implicit commitment to ideals of objectivity, see Baym, *From Cronkite to Colbert.* See also Jeffrey P. Jones, *Entertaining Politics: New Political Television and Civic Culture* (Lanham: Rowman & Littlefield, 2005).

26 *New York Times*, October 25, 2005, E1.

27 Quoted in Baym, *From Cronkite to Colbert*, 124.

28 Maureen Dowd, "America's Anchors," *Rolling Stone*, November 16, 2006.

29 For more detail, see Howard Kurtz, *Reality Show: Inside the Last Great Television News War* (New York: Free Press, 2007).

30 *New York Times*, August 25, 2005, E1.

31 See Kurtz, *Reality Show.*

32   *New York Times*, January 19, 2005, E5.

33   Quoted in Kurtz, *Reality Show*, 272.

34   See David T. Z. Mindich, *Tuned Out: Why Americans Under 40 Don't Follow the News* (New York: Oxford University Press, 2005); and Thomas E. Patterson, "Young People Flee from the News, Whatever the Source," *Television Quarterly* 38 (Winter 2008): 32–35.

35   *New York Times*, July 17, 2006, C1.

36   *New York Times*, October 12, 2007, C1.

37   See David Tewksbury and Jason Rittenberg, *News on the Internet: Information and Citizenship in the 21st Century* (New York: Oxford University Press, 2012).

38   *New York Times*, November 6, 2008, P8.

39   *New York Times*, January 10, 2010, A1.

40   See Jamieson and Cappella, *Echo Chamber*; and David Brock and Ari Rabin-Havt, *The Fox Effect: How Roger Ailes Turned a Network into a Propaganda Machine* (New York: Anchor, 2012).

41   For more on the complexity of populism in America, see Michael Kazin, *The Populist Persuasion* (New York: Basic Books, 1995); and for its role in modern right-wing discourse, see Edsall, *Building Red America*; and Katie Zernicke, *Boiling Mad: Inside Tea Party America* (New York: Times Books, 2010).

42   *New York Times*, September 8, 2008, C1.

43   *New York Times*, September 12, 2005, E1.

44   See the Pew Research Center's *State of the Media Report 2011*, for details.

45   Toby Miller, "Bank Tellers and Flag Wavers: Cable News in the United States," in Sarah Banet-Weiser, Cynthia Chris, and Anthony Freitas, eds., *Cable Visions: Television beyond Broadcasting* (New York: New York University Press, 2007), 284–301.

46   The best summary is King, *Free for All*. See also Adrienne Russell, *Networked: A Contemporary History of News in Transition* (Malden: Polity, 2011).

47   See Tewksbury and Rittenberg, *News on the Internet*.

INDEX